John Freely was born i~~~~~ ~~~~~~~~~~~~~~~~~~~~ ~~~~~~~~~~~~~~
age of seventeen, ser~~~~~~
China during the last ~~~~~~ New
York, Boston, London, ~~~~~~ ~~~ Istanbul and has written over
thirty travel books and guides, most of them about Greece and
Turkey. He is author of *The Western Shores of Turkey* (also
Tauris Parke Paperbacks) and the bestselling *Strolling Through
Istanbul*.

Tauris Parke Paperbacks is an imprint of I.B.Tauris. It is dedicated to publishing books in accessible paperback editions for the serious general reader within a wide range of categories, including biography, history, travel, art and the ancient world. The list includes select, critically acclaimed works of top quality writing by distinguished authors that continue to challenge, to inform and to inspire. These are books that possess those subtle but intrinsic elements that mark them out as something exceptional.

The colophon of Tauris Parke Paperbacks is a representation of the ancient Egyptian ibis, sacred to the god Thoth, who was himself often depicted in the form of this most elegant of birds. Thoth was credited in antiquity as the scribe of the ancient Egyptian gods and as the inventor of writing and was associated with many aspects of wisdom and learning.

STROLLING
THROUGH
ATHENS

Fourteen Unforgettable Walks
Through Europe's Oldest City

JOHN FREELY

TPP

TAURIS PARKE
PAPERBACKS

Published in 2004 by I.B.Tauris & Co Ltd
6 Salem Road, London W2 4BU
175 Fifth Avenue, New York NY 10010
www.ibtauris.com

In the United States of America and in Canada distributed by
Palgrave Macmillan, a division of St Martin's Press
175 Fifth Avenue, New York NY 10010

First published in 1991 by Penguin Books
Copyright © 1991, 2004 by John Freely
Front cover illustration: The Acropolis of Athens © Clay Perry/CORBIS

ISBN 1 85043 595 2
EAN 978 1 85043 595 2

A full CIP record for this book is available from the British Library
A full CIP record for this book is available from the Library of Congress

Library of Congress catalog card: available

Printed and bound in Great Britain by MPG Books Ltd, Bodmin

FOR TOOTS
In memory of our Athenian years

Contents

List of Diagrams

List of Maps

Acknowledgements

Acknowledgement is due to the author and publishers of John Travlos, *Pictorial Dictionary of Ancient Athens*, London, Thames & Hudson, New York, Praeger, 1971, for permission to reproduce the diagrams on pages 34, 48, 51, 61, 71, 75, 106, 198, 201, 212 and also, slightly adapted, those on pages 100 and 153; to Johnson Editions Ltd for the illustrations in the Glossary from John Freely's *Classical Turkey* (Viking, 1990); the plans in the Glossary, also from John Freely's *Classical Turkey*, were based on original drawings by John Flower for Robin Barker's *Blue Guide: Greece* (A. and C. Black Publishers).

Photographic acknowledgements: Alison Frantz, 6, 10; National Tourist Organisation of Greece, 5, 21; N. Tombazi, Psichico, Athens; all other photographs are by A. E. Baker.

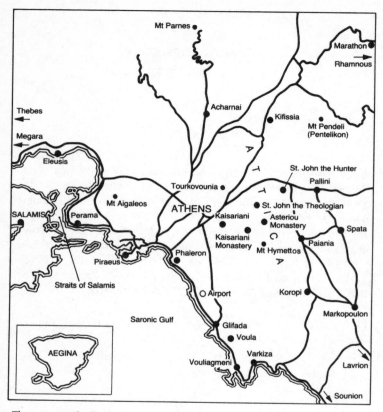

The environs of Athens

Introduction

Strolling Through Athens is a guide to the city, both as it was in ancient times and as it is today.

Ancient Athens is still the heart of the modern metropolis, and on arrival one immediately sees the great roseate rock of the Acropolis rising up out of the vast urban sprawl with its network of chaotic highways. Crowned with the magnificent ruins of the Parthenon and suffused with a golden glow when it is illuminated in the evening, you are reminded that this is the city of Athena, as it is known to the Greeks.

This guide begins with a description of the city's topography and a brief outline of its history, covering a span of time from remote antiquity up through the twenty-first century. The walks begin in the centre of the modern city to look at the ruins on the south slope of the Acropolis and move on to a more detailed investigation of the Acropolis and its monuments, most notably the Parthenon – the temple of Athena Parthenos – the Virgin Goddess. The chapters that follow guide one through the oldest parts of the town, those clustering around the lower slopes of the Acropolis, concentrating first on sites from the Graeco-Roman era and subsequently going on to look at monuments from the Byzantine, Latin, Ottoman Turkish and early modern periods. The guide ends with descriptions of a number of sites in the city outside central Athens, places seldom seen by visitors with limited time at their disposal.

This is not meant to be a scholarly work on Greek architecture and archaeology; nevertheless it does use the technical vocabulary of those disciplines in describing ancient and medieval Athens. Unfamiliar terms are explained in the illustrated glossary in the appendices, which also include a chronology and a bibliography.

Strolling Through Athens is not just a guide to the antiquities of the city. Nor is Athens treated as a mere outdoor museum of the dead past, for its ancient monuments are described in the context of the vibrant modern city of which they are such an integral part. The book is planned so that one visits the archaeological sites and museums in the course of a series of strolls around the city, through interesting and colourful quarters such as Plaka and Monastiraki. During these walks one will become acquainted with the contemporary city while studying the monuments of its past, just as I have done on my strolls through Athens across the years. It is well worth the effort, for modern Athens has a unique character that is often lost sight of in the long shadow of the Parthenon.

On one of my first explorations of the city, early in 1961, I was walking along the new highway that passes the ancient Panathenaic Stadium and I paused to consult my notes. I found that the place where I stopped, just south of the temple of Olympian Zeus, was the site of a ford across the Ilissos river, now canalized beneath the highway, though its waters still burst forth from storm sewers in times of torrential rains. This ford is the site of a scene in Plato's dialogues, where Socrates congratulates his companion for having led him to such a beautiful spot, 'a fair resting-place full of summer sounds and scents My dear Phaedrus, you have been an excellent guide!' I realised then that ancient Athens is still present within and beneath the modern city. Others long before my time had come to the same realisation, as I learned when I read Cicero's *De Finibus* and came across a remark he made to friends while strolling in Athens in 79BC, 'There is no end to it — wherever we walk, we set foot upon some history.'

Only through walking can one really come to know Athens, not just the historic monuments but the cafés and tavernas that Athenians frequent, particularly those off the main tourist trails. The strolls in this guide stop in a number of these places, such as a café called *Ai Aerides*, 'the Windy Ones', so called because it overlooks the ancient monument known as the Tower of the Winds. Our own strolls in Plaka usually end with drinks at *Ai Aerides*, where we can look down and see the pastels of sunset fading upon the marble columns in the Roman Agora, while locals make their way up ancient streets to their homes in Plaka on the north slope of the Acropolis, as they have since time immemorial. As twilight falls, the heather on Mount Hymmetos gives rise to a purple glow on the eastern horizon, reminding us of the lines that Pindar composed twenty-five centuries ago, when he wrote of 'Athens, violet-crowned'. Then we go on to supper at *Planatos*, an old taverna named for a venerable plane tree that has shaded its tables for more than a century, where we are serenaded by wandering musicians while the ever-present Parthenon looms above us. Such were the strolls through Athens that in time gave rise to this guide.

Athens has undergone some superficial changes in the years since this guide was first published, mostly as a result of the work done to prepare the city to host the Olympic Games in 2004. For example, one or two of the museums have been rearranged and archaeological displays have been set up in the new stations of the underground. But otherwise Athens itself is just as it was when the guide first appeared, and the strolls that make up the book still evoke the spirit of this incomparable city that I have known and loved for more than four decades.

1

Athens, the City of Athena

Athens is known to the Greeks as Athena, named for the virgin goddess, daughter of Zeus, who was the protectress of the city in ancient times. This is the oldest city in Europe, and its ancient monuments are testimonials to its glorious past, which profoundly influenced the emerging culture of the western world. But at the same time it is a very new city, for only a few of its existing buildings were erected before the present century. Modern Athens is a megalopolis that now stretches from the Saronic Gulf across the Kephissos plain, limited in its expansion only by the mountains that nearly hem in the city on its landward sides. The plain is bounded on the west by Mt Aigaleos (468 m), on the north by Mt Parnes (1,412 m), on the northeast by Mt Pendeli (1,109 m), and on the east by Mt Hymettos (1,027 m). This vast expanse, about 150 square miles in area, is now inhabited by nearly four million people, more than one third of the population of Greece. The monotony of this almost featureless urban sprawl is interrupted here and there by a low range of hills that cuts through the centre of the Kephissos plain. This range, known in antiquity as the Anchesmos, terminates at its southern end in the steep, conical hill of Lycabettos (278 m), one of the two most conspicuous landmarks in central Athens. The other landmark is the Acropolis, a rocky plateau that rises abruptly and dramatically out of the plain, crowned with the majestic ruins of the Parthenon and other monuments of classical Athens. All visitors are inevitably drawn to the Acropolis upon their arrival in Athens, for this is and always has been the centre of the city.

The Acropolis, or upper city, is an approximately elliptical mass of limestone on a layer of schist, measuring nearly 305 m along its east–west axis and 137 m from north to south. The rock was more sharply peaked in antiquity than it is today, but then as now it reached its maximum elevation of 156 m just to the north-east of the present Parthenon. During the fifth century BC a circuit of retaining walls was built and fill was poured in to provide a level area for the foundations of the Parthenon, creating the plateau that one sees today. The slope of the Acropolis is steep on its western side, but the other three sides are precipitous. The north side of the rock has been heavily eroded by the elements, so that parts of its face have been hollowed out into clefts and caves, while elsewhere huge clumps of earth and bedrock have partially or completely fallen away. Rainwater pouring down on the plateau seeps in between the layers of limestone and schist to emerge in springs or underground pools that can be tapped by wells. Thus the Acropolis was an ideal site for a settlement in prehistoric times, serving as a refuge and natural fortress for those dwelling near it when enemies appeared, with sources of water available to them if the city was besieged.

The earliest evidence of human habitation on and around the Acropolis dates to the Neolithic period, c. 5000 BC. Archaeological excavations have unearthed the foundations of ancient houses, wells, graves and pottery, indicating that the Acropolis and its slopes were continuously inhabited throughout the Bronze Age (c. 3000–1125 BC) and the eras that followed, up to historic times. During the Mycenaean period (c. 1400–1125 BC), the kings of Athens had their palace on the Acropolis, which was then protected by a defence wall. No certain trace of the royal palace remains, but sections of a Mycenaean wall dating to c. 1300 BC can still be seen on the Acropolis.

Greek mythology gives us the names of half a dozen major kings of prehistoric Athens (as well as several more obscure ones); the order of their succession varies from one legend to another, but they are usually listed chronologically as Cecrops, Codrus, Erichthonius, Erechtheus, Pandion, Aegeus and Theseus. The Athenians believed that they were an autochthonous people, that is, that they were the indigenous inhabitants of Attica and were not descended from any of the foreign races that had invaded Greece in prehistoric times. Thus their first king, generally identified as Cecrops, whose upper body was human and whose lower part was like a serpent, was born out of the soil of Attica itself, the son of the Earth-Mother Ge. It was during his reign that Poseidon and Athena quarrelled over the possession of Attica. Poseidon came to the Acropolis and struck the rock with his trident, causing a 'sea' of salt water to burst forth; after which Athena appeared and planted an olive tree on the peak of the hill. Zeus then

appointed a panel of gods and heroes to decide the contest, and when
Cecrops testified that Athena had been the first to plant the olive tree
in Attica she was adjudged the winner, whereupon Poseidon took his
revenge by releasing a deluge to flood the countryside. Thus Athena
became the patron deity of Athens, which thenceforth bore her name.
This was the first act in the deeply layered and many-versioned cycles
of myths surrounding the foundation of Athens, all of which culminate
in the epic adventures of Theseus, the great national hero of Attica,
whose career is set a generation or so before the Trojan War, *c.* 1200
BC. According to tradition, it was Theseus who was responsible for the
political union of the towns of Attica under the aegis of Athens, the
Synoikismos, an historical development most clearly described by
Thucydides:

From the time of Cecrops and the first kings down to the time of Theseus the
inhabitants of Attica had always lived in independent cities, each with its own
town hall and its own government. Only in times of danger did they meet
together and consult the King of Athens; for the rest of the time each state
looked after its own affairs and made its own decisions. There were actually
occasions when some of these states made war on Athens, as Eleusis under
Eumolpus did against King Erechtheus. But when Theseus became king, he
showed himself as intelligent as he was powerful. In his reorganization of the
country one of the most important things he did was to abolish the separate
councils and governments of the small cities and to bring them together into
the present city of Athens, making one deliberative assembly and one seat of
government for all. Individuals could look after their own property just as
before, but Theseus compelled them to have only one centre for their political
life – namely Athens – and, as they all became Athenian citizens, it was a
great city that Theseus handed down to those who came after him. From him
dates the feast of the Synoikia (Union of Attica), which the Athenians still
hold today in honour of Athena and pay for out of public funds.

According to tradition, it was during the late Mycenaean age that
the people of Attica first began to celebrate the Panathenaea, an
annual festival in honour of Athena Polias, a title which the goddess
bore as protectress of the *polis*, or city. As reorganized in the mid sixth
century BC, the usual festival was heightened every fourth year into a
Greater Panathenaea, which from then until the end of antiquity was
the high point of Athenian life. The climax of this festival was a great
procession that began at the principal gateway of Athens and made its
way up to the Acropolis, ending there at Athena's sanctuary, where all
the people of Attica paid homage to the divine protectress of the *polis*.
The Greater Panathenaea was also the occasion for the holding of the

Panathenaic Games, which rivalled and eventually surpassed the Olympic Games in their popularity.

Tradition holds that Athens was the leader of the great Ionian migration to the Aegean coast of Asia Minor, a population movement that began c. 1050 BC. Miletus and Ephesus, the two most famous cities of the Pan-Ionic League, held that they had been founded by sons of King Codrus and, along with all the other Ionian cities, they looked to Athens as their mother city.

Around the tenth century BC the institution of hereditary kingship in Athens was abolished when the land-owning aristocracy took control of the city, which became an oligarchy. This began a protracted struggle between the aristocracy and the rest of the populace, and in the course of this conflict Athens was surpassed by the more highly organized Dorian city-states in the Peloponnesus, particularly Corinth and Sparta. This eventually forced the Athenians to change their laws and reorganize their political institutions, leading to the reforms of Dracon (c. 621) and Solon (c. 594). Solon's reforms were highly successful, so that during the last century of the Archaic period (c. 700–480 BC) Athens once again became the leading city-state in the Greek world.

After the overthrow of the last king the seat of government in Athens was transferred from the palace to the lower town, and the Acropolis was thereafter reserved solely for sanctuaries of Athena and other patron deities of the city. By the beginning of the Archaic period the political institutions of the Athenian state had emerged, although the struggle between oligarchy and democracy would continue throughout the history of Athens as an independent city. The titular head of state was the Archon Basileus, whose duties were principally religious. The armed forces were commanded by the Polemarchos, or General, while the civil service was headed by the eponymous archon, who gave his name to the civil year in which he served. Later a board of six judges called the Thesmothetai was created, thus making a total of nine high magistrates, who were known collectively as the archons. When they completed their term of office the archons became life members of the Areopagus Council, the ancient tribunal that met on the Areopagus hill beneath the Acropolis. During the Archaic period the principal function of the Areopagus Council was to uphold the Athenian constitution. The Ekklesia, the popular assembly of all the people, elected the archons who would eventually become members of the Areopagus Council, but the voters could only choose from among those who were qualified in terms of birth and property. Other than

that, the Ekklesia had no real political power, and its main functi〔
to serve as a forum in which matters of state policy were deba〕
the people.

From the Mycenaean period onwards the people of Attica were enrolled in four tribes (phyle), whose names were perpetuated by many of the Greek cities in Asia Minor and the eastern Aegean isles founded during the Ionian migration. Each of these tribes was divided into three brotherhoods (phratria), the land belonging to which was called a trittys, literally 'a third'. There were thus twelve phratria in Attica, each with its own inalienable trittys; these were further subdivided into localities called demes, the equivalent of an English parish. The men of the phratria consisted of two groups, members of clans and members of guilds. The broad distinction between them was that clansmen owned and worked the land, while guildsmen practised trades and crafts. The clan was a large family group, comprising many households, their origins probably dating back to the original settlement of Attica by the Ionian tribes at the beginning of the second millennium BC. The guilds were a later development. Their members were usually refugees who were granted citizenship in the Athenian polis, but who did not have their roots in the ancient familial system and the original allocation of the land in Attica. When an Athenian youth reached maturity he was enfranchised by being admitted to a phratry either as a clansman or a guildsman. The clans had more social and political power than did the guilds, since they were the social élite, the numerical majority and the possessors of all the fertile land in Attica. In addition there were also large numbers of landless peasants, who, together with other disenfranchised workers, formed the lowest class of Athenian society, the thetes, and it was their persistent demand for equal citizenship and a redistribution of the fertile land of Attica that led to the reforms of Solon.

One of the reforms instituted by Solon was the creation of a Council of Four Hundred, the Boule, with a hundred life members selected by him from each of the four Ionian tribes. The main function of the Boule was to prepare the agenda for the Ekklesia, thus controlling the activities of the popular assembly. Consequently, the Boule and the Areopagus Council together acted as a counterpoise to the often tempestuous Ekklesia. As Solon wrote of this in one of his poems: 'The ship of state, riding upon two anchors, will pitch less in the surf and will make the people less turbulent.' Another of Solon's innovations was to make the Ekklesia function as a judicial body as well as a popular assembly, in which a panel of the people, selected by lot, served as jurors and judges in a court called the Heliaia. This gave the *thetes* their first voice in the government of Athens, a significant development explained by Plutarch in his *Life of Solon*.

All the rest [aside from the clansmen and guildsmen] were called *thetes*; they were not allowed to hold any office, but took part in the administration only as members of the assembly and as jurors. For even in cases which Solon assigned to the magistrates for decision, he allowed also an appeal to a popular court when anyone desired it. Besides, it is said that his laws were obscurely and ambiguously worded on purpose to enhance the power of the popular courts. For since parties to a controversy could not get satisfaction from the laws, the result was that they always wanted jurors to decide it, and every dispute was laid before them, so that they were in a manner masters of the laws.

But within a generation after Solon democracy in Athens was suspended when the Peisistratids came to power. Peisistratus, the founder of this short-lived dynasty, first seized control of the Acropolis in 561. Five years later he was deposed, whereupon he set himself up as an independent ruler in Thrace. He returned to Athens with an army in 546 and captured the city in a surprise attack, after which he ruled as a tyrant until his death in 528. Peisistratus was succeeded by his eldest son, Hippias, who reigned until he was deposed by a popular uprising in 510. (His brother Hipparchus, who shared power with him, had been assassinated in 514.) Although they were tyrants, the Peisistratids were benevolent despots as well as being great builders and patrons of the arts. Peisistratus and his sons are credited with the reorganization of Athena's festival to create a Greater Panathenaea, the editing and publication of Homer's *Iliad* and *Odyssey*, the erection of the first archaic temple of Athena on the Acropolis, and the founding of the colossal temple of Olympian Zeus in the lower city, though the latter was not completed for six and a half centuries. As Thucydides wrote of them: 'The Peisistratids were to the greatest degree honourable in conduct and shrewd in policy; they beautified the city, excelled in war and performed religious acts.'

After the overthrow of the Peisistratids, democracy was restored and the government reorganized by Cleisthenes, beginning in 508 BC. At that time Cleisthenes divided the city-state into three regions, each with the same number of citizens. These were the *asty*, which was made up of Athens and its immediate environs; the *paralia*, or the coastal region from Eleusis to Cape Sounion; and the *mesogeion*, which comprised the Attic hinterland out as far as Marathon. Cleisthenes

then created ten new tribes in Attica, each of which had citizens from
all three regions, cutting across all social and economic classes among
the populace. Every tribe had its own popular assembly, headed by
officials who supervised all their communal activities. And each tribal
group was named after a hero selected by the Pythian oracle at Delphi
from among a hundred names presented by the tribal chiefs.

Cleisthenes also created a new Boule, the Council of Five Hundred.
Each deme, according to its population, elected a fixed number of
delegates, all of whom had to be male citizens over thirty years of age
and the owners of property of a certain value. From this slate of
delegates each of the ten new tribes selected by lot fifty members of
the Boule, which was thus made up of a representative selection of the
population. In order to give the Boule continuity, it was divided by
tribes into standing committees of fifty councillors each, known as the
prytaneis. Each of these committees sat in continuous session during
one tenth of the year, a thirty-five- or thirty-six-day period called a
prytaneia, so that there was always a group of councillors on duty to
handle any emergency that might arise. This was the system by which
Athenian democracy functioned throughout the Classical period (479–
323 BC), during which time the city reached the pinnacle of its
greatness. As Plutarch wrote of the reforms of Cleisthenes: 'The
constitution was admirably suited to promote equanimity and to
preserve the state.'

Athenian history in the first quarter of the fifth century BC is
dominated by the dramatic struggle that took place between the
Greeks and Persians. In 499 Miletus led the Ionian Greeks of Asia
Minor in a revolt against Persian rule, and the following year Athens
sent a contingent of ships to aid them. But the revolt was eventually
crushed at the battle of Lade in 494, after which the Persians wreaked
their revenge by utterly destroying Miletus and enslaving its surviving
population. This catastrophe deeply shocked the Athenians, as Herodotus remarks in a moving passage.

The Athenians . . . showed their profound distress at the destruction of
Miletus in a number of ways, and, in particular, when Phrynichus produced
his play, The Capture of Miletus, the audience in the theatre burst into tears.
The author was fined a thousand drachmas for reminding them of a catastrophe
which touched them so closely, and they forbade anyone ever to put the play
on stage again.

A new leader emerged in Athens at the time in the person of
Themistocles, who was first elected as eponymous archon in 493, and

it was apparent to him that the Greek mainland would soon be invaded by Darius, the Persian king. A Persian fleet set out from the Mediterranean coast of Asia Minor in June 490, and in September it anchored off the beach at Marathon, just twenty-six miles by road from Athens. Soon after the Persians landed they were defeated by the Athenians and their Plataean allies, after which the invaders were forced to abandon their campaign and return to Asia.

Xerxes, son and successor of Darius, invaded Greece in 480 with an army that Herodotus estimated to number more than two million. The Persian horde took more than a month to cross the Hellespont and then advanced down the Aegean coast of Greece. A Spartan contingent fought to the last man defending the pass at Thermopylae, while at the same time the Persian armada accompanying Xerxes' army suffered severe losses in a hurricane and in a subsequent battle with the allied Greek navy off Cape Artemision. But after these checks the Persian army advanced into Attica and their fleet rounded Cape Sounion and sailed up the Saronic Gulf, whereupon the Athenians abandoned their city and took refuge on the peninsula of Troezen and on the islands of Aegina and Salamis. Herodotus writes that 'The Persians found Athens itself abandoned except for a few people in the temple of Athena Polias — temple stewards and needy folk — who had barricaded the Acropolis against the invaders with planks and timbers.' The defenders left the precipitous northern side of the Acropolis unguarded, but some Persian soldiers managed to scramble up the cliff and take the citadel. As Herodotus concludes his account:

When the Athenians saw them on the summit, some leapt from the wall to their death, others sought sanctuary in the inner shrine of the temple; but the Persians who got up first made straight for the gates, flung them open and slaughtered those in sanctuary. Having left not one of them alive, they stripped the temple of its treasures and burnt everything on the Acropolis. Xerxes, now master of Athens, dispatched a rider to Susa with news for Artabanus [his uncle] of his success.

Shortly afterwards the Persian fleet was decisively defeated by the Greeks at the battle of Salamis, in which Themistocles distinguished himself by his brilliant leadership. After the battle Xerxes made his way back to Asia with most of his army, leaving 300,000 picked troops under his general Mardonius to winter in Attica. Mardonius then marched northwards to Thebes, leaving destruction in his wake, as Herodotus writes: 'Before he went, he burnt Athens and reduced to complete ruin anything that remained standing — walls, houses, temples and all.'

The following year the Greek allies routed the Persian army at the battle of Plataea, killing Mardonius. At the same time (tradition says on the same day), the Greeks destroyed the Persian fleet in a battle off Cape Mycale in Asia Minor. The Ionian Greeks, aided by the Athenians, immediately revolted against Persian rule, restoring the freedom of their cities. These battles mark the triumphal beginning of the Classical period (479–323), during the first half century of which Athens would reach the height of its glory as the political and intellectual leader of the liberated Greek world.

After the liberation of Ionia the Athenian warriors went back to Greece to rejoin their families, who had been living in exile during the Persian occupation. Then they returned to their ruined city, which they quickly rebuilt under the spirited leadership of Themistocles. Themistocles took the opportunity to fortify both Athens and the Piraeus, its seaport, using trickery to get round the objections of the Spartans and their allies, who feared the enormous sea power that the Athenians had built up during the Persian Wars.

Shortly thereafter Themistocles fell from power and was supplanted by Cimon, one of the heroes of the Persian War. (Cratinus, one of the leading poets of the Old Comedy described him as 'Cimon the godlike, most generous to strangers,/ In every way the noblest of the Greeks'.) In 478 Cimon also became leader of the Delian League, a confederacy of all the Greek naval states. When the confederacy was founded, all its members agreed to build a certain number of ships for the allied navy. But Cimon encouraged the allies to contribute money instead, leaving to Athens the responsibility of constructing and manning the ships. This soon made Athens the greatest naval power in the Mediterranean, creating a virtual Athenian Empire, and her control of the Delian League's treasury gave the city far more wealth than any other state in Greece. Much of this wealth would soon be used for

(Overleaf) The monuments of ancient Athens in relation to the modern city

1 State burial-ground
2 Monument of Euboulides
3 Shrine of Heracles
4 Altar of Zeus Phratrios and Athena Phratria
5 Eridanos
6 Garden of Theophrastos
7 Kolonos Agoraios
8 Hill of the Nymphs
9 Eleusinion
10 Odeion of Herodes Atticus
11 Lysicrates Monument
12 Shrine of Codrus
13 Arch of Hadrian
14 Delphinium
15 Kronos and Rhea
16 Metroon in Agrai
17 Artemis Agrotera
18 Kynosarges

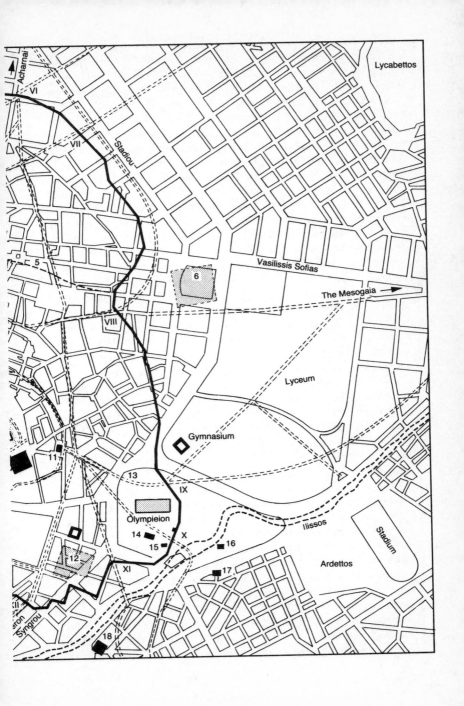

the embellishment of Athens, particularly during the Periclean age.

Pericles rose to power when Cimon was ostracized in 461, and he was first elected general in 454, a post which he held every year from 443 until his death fourteen years later. (During the years 458–456 he may have initiated the building of the Long Walls, the two parallel lines of defence walls that connected the fortifications of Athens and the Piraeus.) Throughout the last quarter century of his life Pericles dominated political life in Athens, the most illustrious era in the city's history, an age of genius that Pericles himself inspired through his oratory and his close personal friendships with some of the most creative men of his age, including the philosophers Anaxagoras and Protagoras, the playwright Sophocles and the sculptor Pheidias, to name only the most renowned in his inner circle. He sponsored the development of Attic drama – Aeschylus, Euripides, Sophocles and Aristophanes were all writing plays at this time. And it was he who was responsible for the erection of the Parthenon, appointing Pheidias to superintend the building and decoration of the magnificent edifice that became the symbol of the golden age of Athens. He also inspired the historian Thucydides, who quotes Pericles in the funeral oration he gave at the end of the first year of the Peloponnesian War: 'Mighty indeed are the marks and monuments of our empire that we have left. Future ages will wonder at us, as the present age wonders now.'

The Peloponnesian War developed out of the political polarization that took place in Hellas in the half century after the victories at Salamis and Plataea, with almost all of the Greek city-states aligning themselves either with Athens or with her arch-rival, Sparta. The war began in March 431 and its first phase ended with the Peace of Nicias in 421, with both sides exhausted by the decade of bitter fighting. The following year Alcibiades became leader of the extreme democratic faction in Athens, and through his brilliant oratory he persuaded the Athenians to resume their struggle with the Spartans in 416 BC. The Athenians were victorious at first, but the war finally ended in 404 with the unconditional surrender of Athens to Sparta.

After their victory, the Spartans forced the Athenians to destroy the Long Walls, and at the same time they stationed a garrison on the Acropolis to control the city. A provisional government was then set up under the so-called Thirty Tyrants, oligarchs who began a reign of terror to eliminate their opponents. But within a year the Spartan garrison had departed and democracy was re-established in Athens. The fortunes of the city revived rapidly, and in 394 the Athenian admiral Conon defeated a Spartan fleet off Cnidus in Asia Minor. Then

the naval supremacy of Athens was restored in 387 with the founding
of the Second Maritime League, which effectively reconstituted the
Athenian Empire of the previous century.

Socrates, the most influential philosopher of the late fifth century,
was executed in 399 BC, after having been convicted on charges of
impiety, importing new gods into the city and corrupting the youth of
Athens. Nevertheless, his ideas and personality lived on in the dialogues of Plato, who had been one of his followers. Soon after his return
from Sicily, in about 386, Plato established the Academy, a school of
philosophical studies that was to continue in existence for more than
nine centuries. Then in 335 Plato's former student Aristotle founded
the Lyceum, a philosophical school that was to rival the Academy in
its influence on the cultural life of Athens. Two other more informal
schools of philosophy were created in Athens during the last decade
or so of the fourth century, both of them founded by Greeks who had
come to the city to study at the Academy; these were Zeno of Citium
(in Cyprus), founder of the Stoic school, and Epicurus of Abdera (in
Thrace), who founded the Epicurean school. Thus the city continued to
perform the role that Pericles had spoken of in his funeral oration,
when he called Athens 'the school of Hellas'.

The middle of the fourth century BC saw the rise of Macedonian
power under King Philip II. The Athenians, stirred by the oratory of
Demosthenes, led the Greek states in a defence league against the
Macedonians, but the allied army was crushed by Philip in 338 at the
battle of Chaeronea. After his victory Philip treated Athens with great
consideration, out of respect for its reputation as the cultural centre of
the Greek world. This policy was continued during the reign of
Philip's son and successor, Alexander the Great, who began his campaign of conquest in Asia in 334, leading the Macedonians deep into
Asia during the remaining eleven years of his life. Athens enjoyed a
period of peace and prosperity during this time, largely because of the
wise financial administration of the orator Lycurgos, who resumed the
ambitious building programme of the Periclean era.

When Alexander died in 323 BC, a date that marks the beginning of
the Hellenistic period, most of the city-states in Greece united in a
revolt against Macedonian rule. This uprising, the Lamian War, ended
in the total defeat and subjugation of the Greeks by Antipater, one of
the Diadochoi, the generals of Alexander who eventually partitioned
his empire in a series of wars that lasted for more than four decades
after his death. The Athenians surrendered their city to Antipater in
September 322. Antipater punished them by disenfranchising all citi-

zens who had taken part in the revolt, after which the Macedonians set up an oligarchy. Cassander, another of the Diadochoi, took control of the city in 317, installing Dimitrios of Phaleron as tyrant. This tyranny was overthrown in 307/6 BC by Dimitrios Poliorcetes (the Besieger of Cities), who liberated Athens and declared it a free city, restoring its democratic government. But the liberation did not bring peace to Athens, for Cassander and his brother Pleistarchus continued to contend with Dimitrios Poliorcetes for control of the city. Then civil war broke out between the supporters of Macedonian rule and those who strove for independence, and during the years 307–261 the government of Athens changed hands seven times.

At the end of the third century a widespread war broke out in Greece, with Rhodes, Pergamum and Rome siding with Athens against Philip V of Macedon, who marched southwards and inflicted severe damage in Attica and in the suburbs of the city. The Romans and their allies finally defeated Philip in 197 BC, a victory that for a time brought Athens some degree of independence and stability. This brought about a renaissance in Athens, where the Academy, the Lyceum and the other philosophical schools of the city attracted students from all over the Greek-speaking world, including princes of the royal houses of the independent kingdoms that had arisen during the Hellenistic period. The rulers of these kingdoms demonstrated their veneration of Athens by endowing the city with splendid monuments, the most notable surviving example being the stoa, now magnificently restored, erected in the Agora by King Attalos II of Pergamum (159–138 BC).

In 146 BC the Roman general Mummius crushed the Achaean League (an ancient confederation of cities in Achaea, refounded in 280 BC) and utterly destroyed Corinth, after which all of Greece became virtually a province of Rome. The Athenians made an attempt to regain their independence in 88 BC, when they sided with King Mithridates of Pontus in his revolt against Rome. Two years later the Roman general Sulla captured Athens after a long and hard-fought siege, inflicting considerable damage on the lower city. This marked the end of independence for Athens, beginning the Roman period in the city's history.

Several battles of the Roman civil wars in the first century BC were fought in Greece. Many of the leading Romans involved in these wars visited Athens during this period, principally Julius Caesar, Pompey, Brutus, Cassius and Mark Antony. Antony was honoured by the Athenians just prior to the battle of Actium in 31 BC, when he and Cleopatra were decisively defeated by Octavian, who four years later became Augustus, beginning the imperial era in Roman history. During the imperial era many eminent Romans came to Athens to study, the most renowned being Cicero, Horace and Ovid. Several Roman emperors visited Athens and were honoured there, most notably Hadrian (AD 117–38), who enlarged the city's boundaries and built a number of important monuments, completing the colossal temple of Olympian Zeus that had been begun six and a half centuries earlier by Peisistratus. Another prominent benefactor was the wealthy Athenian Herodes Atticus, who in AD 161 endowed the splendid odeion on the south slope of the Acropolis that still bears his name. Several Roman emperors came to the city to be initiated into the Eleusinian Mysteries (see p. 95), expressing their devotion to Athens by endowing professorships in its ancient and famous schools. As Dio Cassius of Nicea noted of Marcus Aurelius (161–80) in his *History of Rome*: 'When Marcus had come to Athens and had been initiated into the Mysteries, he not only bestowed honours upon the Athenians, but he also, for the benefit of the whole world, established teachers at Athens in every branch of knowledge, granting them an annual salary.'

We are fortunate to have a detailed description of Athens as it was in the middle of the second century AD, when the ancient city was beginning its last period of splendour. This is contained in the *Description of Greece* by Pausanias, a Greek traveller from Asia Minor. His description of Athens comes mostly in the first of the ten volumes of this work, which Pausanias wrote *c*. 143–61, and there is an additional section in the seventh volume on the recently built Odeion of Herodes Atticus. Pausanias is an invaluable guide to the monuments of Athens, and he has been the most important primary source for scholars studying the topography of the ancient city. His Athenian chapters constitute the earliest guidebook to the monuments of Athens, an informal and chatty series of strolls through the quarters described in the present book, with numerous references to the mythological associations of virtually every stone of the ancient city. As Pausanias writes in his first paragraph on Athens, describing the place where both the Panathenaic and Eleusinian processions began, the former proceeding up to the Acropolis and the latter going westwards to the sanctuary of Demeter in Eleusis: 'When you are inside the city you come to a building for the arrangement of sacred processions (both the annual ones and those that take place at longer intervals). The Temple of Demeter is close to this; its images are Demeter and the Child, and Iachos holding a torch: an inscription in the wall in

Attic lettering says these are by Praxiteles.'

The last monumental structures of ancient Athens date from the early years of the fifth century AD, for after that time the decline of the Roman Empire made it impossible to build on an imperial scale any longer. As the empire declined, barbarian tribes began swarming across its boundaries, ravaging Italy, the Balkans and Greece. Attica was overrun by these barbarian invasions on a number of occasions, and Athens itself was sacked twice, first in 267 by the Heruli, a German tribe, and again c. 590 by the Slavs. After the Herulian sack the Athenians hurriedly constructed a new defence perimeter, the so-called Late Roman fortification wall, which enclosed a much smaller area than the walls of the Classical period. The Athenians then withdrew behind these new walls, which enclosed that part of the city lying just to the north of the Acropolis. This area, which comprises the quarter now known as Plaka, would by and large be the extent of Athens for the following fourteen centuries.

The Byzantine era in Greek history began in AD 330, when Constantinople became capital of the Roman Empire under Constantine the Great. During the first two centuries of the Byzantine era Athens continued to be one of the two most important cultural centres in the Greek world, the other being Alexandria. Several of the early Christian Fathers studied in Athens during that time, the most eminent being St Basil of Caesarea and St Gregory of Nazianzus, both of them Greeks from Asia Minor. Julian the Apostate studied here too before he became emperor, and during his brief reign (361–3) the ancient Greek religion was restored in Athens and elsewhere in the empire. But then in 435 an edict of Theodosius II forbade the worship of the ancient gods and ordered that their sanctuaries be closed throughout the empire. Thenceforth the ancient shrines and sanctuaries in Athens were no longer frequented, although pagan practices undoubtedly continued there in secret on into the sixth century, and possibly even later in remote parts of Greece. By then almost all the monuments of Athens were in ruins, many of them destroyed during the Herulian and Slavic sacks of the city. Others, most notably the Parthenon, survived largely intact because they had been converted into Christian basilicas. Nevertheless, ancient Greek philosophy continued to be taught in the schools of Athens for nearly a century after the Edict of Theodosius. But that period of tolerance came to an end in 529, when the Emperor Justinian closed the ancient Platonic Academy, the last surviving school of philosophical studies in Athens. This severed the city's oldest intellectual link with its classical past, marking the final triumph of Christianity over paganism in the Greek world. Thenceforth Athens declined to the status of a provincial town, and for the next seven centuries it virtually disappeared from the pages of history, mentioned only occasionally by travellers and chroniclers, as Greece entered the Dark Age that followed the end of antiquity.

The next epoch in the history of Athens began in 1205, the year after the Latin knights of the Fourth Crusade sacked Constantinople and dismembered the Byzantine Empire. Constantinople was recaptured by the Greeks in 1261, but much of the former territory of the Byzantine Empire remained under Latin rule. The region comprising Attica, Boeotia, Megara and Locris fell to the share of Othon de la Roche, a Burgundian knight who ruled as Duke of Athens. The dynasty that he founded lasted for more than a century, the most brilliant period of Latin rule in Greece. The last duke of that line was Walter de Brienne, who in 1311 lost his life when his army was annihilated by the Catalans at the battle of the Kopaic marshes, near Thebes. The Catalans, who had been mercenaries in the army of the Byzantine emperor, occupied Athens without a struggle shortly afterwards. The following year the Catalans invited Frederick II of Sicily to send one of his sons to be their ruler, since there was no one of royal lineage among their own company. Frederick sent his second son, Manfred, who began a dynasty that lasted for three quarters of a century. This Catalan–Sicilian regime ended in 1388, when the Acropolis was captured by a Florentine adventurer named Nerio Acciajuoli. This third Latin dynasty lasted until 1456, when Athens was captured by the Ottoman Turks under Ömer Pasha, a general of Mehmet II, the young sultan who three years before had conquered Constantinople and ended the long history of the Byzantine Empire. The church in the Parthenon was converted into a mosque and a Turkish garrison was stationed on the Acropolis, thus beginning the Ottoman occupation of Athens, which would continue almost without interruption for the next 377 years.

Sultan Mehmet himself visited Athens two years later, granting his Greek subjects freedom of worship and a certain degree of self-government under a voivode, or Turkish governor. Early in the seventeenth century Athens became the private property of the Kízlar Ağa, the Chief Black Eunuch, who headed the sultan's harem at the palace of Topkapí in Istanbul. The Kízlar Ağa was represented in Athens by the voivode; the Ottoman civil laws were administered by a *cadi*, or judge; and the garrison on the Acropolis was under the command of an officer called the Dizdar Ağa. Almost all of the actual business of running the city was done by the Archons Demogerontes, or town councillors, whose members had to be approved by the *cadi*. Most legal cases involving Greeks were handled by this body, who acted in cooperation with the *cadi* and the voivode. Thus when the English traveller Bernard Randolph visited Athens, *c.* 1685, he was led to write that 'the Greeks here live better than those in any part of Turkey . . . being a small commonwealth among themselves'.

Jean Giraud, who was French consul in Athens during the second half of the seventeenth century, estimated the population of the town to be about seven thousand, of whom two thirds were Greeks. Evliya Chelebi (1611–*c.* 1680), the great Turkish traveller, devoted one of the ten books of his *Seyahatname*, or *Narrative of Travels*, to a description of Athens, which he visited in 1638. As he writes of the relations between the Greek and Turkish inhabitants of Athens, as well as of their relative status:

Yet since this learned, this foremost city is Greek, its infidel population is numerous whereas its Muslims are few, although they too speak Greek. Night and day they do business with the Greeks and are on good terms with them. Their Greek is even fluent, because that is the language cultivated in this town of Athens, where Plato, Hippocrates, Socrates, the Ptolemies, and other Hellenes of Antiquity promoted the Greek tongue . . . The Muslims in this town are not important; they do not hold positions of honour, nor are they distinguished by gentility or held in high esteem. For the infidels are important merchants and have partnerships in the farthest Frankish lands.

The Turkish occupation of Athens was interrupted twice for brief periods by the Venetians, first in 1466 and again in 1687–8. The latter occupation occurred during the sixth war between Venice and the Ottoman Empire; this conflict lasted from 1684 to 1699, and during its first three years the Venetian forces under Captain-General Francesco Morosini recovered almost all of the Peloponnesus from the Turks. Morosini then sailed on to the Piraeus, landing his army of ten thousand men there on 21 September 1687 and marching them to Athens the following day, taking the Borgo, or Lower Town, without a struggle. He then brought up his artillery and began bombarding the Acropolis, destroying both the Parthenon and the Propylaia, the monumental gateway to the upper city. One of Morosini's artillery officers, the Russian Cristoforo Ivanovich, has left an account of the destruction of the Parthenon (which he refers to as the Temple of Minerva), a catastrophe which even at the time dimmed the glory of the Venetian victory.

On the twenty-third of September Morosini sent to the field four light cannons, two newly invented heavy cannons, and four mortars, all of which were drawn by the galley crews. The army pushed on to the Borgo without any obstruction from the enemy, who was closed up in the fortress. The general drew up the attack the same day, and at the timely arrival of the captain-general himself, who had decided to move to the field to be better able to oversee the undertaking. From the continuous shelling, the besieged suffered considerable damage to the narrow enclosing wall of the fortress. His Excellency, informed that the Turks' ammunition, together with the principal women and children, were in the Temple of Minerva ... ordered Count Mutoni to direct his fire at that part. Even from the beginning, a certain disorder appeared in the tossing of the bombs, which were falling outside ... but through practice and adjustment not a single one of them fell outside, so that one of them, striking the side of the temple, finally succeeded in breaking it. There followed a terrible explosion in the fire of powder and grenades that were inside, and the firing and reverberations of the above munitions made tremble all the houses of the Borgo ... and put a tremendous fear in the besieged. In this way the famous Temple of Minerva, which so many centuries and so many wars had not been able to destroy, was ruined.

[Quoted V. J. Bruno, *The Parthenon.*]

The explosion destroyed the north and south sides of the Parthenon, including the peripteral colonnades and the walls of the cella, or temple building. The ensuing fire burned down the Turkish village that had been built on the Acropolis during the Ottoman occupation, killing three hundred of its occupants, including women and children. This forced the surviving members of the garrison to surrender, after which they and the entire Turkish population of the city were evacuated by sea. Morosini then sent a report of his victory to the Venetian Senate, concluding with his description of the bombardment of the Acropolis (as quoted by V. J. Bruno): 'With a fortunate shot on a powder-store, an inextinguishable fire spread this way and that, demolishing the houses through two whole days, and causing the enemy considerable damage and grievous affliction. Thus the greatly famed and celebrated fortress of Athens has fallen under the sway of Your Serenity's venerable dominion.'

The Venetians held Athens only until 4 April 1688, when they were forced to withdraw from the town because of the threat of a large Turkish force that had been assembled at Chalkis, the main Ottoman base in the region. Before the Venetians evacuated Athens, Morosini tried to remove some of the sculptural decoration from the Acropolis, as he wrote in another report to the Venetian Senate.

In the plans for abandoning Athens, I conceived the project of taking some of the beautiful ornaments, especially those which could add to the splendour of the Republic. With this intention, I instigated the first steps for detaching from the façade of the Temple of Minerva — where there are the most beautiful sculptures — a statue of Jupiter and the reliefs of two magnificent horses. But hardly had the workers started to remove the large cornice than it fell from this extraordinary height, and it is a miracle that no harm came to the workers. The blame for this accident lies in the construction of the temple, built with stones placed on top of one another, without mortar and with a marvellous art, but which were all dislocated by the shock of the explosion.

Morosini then decided to make do with the marble statues of two lions and a lioness, which he shipped off as trophies to Venice. One of these statues was the great lion that gave to the Piraeus the name by which it was known in the Latin period — Porto Leone — and which now stands before the Venetian Arsenal.

When the Venetians abandoned Athens they were accompanied by most of the Greek population of Athens, who feared reprisals from the Turks. Some of those who fled sailed off to the Venetian-held isle of Zakinthos and to those parts of the Peloponnesus controlled by Venice, but most of the refugees moved across to Salamis, just as their ancestors had done in 480 BC. The few Greeks who decided to remain in Athens found themselves defenceless against the local *klepthes*, or bandits, and they were soon forced to flee, as described in a chronicle written in the mid eighteenth century, the *Anargyria Apospasmata*, quoted by Liza Micheli:

... They took whatever they could and escaped to the mountains. Most of the houses collapsed, the streets filled up, and the entire town became a lamentable wilderness. Marauders set fire to the trees, and the flames from these burned down even the ancient monuments. Then it was that the Gymnasium of Hadrian acquired its blackened hue, and one of its sections crumbled. Then the Temple of Panhellenic Zeus turned black from the smoke, and so many other buildings too.

Athens was virtually abandoned until the spring of 1690, when the first refugees began returning from Salamis, responding to an amnesty declared by Sultan Süleyman II. The Athenians then began rebuilding their city, aided by funds provided by the new voivode and a three-year respite from taxes granted by the sultan. Thus the Athenians resumed their former peaceful existence under Ottoman rule, once again enjoying a considerable degree of local autonomy. Their situation is described in the chronicle of John Benizelos, an Athenian writing during the last decades of Ottoman rule (as quoted by Liza Micheli):

Athens, though under the Ottoman yoke, was nevertheless in good condition. It could be set as an example to other cities of Greece, and indeed it was celebrated and envied. Its principal good fortune lay in its excellent citizens, who, like a sort of aristocracy, always undertook the administration of the city.

But all of this changed in 1760, when Athens and many other places in Greece became a *malikhane*, part of the sultan's own lands, as Benizelos writes in his chronicle:

That year Athens too was made a *malikhane*, a state land belonging to the sultan and sold in usufruct, for life only. On top of the regular purchase tax, the buyer paid the sultan a lump sum equivalent to ten times the property's annual revenue. The territory was sold at auction, and its life owner, the Malikhane Sahib, also exercised judicial rights over its inhabitants.

The Athens *malikhane* fell vacant in 1772 and was acquired by the infamous Hadji Ali Haseki, an Anatolian Turk who had been the personal bodyguard of Sultan Abdül Hamit I. After being Malikhane Sahib for three years Hadji Ali was made voivode of Athens, a post to which he was reappointed four times in the following seventeen years. These were the worst years in the history of Athens under Ottoman rule; hundreds of Greeks, women along with men, were imprisoned on Hadji Ali's orders, many of them dying in prison, and the city was impoverished by his extortionate taxes. Attica was twice overrun by hordes of Muslim Albanians during the first three years of his rule, the second time in 1778. This led Hadji Ali to construct a new defence wall around Athens, the so-called Serpentzes, which had a perimeter of about 10 km, indicating that the city had expanded well beyond the quarter now known as Plaka. Hadji Ali enlisted the entire population of Athens in the project, Turks and Greeks alike, and by working them day and night he completed the fortifications in less than four months. Then, as the chronicler Dimitrios Kalephronas writes:

As soon as the work was completed, Hadji Ali presented the Athenians with a bill of 42,500 piastres for supervisors from outside, and they paid it. But, alas, that wall became a prison for the Athenians, though useful to the tyrant. He set guards at the gates, and his tyranny was worse than before. The Athenians suffered much, until in 1784 the curse of his rule was no longer to be borne. The longer he stayed in Athens the more his tyranny took root and grew worse. [Quoted Micheli, *Monastiraki*.]

Hadji Ali's excesses led the Porte (the Sublime Porte, named after the monumental entry-way to the headquarters of the Grand Vizir, was the Foreign Office of the Ottoman government) to bring him back to Istanbul in 1785 for trial, along with the Athenian archons who had supported him. But five years later he was reappointed voivode and returned to Athens, where an outbreak of the plague had killed off one tenth of the population in the previous year. As Benizelos wrote in 1792:

... like a dragon creeping out of the den where he was hiding, he retook possession of the *malikhane* ... In 1791 and this year too there was nothing but oppression, with people fleeing the country and the Athenians fleeing in every direction. The years 1789–92 were the worst in the twenty-year period of Hadji Ali's rule, if not in all the history of Athens.   [Quoted Micheli, *Monas-tiraki.*]

The enormity of Hadji Ali's crimes had by then become evident even to the sultan, the liberal-minded Selim III, who banished him to Chios and had him beheaded there three years later. Hadji Ali's head was then sent to Istanbul and displayed before the main gateway of Topkapí palace, as was customary for those executed by the sultan, as proof that the villain was really dead.

During the latter Ottoman period Athens was visited by a number of travellers from northern Europe, some of whom wrote scholarly descriptions of the city or made drawings of its ancient monuments. Fortunately, two groups made careful studies of the Parthenon shortly before it was blown up in Morosini's bombardment, observing the temple while it was still virtually intact, except for the structural changes and damage that had taken place in its successive conversions, first to a church and then to a mosque. The first of these groups was the entourage of the Marquis de Nointel, ambassador from Louis XIV to the Sublime Porte, who in 1674 received permission from the Dizdar Ağa to have drawings made of the Parthenon sculptures by a painter in his company, who was probably Jacques Carrey of Troyes. The Carrey drawings, which are preserved in the Bibliothèque Nationale in Paris, constitute the only record of many of the sculptures that were destroyed in Morosini's bombardment, and, together with the description by Pausanias, have enabled archaeologists to recon-struct the scenes in both pediments of the Parthenon.

Two years later, in 1676, Jacob Spon and George Wheler came to Athens together to study its antiquities. Both of them afterwards published accounts of their observations, including the last description of the Parthenon and its sculptures before the temple was blown up by Morisini.

The two most important travellers in the following century, in terms of their contribution to knowledge of the ancient city, were the painter James Stuart and the architect Nicholas Revett. Stuart and Revett met in Rome in 1748, where they formed a plan for a systematic study of the monuments of ancient Athens. Later that year they submitted their proposal to the Society of Dilettanti in London, summing up their aims thus:

Athens, the mother of elegance and politeness, whose magnificence scarce yielded to that of Rome, and who for the beauties of a correct style must be allowed to surpass her, as much as an original excels a copy, has been almost completely neglected, and unless exact drawings from them be speedily made, all her beauteous fabricks, her temples, her theatres, her palaces will drop into oblivion, and Posterity will have to reproach us.

After receiving the support of the society, they spent the years 1751–4 together in Athens, Stuart drawing and painting the ancient monuments of the city and Revett measuring them and producing plans. The four volumes of their beautifully illustrated work, *The Antiquities of Athens*, were published between 1762 and 1814, with a supplement in 1830. (Stuart died in 1788, when only the first volume had been published; Revett lived until 1804, by which time the second and third volumes had come out.) The work of Stuart and Revett firmly established the popularity of Greek architecture, and for long it formed the basis for the architectural study of the monuments of ancient Athens.

The first systematic work on the topography of ancient Greece was by William Martin Leake, who carried out his researches during two periods in the years 1805–10 while on active duty as a British officer. Leake's two-volume work on the topography of Athens and Attica was first published in 1821, with a second edition in 1841, and in the interim he also wrote multi-volume works on his travels elsewhere in Greece and in Asia Minor. Leake's *Topography of Athens*, based on his own observations and those of earlier travellers going back as far as Pausanias, laid the foundations for all subsequent researches on the monuments of the ancient city.

Lord Elgin, newly appointed British Ambassador to the Sublime Porte, arrived in Istanbul for the first time in 1799. He then put into operation a plan that he had conceived before leaving London, that is, to remove from Athens examples of classical architecture and sculpture that would be 'beneficial to the progress of the Fine Arts in Great Britain'. This project was supervised by the Neapolitan painter Giovanni Battista Lusieri, with the political side being handled by the British Consul in Athens, Logothetis. Lusieri and his team arrived in Athens in August 1800, but it took six months before Logotheti could obtain permission to enter the Acropolis. Permission was finally granted in February 1801 by the Dizdar Ağa, the commander of the Turkish garrison on the Acropolis, who accepted a payment of five guineas a day to allow Lusieri and his team to begin their work. But the Dizdar Ağa refused permission for them to erect scaffolding on the Parthenon, for fear that the foreigners might be able to see his sequestered women in the garden of his harem; then on 17 May he abruptly closed the Acropolis to all foreigners, having received news from Istanbul that a French fleet was about to sail from Toulon to invade the Ottoman Empire. This led Elgin to begin negotiations with the Porte for a *firman*, or imperial decree, which would allow Lusieri and his men to carry out their work without interference from the Dizdar Ağa. Elgin received the desired *firman* from Sultan Selim III on 6 July 1801, and seventeen days later this was presented to the voivode of Athens, Abdullah Pasha, by the Revd Philip Hunt, Elgin's chaplain. During the next decade Elgin's workmen removed a large part of the Parthenon frieze, fifteen metopes from the south architrave and most of the surviving figures in the pediments, along with sculptures from three other structures on the Acropolis, the Propylaia, the Erechtheion and the Temple of Athena Nike; all these works were shipped to England and were eventually housed in the British Museum. As a result, the Acropolis was denuded of most of its works of art by the time that the Turkish occupation of Athens drew to a close.

The painter Edward Dodwell visited Athens for the first time while Elgin's workmen were stripping the Parthenon of its sculptures, and he wrote of this in his *Classical and Topographical Tour through Greece,* published in 1819.

During my first tour of Greece I had the inexpressible mortification of being present when the Parthenon was despoiled of its finest sculpture, and when some of its architectural members were thrown to the ground. I saw several metopes at the south-east extremity of the temple taken down. They were fixed in between the triglyphs as in a groove; and in order to lift them up, it was necessary to throw to the ground the magnificent cornice by which they were covered. The south-east pediment shared the same fate; and instead of the picturesque beauty and high preservation in which I first saw it, it is now comparatively reduced to a state of shattered desolation.

Lord Byron and his friend John Cam Hobhouse arrived in Athens for the first time on Christmas Day, 1809. Two weeks later they were taken up to the Acropolis by Lusieri, who was still employed by Lord Elgin, arranging for the shipment of forty more cases of antiquities from the Acropolis. By 1810 all but five of the cases had been shipped off to England, and on 22 April 1811 these last boxes of sculptures left port on board the ship *Hydra*, accompanied not only by Lusieri but also Byron and Hobhouse. As the sculptures were being loaded aboard the ship, an old Albanian spoke to Hobhouse. 'Guard them well,' he said, 'for one day we shall ask for them back again.'

Byron had already condemned the stripping of the Acropolis marbles in the 'Curse of Minerva', which he had written before he left Athens, comparing Elgin to Herostratus (whom he calls Eratostratus), the madman who burned down the archaic temple of Ephesus.

> Oh, loath'd in life, nor pardon'd in the dust,
> May hate pursue his sacrilegious lust!
> Link'd with the fool that fired the Ephesian dome
> Shall vengeance follow far beyond the tomb,
> And Eratostratus and Elgin shine
> In many a branding page and burning line;
> Alike reserved for aye to stand accurs'd
> Perchance the second blacker than the first.

The Greek War of Independence began on 16 April 1821, and ten days later the men of Attica rose in revolt. They attacked Athens and succeeded in making their way into the lower town, but they failed to take the Acropolis and were eventually forced to withdraw. The Greeks attacked in greater numbers the following year, led by the partisan chief Androutsos, and on 21 June 1822 the Turkish garrison on the Acropolis surrendered. Then in August 1826 a Turkish army led by Kütahya Pasha took the lower town and put the Acropolis under siege. The Greek defenders on the Acropolis held out until June 1827, when they finally surrendered to the Turkish general Reschid Pasha. The Turks then occupied Athens for the remainder of the war, and their garrison did not leave the Acropolis until 31 March 1833, after the signing of the peace treaty that created the new and independent Kingdom of Greece.

Athens suffered grievously during the Greek War of Independence, and at its close the city was in ruins. Christopher Wordsworth, whose work on the topography of ancient Greece was published in 1839, describes the condition of Athens when he first saw it in 1832:

The streets are almost deserted; nearly all of the houses are without roofs; the churches are reduced to bare walls and heaps of stones and mortar. There is but one church in which divine service is performed. A few new wooden houses, one or two of more modern structure, and two lines of planked sheds which form the bazaar, are all the inhabited houses that Athens can now boast.

The population of Athens at the end of the War of Independence is estimated to have been less than two thousand. But then the Athenians began returning to their city in large numbers after the Turkish garrison departed. Athens was officially proclaimed the capital of the new Greek Kingdom on 14 June 1833, and in December of the following year the young King Otho arrived to take up residence there. Soon afterwards the king and his advisers began an ambitious programme to rebuild and expand the city, preparing it for its new role as one of the national capitals of Europe.

The first plans for the new city of Athens were drawn up in 1833 by the architects Stamatios Cleanthes and Eduard Schaubert. Their plans were later modified by Leo von Klenze, court architect of King Ludwig of Bavaria, Otho's father. Within the next decade a number of imposing buildings were erected in Athens, beginning with the Royal Palace, which was completed in 1840. The University of Athens was founded in 1837, housed in the mansion that Cleanthes had built for himself while he was serving as King Otho's architect, and two years later work began on a much larger edifice to house the growing numbers of students and staff. By that time a network of broad avenues and spacious squares had been laid out, as Athens expanded beyond the confines of the old Ottoman town under the north slope of the Acropolis, on its way towards becoming a modern and sophisticated European city. The population of Athens in 1840 had risen to 26,327, as the new capital began to take form, its public buildings and mansions designed in the neo-classical style then popular in Europe. The intellectual life of the city proceeded apace, as Greece emerged from the torpor of its nearly five centuries of Ottoman occupation to become part of the contemporary Western world. As Eduard Masson wrote in 1842: 'Through her university and her press, Athens has already begun to lead public opinion all over the Levant, in matters of literature, politics and religion.'

Meanwhile, the monuments of ancient Athens were beginning to re-emerge from their ruins. In August 1834 the German archaeologist Ludwig Ross was appointed to excavate the Acropolis and restore its extant structures. He began by clearing away the Byzantine, Latin and

Turkish fortifications, after which he started restoring the Parthenon and the other ancient edifices on the Acropolis. Three years later the Greek Archaeological Society was founded under the leadership of Alexander Rangavis and Kyriakos Pittakis. The society held its first meeting in the Parthenon on 28 April 1837, declaring that 'these stones are our heritage', after which they conducted excavations on and around the Acropolis. They were soon joined by scholars from abroad, whose work was carried out through archaeological schools in Athens founded by the French (1845), Germans (1874), Americans (1882), British (1886), Austrians (1897) and Italians (1909). This led to the restoration of monuments on the Acropolis and in the lower city, work which continues to the present day.

The population of the city increased tremendously during the first century of Greek independence, and by 1940 it had passed one million. A large part of this increase occurred in 1923, during the exchange of minorities after the Graeco-Turkish War of 1919–22, when a million Greeks from Asia Minor were resettled in Greece, many of them creating shantytowns in and around Athens and the Piraeus. The city's population has almost quadrupled in the half century since then, as both islanders and villagers from mainland Greece move into Athens in search of opportunity, creating the vast metropolis that one sees today. This has caused the city to expand far beyond its original limits on all sides, its characterless modern buildings now covering the whole of the Kephissos plain and merging on the south with those of the Piraeus.

But the heart of the city is still the Acropolis. When walking along the crowded streets of central Athens one suddenly sees the immemorial form of the great eroded rock and its ancient walls, its plateau crowned by the majestic ruins of the Parthenon, the temple of the goddess for whom the city was named some three thousand years ago. The view is breathtaking in late afternoon, when the Acropolis and its monuments reflect the oblique light of the sinking sun in a spectrum ranging from umber through ochre and pale gold. Then at twilight a violent glow emanates from the 'purple hills of flowering Hymettos', as Ovid wrote in his *Ars amatoria*, forming the same corona above the city that Pindar praised in his famous 'Dithyramb for Athens', of which only this fragment has survived:

> O shining, violet-crowned, song-famed
>   bulwark of Greece,
> illustrious Athens,
>   city of the gods . . .

2

The South Slope of the Acropolis

The centre of modern Athens is Plateia Syntagma, known in English as Constitution Square, where we will begin our first stroll through the city. The square is dominated by the handsome edifice that was once the Royal Palace, and which has housed the Greek Parliament since 1935. We will look at this and other monuments in central Athens on later strolls through the city, but let us now head for the south slope of the Acropolis, the destination of our first walk.

We start down the right side of Leoforos Amalias, the avenue that runs south past the palace. Beyond the palace on the left side of the avenue are the National Gardens, which were laid out and planted soon after the establishment of the Greek Kingdom in 1833. About 500 m beyond the gardens we see on our left the Arch of Hadrian, and behind that the monumental ruins of the Temple of Olympian Zeus, which we will also visit on a later stroll through the city. But now let us turn right on to Odos Lysikratous, the side street just opposite the Arch of Hadrian. This takes us into the southernmost extension of Plaka, the picturesque old quarter that lies below the Acropolis to the north and east. At the first intersection we pass on our right the church of Ay. Aikaterina (St Catherine), one of the surviving monuments of Byzantine Athens. Then at the next corner we come to a little square surrounding one of the most beautiful and unique antiquities in Athens, the Monument of Lysicrates.

This is the only completely preserved example in Athens of a choregic monument, one built to commemorate the victory of a chorus in the Greater Dionysia, a festival held annually around the time of the autumnal equinox. Each of the ten Attic tribes entered two choruses in the competition, one of fifty men and the other of fifty boys. The choregos, or producer, of each chorus was a wealthy man

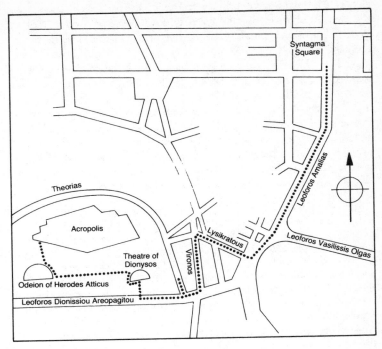

The south slope of the Acropolis

nominated by the tribe and approved by the eponymous archon. The choregos organized the chorus and chose the poet who would write the song which they sang, as well as hiring the flute-player who would accompany them. The first prize for the poet of the winning chorus was a bull, the second an amphora full of wine and the third a goat. The victorious chorus received a tripod; that is, a bronze cauldron with three legs and decorative ring handles. This trophy was dedicated to Dionysos, and placed on a monumental marble base inscribed with the names of the victors.

The Monument of Lysicrates consists of a base some 3 m square and 4 m high, above which a three-stepped platform supports six Corinthian columns arrayed in a circle, the spaces between them filled with curved slabs of marble. The columns support a tripartite architrave and a narrow sculptured frieze, above which is the conical marble roof, carved to resemble a thatch of laurel leaves and surmounted by an elaborate floral monument that once formed the base of the tripod. On the east face of the monument there is the following inscription, written in three lines: 'Lysicrates of Kikynna, son of Lysitheides, was choregos; the tribe Acamantis gained the victory with a chorus of boys; Theon played the flute; Lysiades, an Athenian, trained the chorus; Euainetos was archon.' The name of the eponymous archon dates the monument to 335/4 BC. The sculptures in the frieze represent a scene from the mythical life of Dionysos, undoubtedly the event that served as the theme for the song of the victorious chorus. This is the incident in which Dionysos is kidnapped by pirates, who are at first unaware of just who they have aboard. But then they learn that they are in the presence of a god through the miraculous events that occur aboard the vessel, as related in the second 'Homeric Hymn to Dionysos'.

. . . First of all sweet, fragrant wine ran streaming throughout all the black ship and a heavenly smell arose, so that all the seamen were filled with amazement when they saw it. And all at once a vine spread out both ways along the top of the sail with many clusters hanging down from it, and a dark ivy plant twined about the mast, blossoming with flowers, and with rich berries growing on it; and all the thole-pins were covered with garlands. When the pirates saw all this, then at last they bade the helmsman to put the ship to land. But the god changed into a dreadful lion there on the ship, in the bows, and roared loudly: amidships also he showed his wonders and created a shaggy bear which stood up ravening, while on the forepeak was the lion glaring fiercely with scowling brows. And so the sailors fled into the stern and crowded about the right-minded helmsman, until suddenly the lion sprang upon the master and seized him; and when the sailors saw it they leapt overboard one and all into the bright sea, escaping from a miserable fate, and were turned into dolphins. But on the helmsman Dionysos had mercy and held him back and made him altogether happy, saying to him: 'Take courage, good man; you have found favour with my heart. I am loud-crying Dionysos, whom Cadmus' daughter Semele bare of union with Zeus.'

The Monument of Lysicrates survived largely because it was incorporated within the precincts of the Capuchin monastery, founded in 1669. At some time after the foundation of the monastery several of the curved marble slabs were removed from the structure, which was converted into a small reading-room and study. Byron was a guest in the monastery during his first visit to Athens, describing the scene in a letter to Francis Hodgson, dated 20 January 1811. 'I am living in a Capuchin convent, Hymettos before me, the Acropolis behind, the Temple of Jove to my right, the Stadium in front, the town to my left, sir, there's a situation, there's your picturesque.'

The monastery was burned down in 1821, in the early days of the War of Independence, and the Capuchins abandoned the site. The Monument of Lysicrates was only slightly damaged in the fire, and in the first decade of the Greek Kingdom it was freed of the structures around it and restored to its present condition. In more recent years a little park was laid out around it, making the square one of the most pleasant and picturesque spots in Athens.

The bases of nine other choregic monuments have been unearthed in and around the square. The remnants of one of these bases can be seen on the street to the right, as one comes upon the square from Odos Lysikratous, and the fragments of two others are in the park to the left of the monument, while parts of six others lie under the buildings along the street that passes in front of the square, Odos Tripodon. The ancient street that ran along the course of Odos Tripodon was known by the same name, for it was lined with choregic monuments supporting tripods. Excavations in 1921 and 1955 uncovered the ancient street and the eight monument bases at a depth of 3 m below the present roadway. The choregic monuments were built along this street because it led to the main gateway of the theatre and shrine of Dionysos, the next stop on our tour.

Odos Vironos (Byron) leads from the square out on to Leoforos Dionissiou Areopagitou, the avenue that runs past the south slope of the Acropolis. At the next corner Odos Thrassilou leads up to the right, dividing the southernmost corner of Plaka from the archaeological zone on the south slope of the Acropolis. Making a short excursion up Thrassilou, one can see just inside the archaeological site a number of fragmentary sculptures that have been unearthed in recent excavations.

Returning to the main avenue and continuing along in the same direction, one can now see across the way a huge neo-classical building behind a block-long wall. This is the old Makriyannis Military Hospital, one of the finest buildings that has survived from the early years of the Greek Kingdom. This now serves as the Acropolis Study Centre, exhibiting casts and photographs of the Parthenon sculptures and other antiquities on the Acropolis. The entrance to the precincts is on Odos Makriyanni, the street that leads southwards opposite Odos Vironos.

After walking about 200 m along the avenue we come to the main entry-way to the Theatre of Dionysos. Here we leave the modern city behind for a time, strolling through the ruined-filled fields below the sheer southern cliff of the Acropolis, with the Parthenon looming on

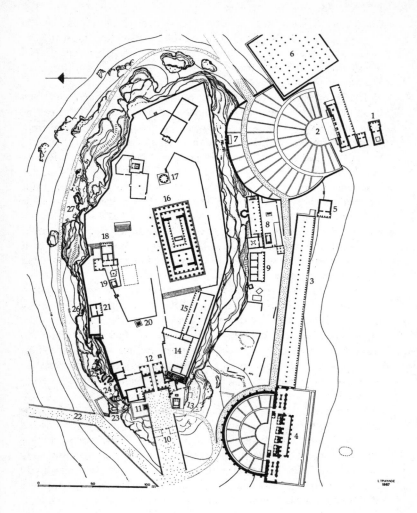

(*Opposite*) The Acropolis and its surrounding shrines and monuments in the second century AD

1 Temple of Dionysos	16 Parthenon
2 Theatre of Dionysos	17 Temple of Rome and Augustus
3 Stoa of Eumenes	18 Erechtheion
4 Odeion of Herodes Atticus	19 Sanctuary of Pandrosos
5 Nikias monument	20 Athena Promachus
6 Odeion of Pericles	21 Arrephorion
7 Thrasyllos monument	22 Panathenaic Way
8 Asklepieion	23 Klepsydra
9 Ionic stoa	24 Apollo Hypokraios
10 Beulé Gate	25 Cave of Pan
11 Monument of Agrippa	26 Cave of Aglauros
12 Propylaia	27 Shrine of Eros and Aphrodite
13 Temple of Athena Nike	
14 Artemis Brauronia	
15 Chalkotheke	

the summit of the rock above the shrine of Dionysos and the other monuments in this very peaceful archaeological site.

The theatre and its surrounding shrine on the south slope of the Acropolis were dedicated to Dionysos Eleutherios, the full name by which the god was worshipped here. The second name stems from the fact that Dionysos, according to the myth, first made his way into Attica at the town of Eleutherai, on the border with Boeotia. The cult of Dionysos Eleutherios appears to have been introduced into Attica in the mid sixth century BC, during the reign of the Peisistratids, for the oldest parts of the shrine date from the period of their tyranny. According to tradition, it was Peisistratus himself who introduced the festival of the Greater Dionysia into Athenian life and it was also he who founded the sanctuary of Dionysos here on the south slope of the Acropolis.

Before we enter the theatre, let us first look at the scattered ruins to the south, in the area just inside the entrance to the archaeological site. This area comprised the temenos, or sacred precinct, of the shrine of Dionysos, separated spatially from the theatre by a long Doric stoa, whose ruins lie behind those of the stage-building. The stoa was erected by Lycurgos *c.* 330 BC, at the same time that he built the present theatre. According to Vitruvius, the stoa was designed as a shelter from the sun and rain, serving both the pilgrims at the sanctuary and the audience at the theatre. Abutting the left wall of the stoa are the foundations of the original sanctuary of Dionysos on this site, dated to the mid sixth century BC. It was apparently a very small sanctuary, 12.5 m long and 8.0 m wide, with a pronaos to the east fronted by two columns *in antis*. Just to the south of this are the fragmentary remains of a later sanctuary also dedicated to Dionysos. This temple was larger than the earlier one, 21.0 m long and 9.6 m wide; its pronaos had a portico with four columns along the front and a pair behind the corners of the colonnade. Both temples were still standing when Pausanias visited Athens in the mid second century AD; as he writes: 'The oldest sanctuary of Dionysos is near the theatre; in the enclosure are two temples and two statues of Dionysos, the god of Eleutherai and the one that Alkamenes made of ivory and gold.' The base of the statue by Alkamenes is still partially preserved among the foundations of this later temple, which has been dated to the last quarter of the fifth century BC. Some 20 m to the south-east of these foundations there is a large marble altar, which probably stood in the centre of the orchestra. It is adorned with a fine sculptural decoration in the form of wreaths and actors' masques, symbolic of Apollo's role as god of the theatre.

A pathway to the left of the ruined stoa leads into the theatre itself. This path follows the course of one of the two *paradoi*, the side aisles that gave entrance to the theatre between the stage building and the auditorium. Once inside one inevitably walks to stage centre, standing back to study the architecture and layout of the ancient theatre.

Those who built the first theatre on the south slope of the Acropolis used the natural contours of the terrain to best advantage. At first the spectators undoubtedly sat on the sloping hillside to watch the performance in the orchestra below. Later, rows of wooden benches may have been placed there, and later still some stone seats may have provided for the high priest of Dionysos and other dignitaries. The present theatre was built by Lycurgos *c.* 330 BC, and altered somewhat in the Hellenistic, Roman and Byzantine periods. When this theatre was built, the hillside was excavated and shaped into a concave form, requiring the construction of massive retaining walls along the side of the cavea, while along its upper arc the Acropolis rock was cut away to receive the top row of seats. The cavea thus formed was horseshoe-shaped, except for a missing sector at the far right-hand corner looking towards the auditorium from the stage. This was due to the intrusion of an existing structure, the Odeion of Pericles, which was located just to the north-east of the theatre.

The number of spectators that could be seated in the theatre is estimated to have been about fifteen thousand. The seats, except in the front row, were of poros limestone. They were arranged vertically into three zones, with thirty-two rows of seats in each of the two lower zones and fourteen in the upper one. These zones were divided by two semicircular *diazomata*, or horizontal aisles. (The upper *diazoma* was part of a public roadway, the Peripatos, that ran right around the Acropolis just below its precipitous cliffs.) The lower zone of seats was made up of thirteen *kekrides*, or wedges, divided by a dozen vertical staircases and flanked by another pair. The angular width of the wedges in the two upper zones was only half as great as in the lower zone, so they had twice the number of staircases. The front row had sixty-seven thrones of Pentelic marble for local and visiting dignitaries, many of them inscribed with the names of those for whom they were reserved. Sixty of these remain today; these date from the first century BC, but are exact copies of fourth-century originals. The central throne in the front row, as its inscription shows, was reserved for the high priest of Dionysos. This throne is grander than the others in the front row, its arms and legs carved inside and out with sculptures in low relief. During Hadrian's reign an imperial box was constructed above and behind the throne of the high priest, and statues of the emperor were erected at the bottom of each wedge of seats. By that time a barrier was erected in front of the auditorium, so as to protect the spectators during the wild-beast shows and gladiatorial combats that were held there in the Roman period. (We learn from an ancient source that in one of these battles the blood of a wounded gladiator actually stained the robe of the high priest himself.)

In the early days of the theatre the circular orchestra was of earth, rolled flat and then trodden firm by the feet of the performers. In its centre was the *thymele*, the altar of Dionysos, which was the focal point of the ritual songs and dances. It was not until much later, probably in Roman times, that the orchestra was paved in marble. At that time a stone drain was constructed around the periphery of the orchestra to carry off rainwater, and this was bridged by marble slabs at the foot of the stairways that led up into the auditorium.

During the great age of Greek drama the plays were acted out against the background of a simple wooden *skene*, the predecessor of the grander stage-buildings of later eras. In ancient Greek *skene* means 'hut' or 'tent', and at the beginning it was probably a temporary wooden structure used for dressing-rooms and storage, undoubtedly rebuilt at the time of each new celebration of the Greater Dionysia. Later the *skene* became a more permanent structure and its inner façade was decorated to provide a scenic background to the play, the first instance of which was probably the *Oresteia* of Aeschylus, produced in 458 BC. The first monumental stone *skene* was undoubtedly part of the theatre constructed by Lycurgos c. 330 BC, built back to back with the long stoa that he erected facing the sanctuary of Dionysos. The central structure of this *skene* was a long hall, 46.3 m in length and 6.4 m wide, with a façade some three or four metres high. This hall had two projecting porticoed wings, the *paraskenia*; these were separated by the *paradoi*, and they flanked the proscenium, the stage where the actors performed. Most modern authorities agree that the actors performed on the same level with the chorus in the theatre, at least in the Classical period. Later, probably during the Hellenistic period, the actors may have performed on an elevated stage, as in a modern theatre. The ruined stage building that one sees today was constructed much later, probably in the early fourth century AD. By that time the theatre was seldom if ever used for the production of plays, and the stage probably served as a pulpit for orators in the popular assembly. This stage was constructed by an official named Phaedrus, identified by the following inscription on the top step of the stairway leading up from the orchestra: 'For thee, delighter in the orgy, Phaedrus, ruler of life-giving Attica, was wrought this beautiful platform of the theatre.' The so-called Stage of Phaedrus used as its base a sculptural relief taken from an earlier structure, perhaps the stage-building that is thought to have been erected in the reign of Nero. It was built hurriedly and with little care, with the sculptured figures from the earlier structure cut down to size so that the stage would be the right height. As a result, all but one of the figures have lost their heads; the only exception is an old bearded Silenus, who has survived only because he is crouching down, thus appearing to support the weight of the stage upon his shoulders. The scenes depicted here are all from the myth of Dionysos Eleutherios, depicting the story of the god's life from the time of his birth until his triumphant entry into Attica, when he was enshrined here in his sanctuary on the south slope of the Acropolis.

The myth depicted on the Stage of Phaedrus formed the basis for the Greater Dionysia, a three-day festival commemorating the triumphal arrival of Dionysos in Attica with singing and dancing and the drinking of considerable amounts of wine. On the eve of the festival an ancient xoanon, or wooden image, of Dionysos was taken from a shrine in the Academy, a sacred precinct outside Athens, and was carried in a torchlit procession to the god's sanctuary below the Acropolis. The god's arrival in Attica was re-enacted on the first day of the festival, with the Archon Basileus playing the part of Dionysos as he is borne through the city on a ship with wheels, similar to the one used in the Panathenaic procession (see p. 47). The ship was pulled to the sanctuary on the south slope of the Acropolis, and there the god was wedded to Basilinna, the queen, whose role was played by the wife of the Archon Basileus. After this sacred wedding there was a drinking competition called Choes, or 'the Jugs', in which the renowned drunkards of Athens sought to outdo one another in the consumption of new wine, 'the gift of bounteous Dionysos'. The final day of the festival was a more sober one in which the hung-over Athenians made pilgrimages to the cemeteries outside the walls bearing votive offerings to their departed relatives, whose own initiation into the cult of Dionysos had assured them of a better life after death.

According to the testimony of several ancient writers, the Theatre of Dionysos was adorned with the statues of famous men, most notably the dramatists whose plays were performed there. As Pausanias writes: 'In the theatre the Athenians have portraits of the poets of tragedy and comedy ... Except for Menander there are none of the famous comic poets. In tragedy there are Euripides and Sophocles who are well known ... I think the image of Aeschylus is much later than his death.'

The sanctuary of Dionysos was finally closed and abandoned in AD 435, when Theodosius II banned pagan practices throughout the empire. But performances of drama in the theatre had ceased long before that time, probably after the Herulian sack of AD 267. A small Christian chapel was erected in the eastern *parados* of the theatre towards the end of the fifth century AD, with the orchestra serving as its courtyard. The chapel was destroyed in the eleventh century, when the Byzantines built a new line of fortifications below the Acropolis. This defence wall, the Rizocastron, cut through the theatre along the two *paradoi*, destroying much of its structure in the process. Then in the centuries that followed the remains of the theatre and the sanctuary of Dionysos were covered over with earth washed down by rain from the Acropolis. When Leake explored the south slope of the Acropolis, between 1805 and 1810, all that remained above ground was part of one wing of the stage building; nevertheless he was able to identify it as part of the Theatre of Dionysos, and so it proved to be when the site was first excavated in 1862. The orchestra was unearthed by Wilhelm Dörpfeld in 1886, and in the years since then the remainder of the theatre and the sanctuary have been uncovered. In recent years there were hopes that the theatre would be fully restored to its original condition, so that it could be used to stage productions of the great plays that were performed here during the golden age of Greek drama, but unfortunately these plans have been put aside for the time being. But at least the ancient theatre and sanctuary of Dionysos have survived, and even without restoration their ruins evoke the richness of the ancient rituals and drama that were enacted here on the south slope of the Acropolis.

We now walk back to examine the ruins of the vast arcade that marches westwards from the Theatre of Dionysos, its ruined arches extending as far as the Odeion of Herodes Atticus, a distance of 163 m. These are the remains of a stoa built by Eumenes II, King of Pergamum (197–159 BC), as a gift to the beloved city where he and his younger brother Attalos had studied in their youth. (His brother, who ruled from 159 to 138 as Attalos II, would later endow Athens with the stoa that now bears his name in the Agora.) The Stoa of Eumenes was designed as an additional shelter for spectators at the Theatre of Dionysos, for the stoa behind the stage-building was too small to accommodate a full house. The Stoa of Eumenes had two storeys, with a Doric portico of sixty-four columns in front and an Ionic colonnade of thirty-two columns along its central axis. In front there was an immense courtyard, which served as a promenade during intermissions at the theatrical performances. When the Odeion of Herodes Atticus was built, c. AD 161–74, the stoa was connected structurally with its stage-building, so that spectators could pass from its second storey into the upper tier of the theatre. The back wall of the stoa abutted the retaining wall of the Peripatos, which ran directly behind it at the level of its hipped roof. This retaining wall was supported by forty buttresses connected by semicircular arches. These arches were once concealed behind the Stoa of Eumenes, but after the destruction of the main portico they were exposed to view, creating the distinctive landmark that one sees today.

At the south-east corner of the stoa there are the foundations of an ancient structure, which has been identified as the choregic monument of Nikias. This monument, erected in 320/19 BC, was designed in the form of a prostyle temple, with a western pronaos fronted by six Doric columns. The monument of Nikias was destroyed during the Herulian raid of AD 267, after which its stones were used in the construction of one of the main portals in the Late Roman fortification walls; this is the so-called Beulé Gate, through which one passes on the way up to the Acropolis.

In the sanctuary of Dionysos, at the south-east corner of the theatre, we find a partially excavated area, identified as the site of an odeion built in 445 BC by Pericles. The Odeion of Pericles was designed as a covered auditorium for the musical programme and competitions that were held during the celebrations of the Greater Dionysia and the Panathenaic festival. The Periclean structure was destroyed during Sulla's sack of the city in 86 BC, but it was rebuilt to the same design a quarter of a century later by Ariobarzanes II, King of Cappadocia, who in his youth had been a student in one of the ancient philosophical schools of Athens.

The site of the odeion has been excavated only to the extent of unearthing part of its foundation. The exterior dimensions of the structure were 62.4 × 68.6 m, and within there were three rows of columns on all four sides, leaving an open space in the middle for the performers. These columns, seventy-two in all, were surmounted by architraves and an upper colonnade, which supported an extremely steep pyramidal roof. Some ancient sources say that this roof was built in imitation of the King of Persia's royal tent, but one wag, the comic poet Cratinus, claimed that it represented the head of Pericles himself. As Cratinus wrote in his *Thrattae*: 'He wears a cap for his odeion/ Our Pericles pointed of pate.'

Pericles took great interest in the musical contests performed in his odeion. He used his influence to establish prizes for the best singers and musicians, and he himself acted as one of the judges. The odeion was undoubtedly wrecked when the Herulians sacked the city in AD 267. Whatever was left of it suffered additional damage when the Byzantine defence wall was built in the eleventh century, cutting right through the centre of the odeion. Subsequently the Odeion of Pericles was covered with soil washed down by rain from the Acropolis, and it totally disappeared until the site was partially excavated in the 1920s by the Greek Archaeological Society.

We now make our way up from the Odeion of Pericles to the rocks underneath the south cliff of the Acropolis, stopping just above the central axis of the Theatre of Dionysos. There we come upon a cave closed off by an iron grille, with a pair of isolated Corinthian columns standing tall on the ledge above. As Pausanias says, 'On the brow over the theatre is a cave in the rocks under the Acropolis; it has a tripod on it, and inside Apollo and Artemis are slaughtering the children of Niobe.' One authority holds that the cave was formerly a shrine of Artemis, converted into a Christian chapel early in the Byzantine period. The chapel continues in existence to the present day as a shrine of the Panayia Spiliotissa, Our Lady of the Cave. The chapel was in times past much frequented by Athenian women: mothers praying for their sick children; barren women asking for the gift of a child; spinsters hoping for a husband; requests that would have been made to Artemis in ancient times.

The tripod that Pausanias mentions in connection with the cave was part of the choregic monument of Thrasyllos. This monument was destroyed during the Turkish siege of the Acropolis in 1826–7, but it can be reconstructed from the drawings in Stuart and Revett. The façade consisted of three Doric pilasters standing on a two-stepped platform; these supported an architrave, a frieze decorated with sculptured garlands in relief, and a cornice, all made of white Pentelic marble. On top of the monument there was a three-stepped pedestal on which stood the tripod, the prize for victory in a choral competition. The inscription on the architrave was copied by Stuart, who translated it as follows: 'Thrasyllos, the son of Thrasyllos of Dekelia, dedicated this; he was victor as choregos with the men of the tribe of Hippothoon; Eyios the Chalcidian played the flute; Neachismos was the archon; Karchidamos the Sotian taught the chorus.'

Half a century later another pair of pedestals were set up on the monument by Thrasykles, a son of Thrasyllos. These pedestals also supported prize tripods, won when Thrasykles was agonothetes, the president and chief judge of the choral competition. Fragments of the two pedestals can still be seen to the left of the cave. The inscription on the one that originally stood on the left side of the monument has been translated thus: 'The people gave the chorus, Pytharatos was archon; Thrasykles of Dekelia, the son of Thrasyllos, was agonothetes; the tribe of Hippothoon won the victory among the boys; Theon the Theban played the flute: Pronomos the Theban taught the chorus.' The inscription on the right-hand base began with the same introduction, naming the same agonothetes and archon, and then identified the chorus thus: 'The tribe of Pandion won the victory among the men; Nikoles of Ambracia played the flute; Lysippos the Arcadian taught the chorus.' The names of the archons reveal that the inscription by Thrasyllos dates from 320/19 BC and that of Thrasykles from 271/70 BC.

At some time during the Roman period the three trophies were removed from the monument and replaced by statues, one of which was still in place when Stuart made his drawing. This work, a headless figure thought to represent Dionysos, is now in the British Museum.

The two tall Corinthian columns on the rock above the cave also date from the Roman period. Each of the three-sided capitals on these columns once supported a prize tripod, but the dates and circumstances of the choral victories that they commemorated are unknown.

Notice the ancient sundial on the rock face above and to the right of the cave. This was first described by a European who visited Athens just after the Turkish conquest in 1456. This traveller, the so-called 'Anonymous of Vienna', wrote a short guide to the antiquities of Athens, the first description of the city since that of Pausanias, thirteen centuries earlier.

Some 50 m west of the cave there is a little terrace above the north-west corner of the Theatre of Dionysos. From there one can look down upon the ruins of the Asklepieion, the sanctuary of Asklepios, the Greek god of health. According to mythology, Asklepios was the son of Apollo and the nymph Coronis, a granddaughter of Ares. The cult of Asklepios as a healing deity had its roots in several places in the Greek world, but in the Classical period Epidauros was generally acknowledged to be the birthplace of the god, and his principal sanctuary was established there. The cult of Asklepios spread to Attica in the mid fifth century BC. According to tradition, when the healing god first came to Athens he was received by Sophocles. The playwright made his own house a place of worship for Asklepios until the completion of the sanctuary on the south slope of the Acropolis. Inscriptions found on the site indicate that the original Asklepieion was established here in 420 BC. Associated with Asklepios in this cult was his daughter Hygieia, the personification of health, which formerly had been one of Athena's divine attributes. In the Hippocratic oath the name of Hygieia follows immediately after that of her father and before Panacea, her younger sister.

Before descending to look at the Asklepieion we might pause for a moment on the terrace below, for this is where the great Neoplatonist philosopher Proclus (c. 410–85) lived for most of his life. Proclus served as director of the Platonic Academy until the time of his death. He was the most prolific and creative thinker of late antiquity, the author of books in philosophy, mathematics and astronomy; and it was his interpretation of Plato's thought that came to influence the cultures of Byzantium, Islam and medieval Europe.

We now make our way down to the Asklepieion, entering the site through the ruins of its propylon, a gateway of Roman date. Passing through the gateway, we see to our right a ruined stoa of Roman date, and on our left a long array of marble fragments piled neatly along the southern side of the terrace. The latter are the remains of a Doric stoa of the early fourth century BC, which probably served as a dormitory for the patients at the Asklepieion. The stoa, which had two storeys, was nearly 50 m long and 10 m deep, backing against the Acropolis scarp. There were seventeen Doric columns on the façade of each floor, and along the central axis on both storeys there was an inner colonnade of six Ionic columns, with the upper columns supporting a sloping roof with a hip at each end.

Fifteen metres from the east end of the stoa a circular chamber with a domed roof has been hollowed out of the Acropolis rock, enlarging what had originally been a natural cave with a spring issuing from the ground. This cave and its natural spring were undoubtedly part of a sanctuary even before the establishment of the Asklepieion, although the name of the deity to whom it was dedicated is not known. Like so many pagan shrines, it was converted into a Christian chapel early in the Byzantine period and continued as such until Athens was captured by the Turks in 1456. During the Turkish occupation of Athens the sanctuary was within the fortifications of the Acropolis and thus was inaccessible to the Greeks. But when the Turkish occupation ended in 1833 the chapel was reconsecrated, and it continues to serve as a place of worship to the present day. Such is the tenacity of Greek popular religion.

At the west end of the stoa the Acropolis rock was cut back some 4 m deeper than the rest of the structure, thus making room for a square chamber measuring approximately 10 m on each side. The floor of this chamber was raised 4.5 m above the ground floor of the stoa, and was reached by a flight of steps that ascended from the western end of the portico. In the floor of this chamber there was a *botrhos*, or pit, 2.7 m in diameter and 2.2 m deep. The purpose of this pit is uncertain, but it may have been the home of the sacred serpents that are known to have played a part in the mystical healing rites practised in the Asklepieion.

Numerous votive offerings have been found in the Asklepieion, as well as a great many inscriptions attesting to miraculous cures. These offerings were in the form of stone or metal tablets, on which are represented in low relief the particular part of the body involved in the cure. The excavations also unearthed a number of votive reliefs showing scenes from the myth of Asklepios. Another relief, found on a statue base, depicts an array of surgical and cupping instruments, showing that the Asklepieion was a medical centre as well as a religious shrine. The founder of scientific medicine, Hippocrates of Cos, was a member of the Asklepiades, or descendants of Asklepios; he was a contemporary of Socrates, and he may have visited the Athenian Asklepieion.

The foundations of a small temple dedicated to Asklepios and Hygieia have been found at the west end of the stoa. Also, in the centre of the Asklepieion's temenos, excavations have revealed the foundations of a large altar, probably the one mentioned in many of the inscriptions commemorating cures by Asklepios.

A Christian basilica was built on the site of the Asklepieion in the mid fifth century AD, and many of the marble architectural fragments that one sees on the site today are from that structure. This church is thought to have been dedicated to St Cosmos and St Damian, who are known in Greek as Ay. Anargyroi, the 'Penniless Saints', so called, according to tradition, because they would not accept payment for the medical care that they gave to the poor people of Athens. These saints have been popular in Athens since the early Byzantine period, and there are several churches in the modern city dedicated to them. The iconostases of all the churches of Ay. Anargyroi are covered with metallic ex-votos attesting to miraculous cures performed by the saints, indicating that they inherited the healing power of Asklepios along with his shrine here on the south slope of the Acropolis.

We now walk across to the western part of the Asklepieion, which is on a terrace slightly higher than the eastern part of the sanctuary. The fragmentary ruins on the northern half of the terrace are all that remains of an Ionic stoa, dated to c. 400 BC. At the rear of the stoa there were four rooms with pebble mosaic floors, and at the front there was a portico with a colonnade of twelve Ionic columns. It is thought that this stoa, like the one on the eastern terrace, was used as a dormitory for patients at the Asklepieion.

Just to the west of the Ionic stoa there are the remains of an ancient spring-house, of which only the eastern half of the draw-basin has survived. The western half of the basin was destroyed at some time in the medieval period, when a vaulted cistern was built to store water from the spring that issued forth at the bottom of the well. This sacred spring, whose well is dated to the end of the sixth century BC, is thought to have been a sanctuary of the nymph Alkippe. The temenos of this shrine extended from the Acropolis rock as far as the Stoa of Eumenes, which was bordered by the Peripatos. A boundary-stone still standing on the Peripatos, directly below the well, bears the inscription HOROS KRENES, or 'Boundary of the Spring'. South of the boundary-stone there is a large vaulted cistern, which is thought to date from the Byzantine period.

Just to the south of the sacred spring there are the remains of two small monuments. The one to the west is a crudely built structure dating from the Byzantine era. The other, which abuts the spring-house, was apparently a small classical temple *in antis*, with its entrance facing south-east. Some authorities think that this was a sanctuary of Themis, mother of Prometheus, while others believe that it was the original temple of Asklepios on this site.

We now continue westwards along the south slope of the Acropolis, passing on the right a pit that is believed to have been used in ancient times for the casting of colossal bronze statues. This brings us to the heights above the Odeion of Herodes Atticus, which we will visit on a later stroll. Above the odeion we take a path that leads steeply uphill towards the Nike bastion, where there is a gate that opens into the area below the entrance to the Acropolis. There we complete our stroll along the south slope of the Acropolis, one of the least-known parts of the ancient city.

3

The Acropolis

On our last stroll we approached the entrance to the Acropolis along the south slope of the hill. But most travellers approach it from the west, as the Greeks did in ancient times, for the ascent is more gradual there than on the other sides, which are all precipitous. One begins the final part of the ascent in that direction from the open area below the Areopagus, the rocky spur just to the north-west of the Acropolis. This is where the procession of the Panathenaic festival paused in order to anchor the ship on wheels that had been pulled up from the main gate of the city, its mast draped with the sacred *peplos*, a gown which had been woven by a group of Athenian maidens during the previous year. When the ship halted the maidens removed the *peplos* from the mast and carried it with them on the final stage of the procession, which ended up in front of a sanctuary of Athena on the Parthenon. There the maidens presented the *peplos* to the Archon Basileus, and he in turn placed it on the xoanon, the ancient wooden image of Athena. The last stage of the Panathenaic procession followed the same route that most people take today in going up to the Acropolis. This leads one by a series of stepped paths to the Beulé Gate, the main entrance to the archaeological site.

The Beulé Gate is named after the French archaeologist who unearthed it in 1852. The gateway consists of two large towers flanking a central doorway aligned with the axis of the Propylaia, the monumental entrance to the Acropolis. The date of construction of the gateway is uncertain, but it is thought to have been erected soon after the Herulian raid of AD 267, using architectural fragments taken from older monuments. The central part is constructed largely of blocks from the choregic monument of Nikias, the foundations of which we saw earlier in the precincts of the sanctuary of Dionysos. The

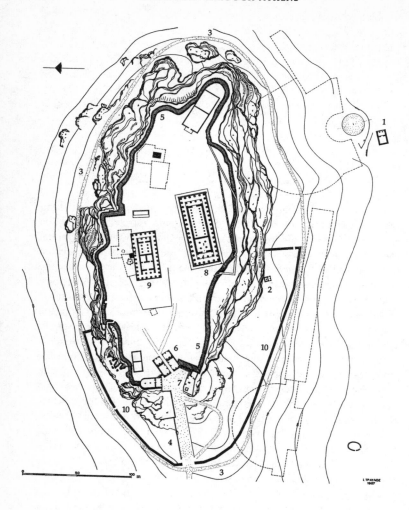

The Acropolis on the eve of the Persian invasion in 480 BC

1 Asklepieion spring house
2 Shrine of Dionysos
3 Peripatos
4 Ramp
5 Ancient wall

6 Old Propylon
7 Shrine of Athena Nike
7 Older Parthenon
9 Old Temple of Athena

entablature of the monument, with its architrave, triglyphs, metopes and cornice, forms the upper part of the central gateway. Across the architrave there is this inscription: 'Nikias, son of Nikodemos of Xypete, dedicated this, having won with a chorus of boys from the tribe Cecropis; Pantaleon the Sicyonian played the flute; the Elpenor of Timotheus was the song; Neachmus was archon.' The name of the archon dates the monument to 320/19 BC. Leake deciphered another inscription on the architrave, in which a Roman named Flavius Septimus Marcellinus is commemorated as having presented the gateway to the city. Presumably this would have been after the Herulian raid of AD 267, when the Beulé Gate was incorporated into the Late Roman fortification wall.

Passing through the Beulé Gate, we ascend a flight of steps that leads directly up to the Propylaia, with the Temple of Athena Nike standing on its bastion above and to the right. Along the left side of the steps there is a polygonal wall running uphill nearly parallel to the central axis of the Propylaia. This has been tentatively dated to the late sixth century BC; it is undoubtedly the retaining wall for the ramp to the archaic Propylon, the main gate to the Acropolis at that time. The gateway of the archaic Propylon stood at the same place as that of the Propylaia, but it faced south-west, whereas the classical entry-way opens to the west.

Beyond the polygonal retaining wall, in front of the north tower of the Beulé Gate, there is an altar dated to the sixth century BC. On top of the wall to the right of the stairway there are four fragments of an architrave, adorned with the figures in relief of doves with fillets in their beaks. An inscription on the architrave identifies the fragments as being from a sanctuary of Aphrodite Pandemos (Of All the People). Excavations in 1960 revealed that this was a small sanctuary that stood in the level area just below the Nike bastion to its south, where a number of architectural fragments have been assembled.

One might now take the opportunity to examine the Nike bastion. In Mycenaean times this was a *pyrgos*, or tower, which guarded the entrance to the Acropolis. The bastion was sheathed in dressed poros stone during the classical period, but boulders of the original Mycenaean tower can still be seen projecting through the revetment. The window-like niches are part of the classical structure, marking spots that had evidently been held sacred since Mycenaean times. Notice the rough steps cut into the living rock beneath the bastion; these were hewn in the Mycenaean period to provide a firmer footing for sacrificial animals being led up to the Acropolis.

Above the left side of the stairway, almost directly opposite the Nike bastion, there stands a colossal pedestal of bluish-grey Hymettos marble, the so-called Monument of Agrippa. Cuttings on the upper surface of the pedestal show that on two occasions it was surmounted by a bronze quadriga, or four-horse chariot. The pedestal was erected in 178 BC by King Eumenes II of Pergamum, commemorating a victory that he and his brother Attalos won in a chariot race that year at the Panathenaic Games. The quadriga was later removed and replaced by statues of Antony and Cleopatra, probably in 39 BC, when they began their extended stay in Athens. Their statues were toppled by a hurricane in 31 BC, soon after they were defeated by Octavian at the battle of Actium. After his victory Octavian wintered in Athens with his bosom friend, Marcus Vipsanius Agrippa, who had been his commander-in-chief at Actium. When Octavian became Augustus, in 27 BC, Agrippa became his first minister, and while holding that post he treated Athens with great favour. Among other benefactions, he built a monumental odeion in the Agora, where its impressive ruins can still be seen today. The Athenians responded to Agrippa's generosity by mounting a quadriga in his honour on the pedestal originally erected by Eumenes. Traces of an inscription high on the west face of the pedestal record this latter dedication: 'The people [dedicated this statue of] Marcus Agrippa, son of Lucius, thrice consul, their benefactor.'

The terrace on which the Monument of Agrippa stands dates from the same period as the Propylaia, and it has been suggested that it was originally designed as the lower forecourt of the classical entry-way. On the eastern side of the terrace there is a mound of marble fragments found at various places on the Acropolis. Many of these are Turkish tombstones dating from the Ottoman occupation of Athens. The tombstones of the men are topped with turbans; those of the women are adorned with floral reliefs; and a number of them have finely carved epitaphs in old Ottoman script.

At this point one might pause to look up at the Propylaia and study its structure, for this is the most magnificent entry-way ever erected in the ancient Greek world. The Propylaia was built in the period 437–432 BC, just after the completion of the Parthenon, and it was the last structure to be erected on the Acropolis in the Periclean Age. The architect was Mnesikles, an associate of Pheidias, who undoubtedly worked closely with him on the design and construction of the Propylaia.

It is probable that the original plan conceived by Mnesikles

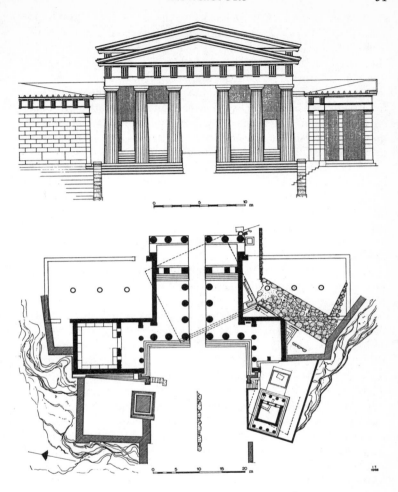

The Propylaia
(*Above*) The Propylaia flanked by north and south wings (restored)
(*Below*) The Mnesiklean Propylaia with the Agrippa Monument and the Temple of
Athena Nike. Broken lines indicate the Old Propylon and the earlier shrine of Athena
Nike

envisioned a structure that would take up the entire western end of the Acropolis. This would have consisted of the central gateway itself, along with a pair of outer wings extending to the north-west and the south-west, and also a pair of inner halls to the north-east and south-east. But for various reasons the original plan was never carried out. When construction was halted in 432 BC, because of the outbreak of the Peloponnesian War, only the central gateway and the two outer wings had been completed. Even then, the south-west wing was a good deal smaller than originally planned, and the two inner halls had hardly been started. The curtailment of the south-west wing was due to the fact that it abutted on to the Temple of Athena Nike, while the south-east hall would have encroached upon the precincts of the sanctuary of Artemis Brauronia. Construction was resumed for a time after the Peloponnesian War, but it was never carried through to completion. Nevertheless, the structure erected by Mnesikles was remarkably successful, creating a monumental entrance with a grandeur appropriate to the site.

As originally constructed, the entry-way consisted of a cross-wall pierced by five gates, with a large central portal flanked by two pairs of successive smaller gates. Porches with pedimented roofs projected from both sides, with the outer porticoes flanked by a pair of wings that projected to the north-west and south-west. Processions, chariots and sacrificial animals entered the Acropolis along the sloping ramp that ran up the central axis of the Propylaia. Pedestrians would first have to climb a set of four marble steps to enter the outer portico, and after passing through this they would have to ascend a second stairway of five steps before entering the inner porch through one of the side doors. The façades of the two porches were formed by colonnades of six Doric columns, each supporting its entablature of architrave, frieze and cornice. The spacing between the two central columns in both colonnades was made wider than the other inter-columniations to accommodate the wide ramp. This ramp was flanked in the outer porch by three pairs of exceptionally tall columns, whose Ionic capitals are considered to be the finest extant examples of their type. These columns provided internal support for the roof of the outer porch, which was more than twice as long as the inner one. Marble beams passed between the north and south walls of the outer porch and the architraves of the central columns. These beams, each of which weighed more than eleven tons, formed the basis for a coffered ceiling decorated with eight-pointed gold stars on a blue ground. A similar ceiling covered the inner porch, though there the beams were laid parallel to the central axis of the Propylaia, and the coffers were decorated with palmettes rather than stars. The great ceiling of the Propylaia is considered to have been the supreme work of its type in the Greek world. As Pausanias described it, the Propylaia 'has a roof of white marble, which down to my own times is still incomparable for the size and beauty of the stone'.

The two outer wings of the Propylaia were erected at right angles to the central gateway, with their stylobates and steps being extensions of those of the outer porch. The façades of both wings have three Doric columns *in antis*. The wing to the right was purely decorative, but the one on the left formed the porch for a large hall; this served as a lounge where visitors to the Acropolis could take their ease, and for that purpose seventeen couches were laid out head to foot round the four walls of the room, leaving room only for the door leading in from the north-west porch. Pausanias identifies this hall as the Pinakotheke, or Picture Gallery, and he describes a number of paintings that were exhibited there in his time, most of them scenes from Greek mythology and Homer's epics.

At some time during the Roman era the unfinished north-east hall was made into a cistern, and it continued to serve as such up until the nineteenth century. After the Herulian raid of AD 267, the Propylaia was enclosed within the Late Roman fortification wall, so that the Acropolis once again became a fortress. The Propylaia itself may have been fortified during the reign of Justinian (527–65), who built a new circuit of defence walls around the city. The south-west wing was converted into a Christian chapel at that time, and in the tenth century the north-west wing also became a church, requiring a modification of its structure. During the middle Byzantine period a second floor was added to the north-west wing, creating a residence for the Greek Orthodox Bishop of Athens. After the capture of Athens by the Latins in 1205, this became the home of the Roman Catholic Archbishop of Athens. During the reign of Nerio I Acciajuoli, in the latter years of the fourteenth century, the back half of the south-west wing was converted into a huge *pyrgos*, a building of square cross-section that rose some 30 m above the stylobate of the Propylaia and extended as far back as the south-west corner of the Acropolis wall. This *pyrgos* served as both a watchtower and as the palace of the Latin kings of Athens. After the Turkish conquest of 1456 the Propylaia became a fortress once again; the former residence of the archbishop housed the garrison commander, with the lower floor serving as a powder maga- zine. A bolt of lightning struck the magazine on 26 October 1656 and it exploded, severely damaging the Propylaia and causing many casualties among the Turkish garrison. The Propylaia was damaged again during Morosini's bombardment of the Acropolis in 1687, and it suffered additional ruination during the Turkish siege of 1826–7. The long task of repair and restoration began shortly after the War of Independence, when archaeologists cleared away all of the Byzantine, Latin and Turkish structures that had been built on and around the Propylaia. The Latin *pyrgos* survived until 1875, however, when it was finally pulled down by Heinrich Schliemann. A long-term project to restore the Propylaia was begun under the direction of Nicolas Balanos in 1909; a second programme was completed by A. K. Orlandos in 1963; and still another restoration programme is under way at the present moment.

We now pass through the Propylaia, walking up a wooden stairway that has been laid down to protect the marble ramp. In passing through, notice the superb Ionic capital atop the last column on the left of the central colonnade, where a section of the coffered ceiling has been put back in place. Another fragment of the ceiling can be seen on the ground below, with its painted stellar decoration still visible. Finally we pass through the central columns of the inner porch and emerge upon the plateau of the Acropolis, where suddenly one is confronted with the magnificent spectacle of the Parthenon, framed in the columns of the Propylaia's inner porch.

Before walking over to the Parthenon, let us look at the antiquities in the south-west corner of the Acropolis. (This area has now been roped off for preservation and repair, and so one must make do with a longer-range observation from the high ground of the Acropolis or from the stairway leading up to the Propylaia.) We begin by turning right to walk past the inner colonnade of the Propylaia. Before going on, notice the semicircular marble drum resting against the corner column. An inscription on the stone identifies it as having been the base of a statue of Athena Hygieia, an attribute of the goddess recognizing her powers as a healer. According to Plutarch, Pericles dedicated this statue to Athena after she restored the health of one of his workmen, who was on the verge of death after having fallen here from a scaffold while the Propylaia was under construction.

The ruins just to the south of the Propylaia occupy the site of what would have been the south-east hall of the entry-way. Cutting diagonally across the site of this hall are the remains of an ancient wall; this and the original Nike bastion were part of the Mycenaean fortifications at the south-east corner of the Acropolis. According to tradition, this is where King Aegeus of Athens met his end, a tale told by Pausanias:

... they say that this is where Aegeus leapt to his death. The ship carrying the children to Crete started out with black sails, and Theseus, who was sailing to prove his courage against the Minotaur, promised his father that he would use white sails for the voyage home provided he had overcome the monster; but in the loss of Ariadne he forgot this promise, so when Aegeus saw the ship coming in under black sails the old man thought his son was dead, and threw himself down and was killed.

At the inner end of the Mycenaean wall, where it abuts the south wall of the Propylaia, one can see a surviving corner of the archaic Propylon. This gateway has been dated to the sixth century BC, and was probably commissioned by Peisistratus. The archaic gateway was destroyed during the Persian sack of Athens in 480 BC, and its ruins were incorporated within the structure of the classical entry-way, leaving only this corner of the original structure intact.

The beautiful little Temple of Athena Nike on the bastion is one of the landmarks on the Acropolis, and Pausanias mentions passing it on his way up to the Propylaia. Pausanias calls it the Temple of Wingless Victory, in Greek, Nike Apteros. The ancient goddess Nike, the personification of Victory, was represented as winged and flying with great speed. Later the Athenians assimilated her cult with that of their patron deity, who here became Athena Nike, but since the goddess in this role was represented without wings she became Nike Apteros. (Pausanias mentions in another place that 'in Athens they believe Victory will stay with them for ever because she has no wings'.) Thenceforth Nikes were represented in Greek art as winged maidens who served as attendants to Athena, the Bringer of Victory.

Excavations on the bastion shortly before the Second World War unearthed an altar and a small sanctuary dedicated to Athena Nike, with an inscription dated to the mid sixth century BC. The cult of Athena Nike seems to have been established in Athens by that time, although it did not become part of the state religion until a century later. A decree issued in 448 BC authorized the construction of a temple on the bastion under the direction of Kallikrates. But it appears that work on the temple did not begin until 427 BC, two years after the death of Pericles. The temple itself was completed in 424, but work on the sculptured parapet was not finished until c. 410. the temple survived intact until 1686, when the Turkish garrison demolished it and used its stones to build a redoubt at the south-western corner of the Acropolis, which was severely damaged the following year during Morosini's bombardment. The temple was reconstructed by Ludwig Ross in 1835–6, using the fragments he found embedded in the

Turkish fortifications. A more thorough and scientific restoration was done in the decade before the First World War, a project that produced the temple as we see it today.

The temple stands on a platform of four steps, with the lowest step at the rear standing flush against the edge of the bastion and close to its north-western corner. Its proximity to the edge of the bastion made it necessary to build a parapet behind the temple and along the two adjacent sides. This wall, which was a little more than a metre high and topped by a brass grille, ended on the northern side at a stairway that led down to the steps below the Propylaia. The parapet was decorated on its outer surface with panels sculptured in relief. The focal point of this decoration was a panel in the middle of the west parapet, where Athena was shown receiving adulation from two processions of winged maidens representing Nikes. These processions moved generally towards the west on both the north and south parapets, and then they turned the corner to proceed towards the goddess. About a third of these panels have survived, and the best are now on exhibit in the Acropolis Museum. The most famous of the reliefs is the headless figure of a Nike who is shown bending down to adjust her sandal. These reliefs are generally acknowledged to be among the finest sculptures that have survived from the classical era.

The temple is of the Ionic order and is amphiprostyle-tetrastyle; that is, with porticoes of four columns at the front and rear only. The cella, or main structure of the temple, has solid walls on all sides except the east, where two rectangular pillars stand between the antae. The space between each of these pillars and the adjacent anta was closed off by a bronze grille, leaving a central portal opening out between the pillars on to the front portico. The triple Ionic architrave is supported by the porticoes and the side walls of the cella, and above this there is a sculptured frieze of figures in relatively high relief extending around the four sides of the building. The only panels of the original reliefs that have survived *in situ* are those on the east frieze. The panels on the other three sides are copies in cement of the originals, now in the British Museum. The figures on the east frieze are badly weathered and all of them have lost their heads, but Athena can be identified by her shield. Beside her is a figure who is probably Zeus, and arrayed on either side of them are the figures of a score of other deities. The other sides of the frieze show scenes from the battle of Plataea, with Greeks fighting the Boeotian allies of Xerxes on the north side, and doing battle with the Persians on the west frieze.

According to the testimony of ancient writers, the cella of the temple housed the wooden cult-statue of Athena Nike, the Wingless Victory, representing the goddess with a pomegranate in one hand and her crested helmet in the other. The pomegranate symbolized fertility, a reminder that Athena was originally a fertility goddess, while the helmet signified that she was a warrior, the protectress of the city and the bringer of victory.

We now head back towards the Parthenon, keeping close to the south wall of the Acropolis. As we do so we pass through what was once the temenos of the sanctuary of Brauronian Artemis, the Bear-Goddess. The original sanctuary of Artemis on this site was probably founded by Peisistratus, for he was born in the village of Brauron in Attica. The temple at Brauron enshrined the ancient wooden xoanon of Artemis which Iphigenia was supposed to have brought back with her from the land of Tauris. The sanctuary of Brauronian Artemis was a long stoa whose back wall ran along the southern rampart of the Acropolis, with porticoed wings extending from its eastern and western extremities. These wings were used to house two statues of Artemis, and they also served as treasuries for the safe keeping of votive-offerings presented to the goddess. The oldest of these statues was the wooden cult-image of Artemis, probably dating from the time of Peisistratus, undoubtedly a copy of the ancient xoanon of the goddess at Brauron. The second was a bronze statue of the goddess by Praxiteles that Pausanias saw in the sanctuary of Brauronian Artemis on the Acropolis. The latter work, dated 346 BC, is believed to be the original of the so-called Artemis of Gabii in the Louvre.

Since Artemis was a fertility goddess, her shrines at Brauron and here on the Acropolis were very popular among mothers and pregnant women, for she was the patron of childbirth. The attendants in her sanctuary were very young girls, perhaps five or six years old, and they dressed in bearskins to symbolize the fact that Artemis was also the protectress of animals. (In the Brauronian myth, Artemis substituted a bear for Iphigenia when Agamemnon was about to sacrifice his daughter there.) There is a reference to this in the play *Lysistrata*, where Aristophanes has the chorus-leader tell of the state ceremonies in which she participated as a girl, mentioning the occasion when 'wearing the saffron robe I was a bear at the Brauronian festival'.

Just beyond the temenos of Brauronian Artemis there are a number of squared poros stones *in situ* as well foundations for walls hewn into the rock, one of which cuts into the western steps of the Parthenon. This is believed to be the Chalkotheke, or Bronze Storeroom, a treasury for storing bronze vessels and votive offerings belonging to the various sanctuaries on the Acropolis. The Chalkotheke itself was built up against the southern rampart of the Acropolis, probably in the mid fifth century BC; then in the beginning of the next century a stoa was added along the length of its north façade, its north-eastern corner cutting into the adjacent steps of the Parthenon. The building was apparently restored extensively during the Roman period, as is suggested by architectural fragments found all over the Acropolis that seem to have come from a structure with the dimensions of the Chalkotheke.

We now approach the area between the south-west corner of the Parthenon and the south wall of the Acropolis, where we come upon two deep pits walled off by parapets. These pits have been left open so that one can see the older fortification walls that run along the south side of the plateau below the present ground level.

The Acropolis was first fortified during the Mycenaean period, probably in the second half of the thirteenth century BC. The Peisistratids rebuilt this wall in the mid sixth century BC and erected the first monumental entry-way, the Propylon. After Hippias was overthrown in 510 BC these walls were demolished, so that no future tyrant could set himself up in a fortress on the Acropolis. The next period of wall-building on the Acropolis took place soon after the Greek victory at Marathon in 490 BC. At that time the Athenians decided to build a huge new sanctuary of Athena on the Acropolis, and to do this they had to create an artificial terrace on which the temple would stand. They accomplished this by building a series of retaining walls to the south of the present Parthenon, where the rock slopes sharply downwards, and then pouring in earth and debris to form a plateau at the peak of the Acropolis. (This fill was temporarily removed during excavations in the late nineteenth century, when the Acropolis was stripped down to bedrock here in order to study the foundations of the Parthenon. It was found that the fill was deepest near the southeast corner of the Parthenon, where there are twenty-two courses of poros foundation blocks between the bedrock and the first step of the temple platform.)

The classical defence walls of the Acropolis were built in two stages, beginning the year after the Greek victories at Salamis and Plataea. The northern ramparts were built by Themistocles in 479/8 BC, at the same time that he built the outer defence walls of the city. Then in 467 BC Cimon began to build the southern ramparts, which served not only as a fortification but as the outer retaining wall for the fill that had been poured in to create the terrace. The last courses of this wall were laid down by Pericles, and it was he who finally filled in the terrace to its present level, undoubtedly just before construction began on the present Parthenon.

In the first pit, the one closest to the Acropolis wall, we see the corner of a wall of poros limestone in ashlar construction. This is thought to have been built by Cimon as a retaining wall to extend the area of the terrace, in which case it would have been erected just before he constructed the southern rampart of the Acropolis.

In the second pit we see a polygonal retaining wall of Acropolis limestone on top of a section of the Mycenaean wall, with a staircase descending from one level to the other. It is believed that the retaining wall here was erected in the late sixth century BC or early in the following century when the artificial plateau was first created at the peak of the Acropolis. Presumably this would have been when the first monumental temple of Athena was built on that site, the ancestor of the present Parthenon.

There has been considerable controversy about the architectural ancestry of the present Parthenon, particularly about the possibility that one or more temples were built on this site in the sixth century BC. One prevalent theory has it that the first monumental temple on this site was erected in the second half of the sixth century, probably during the reign of the Peisistratids. This is sometimes referred to as the Hekatompedon, the 'Hundred Footer', presumably because it was one hundred Attic feet in length. This name has also been applied to one or more later temples on the site, and is one of the factors responsible for some of the confusion regarding the prehistory of the present Parthenon. Another factor in the confusion is that there was a second sanctuary of Athena close by, just to the north of the Parthenon, where its foundation stones have been arrayed. This was the Temple of Athena Polias, which enshrined the ancient wooden xoanon of the goddess. This sanctuary is generally referred to as the Old Temple of Athena, and there has also been a great deal of discussion about whether it too had one or more predecessors on the site, further adding to the confusion.

In any event, it is now generally believed that the archaic Parthenon was demolished shortly after the victory at Marathon to make way for the construction of a new temple of Athena. The temple was only partly completed when it was destroyed during the Persian sack of Athens in 480 BC. Numerous fragments of this temple, now generally referred to as the Older Parthenon, have been discovered on the Acropolis, some of them built into the structure of the present Parthenon.

The sanctuaries on the Acropolis remained in ruins for three decades after the Persian sack. Plutarch, in his *Life of Pericles*, writes that the Greek allies took an oath after their victory at Plataea in 479 BC; they swore that they would not rebuild the temples destroyed by the Persians, but would leave them as memorials to the barbarism of the invaders. According to Plutarch, Pericles called a conference of the Greek city-states, *c.* 450 BC, asking them to revoke the oath taken at Plataea. Historians now doubt Plutarch's story about the Plataean oath and the purported attempt by Pericles to revoke it. In any event, in 450 Pericles did persuade the Athenians to build a new sanctuary of Athena on the Acropolis, appropriating the necessary funds from the treasury of the Delian League. Pheidias was placed in overall charge of the project, 'controlling everything and supervisor of all', particularly the sculptural decoration of the Parthenon, while the architects Iktinos and Kallikrates were appointed to design and build the temple itself. Construction of the temple began in 447 and was completed in 438, although work on the sculptural decoration was not finished until 432. Nevertheless, the new sanctuary of Athena was dedicated as soon as the building itself was finished, and it was opened to the public at the climax of the Great Panathenaea in 438.

Before studying the design and construction of the Parthenon, a word might be said about the name of the temple. At first it inherited the name Hekatompedon from one or more of its predecessors on the site, although strictly speaking this applied only to the cella (*hekatompedos naos*), for it was in fact about one hundred Attic feet in length. The name Parthenon comes from the colossal cult-statue of Athena Parthenos – the Virgin Goddess – that stood in the cella. During the Periclean Age the name Parthenon seems to have referred only to the smaller room at the rear of the temple, behind the cella. This perhaps stems from the fact that the rear chamber may have been used by the virgins who served as priestesses of Athena. In any event, the name Parthenon was eventually applied to the whole temple, as it is today.

As Plutarch describes it, the whole of Athens pitched in to build and adorn the Parthenon and the other monuments of the Periclean Age, 'so the works arose, no less towering in their grandeur than inimitable in the grace of their outlines, since the workmen eagerly strove to surpass themselves in the beauty of their handicraft. And yet the most wonderful thing about them was the speed with which they rose.' Plutarch then goes on to list the various guilds that were employed in the project; there were, he writes:

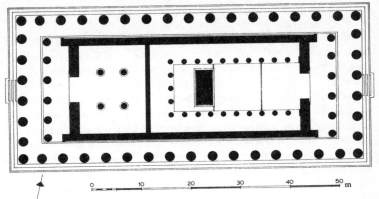

Plan of the Periclean Parthenon

carpenters, coppersmiths, stonemasons, gilders, softeners of ivory, painters, broiderers, turners ... [and also] attendants of them and guardians,
merchants and sailors and helmsmen by sea, and further, by land wagoners
and horse-breeders and charioteers and rope-twiners and linen-makers and
leather-workers and road-makers and metal miners ... and since each particular art, like a general with the army under his separate command, kept
his own throng of unskilled and untrained labourers in compact array, to
be as instruments unto player and as body unto soul in subordinate service, it came to pass that for every age, almost, and every capacity, the
city's great abundance was distributed and scattered abroad by such
demands.

Pericles and his architects decided at the outset to build largely on
the foundations of the Older Parthenon, using as much material as
possible from the temple that had been destroyed by the Persians in
480 BC. Their design placed eight columns in the front and rear
colonnades, rather than six as in the Older Parthenon, so that the new
temple required a somewhat wider and longer foundation than the
preceding structure. The extension to the foundation was made principally to the north, where the bedrock of the Acropolis came right up
to the surface. Except for the poros foundations and the wooden doors
and inner ceilings, the entire temple was made of marble, with stone
from Mt Pendeli quarried for the structure itself and finer-grained
Parian marble carved for its sculptural decoration. The Periclean Parthenon was the first monumental sanctuary in mainland Greece to be
constructed virtually entirely from marble, including its roof tiles,
which were quarried on Naxos.

The temple stands on the usual three-stepped Doric crepidoma, which at its top step, the stylobate, measures 69.62 × 26.19 m. The outer peripteral colonnade, the pteron, was erected around the edge of the crepidoma, with eight columns to front and rear and seventeen along the sides, counting corner columns twice. This arrangement, known as peripteral-octastyle, was an unusual one, since most Doric columns, including the Older Parthenon, had six columns to front and rear and thirteen along the sides. The intercolumniation, or spacing between column centres, is directly related to the dimensions of the stylobate and the height of the temple. The ratio of the length of the stylobate to its width is 9:4. If one imagines the front of the Parthenon without its pediment or steps it forms a rectangle where the ratio of width to height is also 9:4. The ratio of the intercolumniation to the diameter of the columns at their base is once again 9:4, a proportion that the Greeks called 'eustyle', or the 'good' system of column spacing.

The peripteral columns, which are in most cases made up of twelve fluted drums weighing six and a half tons each, are 10.43 m tall and have diameters ranging from 1.91 m at the ground to 1.48 m at the top. The columns do not taper uniformly, but have a slight swelling about two thirds of the way up. The variation of column diameter was a principle of design that the Greeks called entasis; this was meant to allow for the optical illusion that occurs when looking upwards along a tall and perfectly cylindrical column, which appears to taper outwards as it rises. Entasis was one of several refinements introduced to correct unsightly optical illusions in the Parthenon and to give a feeling of vitality to the structure. For example, the column drums were displaced inwards as they were stacked, so that the centre of the top cylinder is more than six centimetres farther in than that of the bottom one. Furthermore, the columns of the peristyle were not arrayed in a straight line, but were placed on a curve that was concave inwards on all sides. And the crepidoma was not designed as a flat plane but curved downwards on all sides. All of this has given rise to the remark that there is hardly a Euclidian straight line or flat plane in the design of the Parthenon.

The columns of the peristyle were surmounted by the usual plain Doric capitals, above which was the entablature, with its architrave, frieze and cornice. The frieze, as was customary in Doric temples, was divided into alternate triglyphs and metopes. The triglyphs were rectangles divided into three vertical bands by two deep grooves, whereas the metopes were broader panels whose surfaces were sculptured with figures in high relief. The placement of the triglyphs and metopes involved geometrical problems, which the architects of the Parthenon solved with their usual ingenuity. One possible arrangement was to have a triglyph above each column and one at the centre of each intercolumniation, with a metope in between. This arrangement presented no problem as long as the metopes were plain, but if they were decorated with sculptures, as on the Parthenon, then a difficulty arose. For the corner metopes would then be much smaller than the others, marring the rhythm of the decoration. The architects of the Parthenon resolved this difficulty by slightly reducing the width of each metope outwards from the central one, so that the frieze ended on each side with triglyphs at the corners rather than metopes. This slight reduction of the metope widths was imperceptible, and thus it preserved the harmony of the sculptured decoration on the frieze. Also, the triglyphs at the corners of the frieze somehow gave the structure an appearance of added strength and stability.

There were 14 metopes at each end of the temple and 32 on each side, a total of 92. Each metope represented a separate scene and contained two figures sculptured in high relief, almost in the round. The metopes were worked on by a number of different sculptors, and from those that have survived one can see that their artistic merit varies considerably. Many of the metope sculptures were destroyed during the Venetian bombardment in 1687, particularly on the north side, and those that remain *in situ* have in most cases been badly weathered. Nevertheless, the Carrey drawings and the metopes preserved in the British Museum and elsewhere have enabled archaeologists to identify the decorative themes that were used on the four sides of the temple. Thus we know that the east metopes depicted a Gigantomachy, a battle between the Olympian gods and the ancient Giants; the west an Amazonomachy, a fight between Greeks and Amazons; the south a Centauromachy, the struggle between the Lapiths and Centaurs; and on the north scenes from the Trojan War. And so one sees that the overall theme of the metope decoration was the triumph of the Greeks and their gods over their enemies, both human and mythical, undoubtedly an allegory of their recent victories in the Persian Wars.

Above the frieze in the peristyle is the usual horizontal cornice, which on the long sides of the temple was surmounted by a marble gutter with ornamental rain spouts in the form of lion heads. The joints in the marble roof tiles above the cornice were covered with antefixes in the shape of palmettes, which thus formed an ornamental fringe above the four sides of the temple. At the front and rear of the temple the raking cornice sloped back at an angle of 13.5° to form the pediments. On the summits and corners of the pediments there were colossal acroteria in the form of scrolls and palmettes.

Both pediments were adorned with sculptures, some fifty figures in all, of which only a few figures remain *in situ*. Most of the pedimental figures that survived the Venetian bombardment were taken down by Lord Elgin, during the course of which the pediments suffered additional damage. The statues removed by Elgin are now in the British Museum, while portions of other figures are preserved in the Acropolis Museum and in the Louvre. These and the Carrey drawings help in reconstructing the pedimental scenes, but the identity of the central figures in the east pediment is still uncertain. In any event, Pausanias has identified the main decorative themes in the pediments; as he writes: 'As you go into the temple called the Parthenon, everything on the pediment has to do with the birth of Athena; the far side shows Poseidon quarrelling with Athena over the country.'

The centre of the east pediment was undoubtedly occupied by Zeus enthroned. To his left stood Athena, who had just emerged newborn from her father's head, and to the right stood Hephaistos. Other deities looked on from either side, with those who are farthest away shown seated or reclining under the narrowing gap of the raking cornice. At the left corner the quadriga of Helios, the sun god, was shown as if emerging from the sea, symbolizing the beginning of the great day on which Athena was born, and in the right corner the chariot of Selene, goddess of the moon, is entering the depths at the fateful day's end. All that remains *in situ* is the heads of the two rear horses in the quadriga of Helios and some fragments of the last pair of horses pulling Selene's chariot. The rest are copies of originals in the British Museum, including the reclining figure in the left angle, who is thought to represent Dionysos.

The central figures in the west pediment were Athena and Poseidon. Beside them were their quadrigas, with Athena's horses being handled by a Nike and Poseidon's by Amphitrite, his wife. On either side there was an assemblage of gods and heroes from Attica, who were shown as they looked on as judges in the contest. Fragments of only three of these figures remain on the pediment; the others were either destroyed in the Venetian bombardment or shortly afterwards, when Morosini tried to remove the horses of Athena's quadriga, only to have them fall and shatter on the ground. Two of the surviving sculptures are to be seen midway along the left side of the pediment; these are thought to represent Cecrops, King of Athens, and his daughter Pandrosos. The third figure, in the angle to the right, is believed to be the Athenian nymph Kallirhoë.

The peristyle enclosed a covered walkway, the ambulatory, which was 4.84 m in width at the front and back of the temple and 4.26 m wide at the sides. The ambulatory had a coffered ceiling painted in brilliant blue with golden stars, as did the pronaos and opisthodomos, the front and rear porches. This ambulatory was the only place from which one could easily look up at the Ionic frieze, a continuous sculptured band almost 160 m in length above the architrave, extending completely around the *sekos*, or temple building. The frieze originally consisted of 111 panels of varying length, each about one metre high, on which were represented in low relief the figures of 360 humans, deities and animals. Only sixteen of these panels still remain *in situ* on the Parthenon. All or part of twenty-four panels have been lost, but fortunately all except one of these were recorded in the Carrey drawings. As a result, it has been possible to establish that the theme of the decoration was the procession that formed the climax of the Great Panathenaea, the quadrennial celebration in honour of Athena. It has been suggested that the procession depicted in the frieze was the last one that took place before the battle of Marathon. In support of this, one authority has counted 192 men in the frieze exclusive of charioteers, exactly the number of Greeks who died at Marathon. And thus one is led to believe that this is also a memorial to the fallen heroes of Marathon, who are here being received by the gods into the pantheon of immortality.

The procession, as represented in the frieze, began at the southwestern corner of the Parthenon. One group in the procession headed along the west and north faces of the frieze and the other along the south, after which the two of them turned the corners on to the east face, where the procession culminated.

One might begin with the west frieze, since that contains most of what is left *in situ* on the Parthenon, fourteen of the original sixteen panels on that side. The first figure on the right is a naked youth, who looks as if he had just awakened on the morning of the great festival. The next figure is another naked youth, who is adjusting his sandal on a rock, preparing to mount the horse beside him. The remainder of this first panel shows a figure standing in front of a horse, perhaps a groom awaiting the arrival of his master. The other surviving thirteen panels on this side show a spirited assemblage of cavalry soldiers, some on horseback and others attempting to control their excited mounts, giving one the feeling that this part of the procession is about to get under way. The last two panels on this side are now in the British Museum; the one that would have been on the left end shows a marshal with his right hand raised, as if he is signalling for the procession to halt momentarily, and the panel that was just to the right of this shows two riders on rearing steeds, looking as if they had just reined in their horses at the marshal's command.

None of the original slabs remain in place on the north and east sides of the temple. The procession, as it was represented here, proceeding from right to left, continued the march of the cavalry from the west frieze. About half-way along this side there were represented a number of chariots, the ones to the rear at rest and those in front moving, interspersed with the figures of marshals attempting to keep the drivers and spectators in order. Ahead of them were the pedestrians, some conversing with one another as they strolled along, others bearing pitchers, playing lyres, carrying firewood, or leading sacrificial animals. Then the procession turned the corner on to the east face of the temple, where a solemn line of pilgrims approached a group of deities, the Olympian gods.

At this point one should go back to the south-west corner of the Parthenon, in order to follow the second group in the procession as it moves along the south side of the temple before turning on to the east face.

The first slab on the south face, starting from the left, is one of the two reliefs still in place on that side. But this and the other surviving slab on that side, the fourth from the left, are both so badly weathered that one can hardly make out the figures, other than to see that they are mounted soldiers, just as on the adjacent west face. The procession on this side was almost identical to that on the north frieze, with the cavalry following after chariots, marshals, pedestrians and youths leading sacrificial animals. Here again the procession changed character as it turned the corner on to the east face, where a group of reverential Athenians approach the assembled Olympians.

The deities represented on the east frieze were in two groups of six, each flanking the central scene, the figures in each group looking towards the pilgrims approaching them. The deities were the twelve Olympians: Zeus, Hera, Athena, Poseidon, Hephaistos, Ares, Apollo, Artemis, Demeter, Aphrodite, Hermes and Dionysos. (Dionysos is a latecomer to this group, replacing Hestia, Goddess of the Hearth, who, as Plato put it, 'always stayed at home when the Olympians went abroad'.) The principal figures in the central group were those of a young girl and a dignitary who is thought to be the Archon Basileus. The girl is handing to the archon a bundle presumed to be the *peplos*, the robe that he will place on the ancient xoanon of Athena. This panel is now in the British Museum, and seeing it there one is struck by the power and beauty of the scene, the procession of the Great Panathenaea at its climax here on the Acropolis.

Let us now look at the temple building itself, which consisted of two rooms separated by a solid wall. The largest of these two rooms was the cella, or sanctuary proper, which was two and a quarter times the length of the rear chamber. The cella faced east and looked out on to the pronaos, the front porch, while the small chamber at the rear, originally the Parthenon proper, opened on to the opisthodomos, the rear porch. Both porches were formed by colonnades of six Doric columns and short side walls ending *in antae* one intercolumniation behind the corner columns. The spaces between the columns were closed to the height of the capitals by bronze trellises, as were the spaces between the corner columns and the antae, thus forming closed chambers at the front and rear of the temple that could be used as storage areas for precious objects.

The cella, also known as the naos, was entered from the pronaos through a great doorway 10 m high and nearly 5 m wide. The cella was divided by a π-shaped colonnade into a central naos, two side aisles and a rear passage. Two tiers of pillars formed the four corners of the colonnade, and between them on each storey there were nine Doric columns on either side and three at the west end. The columns in the upper storey provided internal support for the huge wooden beams of the ceiling, and above this was the gabled roof, which was covered with thin marble tiles.

Towards the rear of the nave there was a pedestal on which stood the famous chryselephantine (gold and ivory) cult-statue of Athena Parthenos by Pheidias, so tall (about 10 m) that her spear almost touched the ceiling. The core of the statue was a wooden frame on which were fastened thin plates of gold and ivory: ivory for the flesh of the goddess and gold for her robes, spear and helmet. The pupils of Athena's eyes were probably made of precious stones. Pausanias saw the statue when he visited the Parthenon, and his description is the most detailed of any ancient writer:

The statue is made of ivory and gold. She has a sphinx on the middle of her helmet, and griffins worked on either side of it . . . the statue of Athena stands upright in the ankle-length tunic with the head of Medusa carved in ivory on her breast. She has a Victory about eight feet high, and a spear in her hand and a shield at her feet, and a snake beside the shield; this snake might be Erichthonios. The plinth of the statue is carved with the birth of Pandora. Hesiod and others say Pandora was the first woman ever born, and the female sex did not exist before her birth.

Descriptions by other ancient writers give additional information about the decoration of the statue. The inside of Athena's shield was painted with a scene showing a Gigantomachy, while the outside was decorated with an Amazonomachy. Even the rims of her sandals were adorned with gold reliefs, representing a Centauromachy. These scenes of mythical combat recurred frequently in Greek art, and, as we have seen, all three of them were used in the sculptural decoration of the Parthenon metopes.

According to Plutarch, Pheidias was accused of having represented himself and his patron Pericles in the decorations on Athena's shield. As Plutarch says in his *Life of Pericles*, 'The reputation of his works was what brought envy upon Pheidias. Where he represents the fight with Amazons upon Athena's shield, he introduced a likeness of himself as an old man holding up a great stone with both hands, and puts in a very fine figure of Pericles fighting with an Amazon.'

The weight of gold on Athena's statue amounted to forty-four talents, more than a ton, which at today's prices would be worth about £7m sterling. The gold plates could easily be removed from the statue and so their weight could be checked to make sure that nothing was missing. According to Plutarch, Pheidias was actually accused by his enemies of having taken some of the gold for himself. But he was able to prove his innocence by removing the gold plates from the statue and demonstrating that the full weight of forty-four talents was there, or so the story goes. The gold was in fact stripped from the statue in 296 BC by the tyrant Lachares, who governed Athens for King Cassander of Macedonia, 'leaving Athena nude', as one contemporary writer put it. But Lachares was soon afterwards overthrown and had to flee the city, leaving most of the gold behind him. The gold plates must then have been restored to Athena's statue in the Parthenon, for there are references to it up until the end of antiquity.

There was no communication between the cella and the smaller chamber to its rear. One entered that room from the rear porch, the opisthodomos, passing through a great portal identical to the one at the front of the temple. This rear chamber was divided into three sections of approximately equal width by two pairs of Ionic columns that gave internal support to the wooden ceiling. This room and the opisthodomos served primarily as storage areas for the safekeeping of sacred and precious objects. An inscription reveals that this part of the temple also served as the Treasury of Athens.

There is evidence that the Parthenon was gutted by fire at some time during the Roman period. According to one authority, John Travlos, this occurred when Athens was sacked by the Heruli in AD 267, at which time the two-tiered colonnade in the cella was destroyed. A study made in 1888 showed that the colonnade had been restored in late antiquity, using columns from a Roman structure in the lower city. This led Travlos to suggest that the repair was done during the brief reign of Julian the Apostate, AD 361–3.

The Parthenon ceased to be a sanctuary of Athena in AD 435, when an edict issued by Theodosius II in Constantinople closed all pagan temples in the empire. The chronicler Marianus tells a poignant story about the closing of the Parthenon as a temple of Athena. It seems that Proclus, the great Neoplatonist philosopher, was at that time living in his house on the south slope of the Acropolis. One night while he was sleeping there, according to Marianus, a beautiful woman dressed in the costume of Athena Parthenos appeared to him in a dream, imploring him to prepare a room in his house for the Queen of Athens, who had been evicted from her ancient sanctuary in the Parthenon. The statue of Athena Parthenos seems to have disappeared at this time, for there is no mention of it by ancient sources after Proclus.

Some modern writers maintain that the Parthenon was converted into a Christian sanctuary during the reign of Justinian (527–65), and that it was then dedicated to Haghia Sophia, the Divine Wisdom, like the great cathedral in Constantinople. This would have perpetuated the original dedication of the Parthenon to Athena, the Goddess of Wisdom. But there is no evidence to support this in the ancient sources. The existing evidence suggests that the Parthenon was converted into a Christian basilica in the last decade of the sixth century, after Athens had been sacked by the Slavs. The Parthenon was then dedicated to the Theotokos Atheniotissa – the Virgin of Athens, Mother of God. (Michael Akominatos, the last Greek Orthodox Patriarch of Athens before the Latin conquest, referred to Athena as pseudo-Parthenos, the 'False Virgin'.)

The conversion of the Parthenon into a church required changes in the structure of the building. The orientation of the building was reversed, so that the main entrance was at the west, rather than at the east. Also, the solid wall between the cella and the rear chamber was opened up, creating a large portal in the centre and smaller doorways on either side. Thus the rear room became the narthex of the church and the cella served as the nave. An altar and an iconostasis wall pierced by three portals closed off what had been the main entrance from the pronaos. A shallow apse was constructed behind that, with its rear wall including the two central columns of the pronaos. The spaces between the columns of the opisthodomos were walled up, except for a large central portal and smaller doorways between the last columns on either side. The peristyle was also walled up except for eight small doorways, two in the front and three on each side. During the medieval Byzantine period a wooden roof was put on the church, and a campanile was erected at the south-east corner of the opisthodomos. By that time the church was known as the Panayia, the Blessed Virgin, and it served as the cathedral of the bishopric of Athens. The most momentous event in the history of the Parthenon during the Byzantine era occurred in 1019, when Basil II came to Athens to celebrate his triumph over the Bulgars, offering a mass of thanksgiving in the church of the Panayia.

After the Latin Conquest in 1205 the Parthenon became a Roman Catholic cathedral, dedicated to Our Lady of Athens, but apparently no changes were made in its structure. Then, shortly after the Turkish conquest in 1456, the Parthenon was converted into a mosque. The only changes made then were the construction within the building of a mihrab, or niche, to indicate the direction of Mecca, and a mimbar, the pulpit used by the imam of the mosque during the noon prayer on Friday, the Muslim holy day. But none of these changes in the Christian and Muslim periods really altered the basic structure of the Parthenon, which was essentially intact up until 26 September 1687, when it was blown up during the Venetian siege of Athens. Morosini's bombardment destroyed fourteen of the forty-six columns of the peristyle, eight of them on the north side and six on the south, along with their entablature. It also demolished the roof and all of the inner structure except the rear chamber, so that the building was literally cut into two, with both halves in ruins. A few years afterwards the Turks built a small mosque within the ruins of the cella, constructing it largely from the debris of the temple.

After the removal of the Parthenon sculptures by Lord Elgin, the building suffered additional damage during the sieges of 1822–3 and 1826–7. During the first decade of the Greek Kingdom the temple was cleared of almost all accretions from the Byzantine, Frankish and

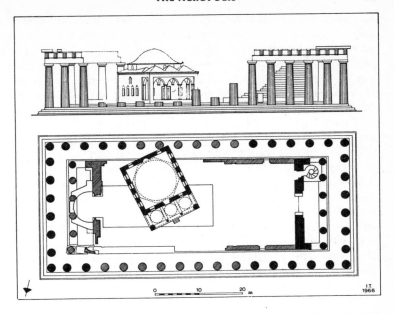

The Parthenon after the explosion of 1687, with a small mosque constructed in the cella

Turkish periods, and some modest attempts at restoration were made. More scientific repairs were carried out during the years 1898–1903 and again in 1921–3, when the north side of the peristyle was rebuilt. Another programme of restoration began soon after the Second World War and has continued ever since, with present efforts concentrated on rebuilding the south side of the peristyle and arresting the deterioration of the structure due to pollutants in the atmosphere of modern Athens.

Some 20–30 m east of the Parthenon, aligned with its central axis, there is an irregular foundation of rectangular poros blocks, upon which stand the lower drums of a circlet of fluted columns. These and other architectural fragments arrayed on the foundations were found at various places on the Acropolis, to be reassembled here after they were identified as belonging to the same structure. This has made it possible for archaeologists to determine the plan of the structure, which was a circular Ionic monopteral temple, that is, one with columns only, without a cella. The circular colonnade, whose outside diameter was 8.6 m, had nine Ionic columns supporting an entablature and a conical marble roof. The intercolumniation was uniform through-out except at the east, where two columns were placed farther apart to create an entrance portal. The slab of the circular epistyle, or architrave, that stood above this portal has survived, and it has been set up on poros blocks at the east end of the site. An inscription on the epistyle (first copied by Cyriacus of Ancona in 1437) begins thus: 'The people have [dedicated this sanctuary] to the goddess Rome and to Caesar Augustus . . .' Thus the temple can be dated to soon after 27 BC, the year when Octavian assumed the title of Augustus, and was probably erected within a decade of that time.

North of the Parthenon, between the temple and the Erechtheion, the sanctuary with the famous Caryatid Porch, there is a roped-off area where one sees the foundations of an ancient structure, unearthed in 1885 by Dörpfeld. There has been controversy about the identity of this building, but it is now generally agreed that it is the Old Temple (Archaios Naos) of Athena that is mentioned in ancient sources. (Pausanias does not mention it, so it must have been destroyed and covered over by his time.) Archaeologists now agree that the Old Temple of Athena was preceded in turn by two earlier sanctuaries. The first of these is what the architectural historian William Bell Dinsmoor refers to as 'the hypothetical but necessary' temple of Athena referred to in the *Iliad* and the *Odyssey* by Homer, who in both cases mentions it in connection with the palace of Erechtheus, one of the legendary kings of Athens. This has been tentatively dated to the Geometrical period, *c.* 750–700 BC, which is named for the style of Athenian pottery at that time. Travlos maintains that the Geometrical sanctuary was replaced by a much larger temple at the end of the seventh century or the beginning of the following century, and that this in turn was supplanted in the Peisistratid period, *c.* 529–520 BC, by the one currently known as the Old Temple of Athena. The Old Temple of Athena was then destroyed during the Persian sack of the Acropolis in 480 BC, although its western part may have been restored and perhaps used to house the Treasury of the Delian League. What survived of the structure seems to have been utterly destroyed in 406/5 BC just before the end of the Peloponnesian War, when Xenophon mentions that 'the Old Temple of Athena was burnt', though there is some uncertainty that he is referring to the building represented by the present foundations. By that time the Erechtheion had been built up against the north side of the site of the Old Temple of Athena, assimilating its ancient cults.

If you stand on one of the marble blocks near the foundations, you can readily make out the ground plan of the Old Temple of Athena. It was a Doric peripteral temple, amphidistyle *in antis*, with six columns to the front and rear and twelve along the sides. At the eastern end of the temple there was a pronaos, with a portico formed by two columns *in antis*. From there one passed through a portal into an almost square cella, which was divided into a nave and side aisles by a pair of colonnades with three columns in each line. The cult-statue in the cella appears to have been the ancient xoanon of Athena, the 'heaven-fallen idol of olive wood' which was clothed in a new *peplos* at the climax of each celebration of the Greater Panathenaea. The goddess was worshipped here as Athena Polias, the Protectress of the City. Classical sources refer to her sanctuary here as the 'Old Temple of Athena Polias', or more indirectly as 'the Temple in the city in which is the old statue'. Behind the cella, closed off from it by a solid wall, there were two smaller rooms that opened into a chamber at the western end of the temple. And beyond that there was an opisthodomos identical in plan to the pronaos, with a portico consisting of two columns *in antis*. The rear rooms of the temple, judging from the subsequent design of the Erechtheion, were probably dedicated to the cults of Poseidon–Erechtheus, Hephaistos and the hero Boutes, the brother of Erechtheus.

Before leaving the Old Temple of Athena, one might look at the two column bases surrounded by railings within the northern side of its cella, just to the south-east of the Caryatid Porch. These have been identified as belonging to the Geometrical temple, the first sanctuary on the site of the Old Temple of Athena. It was formerly believed that the bases were from the Mycenaean palace that is known to have been located in this part of the Acropolis. But now it is generally believed that they were the bases of the wooden columns that stood in the pronaos of the Geometric temple. In the *Odyssey* Homer mentions that Athena dwelt in 'the close-built house of Erechtheus', and in the *Iliad* he describes how the goddess nurtured the future kings of Athens there after he had been born out of the very earth of Attica. The latter description occurs in Book II of the *Iliad*, in the section known as the 'Catalogue of Ships', where Homer lists the contingents of the various Greek cities that fought in Agamemnon's army at the siege of Troy.

But the men who held Athens, the strong-founded citadel, the deme of great-hearted Erechtheus, whom once Athena, Zeus' daughter, tended after the grain-giving fields had born him, and established him to be in Athens in her own rich temple . . .

We now walk around the east end of the Old Temple of Athena. This brings us to the Erechtheion, which is surely one of the most peculiar buildings ever created by Greek architecture. The name of the building means the House of Erechtheus, the 'Earth-born' (chthonic) King of Athens, who was sometimes, like Cecrops, represented as half-human and half-serpent. In early versions of the myth he is indistinguishable from Erichthonius, the son of Hephaistos and the Earth-Mother Ge, while later, when he was included in the chronology of the kings of Athens, he and his brother Boutes were listed as sons of King Pandion I. Still later Erechtheus seems to have been identified with Poseidon, probably when the Olympian gods supplanted the primitive deities of the late Bronze Age. At that time Athena was venerated here as well, sharing the sanctuary with Poseidon–Erechtheus.

It was once thought that the Erechtheion was begun during the Periclean Age, but evidence now indicates that it was built during the years 421–406 BC, with some interruptions. The Erechtheion was really two Ionic sanctuaries, one facing east and the other west. There is now general agreement that the eastern sanctuary was dedicated to Athena Polias and the western one to Poseidon–Erechtheus. The *sekos* was rectangular in plan, measuring 11·5 × 22.8 m, with the western sanctuary being half as long again as the eastern one and divided into two parts. At the eastern end of the building there was a pronaos consisting of six Ionic columns, which supported the usual entablature and pediment. (The column to the north is a copy of the original, now in the British Museum.) The ground at the western end of the temple was some 3 m lower than at the east, and so the façade there was designed with two storeys, with a wall below supporting four Ionic columns *in antis* in the upper storey, surmounted by their entablature and pediment. The colonnade was closed off with a parapet below and wooden grilles above, except for an opening at the southern end. Then, to complete the unusual plan, there were porches at the western ends of the two long sides, with the larger northern portico rising from a lower level than the one to the south and also extending beyond the western end of the *sekos*.

There were no sculptures on the three pediments of the building, those on the east and west ends and on the northern portico. But the frieze was adorned with sculptures in low relief, a decoration that extended around all four sides of the building, with an additional band at a lower level on the entablature of the northern portico. The theme of the sculptural decoration of the frieze is not known for certain, but

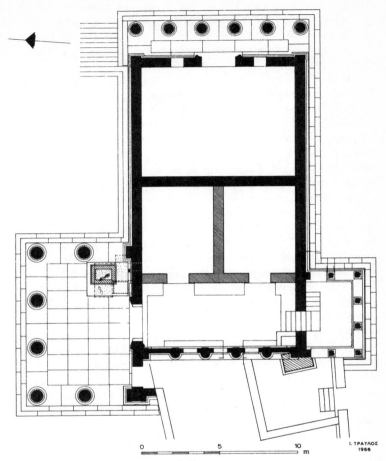

The Erechtheion, 421–405 BC, restored plan

from pieces preserved in the Acropolis Museum it appears that it
represented scenes involving the legendary kings of ancient Athens.

The Erechtheion is famous for the elegance of its architectural
details. The tall and slender Ionic columns have ornate bases and their
capitals are perhaps the most beautiful ever created in the Greek
world. Notice also the sculptured band that decorates the antae of the

cella and extends along the north and south sides of the temple. This decoration was in the form of anthemia, a continuous pattern of alternating palmette and lotus, periodically arising from nests of acanthus leaves and interconnected with scrolls, all of it once painted in polychrome.

The shallow eastern pronaos once had a coffered marble ceiling, similar in design to those in the Parthenon and the Propylaia. From there one entered the eastern cella through a large portal flanked by two windows. Most authorities agreed that this was the sanctuary of Athena Polias, which replaced the earlier one in the Old Temple of Athena. After the completion of the Erechtheion the sacred xoanon of Athena was enshrined here, and so thenceforth this was where the *peplos* was brought at the climax of the Greater Panathenaea.

The western sanctuary was entered through the magnificent northern portico. This porch, which stood on a three-stepped crepidoma, was formed by six Ionic columns, four in front and two behind; above this was the entablature, with its sculptured frieze, and the unadorned pediment. The columns also supported a marble ceiling whose coffers were adorned with delicate mouldings and painted with gilded rosettes. One of the coffers was left open to show where Poseidon's trident passed through during his contest with Athena, when he caused a well of sea water to come gushing forth from the rock below. According to another legend, this is where a thunderbolt hurled by Zeus passed when he killed Erechtheus, who was afterwards buried here in a crypt beneath his palace. A gap was also left in the marble paving of the porch so that one could look down and see the momentous marks below, whether they be of Poseidon's trident or the thunderbolt of Zeus; in any event both are still evident. Beside the gap there was an altar dedicated to Zeus Hypatos (the Supreme), where a priest offered up honey cakes to the god, after which he dropped them through the hole and poured a libation of dissolved sweets into the crypt where Erechtheus was buried. These offerings were also intended as food for the sacred serpent who was believed to dwell within the Acropolis rock, and who was apparently worshipped there in very ancient times. The earth-born Erechtheus was undoubtedly a personification of this mythical serpent, who was represented beside Athena's shield in her colossal cult-statue in the Parthenon.

Passing through the northern portico, one entered the cella through a large portal with a richly decorated frame. This brought one into a broad and shallow chamber identified by inscriptions as the *prostomiaion*, which was the anteroom to the western sanctuary. During the medieval period a cistern was constructed beneath this chamber, destroying whatever was there in ancient times. According to tradition, this was where the legendary 'salt sea' of Poseidon was located, having gushed forth there when his trident struck the rock below. After passing through this anteroom one turned left to enter the western sanctuary, which was some 3 m lower than the eastern one. Most authorities now agree that this was a shrine of Poseidon– Erechtheus, but Hephaistos is also thought to have been worshipped here, along with Boutes.

A stairway led up from the southern end of the anteroom to a balcony at the south-west corner of the Erechtheion. This is the famous portico known originally as the Korai, named for the figures of the draped maidens (in Greek, maiden is *kore*, plural *korai*) which are used instead of columns to support the entablature and coffered ceiling upon their heads, the capitals in the form of basket-like head-dresses carved with the Ionic ovolvo. Later the balcony came to be called the Porch of the Caryatids; according to Vitruvius, this name derived from the maidens of Caryae, a city in Laconia, who apparently wore such a head-dress when they were performing their local dance in honour of the Caryatid Artemis. The six maidens, who are one and a half times life size, are arrayed in the same manner as the columns on the north porch, that is, four in front and a pair behind at the sides, standing on a parapet 1.77 m high. All the present *korai* are copies of the originals; the rear statue on the right disappeared during the Turkish period; the second from the right in front was removed by Lord Elgin and is now in the British Museum; and the other four remained in place until their recent removal to the Acropolis Museum. Nevertheless, the Caryatid Porch is one of the supreme masterpieces of Greek architecture, and even in its present ruined and despoiled state it is still exceedingly beautiful.

A doorway led from the *prostomiaion* into the area immediately west of the Erechtheion. This was part of the sacred precincts of the temple, and it contained several shrines and sacred places associated with the Erechtheion. According to ancient sources, one of these was a sanctuary dedicated to Pandrosos, daughter of King Cecrops. Cecrops himself was also venerated here; his shrine was probably beneath the Caryatid Porch, where there is an open space spanned by a huge marble block now supported by an iron post. This may have been the grave of Cecrops, in which case it was perhaps a shrine in the Mycenaean palace. Another holy place in this area mentioned by ancient writers was the altar of Zeus Herkaios, god of the hearth.

According to several of these sources, this altar stood beneath the sacred olive tree of Athena, the gift to Attica that made the Athenians choose her over Poseidon as their patron deity. Herodotus tells us that Athena's olive tree was burned down during the Persian sack of the Acropolis in 480 BC, but immediately afterwards a fresh shoot sprang out from the old trunk and took root, so that a new tree grew up in the same place. The tree was still standing in the time of Pliny the Elder (AD 23/4–79), who mentions it in his *Natural History*, and it was looked upon as the progenitor of the sacred olive grove in the Academy, the suburb of Athens where Plato founded his school. (The olive tree now standing to the west of the Erechtheion is a modern growth, planted in 1917.)

The Erechtheion was badly damaged by fire at the end of the first century BC and was repaired shortly afterwards, although with some modifications in its original design. During the Christian era it was converted into a church, probably at about the same time as the Parthenon. The principal alteration resulting from this was the construction of an apse in the eastern pronaos, along with the erection of internal colonnades to create a nave and side aisles in the church, which undoubtedly combined the two sanctuaries of the Erechtheion. During the Latin period the building served as a second residence for the Dukes of Athens, who had their headquarters in the Propylaia, and in the Turkish era it housed the harem of the voivode. The building was badly damaged in 1827 by a Turkish bombardment, which ruined the Caryatid Porch and the south wall of the cella. The Caryatid Porch was partially reconstructed in 1841, but a thorough and scientific restoration was not made until the first decade of the present century. Yet another restoration began in recent years, and in the course of this project the four original *korai* still standing in the Porch of the Caryatids were removed to the Acropolis Museum for preservation.

We now walk westwards from the Erechtheion, stopping at a point about midway between the western end of the Old Temple of Athena and the inner portico of the Propylaia. Here you will notice cuttings in the Acropolis rock and several blocks of marble, including one carved in the classical 'egg-and-dart' design. This is all that remains of the base that supported the colossal bronze statue of Athena Promachos (Leader in Battle), which was erected by the Athenians immediately after their victory over the Persians in 465 BC at the River Eurymedon in Asia Minor. This was the most prominent of a group of monuments described by Pausanias as standing in that part of the Acropolis:

In addition . . . there are two Athenian dedications from a tithe of the spoils, a bronze statue of Athena by Pheidias from the Persian landing at Marathon, and a bronze chariot from Boeotia and from Chalkis in Euboia. They say the battle of Lapiths and Centaurs and the other work on Athena's shield was engraved by Mys, but like everything else he did it was designed by Parrhasios. The spear-tip and helmet-crest of this Athena can be seen as you come in by sea from Sounion.

Rock cuttings near the base of Athena's statue have been identified as being the base of the bronze chariot mentioned by Pausanias; this was set up by the Athenians after their victory over the Boeotians and Chalcidians in 507 BC.

We now walk over to the north-west corner of the Acropolis, where we will begin a stroll around the northern ramparts. Looking towards the Propylaia, one notices the finely cut blocks that form the east wall of the Pinakotheka and the north wall of the gateway, with their lifting-bosses still in place. The area here was originally designed to be the north-east hall of the Propylaia, but it was never completed. This part of the Acropolis was taken up by water reservoirs as far back as the archaic period. Remnants of a number of cisterns can still be seen there, most of them of Roman date, along with the ancient rock-cut drain that conducted rainwater to them.

Beyond the proposed site of the Propylaia's north-east hall and to its right are the poros foundations of an ancient building. This structure seems to have had two rooms, with its rear wall abutting the northern ramparts and with a portico of six Doric columns in front. The building is believed to pre-date the Propylaia, and it is thought that its front portico was destroyed when the Periclean entry-way was built.

About 30 m east of these foundations the Acropolis wall bends sharply north for a short way and then bends back to continue west. Here one sees the poros foundations of a square building dating to the fifth century BC, consisting of a hall with a stoa opening to the south. This building is obviously connected with the two staircases at the eastern and western angles of the ramparts. The one at the north-west corner goes out through the ramparts and joins a path that leads down to the foot of the Acropolis, ending outside the Cave of Pan. The other stairway leads down to the Cave of Aglauros, eldest daughter of Cecrops. (These and the other caves in the north slope of the Acropolis will be described in the next chapter.)

Its proximity to these two staircases has led to the identification of the square building as the Arrephorion, which Pausanias describes as being not far from the temple of Athena Polias, which would then have been in the Erechtheion. The Arrephorion was the dwelling-place of the Arrephoroi, or Bearers of the Sacred Offerings. The word is derived from *arreta pherein*; that is, 'those who carry things that cannot be spoken of. The Arrephoroi were four little girls of seven to eleven years of age, chosen by the Archon Basileus to weave the *peplos* robe which was draped over the xoanon of Athena at the climax of the Greater Panathenaea. The girls dwelt in the temple of Athena Polias while they were weaving the robe, but then one night in midsummer two of them were taken to the Arrephorion to participate in a secret rite called the Arrephoria. This rite is mentioned by several ancient writers, the most complete account being that of Pausanias.

There was one thing that amazed me which not everyone knows; I shall describe what happens. Two virgin girls live not far from the temple of Athena of the City; the Athenians call them the Bearers. For a certain time they have their living from the goddess: and when the festival comes round they have to perform certain ceremonies during the night. They carry on their heads what Athena's priestess gives them to carry, and neither she who gives it nor they who carry it know what it is she gives them. In the city not far from Aphrodite-in-the-Gardens is an enclosed place with a natural entrance to an underground descent; this is where the virgin girls go down. They leave down there what they were carrying, and take another thing and bring it back covered up. They are then sent away, and other virgin girls are brought to the Acropolis instead of them.

According to another ancient source, the packages that the maidens carried contained sacred objects made of dough, representing serpents, phallic symbols and shoots of plants, indicating that the Arrephoria was a fertility rite. The shrine of Aphrodite in the Gardens to which they went in transferring these objects has been identified on the north slope of the Acropolis, and will be one of the places visited on the next stroll.

The stairway used by the Arrephoroi on their way to and from the shrine of Aphrodite has been identified as the one that leads down to the Cave of Aglauros. This cave was excavated in 1937, and within it a stairway was discovered descending some 35 m to a subterranean spring. Pottery shards found in the spring all date to a period of thirty or forty years in the second half of the thirteenth century BC, a time when Troy, Mycenae and most other great cities of the late Bronze Age were destroyed, presumably by invaders. Athens must have been besieged at the same time, but the Athenians were fortunate to have a secret spring within the Acropolis itself, and this seems to have enabled them to hold out against their enemies, so that their city remained unconquered throughout the Mycenaean age. The stairway that led down from the Cave of Aglauros to this spring may have been destroyed in an earthquake *c.* 1200 BC, after which the secret passageway was sealed up and never again used.

We now go past the Erechtheion and the Old Temple of Athena and continue our stroll along the northern ramparts. The parapet of the ramparts here is to a large extent formed by column drums and capitals from the Older Parthenon. Farther to the west it is made up of fragments from the entablature of the Old Temple of Athena, including triglyphs, metopes and pieces of the cornice, all of which are displayed on the ramparts as memorials of the barbaric Persian sack of 480 BC. Beyond this section the wall bends again and stretches off to the south-west. Here one must turn inwards to pass around a walled-in cleft; in Mycenaean times this served as the rear entrance to the Acropolis, as evidenced by an ancient stairway discovered there. Once around this we continue walking along the ramparts until we reach the Belvedere, a look-out post on the north-east corner of the Acropolis. This is an excellent place from which to look down upon Plaka, the picturesque old quarter on the north slope of the Acropolis.

After leaving the Belvedere we walk along the eastern ramparts. When doing so one notices here and there short stretches of the Mycenaean defence wall, which winds around the eastern end of the Acropolis just inside the classical fortifications. This gives one a good idea as to how the peak of the Acropolis was formed into a plateau in the fifth century BC by the earth filled into the area between the Mycenaean and classical walls.

We now come to the Acropolis Museum, which is set low in the south-east corner of the plateau. But before entering the museum, one might peer into the fenced-off area to its south, just inside the Acropolis wall. This is a storage area for architectural members and fragments of sculptures and inscriptions found on the Acropolis. Among these are all or part of thirty-four Doric capitals and column drums from a peripteral temple of the sixth century BC, probably one that stood on the site of the present Parthenon. This archaic building is referred to by Greek archaeologists as Parthenon I, and a number of sculptures within the museum have been identified with it.

A flight of steps leads down to the outer courtyard of the museum. Among the objects on display in the courtyard the most noteworthy are two marble horses. These originally stood in the west pediment of the Parthenon, where they were part of Athena's quadriga. The horses were badly damaged when Morosini tried to remove them in 1687, but they were repaired and put on display here soon after the museum opened in 1878.

The museum was reorganized after the Second World War by Yiannis Miliadis, whose *Concise Guide to the Acropolis Museum* was published in 1965. A more recent and selective description of the exhibits is contained in *The Acropolis and its Museum*, published in 1988 by George Dontas, General Director of Antiquities and Director of the Acropolis. Readers can refer to these two works for a more detailed description of the works of art in the museum, so the present book will simply mention some of the most important exhibits.

Among the objects on display in the museum lobby there are a number of sculptures from the fifth century BC to the early Roman period. The most interesting is a relief from a choregic monument, dating from the last quarter of the fourth century BC, showing a group of naked youths performing the Pyrrhic dance. Also noteworthy is the large marble figure of an owl, symbol of Athena's wisdom, which is exhibited to the right of the door leading into Gallery I; this dates from the early fifth century BC and once stood on a high base near the sanctuary of Brauronian Artemis.

Gallery I contains pedimental sculpture from poros temples of the archaic period. These sculptures, along with most of the other archaic works of art in the museum, were discovered during the excavation of the filled-in area south of the Parthenon. They were, in effect, piously buried there when the ruined archaic sanctuaries on the Acropolis were removed to make way for later structures. The most impressive sculpture here shows a lioness devouring a calf; this dates from the early sixth century BC and was probably among the central figures in the pediment of Parthenon I.

Gallery II contains more sculptures from the archaic period. The room is dominated by the two large pedimental sculptures at the centre of the right and left walls. In the sculptures on the right wall the central figures are missing, but the dramatic reliefs in the angles of the pediment have survived. In the left angle the headless figure of Heracles is seen struggling with a serpent-tailed monster identified as Triton, the son of Poseidon and Amphitrite; and in the right angle one sees a monster with three human heads and torsos emerging from three intertwined serpentine bodies, a figure identified as Nereus, the archetype for 'the Old Man of the Sea'. The reconstructed pediment on the left wall contains in its two angles a pair of enormous serpents confronting one another. These and the sculptures on the opposite wall have been dated to the sixth century BC, and they are thought to belong either to Parthenon I or to the Old Temple of Athena. Two other notable archaic sculptures stand just to the left of the door leading in from the previous room. One of these is a charming group of four marble horses; these were originally part of a quadriga and are dated *c.* 570 BC. Near by is a statue of a sphinx, a mythical creature with the body of a winged lioness and the head of a woman, dated to the mid sixth century BC. At the far end of the room we see the famous Moschophorus, the Calf-bearer, dated *c.* 570 BC. This is the marble statue of a *kouros,* or youth, who is carrying on his shoulders a calf that he is offering to Athena.

Gallery III is dominated by the pedimental sculpture on the left wall. The central figure there is that of a fallen bull, which is being torn to pieces by two lions, of which the only surviving fragments are the hind legs. It is thought that these figures made up the central scene in one of the pediments of Parthenon I.

The three alcoves of Gallery IV contain some of the most superb archaic statues in existence. Most of these statues are of *korai,* beautiful maidens garbed in the dress of their day, which in the mid sixth century BC was undergoing a gradual transition from the Doric to the Ionic. Also in this gallery is the Rampin Rider, a votive statue of a naked youth on horseback. (The rider's head is a plaster copy of the original, now in the Louvre.) Next to this statue there are arrayed a few fragments of another mounted figure. It has been suggested that this and the Rampin Rider represent Hippias and Hipparchus, the sons of Peisistratus; in any case the group dates to the third quarter of the sixth century BC, and they are thus the oldest equestrian statues in Greek art.

Gallery V contains the most extraordinary work of art in the museum, a larger than life statue of Athena wearing her *aegis,* a wolf-skin cloak hemmed with intertwined serpents. The goddess is poised dramatically as she leans to her left to confront a fallen enemy, thrusting out with her left hand one of the serpents in her flared *aegis.* This statue was one of the central figures in the eastern pediment of the Old Temple of Athena, the other being that of Zeus. The scene was a Gigantomachy, in which Zeus and Athena led the Olympian gods to victory in a battle with the Giants of the primitive world, symbolizing the triumph of Greek civilization over barbarism. All that has survived of Zeus is his right hand and part of the thunderbolt that it held, now on exhibit in a showcase elsewhere in the room. Two of the giants have survived, those who crouched in the two angles of the pediment, and these are now exhibited in the corners of the room, flanking the statue of Athena. All of these pedimental sculptures date to *c.* 525 BC.

Gallery VI contains some of the finest works of art surviving from the first half of the fifth century BC. This was a period characterized by the so-called 'austere style' in Greek art, in which the richness in decoration of the archaic age is replaced by the more restrained mode of the classical period. Just to the left of the doorway is the famous funerary relief known as the Mournful Athena, dated *c.* 460 BC. Just beyond this is the beautiful marble head known as the Blond Youth, so called because when it was discovered traces of yellow colour still adhered to the young man's hair. Both this and the handsome *kouros* beside it, the Kritios Boy, are dated *c.* 480 BC. Also on exhibit here is the magnificent forepart of a horse, also dated *c.* 480 BC, perhaps the finest equine statue in Greek art.

Gallery VII contains sculptures that have survived from the pediments and metopes of the Parthenon. There are small plaster reconstructions of the Parthenon pediments placed high on the walls of the room, and a careful examination of these will help you in placing the few sculptures that are exhibited here. On the wall to the left there is an almost perfectly preserved metope from the southern architrave of the Parthenon; this is a scene from the Centauromachy that was represented there, showing a Centaur trying to abduct a struggling Lapith woman.

Gallery VIII contains most of the reliefs that still survive in Athens from the three principal extant sanctuaries on the Acropolis: these are the frieze of the Parthenon, the frieze of the Erechtheion and the parapet of the Temple of Athena Nike.

The panels of the Parthenon frieze are placed facing in the same direction as they were when they were affixed to the temple itself, so that the south frieze is exhibited on the north wall and the north frieze on the south, while the east frieze remains on the east. (The west frieze is still *in situ* on the Parthenon, except for the two panels that are now in the British Museum.) The panels here have been arranged in the order in which they originally appeared in the frieze, leaving space for those that have been lost or are now in the British Museum, and their subjects are identified in a wall diagram.

On the partition projecting from the north wall of the gallery there are exhibited fragments of the Erechtheion frieze. The order of the figures is somewhat arbitrary, since the panels were reassembled after the Erechtheion was damaged in the War of Independence. On the walls of the north-west angle of Room VIII there are exhibited fifteen panels, some of them fragmentary, from the parapet of the Temple of Athena Nike. The most beautiful of these is one in which the headless figure of a Nike is shown bending to adjust her sandal. The folds of her clinging garments are shown with such consummate skill that the fabric seems almost transparent.

Room IX is devoted to sculptures and reliefs ranging in date from the fifth century BC to the fifth century AD. The most famous works in the gallery are the *korai* from the Caryatid Porch of the Erechtheion, exhibited here in a special climate-controlled case to preserve them from further decay. Otherwise, the most noteworthy exhibit is a head of Alexander; this is believed to be a work of the sculptor Leochares, who may have done it from life at the time of Alexander's visit to Athens in 338 BC.

This completes our tour of the museum, after which we walk back across the Acropolis to the Propylaia, perhaps pausing for a last look at the Parthenon. We may linger once again on the steps of the Propylaia to take in the splendid view, with Hymettos looming in the background above the massed buildings of the modern city. Here one might recall the words of Michael Akominatos, describing the view from the Archbishop's Palace in the Propylaia in the early years of the thirteenth century, just before the Latin Conquest of Athens:

We may still enjoy here in Attica the same loveliness of the countryside, the temperate climate, the fruit-raising, the fertile lands, Hymettos rich in honey, the horse-ridden plain of the Marathonian warriors, the same Acropolis where I sit now, as I write, and seem to bestride the very peak of heaven.

4

From the Acropolis to the Agora

This stroll will be a rather short one, taking us from the Acropolis to the Agora of ancient Athens. We will see no monuments of any importance on this tour, but the very ground on which we will walk or look upon is deeply steeped in myth and history.

We will commence this stroll in the open area below the main approach to the Acropolis, and from there we will head off along the roadway that extends around the north slope of the great rock. The first stretch of this roadway takes us across the saddle between the Acropolis and the Areopagus, the Hill of Ares. Two of the most important roadways of Athens intersected at this point. One of these was the Peripatos, which extended around the periphery of the Acropolis on its lower slope. The other was the Dromos (literally, 'the road'), which led off to the right from the Peripatos, descending to the Agora and thence to the Dipylon, the main gate of ancient Athens to the north-west. This road was also known as the Panathenaic Way, because it was the route taken by the sacred procession during the celebration of the Greater Panathenaea. The modern roadway that goes around the north slope of the Acropolis runs just below the level of the Peripatos, and we will stroll along this for about 200 m to look up at some of the ancient cave-sanctuaries that have been identified in the cliff below the classical defence walls. Then we will return to our starting-point to visit the Areopagus, after which we will follow the course of the ancient Dromos down to the south-eastern entrance of the Agora.

The point where the Dromos and the Peripatos diverged was just below the bastion that supports the Monument of Agrippa. We will begin our brief exploration of the north slope of the Acropolis at this point, walking up to the western end of the fence that closes off the

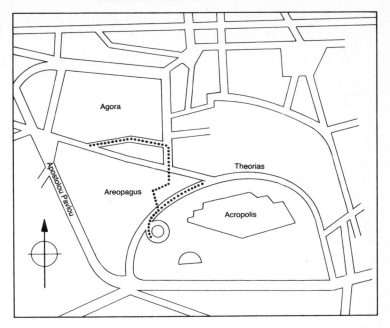

From the Acropolis to the Agora

archaeological area below the classical defence walls. Through the
fence there one can see the remains of Klepsydra, a classical fountain-
house that is one of the most important reference points in studying
the topography of ancient Athens. Those who first settled below the
north-west slope of the Acropolis in the Neolithic period, *c.* 5000 BC,
sank some thirty wells in this area, all of them fed by the subterranean
vein of water that issues forth in the Klepsydra spring. The spring
itself seems to have eluded the first settlers, for it was located in the
bowels of a cave below the north-west cliff of the Acropolis. It was
probably discovered only in the second half of the thirteenth century
BC, when the first large-scale fortifications were built around the
upper city. Thenceforth the spring was the principal source of water
for those dwelling on and around the Acropolis. It was originally
called Empedo, or 'never-failing', after a nymph of that name whose
nymphaion, or fountain-shrine, is placed there by several ancient writers.
Later it came to be called Klepsydra, or 'secretly flowing', since it had
no visible source and its outlet was hidden deep within the cave. The

present fountain-house and its associated courtyard and reservoir were constructed in the years 470–460 BC, their very simple architecture based largely on the shape of the cave and its subterranean spring. Numerous legends were associated with Klepsydra, whose name also means 'hiding the water', since sometimes it ran dry, and also because it was believed to have a subterranean channel that connected it with the sea. These legends are mentioned by an ancient commentator on Aristophanes, who refers to the fountain-house in two of his plays, *Lysistrata* and *Wasps*: 'The spring received its name because it was filled when the Etesian winds blow, and ceases when they stop, like the Nile and the fountain on Delos. A bloody cup that fell into it was afterwards found in the bay of Phaleron, twenty furlongs away. They say that the spring has no bottom, and that the water is salty.'

Early in the Byzantine era the Klepsydra fountain-house was converted into a chapel dedicated to the Holy Apostles, but this was abandoned after the Turkish conquest. By the end of the Ottoman occupation the fountain-house had been totally destroyed and was buried under earth and rubble; nevertheless the spring continued to flow, emerging from the earth in a Turkish fountain farther down the slope. When the Greeks besieged the Acropolis at the beginning of the War of Independence this fountain was outside the Turkish fortifications, and so in 1822 the Ottoman garrison on the Acropolis were forced to surrender principally because of lack of water. After their capture of the Acropolis the Greeks began searching for a source of water, and later that year the Klepsydra spring was rediscovered by the archaeologist Kyriakos Pittakis. The Greek commander Odysseus Androutsos then built a bastion around the spring so as to enclose it within the fortifications of the Acropolis, constructing a stairway down to the cave from the Agrippa bastion. This enabled the Greeks to hold out for ten months on the Acropolis when they were besieged by the Turks in 1826–7, and when they surrendered it was because they had run out of food and ammunition rather than water. The bastion of Odysseus, as it came to be called, was demolished in the mid nineteenth century, and in 1897 the remains of all other later structures were cleared away from the ancient Klepsydra fountain-house. The site was systematically excavated in 1936–40 by the American archaeologist A. W. Parsons, but it has never been opened to the public.

If you look at the cliff face just above Klepsydra you will see a grotto partly carved out of the precipice, with several tiers of rock-hewn seats at its base. This was probably a sanctuary in ancient times, and its proximity to Klepsydra suggests that it may have been part of the Empedo *nymphaion*.

A short distance to the east of this grotto, and a little higher up, there is an almost inaccessible terrace that has been identified as the Long Rocks that Euripides writes about in his play *Ion*. Five caves of various sizes and depths cleave the Acropolis rock above this terrace, and all of them have been identified as ancient sanctuaries, although there is some disagreement as to which deities were worshipped in each of them. Going from west to east (or right to left as one looks up at the Acropolis), they are generally identified as follows: first a shrine of Apollo Hypokraios (All Powerful), in the grotto to the east of the one above Klepsydra; next a cave-sanctuary of Zeus Olympios; and then three caves that were devoted to the cult of Pan.

The Cave of Apollo was also called the Pythion, after the dragon Python that the god slew at Delphi. This was one of the most important shrines in Athens, for the archons of the city took their oath of office at an altar in the Pythion, as is shown by the tablets which were found there dedicated by them to Apollo 'below the heights' or 'below the Long Rocks'. According to the version of the myth given by Euripides, it was here that Apollo made love to Creusa, daughter of Erechtheus. From this union came Ion, progenitor of the Ionian tribes of Attica, and thus the eponymous ancestor of those who founded the Greek cities of Ionia in Asia Minor. As Hermes sets the scene in the prologue to Euripides' *Ion*:

> A citadel there is in Hellas famed,
> Called after Pallas of the golden spear,
> And, where the northern rocks 'neath Pallas' hill
> Are called the Long Rocks, Phoebus there by force
> Did wed Creusa.

According to Herodotus, the cave-sanctuary of Pan was dedicated by the Greeks after their victory over the Persians at Marathon in 490 BC. As Herodotus tells the story, beginning at the point where the Athenian forces left Athens to confront the Persians:

Before they left the city, the Athenian generals sent off a message to Sparta. The messenger was an Athenian named Pheidippides, a professional long-distance runner. According to the account he gave the Athenians on his return, Pheidippides met the god Pan on Mount Parthenium, above Tegea. Pan, he said, called him by name and told him to ask the Athenians why they paid him no attention, in spite of his friendliness towards them and the fact that he had often been useful to them in the past, and would be so again in the future. The Athenians believed Pheidippides' story, and when their affairs were once more in a prosperous state, they built a shrine to Pan under the Acropolis, and from the time his message was received they have held an annual ceremony, with a torch race and sacrifices, to court his protection.

Rock cuttings in and around the easternmost of the three caves of Pan held votive-offerings to the mountain god and the nymphs and other deities who were also worshipped there with him. One votive relief now in the Acropolis Museum shows a fragmentary figure of Pan and a mysterious nun-like woman identified as a nymph. Aristophanes mentions the Cave of Pan in his *Lysistrata*; its seclusion made it a natural trysting place for lovers, with the Klepsydra close by for those who afterwards would want to cleanse and purify themselves. The easternmost cave was converted into a Christian sanctuary in the Byzantine period, and one can still see there the ruins and floor of the little chapel of Ay. Athanasios, along with the faded fresco portrait of a saint.

Some 70 m east of the Cave of Pan we see another grotto high up on the cliff face of the Acropolis. This has been identified as the Cave of Aglauros, based on the testimony of several ancient writers. One of these is Euripides, who in his *Ion* describes rites performed by the Aglaurids, the priestesses of Aglauros, in a place close to the caves of Pan.

> O seats of Pan and rock hard by
> To where the hollow Long Rocks lie
> Where, before Pallas' temple-bound
> Aglauros' daughters three go round
> Upon their grassy dancing-ground
> To nimble reedy staves.
> Where thou O Pan art piping found
> Within thy shepherd caves.

The shrine of Aglauros has been identified within this deep grotto, half-way down the Mycenaean stairway that led from the Acropolis to the secret spring used briefly in the thirteenth century BC. The fact that Aglauros was worshipped here as a nymph, a water deity, indicates that her cult preserved a memory of the forgotten spring in later times. Several ancient sources place her cave-sanctuary in this area. Herodotus gives a vivid account of how the Persians scaled the sheer cliff of the Acropolis at this point in 480 BC, making the last part of the ascent from the Cave of Aglauros, perhaps using the upper part of the ancient Mycenaean stairway. The cave-sanctuary must have been a very ancient one, for it was associated with Erichthonius, one of the 'earth-born' god-kings of the Mycenaean age. As Pausanias tells the story, 'They say Athena put Erichthonius into a chest and gave him to Aglauros and her sisters Herse and Pandrosos; she commanded them not to meddle with the things she committed to their care. Pandrosos obeyed, but the other two opened the chest and saw Erichthonius and went raving mad; they threw themselves off from the very steep side of the Acropolis.'

The terrace below the Cave of Aglauros has been identified as the site of the Anakeion. This was a sanctuary of Castor and Polydeukes (Pollux in Latin), the twin sons of Zeus and Leda, wife of King Tyndareos of Sparta. Zeus had fallen in love with Leda, and one day while she was bathing he came to her in the form of a swan and raped her. Leda subsequently gave birth to two sets of twins, each pair encapsulated in a single egg, with Castor and Polydeukes in one, and Helen and Clytemnestra in the other. But it was Castor and Polydeukes who were known to the Greeks as the Dioskouri, or the Twins; among their other exploits they took part in Jason's voyage aboard the *Argo* in his search for the Golden Fleece, and for that reason they became the patron deities of mariners in the ancient Greek world. The temenos of their sanctuary beneath the north cliff of the Acropolis must have been quite extensive, for in classical times it was used as a place of muster by the Athenian cavalry. Demosthenes mentions in one of his orations that slaves who hired themselves out as day-labourers could be found waiting at the Anakeion.

The Anakeion was near the very ancient defence wall known as the Pelargikon, which seems to have been an outer line of fortifications built around the lower western slopes of the Acropolis in the second half of the thirteenth century BC.

About fifty metres farther to the east there is another ancient sanctuary, located on a terrace beneath the point where the Acropolis wall bends sharply to the south-east past the Erechtheion. (Notice the massive column drums built into the Acropolis ramparts directly above the site; these are from the half-finished temple known as the Older Parthenon, which was destroyed by the Persians in 480 BC.) The precincts of the sanctuary included several terraces and natural grottoes, within which have been found phallic stones as well as reliefs depicting both the male and female reproductive organs. The cave-sanctuary here has been identified by inscriptions as a shrine of Aphrodite and her son Eros (in Latin, Venus and Cupid). This would have been the sanctuary of Aphrodite in the Gardens to which the young girls descended with their mysterious burdens on the night of the secret rites of the Arrephoria.

We now retrace our steps to the Areopagus hill, which we ascend by a flight of rock-hewn steps. Once on top we might sit down to enjoy the view from this hallowed rock, reflecting upon its deeply layered history and mythology. Aeschylus, in his play *Eumenides*, describes how the Amazons pitched their tents on this rock when they invaded Attica and besieged the Acropolis, after which they 'sacrificed to Ares, whence is the name of the Hill of Ares'.

Looking at the peak of the rock near its south-east apex, one can see that a flat area has been cut out of its surface. It is believed that this was the meeting-place of the Areopagus, the ancient Council of Athens. Originally the Areopagus court was chosen from among the aristocracy of Athens to serve as an advisory board to the Archon Basileus. After the establishment of democracy the Areopagus had little or no political power. Nevertheless, it still continued to function as a court, with special jurisdiction in the case of murder and crimes of a religious nature, a prerogative that it had apparently had since prehistoric times. According to mythology, Ares himself was the first to be tried here. This was after he killed Halirrhothios, a son of Poseidon, who was trying to rape Alkippe, Ares' daughter by Aglauros. Pausanias writes of this in his description of the Areopagus hill, where he also mentions that Orestes was tried here after he murdered his mother Clytemnestra.

The Areopagus is so called because Ares was the first to be tried there. I have already explained that he killed Halirrhothios and why. Later they say Orestes was tried here for the murder of his mother; he dedicated the altar here of Athena Areia when he was acquitted. They call the natural rocks where men on trial and the prosecutors stand the Rock of Shamelessness and the Rock of Arrogance.

Euripides, in his play *Iphigenia in Taurus*, at one point has Orestes say:

> But when I first came to Ares' Hill and rose for trial
> Myself upon one stand, while over opposite
> The eldest of the Furies took the other place . . .

The Furies, known in Greek as the Erinyes, were three weird sisters: Alecto, Megaera and Tissiphone; according to Hesiod, in his *Theogony*, they were born from the blood that Uranus shed when he was castrated by his son Cronus. In ancient Greek literature and art the Erinyes were depicted as terrifying creatures with serpents growing from their hair, brandishing torches and scourges while they screamed ritual maledictions known in Greek as *areia*, which some think to be the origin of the name Areopagus. They were also known as the Eumenides, which means 'the kindly ones'; this was a name meant to flatter them, so that if someone mentioned their name he would not bring down upon himself their deadly wrath. The Erinyes represented the primitive order of justice that had existed in late Bronze Age Greece, with its code of bloody retribution in crimes of murder. In his *Eumenides*, Aeschylus has Orestes pursued by the avenging Furies after his murder of Clytemnestra, until ultimately he is driven to the brink of madness. Finally, on the advice of Apollo, Orestes fled to Athens and pleaded his case before the ancient tribunal on the Areopagus. Athena presided over the trial, and Apollo defended Orestes while the Erinyes demanded their vengeance. Athena cast the deciding vote for the acquittal of Orestes, proclaiming that a son's duty towards his father outweighed all else. Thus the curse that had been placed upon the House of Atreus was finally lifted, whereupon the Erinyes were driven from the Areopagus.

The Areopagus is celebrated in the history of Christianity as the place where St Paul made his memorable speech to the Athenian people, known as the Sermon on the Unknown God. Paul came to Athens in the spring of AD 49, and began arguing about theological questions with those he met in the streets or in the Agora. His activities soon came to the attention of the authorities and he was summoned to explain himself before the Areopagus. Thus he began his sermon, the Greek text of which is inscribed on the tablet at the foot of the stairway leading up to the summit of the Areopagus hill:

Men of Athens, I perceive that in every way you are very religious. For as I passed along, and observed the objects of your worship, I found also an altar with this inscription, 'To an unknown god'. What therefore you worship as unknown, this I proclaim to you. The God who made the world and everything in it, being Lord of heaven and earth, does not live in shrines made by man, nor is he served by human hands . . .

As one reads in the Acts of the Apostles, many of those who heard Paul speak before the Areopagus mocked him, but a few became his followers, 'among them Dionysius the Areopagite and a woman named Damaris and others with them'. According to tradition, Dionysius the Areopagite was converted by St Paul and was appointed by him as first Bishop of Athens, remaining head of the small Christian community there until he was martyred towards the end of the first century. After his canonization he was made the patron saint of Athens, a veneration that is still accorded to him today in both the Greek Orthodox and Roman Catholic Churches. (The Roman Catholic Cathedral of Athens is dedicated to St Denis, the Latin form of his name.)

We now climb down from the Areopagus, turning left on the road below. At the south-eastern corner of the rock we pass through a gate in the wire fence that encloses the wooded area below the road that runs round the Acropolis. This opens on to a path that will take us down to the site of the Agora, following the course of the ancient Dromos, the Panathenaic Way.

If you look to the left at the beginning of the path, you will see a large cleft in the apex of the Areopagus rock. According to tradition, this is the mythical Cave of the Furies, the place to which Aeschylus has the Erinyes flee after the acquittal of Orestes. In the final scene of the *Eumenides*, Athena leads the Furies down into the depths of the cave. As they go, they are escorted by a choir of Athenian women, who, in the last lines of the tragedy, warn their listeners not to speak and arouse the wrath of the departing Furies.

> With loyalty we lead you, proudly go
> Night's childless children, to your homes below!
> (O Citizens, a while from words forbear!)

The Cave of the Furies was evidently dedicated as a sanctuary in ancient times, as one gathers from this description of the site by Pausanias:

Near by is a sanctuary of what the Athenians call the Awful Goddesses; Hesiod in the *Theogony* calls them the Furies. Aeschylus was the first to introduce snakes among the hair of their heads, but their statues, and those of all the underworld gods, have nothing fearful about them. A representation is here of Pluto and Hermes and Earth; this is where they sacrifice for men acquitted on the Areopagus, and there are also other sacrifices by foreigners and by people of the city. Inside the enclosure is Oedipus' memorial; by making a nuisance of myself I discovered his bones were brought here from Thebes . . .

At this point let us leave the path for a moment, veering off to the left so as to follow the rock face of the Areopagus. A short way along we see foundations identified by a sign as those of the church of St Dionysius the Areopagite. These foundations belong to a basilica erected in the mid sixteenth century, but Christian graves in the vicinity indicate that there was a church on this site as early as the sixth or seventh century. The Archbishopric of Athens was housed in an annexe to the right of the church from the middle of the sixteenth century until the latter part of the following century. The buildings here were apparently destroyed during the Venetian siege of the Acropolis in 1687, for when the Athenians returned to their city in 1690 they abandoned this site and rebuilt the church of St Dionysius and the Archbishopric in another part of the city.

We now return to the path and begin strolling down towards the Agora. As we approach the south-eastern entrance to the archaeological site, we come upon a paved section of the ancient Panathenaic Way, with huge cobblestones bearing the marks of wheeled traffic. On the left side of the roadway we see the remains of an ancient aqueduct. This has been identified as part of the waterworks endowed by the Emperor Hadrian, and has been dated *c.* AD 140. This aqueduct carried water down to a *nymphaion* known today as the South-east Fountain-house, whose remains we will see in the Agora.

Some fifty metres from the Agora entrance there is a sign on the right identifying the Eleusinion, of which only part of the foundations remain. According to ancient sources, the Eleusinion was one of the three most venerated sanctuaries in Athens, the others being the Parthenon and the Thesion, the tomb of Theseus. The site of the Thesion is still unknown, and that of the Eleusinion has been identified here on the east side of the Panathenaic Way only after many years of study. The identification of the Eleusinion was based partly on the description by Pausanias and also by inscriptions and other objects found on the site.

The Eleusinion was a shrine of Demeter and Persephone, whose main sanctuary was in Eleusis. The Greater Eleusinian Mysteries were celebrated annually at the main shrine in late September, commemorating the descent of Demeter into the Underworld in search of her daughter Persephone. This was an international festival, with people coming from all over the Graeco-Roman world to celebrate the Mysteries. Several Roman emperors were initiated into the cult, including Nero, Hadrian and Marcus Aurelius. On the day before the festival began, sacred objects of the cult were carried by priestesses of Demeter and Persephone leading a procession from Eleusis to Athens. When they reached the Dipylon they were met by mounted ephebes, young military recruits, who escorted them to the Eleusinion. After three days of secret rites, the Archon Basileus presided over a great feast of sacrificial animals at the Eleusinion, and two days after that all the initiates in the cult set out on their pilgrimage to the main sanctuary in Eleusis.

The foundations of the temple of the Eleusinion can be seen at the centre of the site. It was a rectangular building, about 10 × 16 m, consisting of a large room opening to the south. The Eleusinion has been dated to the beginning of the fifth century BC, but there is evidence that there may have been a sanctuary of Demeter and Persephone here as early as the mid sixth century BC. Among the objects found on the site are many fragmentary stelai recording the sale of property confiscated from Alcibiades and his companions in 415 BC; they incurred this penalty when they were found guilty of parodying the Eleusinian Mysteries and mutilating the Herms. (A herm is a stela topped by a human head, originally of Hermes, with a phallus half-way up the stone; they stood outside temples and homes and at crossroads.) The discovery of these stelai is one of the factors that determined the identification of the sanctuary, since they are known to have stood in the Eleusinion. It is believed that the Eleusinion was built on the site of the original Bouleuterion, or Council House, founded by Theseus when he amalgamated the towns of Attica under one rule in his Synoikismos.

The Eleusinion was a prominent landmark in the Panathenaic Festival, since the procession re-formed its ranks there before starting up the last, steep stretch of the Dromos towards the Areopagus and the Acropolis. Also, it was an excellent vantage-point from which the dignitaries of Athens could watch the various activities associated with the festival that took place down in the Agora below. On the eve of the Greater Panathenaea there was a nocturnal celebration with music and dancing, climaxing in a torch race that began at the Academy, a sacred precinct one mile outside the walls of Athens. There the competitors lit their torches at a hearth in a shrine of Prometheus and then ran in relays to the Acropolis, where the winner ignited the sacred fire on the altar of Athena. At dawn the next day the great procession assembled at the Dipylon, where the *peplos* of Athena was draped on the mast of the Panathenaic Ship. Then, as Philostratus described the scene, 'Putting out from the Kerameikos [the quarter just outside the Dipylon], the ship made for the Eleusinion with a thousand oars; rounding the shrine it passed the Pelargikon and reached the Pythion, where it is now moored.'

Leaving the Eleusinion, we continue our approach to the south-eastern entrance of the Agora. As we do so we see on our right a well-preserved section of the Late Roman fortification wall. As was mentioned earlier, this wall was built after the Herulian sack of Athens in AD 267, and was probably completed by c. 280. The purpose of the wall was to enclose a smaller and more easily defensible area, so that the Athenians could be protected from further attacks by the barbarians who were overrunning Greece. Starting at the western apex of the Acropolis, the wall ran just inside the Dromos as far as the Stoa of Attalos, the splendidly restored structure that forms most of the east side of the Agora as we see it today. The stoa itself formed the last stretch of the wall on that side. At the northern end of the stoa the line of fortifications turned east, incorporating within its structure the south wall of the Library of Hadrian, continuing in that direction until it met the eastern line of the fortifications, which extended down from the eastern apex of the Acropolis. The wall was built very hurriedly, using fragments from structures that had been destroyed during the Herulian raid. If you look at the inside of the wall farther on down the slope you will see that virtually every type of architectural member was used in its construction: column drums, capitals, architraves, lintels, triglyphs and metopes, even fragments of statues and inscribed stelai. Except for the Beulé Gate and one small section that we will see later on, this is the only major stretch of the Late Roman fortification wall that has survived. Along this stretch one can see the remains of two defence towers and the curtain-wall between them. The northern-most of these two towers was one of a pair that flanked a gateway opening on to a road leading east from the Agora to the later market-place that developed in Roman times.

Before entering the Agora, let us stroll along the pathway that extends westwards above the archaeological site. This path follows the course of a very ancient road that extended around the northern slope of the Areopagus. The area above this path served as a burial ground for about six centuries beginning in the fourteenth century BC, and many of the excavations that one sees there are of remains from that period. Excavations have also revealed that the north slope of the Areopagus hill was a densely settled urban area for two centuries beginning in the sixth century BC. The foundations of many of these houses can still be seen, several of them with elaborate mosaic floors. Sculptures and other objects found in these houses and in the earlier grave sites are now on exhibit in the Agora Museum. If we leave the path and wander over to the hillside of the Areopagus itself, we see that in many places there are niches cut into the rock face. These undoubtedly mark the site of ancient sanctuaries, but the deities worshipped there have not been identified.

Having completed our stroll along this path, let us finally enter the site of the ancient Agora through its south-eastern gateway.

5

The Agora

We will begin our tour of the Agora by taking the broad path that leads from the south-eastern gate to the main entrance on the northern side of the archaeological site, passing on our right the Stoa of Attalos. This path follows the course of the ancient Panathenaic Way, named for the procession that passed along it during the celebration of the Greater Panathenaea. As we approach the northern gate we turn left and head towards Kolonos Agoraios, the hill at the north-western corner of the archaeological site, which we ascend by a modern flight of steps. This brings us to the Hephaisteion, the Temple of Hephaistos, where we might pause for a while to look out over the Agora while we study its topography and history.

The area that was to become the Agora of ancient Athens comprises the gently sloping region north of the Areopagus and east of Kolonos Agoraios. Throughout the Bronze Age this area was used as a burial ground, and graves have been found there dating back as far as 3000 BC. The earliest wells in the area date back to the twelfth century BC, but there is no certain evidence of houses having been built there until the sixth century BC, by which time it had ceased to be a burial ground. Early in that century, perhaps in the time of Solon, the area was officially designated as the Agora, the market square and civic centre of the *polis*, the Athenian city-state. As John M. Camp writes in his book on *The Athenian Agora: Excavations in the Heart of Classical Athens*, 'The first concrete evidence concerning the Athenian constitution coincides with the laying out of the Agora as the civic centre. The area chosen was the gently sloping land north-west of the Acropolis, bounded on the south by the Areopagus hill, on the north by the Eridanos river, and along the west by the low hill that came to be known as Kolonos Agoraios (Market Hill).'

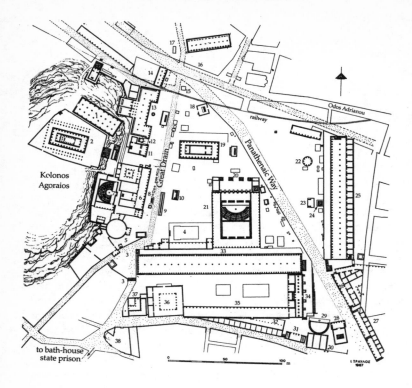

The Agora near the end of the second century AD

1 Hellenistic building
2 Hephaisteion
3 Strategeion
4 South-west temple
5 Tholos
6 Old Bouleuterion
7 New Bouleuterion
8 Metroon
9 Eponymous Heroes
10 Alter of Zeus Agoraios
11 Temple of Apollo Patroos
12 Temple of Zeus Phratrios and Athena Phratria
13 Stoa of Zeus Eleutherios
14 Stoa Basileios (Royal Stoa)
15 Stoa of the Roman period

16 Stoa Poikile
17 Temple of Aphrodite Ourania
18 Stoa of the Herms
19 Sanctuary of the Twelve Gods
20 Temple of Ares
21 Odeion of Agrippa
22 North-east stoa
23 Stoa of Attalos
24 Temple of the second century AD
25 Bema
26 Library of Pantainos
27 South-east stoa
28 Nymphaion
29 Argyrokopeion (mint)
30 South-east fountain house
31 South Stoa I

The first public buildings in the Agora, which were used by the governing council of the city, were erected on the west side of the square, up against Kolonos Agoraios, early in the sixth century BC. There was little construction in the Agora during the time of the Peisistratids, but after the democratic reforms of Cleisthenes the Agora began to take shape as the civic centre of Athens. The first monumental public edifices were erected in the Agora early in the fifth century BC, beginning a state building programme that would continue, with interruptions, for nearly a thousand years, with monumental structures continuing to be built there as late as the fifth century AD. The Agora suffered partial or total destruction on a number of occasions, being wrecked by the Persians in 480 BC, the Romans under Sulla in 86 BC, the Heruli in AD 267, the Goths under Alaric in 396, and the Slavs c. 590. When the Agora was rebuilt, as it was after all the catastrophes that it suffered prior to AD 590, new structures were erected on the ruins of older ones, often with a changed function and to a different design. Consequently, the ruins that one sees today are a palimpsest of a thousand years of Athenian history.

The Herulian sack in AD 267 effectively ended the Agora's role as a civic centre, for when the Late Roman fortification wall was built the ancient market square lay outside the city. But some of the philosophical schools for which Athens was still famous even in late antiquity seem to have been located in the Agora, so that the ancient square continued to be a place where people exchanged opinions and ideas as in the days of Socrates. But this ended when Justinian closed the Platonic Academy and other pagan schools in 529, after which the Agora was no longer even an intellectual centre. Thenceforth, through the Byzantine, Latin and Turkish periods, the Agora was a residential area, with a cluster of simple houses and half a dozen churches standing among the ruins of its ancient monuments. Most of the houses were destroyed during the Greek War of Independence, but after the end of the Turkish occupation a little village once again developed on the site of the ancient market square.

The first archaeological excavations on the site of the Agora began in 1859, the first step in a long series of campaigns throughout the remainder of the nineteenth century. In 1890–91 a deep trench was cut through the northern part of the site for the Athens–Piraeus railway, bringing to light several more ancient buildings. This stimulated interest among archaeologists to excavate the entire area, but the decision to do so was not made for another forty years. By that time the Agora had become one of the most densely populated quarters of Athens, with about five thousand people dwelling in some three hundred houses on the site of the ancient square. The Greek government was then faced with the alternatives of either allowing the Agora to develop as a modern industrial area or of clearing it of houses altogether to proceed with a programme of large-scale excavations. The American School of Classical Studies, with the financial support of John D. Rockefeller, Jr, proposed that the site be cleared and that property owners be reimbursed by them. The Greek government came to an agreement with the American School and the necessary legislation was passed, so that virtually the entire area of the ancient Agora became an official archaeological site. The site was cleared and archaeological excavations began on 25 May 1931, continuing in a series of annual campaigns until 1940, when the outbreak of the Second World War forced the cessation of archaeological work. By that time most of the area had been opened up and excavated down to the level of the ancient square, which in places lay as much as 12 m below the level of the surrounding streets. Work resumed in 1946 and continued in a second series of annual campaigns until 1960, by which time nearly all the major monuments on the site had been excavated and identified. Also during this period, the Stoa of Attalos was restored and converted into a museum to exhibit antiquities discovered during the excavations, and to house the workrooms and offices of the archaeologists working on the site. The third and most recent campaign by the American School began in 1969 and has continued to the present. The major goal of this campaign now is to excavate the northern side of the Agora, part of which lies on the other side of the railway line, and also to unearth the ancient street that connected the Agora with the Roman market-place to its east. We will look at both of these excavation areas after touring the rest of the Agora.

In strolling through the Agora, one should remember that it was not only the civic centre of ancient Athens, but the focal point for virtually all aspects of the turbulent everyday life of the city. Along with the administrative, judicial and religious buildings, there were, at one point or another, gymnasia, theatres, private homes, stores, workshops and the temporary stalls and barrows of the market-place. Each part of the market was given over to one particular commercial activity or the sale of one sort of commodity, which gave its name to that area of the bazaar. Thus a character in an Athenian comedy remarks: 'I went round to the garlic and the onions and the frankincense and the perfume.' According to Xenophon, writing *c.* 360 BC: 'Any servant you tell to go and buy something for you in the Agora will have no difficulty, he will certainly know where to go and find such things. The reason is that each is in its appointed place.' And as the comic poet Euboulus wrote: 'You will find everything sold together in the same place in Athens: figs, witnesses to summons, bunches of grapes, turnips, pears, apples, givers of evidence, roses, medlars, porridge, honeycombs, chick-peas, lawsuits, beestings puddings, myrtle, allotment machines, irises, lambs, water-clocks, laws, indictments.' The profusion of things to buy was such that Socrates once remarked, as quoted by Diogenes Laertius: 'How many things I do not need!'

The Agora was always the favourite haunt of Socrates, and in his time, 466–399 BC, he was a familiar sight in the market square. According to Xenophon, who was a younger contemporary of the philosopher, 'He was always on public view; for early in the morning he used to go to the walkways and gymnasia, to appear in the Agora as it filled up, and to be present wherever he could meet with the most people.' And Socrates himself said, as quoted by Plato in the *Apology*, 'If you hear me making my defence in the same language I customarily use, both elsewhere and in the Agora at the tables where many of you have heard me, do not marvel or raise a clamour on that account.' Plato has Phaedrus address him: 'How very strange you are, sir ... You apparently never set foot in the country or go outside the city walls.' To which Socrates replies, obviously referring to his favourite haunts in the Agora, 'Look at it my way, my good friend. It is because I love knowledge, and it is the people in the city who teach me, not the country or the trees.'

Above all, the Agora was the living heart of Greek democracy, in which every Greek citizen could expect that at some point in his life he would participate in the government of his city or to fight in its defence. The Agora was devoted to the communal life of Athens, and its precincts were as sacred as the temenos of a temple, with laws forbidding entrance to those who might bring harm or dishonour to the city. Nowhere is this communal spirit more proudly communicated than in the impassioned speech that Demosthenes made against Androtion, whom he accused of making an illegal proposal that would damage Athenian interests:

The Athenian democracy, never eager to acquire riches, coveted glory more than any other possession in the world. Here is the proof: once they possessed greater wealth than any other Hellenic people, but they spent it all for love of honour; they laid their private fortunes under contribution and recoiled from no peril for glory's sake. Hence the people inherit possessions that will never die; on the one hand the memory of their achievements, on the other hand the beauty of the memorials set up in their honour ... And so they have bequeathed to us their imperishable glory and excluded from the Agora men whose habits of life were what yours have always been.

Let us now begin our tour by examining the Hephaisteion, the Temple of Hephaistos. The identity and date of foundation of this temple were for long the subjects of controversy. The temple was formerly known as the Thesion, and most Athenians still refer to it by that name. (In fact the neighbourhood just to the north of the temple is called the Thesion.) This was because the exploits of Theseus were represented on the side metopes of the temple and on the frieze above the inner porch of the pronaos, giving rise to the belief that this was the sanctuary built by Cimon in 475 BC, when he brought the hero's supposed bones back from Skyros. But that date would have been much too early for the temple on Kolonos Agoraios, and, besides, there is literary evidence that the Thesion was probably on the east side of the Agora, near the base of the Acropolis. Authorities are now agreed that the temple here was dedicated to Hephaistos, who shared the sanctuary with his sister Athena. This identification is based principally on descriptions by Pausanias and other ancient writers, all of whom place the Hephaisteion above the north-west corner of the Agora. This is reinforced by the discovery that the area around the temple was in ancient times an industrial quarter inhabited by blacksmiths, bronze-workers and potters, an appropriate place to build a sanctuary dedicated to the god of the forge. Both Hephaistos and Athena were worshipped in Athens as patron divinities of the arts and crafts; her knowledge and wisdom complementing his skill and artistry. Plato, in his *Kritias*, explains why the two of them were particularly venerated in Athens: 'Hephaistos and Athena, who were brother and sister, both obtained as their allotted region this land [Attica], which was naturally adapted for wisdom and virtue, and there they implanted brave children of the soil and put in their mind the order of government.'

Authorities are also agreed that construction of the Hephaisteion began in 449 BC or soon afterwards, that is, about two years before work started on the Parthenon. The name of the architect is unknown, but he is believed to be the same man who designed three other Doric temples in Attica during the third quarter of the fifth century BC, the temple of Nemesis at Rhamnous, the temple of Poseidon at Cape Sounion and the temple of Ares in Acharnai. (This last temple was later disassembled and reconstructed in the Athenian Agora, where we will see its remains later on this tour.)

There is no certain evidence as to when the Hephaisteion was completed (a date of 444 BC has been suggested by some authorities), but it is known that the cult-statues of Hephaistos and Athena were created by the sculptor Alkamenes in the years 421–415 BC.

The Hephaisteion is the finest and best-preserved extant example of a Doric hexastyle peripteral temple. The temple, which measures 13.7 × 31.8 m along the stylobate, is built almost entirely of Pentelic marble, with the foundations and the lower step in poros stone and the sculptures carved from Parian marble. A Doric peristyle of six by thirteen columns surrounded a cella with naos, pronaos and opisthodomos, with both front and rear porches distyle *in antis*. The pronaos columns and antae were exactly aligned with the third column from the east in the side colonnades. This arrangement, which set off the front porch as an enframed compartment, was a design feature that appeared in all three of the later temples with which the so-called 'Thesion Architect' is credited. It also provided an additional artistic advantage, in that the sculptural decoration of the continuous frieze above the inner porch of the pronaos could be related to those of the metopes to the side, joining them in one continuous design. We will examine these sculptures in a moment, after we have completed our study of the temple itself.

A large portal gave entry from the pronaos into the naos. The central area of the nave was divided from the side and rear walls by a π-shaped colonnade similar to that in the naos of the Parthenon. The colonnade consisted of two storeys of Doric columns, seven on each side and four in the back row, with the epistyle of the upper row supporting the wooden roof. However, this arrangement did not have the effect of creating a central nave with side and rear aisles, as it did in the Parthenon, for the columns were placed so close to the walls that it would be a tight squeeze to pass behind them.

The naos was dominated by the colossal cult-statues of Hephaistos and Athena, which stood on a pedestal at the rear of the naos. These statues were much admired in antiquity, particularly that of Hephaistos, for Alkamenes had represented him as a great deity and not as the pathetic figure of fun that Homer and others made him. As Cicero

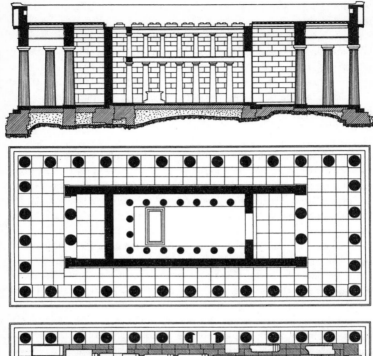

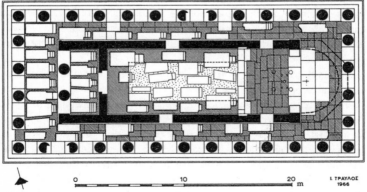

The Hephaisteion
(*Above*) Restored section and plan of the temple of Hephaistos, 449–444 BC
(*Below*) The temple after conversion into a Christian church in the seventh century

wrote of the cult-statue of Hephaistos, who is known in Latin as Vulcan, 'We praise the Vulcan of Alkamenes; the god's lameness is shown unobtrusively and is not unsightly.' Pausanias tells us that Athena was represented with flashing blue-grey eyes. From his description and those of other ancient sources it appears that the pedestal on which the statue stood was sculptured in low relief, and that the decorative theme was the birth of Erichthonius.

Let us now look at the sculptural decoration in the frieze and metopes of the temple, where the decorative themes were the labours of Heracles and Theseus. At first one might wonder why Hephaistos himself was not represented, but the reason is surely that the lame god of the forge had no suitable heroic exploits that could serve as a suitable decorative theme. Besides, the sculptors decorating a temple were under no constraints to confine themselves to subjects connected with the cult; so that, for example, Heracles and Theseus were represented on the Treasury of the Athenians at Delphi, which was dedicated to Apollo.

Only eighteen of the sixty-eight metopes were adorned with sculptures, just those on the front and rear sides of the porch, though it is possible that the remaining fifty panels may have been decorated with paintings. The ten metopes in front depict nine of the Twelve Labours of Heracles. They are, from left to right: the Nemean Lion; the Lernaean Hydra; the Cernean Stag; the Erymanthian Boar; the Mares of Diomedes; Cerberus, the Hound of Hell; the Girdle of Hippolyta, Queen of the Amazons; and the Cattle of Geryon. (The three labours that are not represented in the metopes are: the Augean Stables, the Stamphylian Birds and the Cretan Bull.) These labours were part of the purification process that Heracles went through on the advice of the priestess of Apollo at Delphi, after he had slain his wife Megara and their children in a fit of madness. The priestess advised him to go to Tiryns and work out his punishment through the labours that would be imposed on him by King Eurystheus.

Eight of the legendary deeds of Theseus are represented in the metopes on the north and south sides of the east portico. On the north side, from left to right, are the following scenes: Theseus battling in turn with the brigands Procrustes, Kerkyon and Skiron, and fighting with the man-eating Boar of Crommyon. And on the north side, again from left to right, he is shown struggling in turn with Periphetes, Sinis, the Bull of Marathon and the Minotaur. A ninth heroic deed of Theseus is depicted on the continuous frieze over the inner part of the pronaos, extending north and south as far as the inner colonnade, thus completing the rectangle of sculptural decoration. The theme of the latter frieze is the struggle between Theseus and the sons of his uncle Pallas, who were his rivals for the kingship of Athens. Theseus is the central figure in this scene, battling against his enemies, while six seated deities look on; on the left there are Athena, Hera and Zeus; on the right Hephaistos, Hippodameia and Poseidon. A corresponding frieze above the porch of the opisthodomos (here confined to the width of the porch) depicts a Centauromachy; Theseus is again shown in the centre of the action, aiding a Lapith who is being attacked by two Centaurs.

The pediments of the Hephaisteion were also adorned with sculptures, none of which have survived. It is believed that the decorative themes of the pedimental sculptures were once again the exploits of Theseus and Heracles. It has been suggested that the sculptures in the west pediment depicted another scene from a Centauromachy, perhaps the one in which Theseus aids King Peirithous in the fight during his wedding feast, when the drunken Centaurs tried to rape the Lapith women. The scene represented in the east pediment is thought to have been the Apotheosis of Heracles, his introduction to Zeus and the other Olympians upon his exaltation to divine status.

The Hephaisteion somehow escaped destruction on the several occasions when Athens was sacked in Roman and early Byzantine times, so that the temple was virtually intact until perhaps as late as the mid seventh century AD. At about that time the Hephaisteion was converted into a Christian basilica, dedicated to St George, and this required some changes in its internal structure. The interior colonnade was demolished and the two columns at the entrance from the pronaos to the naos were taken out to make way for an apse. At the same time the east cross-wall was torn down and a large door was opened in the west cross-wall, but this was closed during the Ottoman period (to keep the Turks from riding in on horseback), and two pairs of smaller doors were opened in the sides of the building. Also, a vaulted roof of stone and concrete was constructed over the nave of the church, and the piers supporting the apse were crowned with new capitals carved with a cross as the central element of the design. (The present vault is a later construction, dating to the final years of the Ottoman occupation.) Early in the Byzantine era the zealous Christians of Athens defaced all the figures in the metopes and frieze of the Hephaisteion, but for some unknown reason they left the Minotaur untouched.

During the Byzantine and Latin periods the Hephaisteion was used as a mausoleum by its parishioners, and many family vaults and individual tombs were cut into the floor. During the Turkish occupation the Hephaisteion fell into disuse, as the Greeks living in the Agora below Kolonos Agoraios apparently preferred to worship in one or another of the half-dozen smaller churches that they had built there. Divine services were then held in the Hephaisteion only once a year on the feast day of its patron saint, who thus became known locally as Ay. Yorgios Akamates, or St George the Idler.

During the latter years of the Turkish occupation the Hephaisteion was used as a burial ground for foreign travellers. The first of these was a young Englishman named George Tweddell, who died in Athens on 25 July 1799. There were cemeteries in Athens for Greeks and Roman Catholics, but none for Protestants, and so the French consul Fauvel arranged for Tweddell to be buried in the Thesion, as the Hephaisteion was then called. (Fauvel was an enthusiastic amateur archaeologist, and apparently his real reason for burying Tweddell in the Hephaisteion was the hope that in doing so he would discover the bones of Theseus!) Tweddell's grave seems to have become a place of pilgrimage for other English travellers to Athens. Samuel Rickards, in an Oxford prize poem of 1816, evokes the scene in the last stanza of his romantic poem, the 'Temple of Theseus':

> Such the fair pile, where, shrin'd in holy cell,
> The slumb'ring ashes of the mighty dwell,
> Where Tweddell, youthful shade, to classic rest
> Sinks, like a wearied child, on Science' breast,
> And in the sacred scenes he lov'd to roam,
> Finds the last honours of a kindred home,
> While Muses, mourning whom they could not save,
> Still guard his fame; for Athens is his grave.

The second Protestant to be buried in the Thesion was a young Englishman named George Watson, who died in 1810. As Byron wrote of him at the time, 'I knew him not, but I am told that the surgeon of Lord Sligo's brig slew him with an improper potion and a cold bath.' Byron wrote a Latin epigraph which was carved on Watson's tombstone, now set into the wall of the building; it reads, in translation, 'Here lie the bones of George Watson, whom neither virtues of spirit, strength of body, the spring of youth, nor this most salubrious country could preserve.' Watson's remains were discovered when the cella of the Hephaisteion was excavated in 1839, and in the archaeological report it was recorded that he still had a 'lovely head of blond hair', and that 'the thick sacking in which the body was wrapped retained too fully its original freshness'. After the excavation Watson's corpse was reinterred in its original tomb in the wall of the building, where it still remains, marked by Byron's epitaph. The last to be buried in the Hephaisteion was Marius Wohlgemuth, a young Austrian Philhellene who was killed in April 1822 while fighting alongside his Greek comrades against the Turks. His name is roughly carved near the bottom of the north wall of the cella, along with a pair of crossed cannons, a laurel wreath and the year of his death.

The Hephaisteion was damaged by Greek gunfire from the Acropolis in November 1826, when the temple was being used by a Turkish battery. The church of St George was reconsecrated in the Hephaisteion shortly after the foundation of the Greek Kingdom, and a Te Deum was sung there on 13 December 1834, to mark King Otho's arrival in Athens. During the late nineteenth and early twentieth century the building served as a museum and storehouse for antiquities. Some restoration of the Hephaisteion was carried out in the years 1935–9, when the cella and peristyle were excavated, along with the surrounding area on Kolonos Agoraios.

During the excavations around the Hephaisteion the soil was cleared down to the bedrock of Kolonos Agoraios. When this was done, it was discovered that there were two rows of rectangular cuttings along the north and south sides of the temple and a single row across the west end. In each of these cuttings there was found a shattered flowerpot, which led to the conclusion that this was the 'Garden of Hephaistos' referred to by Plato. When the excavations on Kolonos Agoraios were complete the Garden of Hephaistos was replanted with myrtle and pomegranate, so that the environs of the temple are now embowered as they were in ancient times, watered throughout the year to enhance the beauty of the sacred enclosure. As Plato writes in his *Laws*, 'The fountains of water, whether of rivers or of springs, shall be ornamented with plantings and buildings for beauty. If there be a sacred grove or dedicated precinct in the neighbourhood, let water be conducted to the very temples of the gods to beautify them at all seasons of the year.'

Before descending from the Hephaisteion to the Agora proper, we might stroll for a while along the paths that lead off behind the temple along the north-west slope of Kolonos Agoraios. This part of the archaeological site has not been systematically excavated, and here and there along the way one finds fragments of ancient structures half-hidden in the undergrowth. This is a delightful place for a midday picnic, particularly in the spring, when the whole area is bright with blossoming trees and wild flowers. The English traveller Edward Dodwell passed this way in the early years of the nineteenth century, sketching the antiquities of ancient Athens, and he has left this description of a festival that he witnessed here on Greek Easter: 'At Easter the Athenians celebrate a festival and dance near the Temple of Theseus; some thousands of people fill the plain ... Turks, Greeks, Albanians, and Blacks, were collected in one busy mass, and formed a gay and singular mixture of variegated costumes, the brilliant colours of which waved like a field of anemones agitated by the wind.'

Dodwell's evocative description reminds one that the religious festivals of modern Greece, the *paniyiria*, are usually survivals of ancient pagan feasts. The Easter celebration that Dodwell described could just as well have been that of the Anthesteria, the ancient spring festival marking the annual renewal of life on earth. At the close of this festival the whole of Athens made a pilgrimage to honour the dead at the principal cemetery of the city, which in classical times was in the Kerameikos, just to the north-west of Kolonos Agoraios, outside the city walls by the Dipylon. And in October the local bronze workers celebrated the beginning of autumn here on the Kolonos Agoraios in a festival called the Chalkeia, the Feast of the Bronzes, during the course of which the young girls chosen for the task began to weave the *peplos* for the Panathenaic festival of the coming year.

We now return to the Hephaisteion, after which we make our way southwards along the western slope of Kolonos Agoraios to the belvedere, an area with benches and a map of the archaeological site in the Agora below. A path leads down from the belvedere to the south-west corner of the ancient market square, which is still marked by two ancient boundary-stones. These were discovered in 1938 at the points where two ancient streets entered the south-west corner of the market square; they date to *c.* 500 BC and bear the same inscription: 'I am the boundary of the Agora.' At this and other entrances to the Agora there were *perirrhanteria*, or basins for holy water, and no one could pass the boundary-stones and approach these unless they were deemed worthy. As Aeschines, a contemporary of Demosthenes, said in one of his orations, referring to the boundary-stones of the market square: 'So the lawmaker keeps outside the *perirrhanteria* of the Agora the man who avoids military service, or plays the coward or deserts, and does not allow him to be crowned nor to enter public shrines.' And as Demosthenes himself said: 'Surely those who are traitors to the commonwealth, those who mistreat their parents, and those who do not have clean hands, do wrong by entering the Agora.'

Just behind one of these two boundary stones, in the acute angle made by the two ancient streets, there are the foundations of an ancient structure of some historic interest. Excavations on the site revealed a large number of hobnails and small bone rings that were probably eyelets for boots. Just outside the building, together with pottery dating from the third quarter of the fifth century BC, there was found the base of a drinking-cup with the name Simon scratched upon it. Thus the structure has been identified as the house and shop of Simon the Cobbler, a contemporary of Socrates who is mentioned by several ancient sources. Xenophon writes that Socrates, when he wished to converse with pupils who were too young to be allowed entrance to the Agora, would meet them at a leather-worker's shop outside the market square. Plutarch seems to be referring to the same man when he writes that 'I wish I were a shoemaker in ancient Athens so that Socrates could sit beside Pericles in my house and chat with him.' Diogenes Laertius identifies him by name: 'Simon, an Athenian, a shoemaker. When Socrates came to his workshop and discoursed, he used to make notes of what he remembered, whence these dialogues were called "The Shoemaker's". Thirty-three were gathered into a book.'

Standing in Simon's Shop and facing northwards, one looks along the main channel of the Great Drain of the ancient Agora. This drain was built in the early years of the fifth century BC, and was designed primarily to carry off the rainwater that pours into the Agora from the hillsides after a storm. The drain is about a metre wide and a metre deep, and has a heavy stone floor and walls of polygonal blocks of hard breccia carefully fitted together. Side channels led into the Great Drain from subsidiary drains and sewage lines starting at various points within the Agora. This rainwater and sewage then flowed through the Great Drain to the north-west corner of the Agora; bearing westward at that point it joined the Eridanos brook and was piped under the Panathenaic Way and the city walls and out into the countryside. Failure to maintain the Great Drain in early Byzantine times led to the repeated flooding and silting up of the Agora, so that in some places the ancient market square was covered with as much as twelve metres of earth. This flooding seriously hampered the work of archaeologists when they began excavating the Agora in 1931, and it was only after the Great Drain was discovered and cleared that the site could be kept dry.

The two roads that converged at Simon's Shop continued as the main street along the western side of the Agora, with the Great Drain running down the middle of the road. This road is actually older than the Agora itself, for it was already in existence when the first public buildings were erected in the market square towards the end of the sixth century BC. These buidings, the *archaeia*, or public offices, were built at the south-west corner of the square, diagonally opposite the boundary-stone beside Simon's Shop.

The most important of these state buildings was the Bouleuterion, the meeting-place of the Boule, the Council of Five Hundred. Closely associated with this was the Tholos, where a standing committee of fifty senators remained on duty for one tenth of the year. As Aristotle writes in his work on the *Constitution of Athens*, 'Those members of the Tholos who are acting as chairmen [the *prytaneis*] first eat together in the Tholos, receiving pay from the city; afterwards they arrange the meetings of the Council and the Assembly.' The official name of the building was the Prytaneion, the house of the *prytaneis*, and the foundations that one sees today are those of a circular building erected *c.* 465 BC. The name Tholos was given to the building because of its circular shape, reminiscent of the ancient tholoi, the circular dwelling-places and royal tombs of the Mycenaean age. The building was also called the Skias, which in Greek means sun-hat, because of its distinctive conical roof. It had a doorway to the east and six internal columns which supported the marble roof. A small annexe on the north-east corner served as the kitchen, where food was prepared for the *prytaneis* on duty in the Tholos, along with their secretaries and a few other officials. Usually a third of the *prytaneis* remained on duty throughout the night, so as to take care of any nocturnal emergencies, and thus the Tholos also had sleeping arrangements. Sometimes all fifty *prytaneis* slept there in times of crisis as they did in 415 BC, during the controversy that arose over the mutilation of the herms of the Agora. The Tholos also served as a Bureau of Standards, and a set of standard weights and measures was kept there under the care of a state slave, who was supervised by the chairman of the *prytaneis*.

Like all of the *archaeia* in Athens, the Tholos was a sacred building, and was thus under divine protection. According to Pausanias, 'Near the council-house of the Five Hundred stands the "Round-House" where the Council sacrifice. Some of the images are silver, though not very big.' An inscription from the Hellenistic period reveals the names of the principal deities who were worshipped in the Tholos: it informs us that the *prytaneis* offered sacrifice 'to Apollo Prostaterios and Artemis Boulaia and to the other gods to whom it is ancestral custom to sacrifice'.

The Tholos is one of several buildings in the Agora that have dramatic associations with Socrates, who resided here when he himself was one of the *prytaneis*. In Plato's *Apology*, where Socrates is defending himself against the charges levelled against him by his accusers, he points out that he had never yielded to injustice when serving the state:

When the oligarchy of the Thirty was in power, they sent for me and four others into the Tholos, and bade us bring Leon the Salaminian from Salamis, as they wanted to put him to death. This was a specimen of the commands which they were always giving with the idea of implicating as many as possible in their crimes; and then I showed, not in words but in deed, that, if I may be allowed to use such an expression, I cared not a straw for death and my great and only care was lest I should do an unrighteous or unholy thing. For the strong arm of that oppressive power did not frighten me into doing wrong; and when we came out of the Tholos the other four went to Salamis and fetched Leon, but I went quietly home. For which I might have lost my life, had not the power of the Thirty shortly afterwards come to an end. And many will bear witness to my words.

Soon after Cleisthenes instituted his reforms in 508 BC, a large building was erected in the south-east corner of the Agora to house the Boule, the Council of the Five Hundred. This building, the first large public edifice to be erected in the Agora, stood just north of the foundations of the classical Tholos, which was built about four decades later. The first Council House, some foundations of which can be seen to the north of the Tholos, is known to archaeologists as the Old Bouleuterion, to distinguish it from a later structure, the New Bouleuterion, which was erected towards the end of the fifth century BC. The New Bouleuterion was situated just to the north of the older building, standing on a terrace cut into the hillside north-west of the Tholos. The two buildings stood side by side for nearly three centuries, with the older building serving as an archive for the records of the Boule and other state documents. (It was probably the growing need for archival space that made it necessary to build the New Bouleuterion, thus allowing the old one to be used almost exclusively as a repository for records.) Among the documents known to have been preserved here are the official record of the court proceedings that led to the condemnation and death of Socrates; the last will and testament of the philosopher Epicurus; and official copies of the tragedies of Aeschylus, Sophocles and Euripides.

The Old Bouleuterion was demolished in the latter half of the second century BC, and on its site there was erected a new building, the Metroon, which was a sanctuary of Rhea, the Mother (*mitera*) of the Gods. As Pausanias described it, 'They have a sanctuary built to the Mother of gods, whose statue Pheidias made . . .' From other ancient sources we learn that the cult-statue of Rhea represented her as seated and holding a tympanum in her hand, with a lion recumbent beneath her throne. This was one of the archetypal representations of the Great Anatolian Earth-Mother of the Bronze Age, depicted in her role as a fertility goddess and the protectress of animals. The Earth-Mother later became Cybele in Phrygia; later still, in the Greek world, her roles were taken over by Rhea, who became a fertility goddess and mother of the Olympians, and Artemis, who assumed the role of protectress of animals. In classical Greek mythology, Rhea was the sister and wife of Kronus, bearing him Hestia, Demeter, Hera, Hades, Poseidon and Zeus.

The Metroon consisted of four rooms of various sizes opening on to a colonnaded porch that faced eastwards towards the market square. The second of these rooms, counting from the south, was probably Rhea's sanctuary, since it was designed in the form of a small temple, while the first and third rooms housed the archives. The northernmost room was larger than the others and was built on two storeys around an open courtyard with an altar in the centre. This was probably a library and reading-room for those who were consulting the state documents. Only the foundations of the four rooms of the Metroon are still in existence, along with three marble steps and an Ionic column base towards the south of what was once the colonnaded porch.

Entry to the precincts of the New Bouleuterion was through a small propylon, the foundations of which can be seen just to the south of the steps and column base mentioned above. Beyond the propylon a passage led to a courtyard behind the tholos; from there one entered the colonnaded front porch of the New Bouleuterion, a large rectangular building of two storeys. At the right side of the porch a door led into the right front aisle of the auditorium, which faced east, aligned at right angles to the longitudinal axis of the building. Excavations have revealed that the senators originally sat on rows of wooden planks held up by wooden supports, but later tiers of carved wooden seats were installed, as in a theatre. In the centre of the orchestral area there was an altar called Hestia Boule, the Hearth of the Council, where the senators offered prayers to Zeus when they entered the auditorium.

The Boule was the scene of some of the proudest moments of

Athenian democracy. Here again one might refer to Plato's *Apology*, where Socrates reminds those who are sitting in judgement on him of an event that occurred when he himself was a member of the Council:

The only office of state I ever held, O men of Athens, was that of senator. The tribe Antiochus, which is my tribe, had the presidency at the trial of the generals who had not taken up the bodies of the slain after the battle of the Arginusae [in 406 BC]; and you proposed to try them in a body, contrary to law, as you all saw afterwards; but at that time I was the only one of the senators who was opposed to the illegality, and I gave my vote against you. And when the orators threatened to impeach and arrest me, and you called and shouted, I made up my mind that I would run the risk, having law and justice with me, rather than take part in the injustice because I feared imprisonment and death. This happened in the days of democracy.

Directly across the street from the Metroon there are the foundations of a long and narrow pedestal, in front of which there has been re-erected a restored section of the stone fence that once surrounded it. The pedestal has been identified as the base of the ten statues of the Eponymoi, the Eponymous Heroes, after whom the tribes of Attica were named following the reforms of Cleisthenes. The identification is based partly on the description by Pausanias, who says that the monument is near the Tholos. The monument of the Eponymoi also served as the official bulletin-board of Athens, where officials posted notices concerning legislation, litigation, regulations and lists of men drafted for military service. These notices were posted on the tall pedestal that supported the statues of the Eponymous Heroes, and those reading them could lean on the balustrade of the fence that surrounded the monument.

Behind the northern end of the Eponymoi monument there are the remains of a handsome altar, which was approached by a flight of four steps of Pentelic marble. The altar is believed to date from the late fourth century BC, and there is evidence that it once stood on the Pnyx Hill, where the meetings of the Ekklesia, the popular assembly of the Athenians, were held in ancient times. The altar was probably dismantled and taken down from the Pnyx in late Hellenistic times, when the meeting-place of the Ekklesia was changed to the Theatre of Dionysos, after which it was reassembled here in the Agora. The altar has been identified as a shrine of Zeus Agoraios, whom Aeschylus called the God of Persuasion or Oratory. According to Plutarch, 'From the servants of Zeus Boulaios and Agoraios and Polieus we demand deeds not of feet and hands but of counsel and forethought and oratory.' Plutarch also writes of a curious and perhaps apocryphal incident that associates Socrates with the cult of Zeus Agoraios. It seems that when Socrates was born his father, Sophroniscus, went to consult the Delphic oracle for advice on how to raise his son. The oracle responded thus, according to Plutarch: 'Let the boy do whatever comes into his mind and do not restrain him but give him his head, not bothering him except to pray on his behalf to Zeus Agoraios and the Muses.'

On the opposite side of the road, directly in front of the Metroon, there is a row of a dozen monument bases, at the northern end of which there has been set up the marble torso of a Roman emperor. The relief on the emperor's breastplate shows Athena standing on a she-wolf who is suckling Romulus and Remus; she is flanked by her two symbols, the serpent and the owl, and she is being crowned with laurel wreaths by a pair of Nikes. This combination of Athenian and Roman symbols has led to the identification of the imperial figure as Hadrian. It is possible that it was dedicated on the occasion of Hadrian's second visit to the city, in AD 129, when he was made the founder of a new tribe in Attica named in his honour. His statue was probably toppled from its base during the Herulian sack of Athens; later its head and limbs were knocked off and the torso was used as a cover slab for the Great Drain, in front of the Metroon. It was rediscovered there during the excavations and afterwards re-erected on its present site.

We continue walking north on the road that passes the Metroon, and about 10 m farther along on our left we come to the foundations of a small Ionic temple. This has been dated to c. 330 BC and has been identified as a shrine of Apollo Patroos, the Father. Apollo was so named because he was the father of Ion, the eponymous founder of the Ionian race to which the Athenians belonged. Apollo was the patron deity of all the *phratria* of Attica, and children underwent their initiation rites in this temple when they formally enlisted in the various tribes. The temple had a rectangular cella and a porch with four columns *in antis* facing the market square. There was a small, square chamber attached to the north-east corner of the temple, and this served either as a treasury or as an adyton, or inner sanctuary. Beneath the floor of the temple there is evidence of another sanctuary of the mid sixth century BC.

A colossal marble figure found near the temple in 1907 has been identified as the cult-statue of Apollo Patroos. This statue, which is now in the Agora Museum, is missing its head and arms; nevertheless, it can be identified as a representation of Apollo Kitharoidos, the Lyre

Player, symbolizing his role as the god of music. According to
Pausanias, the statue was the work of Euphranor, one of the most
famous Athenian painters and sculptors of the mid fourth century
BC.

Just to the north of the Temple of Apollo there are the remains of a
tiny shrine, which stood directly in front of the side chamber of the
larger structure beside it. This temple has been dated to the mid fourth
century BC, and has been identified as a sanctuary of Zeus Phratrios
and Athena Phratria. As their names imply, Zeus and Athena here
joined Apollo as patron deities of the tribes of Attica. As Plato has
Socrates say in his dialogue *Euthydemos*, 'Apollo is our paternal deity
since we were sprung from Ion; Zeus we do not call Patroos, but
Herkaios or Phratrios, and Athena we call Phratria.' To the east of the
temple there is a massive foundation that supported a porch added in
the second century BC.

Immediately to the north of these two temples there are the poros
foundations of a large structure, identified as the Stoa of Zeus Eleutherios. Zeus received the name Eleutherios, Bringer of Freedom, because
he had saved the Greeks from enslavement by the Persians; in this
respect he was also called Sotir, or the Saviour. The cult of Zeus
Eleutherios is believed to have been founded after the final Greek
victory over the Persians at the battle of Plataea in 479 BC. Thereafter
the Athenians dedicated there the shields of those who died fighting
to preserve the freedom of Greece and of their city. Pausanias records
one such dedication made by the Athenians after the Greek victory
over the barbarian Gauls at Thermopylae in 279 BC:

On that day the Athenians showed the greatest courage in Greece, and the
bravest of them was Kydias, a young man in battle for the first time. The
Gauls killed him, and his kinsmen dedicated his shield to Zeus of Freedom,
with this inscription: 'The shield of a brave man, Zeus's offering,/ pining away
for the youth of Kydias:/ the first shield his left arm ever put on,/ when
raging War went hottest at the Gauls.' This was the inscription in the days
before Sulla's men took away [in 86 BC] the shields from the colonnade [stoa]
of Zeus of Freedom among the loot of Athens.

The Stoa of Zeus was planned at the very end of the great Periclean
construction programme, and it was completed in the last third of the
fifth century BC. It was designed as a long portico flanked by a pair
of projecting wings, both of which resembled the front porch of a
temple. The columns of the outer colonnade were of the Doric order,

with nine along the recessed central section, six at the front of each wing, and four along their inner sides, with a solid wall running along the sides and back. During the early Roman period a large annexe of two rooms was built behind the centre of the western part of the stoa, and in the second century AD a large exedra was built in front of it.

The Stoa of Zeus was one of the great public buildings of Athens, although its function has never been clearly defined. It has been suggested that it formed a single administrative unit with the Stoa Basileios, which adjoined it to the north. Since the Stoa Basileios was one of the principal lawcourts of the city, it is possible that the Stoa of Zeus formed its annexe and had relegated to it some of the functions of the court.

In any event, the Stoa of Zeus was one of the most popular gathering places in Athens, for it provided a shady arcade where one could promenade with one's friends or sit on the steps to watch the passing crowds in the Agora. The stoa forms the setting for two of the Socratic dialogues, *Eryxias* and *Theages*, both of which are thought to have been written by imitators of Plato. In both dialogues Socrates holds forth while sitting in the stoa or strolling through it with friends, so that this must have been one of his favourite haunts in the Agora. Xenophon, who knew Socrates intimately, places him in the stoa in his *Oeconomicus*, which includes fourteen dialogues between the philosopher and his friend Ischomachus. In one of these dialogues Socrates speaks of meeting his friend in the Agora: 'So once seeing him sitting in the Stoa of Zeus Eleutherios, apparently at leisure, I went up and sat beside him, asking, "Why are you sitting here, Ischomachus?"'

A generation after Socrates the Stoa of Zeus was constantly frequented by Diogenes of Sinope, the founder of the Cynic school of philosophy, who apparently lived there in a wooden tub. According to one of his ancient biographers, Diogenes once said to a friend: 'Athens has given me a home in the Stoa of Zeus.' One of the most frequently quoted incidents in the life of Diogenes is his meeting with Alexander the Great, which may be apocryphal, but nevertheless makes a good story. According to Arrian (a Greek historian from Bithynia who wrote a biography of Alexander the Great in the second century AD), Alexander and his guards and companions were on campaign near the Isthmus of Corinth when they came upon Diogenes lying in the sun. Alexander asked Diogenes if there was anything he wanted, and the old cynic answered, 'Nothing, though I should be grateful if you and your friends would move to one side, and not keep the sun off me.' This seems to have deeply impressed Alexander, who is quoted by Plutarch as saying, 'If I were not Alexander, I would like to have been Diogenes.'

The remains of the Stoa Basileios and other buildings on the north side of the Agora were cut off from the rest of the market square in 1890–91, when the trench was dug for the Athens–Piraeus railway line. Some of these buildings were irretrievably lost, including the Sanctuary of Demos and the Graces, which stood just at or outside the north-west corner of the Agora. For a time there were fears that this might have been the fate of the Stoa Basileios too, but in 1970 its foundations were discovered virtually intact on the far side of the railway tracks, along with the remains of other structures. The Stoa Basileios was immediately identified as such because of its location, standing next to the Stoa of Zeus Eleutherios at the intersection of the Panathenaic Way and the road that runs along the west side of the Agora. When Pausanias describes the entrance to the Agora at that point, he writes, 'The King's Colonnade is the first on the right: this is where the king sits for the year of "King's office", as they call it.' This area is not open to the public, but one can view it from the railway bridge or from Odos Adrianou, the street that runs alongside the trench on the far side of the tracks. The Eridanos river is channelled under this street, and the Great Drain flows into it just to the east of the Stoa Basileios, making it easy to locate this long-lost building.

The Stoa Basileios, or the Royal Stoa, as it is known in English, was the headquarters of the Archon Basileus. The reforms of Cleisthenes in the last decade of the sixth century BC defined the role of this office, dividing up the duties that had once been those of the King of Athens between the three chief archons. The Archon Basileus was given the responsibility of supervising religious matters and organizing the celebration of religious rites and festivals, principally that of the Greater Panathenaea. He also retained a share of the former royal judicial powers, in that he served as judge in trials involving violations of religious canons or practice, as well as in cases of homicide. The Stoa Basileios also served as an archive for writings on legal and constitutional matters, and we learn from ancient sources that the laws of both Dracon and Solon were exhibited on the walls of the stoa and on stelai in its precincts. The nine annually elected archons were sworn in there, each taking his oath on a stone outside the building. The Areopagus Council occasionally met there too, since some of its functions paralleled those of the Archon Basileus, namely responsibility for preservation of the laws and dealing with cases of homicide.

After reading of how important the Royal Stoa was in the public life of ancient Athens, one is somewhat surprised to learn how comparatively small and modest a building it was compared to the adjacent Stoa of Zeus, which was twice as high as the headquarters of the Archon Basileus and occupied an area five times as great. The building was 17.72 m wide on the outside and only 7.57 m deep, facing eastward towards the Agora. There were solid walls on all sides except the front, which had a colonnade of eight Doric columns above two steps, and in the interior there were four identical columns (originally two) supporting the roof. This structure, which was erected *c.* 500 BC, was modified about a century later by the addition of columnar wings set against the façade of the stoa, one at either end, each wing having three columns in front and two at each side. The foundations are intact and the north wall is standing to a height of nearly two metres. The column bases are still in place, and the stumps of a few of them remain standing to the height of a few centimetres. If you look at the third column base on the north in the outer colonnade, you will see a large block of unworked poros stone standing just to the outside of it. This is the historic Lithos, the rock on which the archons stood, as the commentator Pollux described it, 'taking their oath at the Stoa Basileios on the stone where were the cut-up offerings, swearing to join in keeping the law and not accepting bribes, otherwise giving in compensation a golden statue'. According to Aristotle, official arbitrators also took their oath on the Lithos, as did witnesses who wished to swear that they had no evidence to give before the court.

In front of the Royal Stoa, on its central axis, there is the foundation for the pedestal of a large statue, the marble female torso of which was discovered near by and which is now in the Agora Museum. The statue has been dated to the second half of the fourth century BC and has been identified as either Demokratia, the personification of democracy, or Themis, the personification of justice and the dispenser of divine retribution.

The Stoa Basileios is famous in history as being the place where, in 399 BC, Socrates was indicted and held over for the trial that would lead to his execution later that year. Plato quotes Socrates in his dialogue *Theaetetus*: 'Now I must present myself at the stoa of the Basileus to answer the indictment which Meletos has brought against me.' The actual trial probably took place in another court, most likely the Heliaia, whose remains we will see later in our tour of the Agora.

A number of other remains have been unearthed on the railway embankment on either side of the Royal Stoa. The most interesting of these lies some 15–20 m east of the south wing of the Royal Stoa, on the other side of the Great Drain. There one sees a small enclosure of poros stone orthostats, 2.8 m square and 1.2 m high, surrounding an outcropping of bedrock. This is a crossroads shrine that stood just inside the north-west corner of the Agora, at the intersection of the Panathenaic Way and the road that ran along the course of the Great Drain. When the site was first excavated, in 1971–2, a large number of votive offerings were found on and around the rock, and even more within the filled-up well just to the north. The oldest of the ex-votos date from the third quarter of the fifth century BC, and all of them are objects that would be given as grave-offerings to women – perfume vases, oil lamps, loom-weights and jewellery. Also found on the site were a number of lekythoi, funerary vases used to adorn the graves of young unmarried women. This led to the identification of the crossroads enclosure as a *heroum*, or tomb-sanctuary, in this case dedicated to a female deity or deities. It has been suggested that this is the famous Leokorion, the object of considerable investigation and discussion ever since the beginning of modern studies of the Agora. According to the myth, the shrine takes its name from the three daughters (*korai*) of the hero Leos, a son of Orpheus who was the eponymous founder of the Attic tribe known as the Leontids. It seems that Leos consulted the Delphic oracle at a time when Athens was being ravaged by a terrible plague, and the priestess told him that he could purify the city and save the Athenians by sacrificing his three daughters: Theope, Praxithea and Eubule. He did so, whereupon the plague passed and the stone that marked the grave of his daughters became a *heroum*, the Leokorion. The plague struck again in 430–429 BC, beginning in the winter after the first year of the Peloponnesian War. The plague was undoubtedly brought on by the great influx of people who moved within the walls of the city to escape the Spartans, and lived there in extremely crowded and unsanitary conditions. Thucydides, who was stricken himself, devotes five pages of his work to a description of the horrors of the plague, during which so many of the Athenians died that the dead were frequently left unburied. The dating of the oldest ex-votos in the Leokorion indicates that the suffering Athenians then remembered that the daughters of Leos had saved them from an earlier plague, and so they made numerous offerings at the Leokorion, which were found there when the site was excavated 2,400 years later.

The Leokorion was one of the most familiar landmarks in Athens, standing, as it did, at this crossroads just inside the entrance to the Agora from the north-west. As the geographer Strabo writes, quoting Hegesias in his sweeping evocation of the wonders of Athens, '"There is the Leokorion, here is the Thesion!"' Being in such a prominent place, it is mentioned frequently by the ancient sources and figures prominently in the history and literature of ancient Athens.

The most dramatic event associated with the Leokorion took place in 514 BC, during the celebration of the Greater Panathenaea. This was when Hipparchus, one of the sons of Peisistratus, was assassinated by Harmodius and Aristogeiton, known to history as the Tyrannicides. When Peisistratus died in 527 he was succeeded as tyrant by his eldest son, Hippias, while Hipparchus became chief minister. Hippias ruled with an iron hand, without the cultured benevolence of his father. This, together with his arrogance and the frequent imprisonments and executions that he ordered, bred a new spirit of rebellion amongst the Athenians. Finally, just before the celebration of the Greater Panathenaea in 514, a group of Athenians decided that the time had come to strike out against the Peisistratids. The rebels were led by two young men named Harmodius and Aristogeiton, who, according to their plan, would begin the revolt by killing Hipparchus as he passed in the Panathenaic procession, whereupon all of the other conspirators would join in the attack and strike down Hippias and his supporters. On the day of the festival Harmodius and Aristogeiton stationed themselves near the Leokorion, concealing their swords in the boughs of myrtle that all the celebrants carried, and when Hipparchus passed in the procession they slew him. But the other rebels failed to make their move and the revolt failed, with Harmodius and Aristogeiton losing their lives in the futile attempt. Nevertheless, four years later Hippias was finally overthrown and democracy returned to Athens. Harmodius and Aristogeiton were thereafter honoured as the Tyrannicides, and their brave deed was commemorated in a song that begins with this stanza:

> In a myrtle bough shall my sword be hid,
> So Harmodius and Aristogeiton did
> The day they struck the tyrant down
> And made this Athens a freeman's town.

Soon after the fall of Hippias in 510, bronze statues of Harmodius and Aristogeiton were erected in the Agora near the Leokorion, the place where they had assassinated Hipparchus. This work, which was known as the Tyrannicides, was by the sculptor Antenor, and represented the two heroes advancing side by side with drawn swords. The statues were carried off by the Persians after their occupation of Athens in 480–479 BC. They were replaced in 477 BC when the sculptors Kritios and Antenor completed a copy of the group, which was probably done to the same design as the original. The original group was recovered by Alexander the Great at the time of his conquest of Persia, and he or one of his successors had it sent back to Athens, where it was re-erected beside its replacement. The two groups of the Tyrannicides stood there side by side for nearly six centuries, mentioned by virtually every scholar who lived in or visited Athens during the Hellenistic and Roman periods. Then, like most other monuments in the Agora, they were destroyed in the Herulian sack of Athens in AD 267. The only trace of the monument that has survived is a small fragment from the base of one of the statues that still retains part of the dedicatory epigram: 'A great light shone for the Athenians when Harmodius and Aristogeiton slew Hipparchus.' Several representations of the Tyrannicides have survived in vase-paintings and on coins, and the most famous copy of the statues themselves is the one in the Naples Museum.

The identification of the Royal Stoa did much to clarify the problem of locating the remaining monuments on the northern side of the railway trench. Excavations in 1981 unearthed a number of foundations on the northern side of Odos Adrianou, almost directly across the street from the Royal Stoa and the Leokorion. On the north-eastern corner of this site archaeologists of the American School believe that they have unearthed part of one of the most famous buildings of the Agora, the Stoa Poikile, known in English as the Painted Stoa. This building, which was 12.5 m in width and at least 36 m long, has been dated to the period 475–450 BC. (Only the western end of the stoa is visible, the rest being still beneath a large commercial building on Odos Adrianou.) The Stoa Poikile was so called because of the famous paintings with which it was adorned, including works by Polygnotos, Mikon and Panainos; according to Pausanias, these depicted battle scenes ranging in time from the siege of Troy to the battle of Marathon. As the orator Aeschines once said, reminding the Athenians of their renowned military prowess, 'Pass on in thought to the Stoa Poikile too; the memorials of all your great deeds are set up in the Agora.'

The Stoa Poikile was also renowned as the meeting-place of the philosopher Zeno and his followers, who thus came to be known as the Stoics. Informal assemblies were occasionally held in the stoa, and the courts of justice sometimes convened there as well. At some time during the year 404/3 BC the Stoa Poikile seems to have been the scene of a mass execution; according to Diogenes Laertius, the Thirty Tyrants had 1,500 Athenians slaughtered there without benefit of trial.

The satirist Lucian used the Stoa Poikile as the setting for one of the most amusing of his dialogues, *Zeus the Tragedian*. In this dialogue, Zeus is strolling around the Agora when he notices a large crowd gathered at the Stoa Poikile. When he approaches the stoa he sees that they have been drawn there by an acrimonious debate between two orators. Thereupon Zeus disguises himself with a long beard 'so as to pass for a philosopher, and elbows his way in. He finds an Epicurean and a Stoic in high dispute. Poseidon proposes to slay the profane Epicureans by lightning, but Heracles, in his rough and ready way, puts an end to the blasphemy of the philosophers by pulling down the whole stoa on their heads.'

Apuleius, in his *Metamorphoses*, describes a bizarre incident that he witnessed one day in the Stoa Poikile. 'And yet at Athens lately, in front of the Painted Stoa, with these two eyes I saw a conjurer devour a cavalry sword sharpened to a very keen point; and presently, with the inducement of a small payment, he also swallowed a hunting spear, point first, until it penetrated deep into his vitals . . . And all of us who witnessed the performance wondered.'

About 10 m west of the Stoa Poikile, almost directly across the street from the Royal Stoa, one sees the remains of a marble altar that was discovered in 1981. Dated to *c.* 500 BC, this is the earliest and most beautiful altar that has been unearthed in the Agora excavations. All that survives is its platform of purplish limestone, measuring 5.1 × 2.4 m, and the southern half of the altar itself, which is made of Parian marble. The altar has been identified as part of a shrine dedicated to Aphrodite Ourania (Heavenly Aphrodite), whose cult-statue was by Pheidias. This identification is based principally on the testimony of Pausanias, who mentions the sanctuary as he approaches the Stoa Poikile along the northern side of the Agora: 'Near by is the sanctuary of Heavenly Aphrodite . . . The statue there now is Parian marble, and by Pheidias.' Two fragments of a marble relief depicting Aphrodite were found in the area around the altar, confirming the identification of the shrine.

The area around the Royal Stoa and the Stoa Poikile, at the north-western corner of the Agora, was known as 'the Herms', from the numerous monuments of that type erected there. As Thucydides says of these stones, 'These square-wrought figures, in accordance with local custom, stood in large numbers both in private entrances and in shrines.' Since they were used to mark entrances and crossroads, the most popular place for erecting herms was at the north-western entrance to the Agora, where the road from the Dipylon passed between the Royal Stoa and the Stoa Poikile as it entered the market square. Valerius Harpokration, in his work on these monuments, composed in Alexandria in the second century AD, wrote, 'From the Poikile and the Royal Stoa extend the so-called Herms. Because they were set up in large numbers there both by private individuals and by magistrates the place has acquired this name.'

Let us now return along Odos Adrianou to re-enter the archaeological site, turning right once inside to walk back along the inner side of the railway trench. About 25 m along we come to the south-east corner of a square enclosure, the remainder of which was destroyed when the railway trench was dug. This has been identified as the Sanctuary of the Twelve Gods, founded in 522/1 BC by Peisistratus the Younger, son of Hippias and grandson of Peisistratus the Tyrant. The original sanctuary was destroyed by the Persians in 480 BC, and was rebuilt in the closing years of that century. The deities who were worshipped here were probably the Twelve Olympians, but originally they may have been the eponymous founders of the ancient tribes of Attica.

At the centre of the sanctuary there was an altar which, according to ancient tradition, served as a place of asylum and as a refuge for suppliants. It is quite possible that this is to be identified with what the Athenians called the Altar of Eleos, or Pity, which is described by Pausanias and other ancient sources. This is the altar which Herodotus mentions in Book VI of his *Histories*, where he explains why the Plataeans fought as allies of the Athenians at the battle of Marathon. There he tells of how the Plataeans, on the advice of the Spartans, threw themselves on the mercy of the Athenians in 519 BC to protect them against the Thebans:

The Plataeans ... when the Lacedaemonians gave them this counsel, complied at once; and when the sacrifice of the Twelve Gods was being offered at Athens, they came and sat as suppliants before the altar, and gave themselves up to the Athenians ... Under such circumstances did the Plataeans give themselves up to Athens; and now they were come to Marathon to aid the Athenians.

The altar in the Sanctuary of the Twelve Gods was also called the Omphalos, or Navel, since it was the reference point from which all distances to points outside of Athens were measured. On a rare ancient Greek milestone, dated *c.* 400 BC, we read: 'The city set me up, a truthful monument to show all mortals the measuring of their journeying; the distance to the Altar of the Twelve Gods from the harbour is forty-five stades.' The altar is undoubtedly the sanctuary that Pindar refers to in one of his odes, when he invites the Olympian gods to come to the festive dance, 'approaching the navel in the holy city of Athens, much frequented, fragrant with incense, and the famous, richly adorned Agora, to receive garlands of violets and songs gathered in the spring'.

Some 20 m south of the Sanctuary of the Twelve Gods we come to a large rectangular area covered with crushed stone. This is the site of the Temple of Ares, god of war. Some architectural fragments of the temple can be seen at the west end of the area and several courses of the foundations are visible at the east end, while 10 m farther to the east there is a large marble altar that was undoubtedly part of the sanctuary. The Temple of Ares has been dated to *c.* 430 BC, and the altar to about a century later. There are definite indications that the temple originally stood elsewhere, probably in Acharnai, at the foot of Mt Parnes, and that it was dismantled and then reassembled here early in the Roman period. An inscription of AD 2 has been found honouring Gaius Caesar, eldest son of Agrippa and Julia, who was also the adopted son of Augustus. Gaius is referred to in the inscription as the 'New Ares', and so the temple had been rebuilt here before that time. A careful study of the foundations and of marble fragments found in the area have led to the conclusion that the Temple of Ares was a twin of the Hephaisteion, and that both of them were works of the so-called 'Thesion architect'. Like the Hephaisteion, it had a peristyle with six columns to front and rear and thirteen along the sides, and the cella undoubtedly had a pronaos and an opisthodomos, each of which would have had a porch with two columns *in antis*. But there is no evidence as to whether the pediments and metopes of the temple were decorated with sculptures, as they were in the Hephaisteion. Pausanias tells us that there were many statues standing in and around the temple: 'there are two images of Aphrodite, Ares by Alkamenes and Athena by a Parian called Locrus. There is an image of Enyo here by the sons of Praxiteles. Around the temple stand Heracles and Theseus and Apollo tying his hair with a ribbon.'

The Enyo mentioned here by Pausanias was a curious deity, the personification of the horrors of war; his sculptors were Timarchus and Cephisodotus, who were sons of Praxiteles and grandsons of an earlier Cephisodotus, a sculptor who carved several statues in the Agora mentioned by Pausanias.

Twenty metres south of the Altar of Ares we see the so-called Stoa of the Giants, which takes its name from the gigantic figures on three of the four massive piers standing there. Originally there were six figures: three giants, or monsters of the earth, each of which had the head and torso of a man, but whose truncated legs ended as the tail of a serpent; and three tritons, or monsters of the sea, who were men above the waist and fish below. Of the three surviving figures the easternmost one is a giant and the other two are tritons. (The head of a third triton has survived and is now in the Agora Museum.) Homer Thompson has pointed out (as quoted by John Travlos) that: 'the Tritons from the waist up are copies of the Poseidon of the Parthenon west pediment; the Giants are modelled on the type of the Hephaistos of the Parthenon east pediment'. The bases of all four pedestals are decorated with the same scene in low relief, showing an olive tree with a serpent twined round its trunk; this is undoubtedly a representation of Athena's sacred olive tree on the Acropolis and the serpent-king Erechtheus.

The Stoa of the Giants was a later addition to the original structure of which it formed the north side; this was a vast odeion erected *c.* 15 BC by Marcus Vipsanius Agrippa, the chief minister of Augustus, a benefaction to which the grateful Athenians responded by erecting the monument that still bears his name below the Propylaia. The Odeion of Agrippa was part of an ambitious city-planning programme that began in the Augustan period, the main purpose being to shift the market area farther to the east, to what is now known as the Roman Agora. The odeion and the Temple of Ares took up virtually all of what had been a large open space at the centre of the ancient market square, an area that had formerly been the orchestra, or dancing-place.

The Odeion of Agrippa was an enormous structure, taller than the Parthenon and occupying a slightly larger area, dwarfing all of the other buildings in the Agora. The core of the odeion, which was 25 m tall from the ground to the peak of its roof, consisted of an auditorium, a stage-building and a lobby; these were surrounded on the east, west and south sides by a balcony that stood on a basement storey, with a small porch at the centre of the northern side. This balcony was on the same level as the terrace of the Middle Stoa, the long building that abutted the odeion to its south, and the audience entered and departed on that side. The balcony formed a pleasant foyer and promenade for those attending performances in the odeion, and its eastern side would have been an excellent place from which to review processions passing below on the Panathenaic Way.

The core of the odeion was enclosed on its east, west and north sides by a thin wall reinforced at intervals by Corinthian pilasters; between each pair of these, except at the corners, there were windows, whereas at the south side there was a Corinthian colonnade with six columns *in antis*. The two ends of the building had pediments, neither one of which seems to have been decorated with sculptures. The pilasters rose from the hipped roof of the balcony below, giving the odeion the appearance of a temple rising high above a colonnaded portico.

The auditorium in the original structure was 25 m square. At the southern end of the auditorium there was a colonnade identical to the one that formed the southern façade of the building. Beams passing between the architraves on either side supported the coffered ceiling, above which was the pitched roof surfaced with terracotta tiles and decorated along its edges with antefixes. The ceiling had no lateral supports to block the audience's view of the stage, making this one of the most daring feats of roofing ever achieved in Graeco-Roman architecture.

The auditorium had eighteen rows of seats arrayed in six wedges on a gentle slope, enough for a thousand spectators. There was a somewhat less than semicircular orchestra with an altar at its centre, and behind that a rather narrow stage with the *scaena frons* at its rear decorated with alternating marble slabs and herms. The orchestra was paved with thin slabs of coloured marble and other stones in an *opus sectile* design. Behind the stage was the dressing-room; this had a door opening on to a porticoed balcony, from which the performers could look out over the Agora during intermissions.

At some time in the mid first century AD the roof of the auditorium collapsed and seriously damaged the interior of the odeion. The roof was rebuilt almost immediately, but to lessen the chance of another such collapse an east–west cross-wall was built midway in the auditorium, reducing its size to just half of what it had been, with the southern half becoming part of a much larger lobby. The Odeion of Agrippa continued to serve as a theatre and concert hall for another century, until *c*. AD 160, after which such productions were generally put on at the much larger Odeion of Herodes Atticus on the south slope of the Acropolis. Thereafter the Odeion of Agrippa served principally as a lecture-hall for the Sophists of Athens. Herodes Atticus undoubtedly lectured here himself, for he was the leading philosopher and orator of his day.

When the Odeion of Agrippa was rebuilt, the north façade of the building was completely remodelled. The small porch was removed and the stage-building was opened up to form a portico, whose architrave was supported by six piers decorated with the colossal figures of the giants and tritons. The odeion was destroyed at the time of the Herulian sack in AD 267, and afterwards its ruins were used as a quarry in constructing the Late Roman fortification wall. Then, c. AD 400, the ruins of the odeion were used for the construction on the same site of a gymnasium, a vast structure that served both as an educational institution and as an athletic facility, as was customary in the ancient Graeco-Roman world. The figures of the giants and tritons, which had somehow survived the Herulian sack, were re-erected to form the northern façade of the gymnasium. But the arrangement of the piers was now different from what it had been in the Odeion of Agrippa, with two double piers interspersed between single piers on either side, each of them once again including either a giant or triton. Arches sprang between the piers to create a tripartite gateway to the Gymnasium, the last monumental structure to be erected in the Agora in ancient times.

Passing through the Portico of the Giants, we enter what was once the great north courtyard of the gymnasium, and earlier the stage-building and auditorium of the odeion, of which there survives *in situ* a few marble seats and the *opus sectile* pavement of the orchestra. Beyond this courtyard there are the remains of a rectangular lobby and a semicircular corridor leading to the south courtyard of the gymnasium, which extends through the centre of the original structures of the Middle and South Stoas; these buildings are flanked on the west by a Roman bath and on the east by a complex of rooms grouped around a third and smaller courtyard.

Leaving the gymnasium, we now walk over to look at the north-eastern part of the Agora, crossing the Panathenaic Way, the ancient Dromos. This level part of the Dromos coincides exactly with the path that cuts diagonally across the Agora between the northern and southern entrances to the archaeological site. The Dromos was the site of a number of events connected with the Panathenaic Games. The athletic contests included sprints, long jumps, javelin and discus throwing, boxing, wrestling and a race for men in armour. Some of these events were transferred to the Panathenaic Stadium when that was

completed in 330 BC, but the more traditional competitions continued
to be held along the ancient road through the Agora. Among these
were the exciting race known as the *apobatai*, in which armed men
leapt on and off their chariots while their horses raced along the
Dromos. In addition, there were musical and poetry competitions, and
performances of the traditional folk-dances of the tribes of Attica, as
well as a contest to determine which tribe had the best-looking men.
The most spectacular event of all seems to have been the cavalry
display put on by the Athenian knights at the end of the Panathenaic
procession. As Xenophon wrote in the *Cavalry Commander*, describing
how he would organize this display:

I think that the processions would be most pleasing to the gods and to the
spectators if the cavalry were to do honour to all of the deities who have
sanctuaries and statues in the Agora by riding around the square and each of
these shrines, starting from the Herms. Then, after riding around the Agora
and reaching the Herms again, it would be a fine thing, in my opinion, for the
cavalry to gallop in tribal contingents as far as the Eleusinion.

After crossing the Panathenaic Way we walk over to the eastern
side of the railway bridge; from there we can look down on the recent
excavations on the far side of the embankment, which have unearthed
structures that formed the east end of the north side of the Agora. The
foundations nearest the bridge have been identified as those of a large
public building of the first century AD, the stumps of whose colonnade
can be seen just inside the wall of the archaeological site. Just to the
west of the colonnade there are more foundations, as well as patches
of mosaic pavements belonging to a basilica of the second century
AD. And beyond these there are the remains of a house and shops
that once abutted the northern end of the Stoa of Attalos.

The scattered ruins and foundations between the railway bridge and
the northern end of the Stoa of Attalos have been identified as the
remains of lawcourts dating from the fifth and fourth centuries BC.
More substantial remains of these structures have been preserved in
the basement of the Stoa of Attalos, the outside entrance to which is
near the southern end of the terrace wall.

We now walk southwards along the terrace wall of the Stoa of
Attalos. About 20 m from the northern end of the wall we find the
foundations of a circular structure some 8 m in diameter. This has been
identified as a monopteral temple of the mid second century AD, with
a circlet of eight columns of green Thessalian marble supporting an
hemispherical dome, one of the earliest known in Greece. The name of

the divinity to which this little sanctuary was dedicated is not known, for it is not mentioned by Pausanias or any of the other ancient sources.

At the centre of the terrace wall we come upon two large rectangular foundations. The one farthest from the wall has been identified as the Bema, or Speaker's Platform, a podium from which orators addressed informal assemblies gathered together in the Agora. The structure is a Roman work dated to the early first century BC. This date and the identification of the monument are based principally on the evidence of the chronicler Athenaeus, who tells of how in 88 BC the orator Athenion persuaded his fellow Athenians to join King Mithridates of Pontus in his revolt against Rome. Athenaeus describes the scene:

Athenion, mounting the Bema that had been constructed for the Roman generals in front of the Stoa of Attalos, looked at the crowd gathered all around. Then, lifting his eyes, he said, 'Men of Athens, let us no longer submit to our closed temples and squalid gymnasia, our deserted theatre, our dumb tribunals, our Pnyx, consecrated by divine oracles, ravished from the people! Shall we endure the sacred voice of Iacchus to be silenced, the venerable temple of the Eleusinian goddesses to be shut up and the schools of the philosophers to be reduced to silence?'

Athenion went on to persuade the Athenians to take up arms against Rome, a political mistake for which they paid dearly in 86 BC, when a Roman army under Sulla sacked the city and slaughtered the citizens who had opposed him.

The foundations closest to the terrace wall have been identified as those of the Donor's Monument, which was erected to honour King Attalos II of Pergamum (159–138 BC), founder of the stoa that bears his name. The pedestal was surmounted by a full-scale model of a quadriga in bronze, undoubtedly containing a statue of King Attalos; this stood so high that it could be seen at eye-level by those standing on the upper storey of the stoa. Like most other structures in the stoa, the Donor's Monument was destroyed in the Herulian sack, after which its stones were used as building material for the Late Roman fortification wall. More than one hundred of these stones were removed from the Roman wall when it was dismantled, and they are now piled up on the eastern side of the Panathenaic Way where it passes the sites of the Bema and the Donor's Monument. On either side of the foundations of these two structures there are numerous bases for statues, many of which were undoubtedly honorific. A short distance to the south we find a piece of marble with an inscription carved in large Greek capital letters; this is the dedicatory inscription that was carved on the architrave of the stoa directly behind the quadriga: 'King Attalos, son of King Attalos [I] and of Queen Apollonius'. Another inscription, now in the Agora archives, informs us that the Athenians later dedicated the quadriga to the Emperor Tiberius (AD 14–37).

We might now pause to look at the Stoa of Attalos, which occupies nearly the whole eastern side of the Agora. The stoa was designed as both a shopping mall and shaded promenade, its position beside the Panathenaic Way obviously making it an extremely desirable location for merchants and artisans. This magnificent stoa remained in use for more than four centuries, until most of it was destroyed in the Herulian sack that levelled the lower city in AD 267. Part of the structure remained standing, principally the north-eastern corner of the stoa and its back wall, which were preserved by being built into the Late Roman fortification wall.

The ruins of the Stoa of Attalos were identified and cleared of debris by Greek archaeologists in the nineteenth century. Then, beginning in 1931, the stoa was studied and explored by archaeologists of the American School of Classical Studies, who completely rebuilt the structure between 1953 and 1956. It was reconstructed to the same design as the original, using all the original architectural members that could be recovered from the Late Roman fortification wall and elsewhere in the Agora excavations. When new materials were used, they were of the same stone as the original structure, and the local artisans who did the work used essentially the same tools and construction techniques as those who erected the building for King Attalos. Since then the stoa has been used for the storage and study of antiquities found in the excavations, with the most interesting of these being exhibited in the Agora Museum.

The reconstructed stoa was erected on its original terrace, which was built to compensate for the downward slope of the ground from south to north. The building stands on a three-stepped platform and is 116 m long and nearly 20 m deep. It has two storeys, on each of which a two-tiered colonnade is backed by a row of twenty-one chambers (there were only eighteen in the original stoa), most of which were shops. The outer colonnade on the ground floor has forty-five Doric columns between end pilasters; these are unfluted for the lower third of their height to avoid unsightly abrasions by the inevitable human contact. The interior colonnade on the ground floor has twenty-two unfluted columns with Ionic capitals. The outer colonnade on the upper floor stands on an entablature with a frieze of triglyphs and metopes. This colonnade has the same number of members as the one below it, but they are in the form of two unfluted half-columns, back and front, joined by a short, straight unfluted section, the pair capped by a double Ionic capital. Between these columns there is a marble parapet carved in the form of a lattice. The twenty-two unfluted columns of the inner colonnade on that floor are four fifths of the height of those below them, and they are crowned by Pergamene palm-leaf capitals, a design adapted from ancient Egyptian architecture. Thus the four colonnades have different columns and are topped by capitals of different types, so as to avoid monotonous repetition in the long arcades. The columns were all made of Pentelic marble; marble from Hymettos was used for the steps and the lower courses of the walls visible from the arcades, while the inner and back walls were made of Piraeus poros. The floors of the ancient structure were of a rough mosaic of marble chips set in mortar, but in the modern building these chips have been polished to a smooth finish, except for a few patches that have been left unpolished to show the form of the original flooring. The upper floor and the roof were originally supported by wooden beams, but in the modern structure the beams are of reinforced concrete enclosed in wooden casings, with the same dimensions and spacings as in the ancient building. The pitched upper roof is decorated along its front edge with palmette antefixes alternating with rain-spouts in the form of lion heads; they are of white marble, as is the front row of roof tiles behind them, while the rest of the roof tiles are terracotta. In the original design, enclosed stairways at either end of the building led up to the second floor; the interior space in each of these was formed into a barrel-vaulted exedra lighted by an arched window; a marble bench was placed around three sides so as to create a pleasant alcove where shoppers in the stoa could sit and rest for a while, with a view down the whole of the arcade. At the top of each of the stair-wells there was a small pedimented porch with three windows framed by piers, providing vistas to the north and south, but the southern stairway was removed c. AD 100, in order to widen the street that led past that end of the stoa between the Agora and the new Roman Agora or Market. Access to the upper floor at that end of the building was then provided by building a stairway in the southernmost room, and this has also been done in the modern structure. The main entrance to the stoa, both today and in ancient times, is at the southern end of the colonnade, where the ground level in the Agora is the same as that of the terrace.

The ground floor of the Stoa of Attalos serves as the Agora

Museum, while the upper floor, which is closed to the public, houses the American School of Classical Studies. The collections of the museum are on display along the porch itself and in the chambers along its inner side, which in antiquity housed shops of various kinds. The antiquities exhibited there have all been discovered in the Agora and its environs, representing every aspect of the rich and varied communal life of ancient Athens. The second chamber along the stoa, the Memorial Room, has on display photographs of the Agora and the Stoa of Attalos before and after the beginnings of the excavations by the American School. In the next chamber, the Sales Room, one can purchase some of the interesting publications of the American School, including an excellent guidebook to the archaeological site and to the antiquities exhibited in the Agora Museum.

After visiting the Agora Museum, we leave the Stoa of Attalos through a doorway at the south-west end of the arcade, ascending a flight of steps that leads up to a small square. At the eastern end of this area we see the threshold block and the lower parts of a pair of piers. This is all that remains of a monumental archway that formed the western entrance to the colonnaded street, built *c.* AD 100, that crossed between the Greek Agora and the Roman Agora that later developed to its east. This was a pedestrian mall and was inaccessible to wheeled traffic; one ascended to its western end by the stairs we have just climbed, and at its eastern end another flight of steps took one up to the monumental entrance of the Roman Agora. This street, which was 10 m wide, was bordered on both sides by Ionic stoas, of which the stylobate and some column bases remain *in situ*. Behind the southern colonnade there was a row of a dozen rooms of various shapes and sizes, most of which apparently served as shops. An inscription discovered in the fourth room to the east records that this was dedicated as a shrine of Trajan (98–117); the donor is recorded as Herodes, father of Herodes Atticus and chief priest of the cult of the deified emperor. Underneath the ruins of this Roman stoa there are foundations dating back to the fifth century BC, apparently the remains of shops and taverns built around the south-eastern entrance to the ancient market square.

We now make our way into the remains of the structure just to the south of the Stoa of Attalos. An inscription identifies this as a library founded during the reign of Trajan by a scholar named T. Flavius Pantainos, which seems to have been built at around the same time as the colonnaded street between the Greek Agora and the Roman Market. This irregularly shaped but handsome building comprised a colonnaded courtyard bordered on the east, west and north by porticoes. The main building of the library proper was a large two-storeyed structure on the east side of the compound, with its main entrance on the central courtyard. An inscription found there, now in the Agora Museum, contains the following injunction: 'No book shall be removed, since we have taken an oath to that effect; open from the first hour until the sixth.' On the west and north sides of the courtyard there were a dozen rooms which seem to have been used as shops and workrooms. The suite of two rooms at the south end of the west portico was found to contain piles of marble chips and a number of statuettes, and so it has been identified as a sculptor's studio.

The site of the library is a particularly good spot to examine the structure of the Late Roman fortification wall, with its astonishing variety of architectural members and statuary fragments. At the north-west corner of the library you can see the foundations of one of the defence towers in the Late Roman wall. Near the south-east corner of these foundations there is a walled trench some 5 m long and 4 m deep. This and the foundations between it and the Late Roman wall are the remains of an ancient flour-mill. The mill was powered by an overshot paddle-wheel turned by water flowing south in the trench from Hadrian's aqueduct. Coins found in the trench indicate that the mill was in use during the period 450–580, making it one of the oldest water-powered mills known in Europe. No doubt it continued to be used until the Slavic sack of Athens in the late sixth century AD.

Just across the Panathenaic Way at this point there are the remains of an ancient olive-oil factory. A massive stone drum formed the lower half of the mill, in which the olives were reduced to pulp by the millstone. Near by is a tear-shaped stone with a channel running around its periphery to a spout at the cusp. Bags of crushed olives were placed on this stone and then subjected to intense pressure by the beam of a massive wooden lever, which squeezed out the olive oil into the channel, through which it ran into a container below the spout. This olive-oil factory is contemporary with the flour-mill across the way; it is typical of many such oil-presses that are still in use in the remoter parts of the Greek countryside.

Immediately to the south of the Library of Pantainos there are the remains of a structure called the South-east Stoa. Only the western half of the building has been excavated, since the remainder lies outside the archaeological site. These excavations have revealed that the stoa had a western façade consisting of an Ionic colonnade; beneath this there was an arcade with eleven chambers, which undoubtedly served as shops. The stoa was built on two levels because of the steep slope of the ground downwards from south to north, with the southern section standing nearly 2 m higher than the one to the north. Part of the shaft of one column of the colonnade is still standing, and in the right light you can see the faint remnants of some ancient graffiti, including the profile of some men's faces, a few animals and a hunting scene.

The stretch of the Panathenaic Way that runs past the South-east Stoa is the best-preserved in the whole course of the Dromos, with wheel ruts still visible in the original cobblestones. Himerios, an Athenian orator of the fourth century BC, must have been referring to this section of the roadway in his description of the Panathenaic procession, where he writes that it passed along 'the Dromos, which, descending from above straight and smooth, divides the stoas extending along it on either side, in which the Athenians and others buy and sell'.

Across the road from the northern part of the South-east Stoa there are the fragmentary remains of a sanctuary known as the South-east Temple. This edifice, which was only slightly smaller in size than the Hephaisteion and the Temple of Ares, faced north, looking down along the Panathenaic Way. In plan it consisted of a cella and a pronaos with a colonnade of six Doric columns; a capital and the top and bottom drums of one of these columns have been re-erected at the north-east corner of the temple. A study of these and other architectural members recovered from the Late Roman fortification wall have led archaeologists to date the temple to the latter part of the fifth century BC. These scholars have also concluded that the temple, which was dedicated to Demeter and Kore, originally stood in Thorikos, a coastal town in Attica. When Thorikos was abandoned by its population in the first century AD, the temple was dismantled and then reconstructed in the Agora, perhaps as part of the same Roman project that relocated the Temple of Ares there. Near the centre of the cella there are the remains of the masonry core of what was once a large statue base. During the excavations of the temple there were unearthed three fragments of the colossal cult-statue that once stood on this pedestal, the two larger pieces of which are preserved under a shed to the south of the temple. This statue is an original work of the fifth century BC, and is a representation of either Demeter or her daughter Kore.

Just to the west of the temple we come to the church of the Holy Apostles, which was erected c. 1000. This was apparently the first Christian sanctuary to have been erected in the Agora, supplanting the church of St George in the Hephaisteion. In later times at least nine other churches were erected in the Agora, but all of these were demolished during the archaeological excavations. Only the church of the Holy Apostles was spared, partly because it was standing in a corner out of the main area of archaeological interest, but also because it was an important historical monument in its own right. During the years 1954–7 the church was restored to its original condition through a grant from the Samuel H. Kress Foundation of New York, and now this elegant Byzantine structure looks just as it did when it was first built about a thousand years ago.

Before entering the church, let us first walk around the building to study its plan. The ground plan of the church is a variant of the Greek cross-in-a-square, with apses in the four cardinal directions and exedrae between them at the ends of the diagonals. The apses to north and south each have two tall and narrow windows topped by circular arches springing from the walls to a slender central pier. The eastern apse has three such windows, while the exedrae flanking it have single windows and the others none. All of these windows as well as those in the drum of the dome have glassed-in marble screens with carved rosette designs. The dome is carried on a high octagonal drum, with pilasters at each of the corners and circular arches springing between them. Each side of the drum has a pair of windows similar to those in the apses and the exedrae below. The lower part of the western apse is masked by a narthex, or vestibule, which has a peaked roof above and three domes below. The side walls of the narthex are pierced by pairs of windows similar to those in the rest of the building, while in the front there is a large central portal flanked by a pair of smaller doors, all three of which are surmounted by marble lunettes with glassed-in rosettes. The walls are in alternating courses of stone and flat bricks, as was customary in virtually all Byzantine structures, while the dome and all the roofs are surfaced with terracotta tiles. The upper courses of the walls are decorated with courses of fretted brickwork, which also outline the extrados of the arches over the doors. The uppermost course of the front door of the narthex is in the form of a brickwork frieze of Kufic letters, an imitation of the angular Arabic calligraphy that is supposed to have developed in the Iraqi city of Kufa.

Inside the narthex, on the south wall, there are plans of the church in the different periods of its architectural history, as well as photographs of the structure at various stages in the restoration process. The frescos in the narthex were not part of the original iconographic decoration of the church, but were taken from the chapel of Ay. Spyridon; this was built on the ruins of the Library of Pantainos and

was demolished during the excavation of that structure. These paintings date from the sixteenth and seventeenth centuries, as do the
frescos within the nave and aisles of the church. The painting in the
left aisle came from St George in the Hephaisteion, while the other
fragmentary frescos are part of the original decoration of the church of
the Holy Apostles itself. In the alcove on the north end of the narthex
there is a slab from the front of a sarcophagus dating from the Latin
occupation of Athens. The decoration in low relief consists of Greek
crosses interwoven with scrolls, and is perhaps the finest example of
carved stonework that has survived from medieval Athens.

We now enter the nave, standing back for a moment to study the
internal plan. The dome is supported principally by four monolithic
columns with reused ancient capitals. Three of the capitals are Corinthian, while the fourth is a hybrid type, with acanthus leaves below
and lotus leaves above, a combination of the Corinthian and Pergamene
styles. Circular arches spring from these capitals, and between them
four pendentives make the transition to the circular cornice of the
dome. There are also reused ancient capitals topping the stumps of
columns that support the marble altar, and a fragment of the original
marble structure of the Byzantine church has been incorporated within
the reconstructed iconostasis, the wall that screens off the inner
sanctum and on which icons were painted or hung.

The church stands on the south-west corner of the foundations of a
semicircular structure that extends as far as the South-east Temple.
This is the Nymphaion, a type of monumental fountain-house so called
because of its resemblance to the cave sanctuaries of the nymphs, who
were minor water deities. The water entered the Nymphaion from the
Hadrianic aqueduct that we saw earlier when we approached the
Agora; it then flowed into the semicircular pool, which was closed off
in front by a low parapet over a three-stepped platform. The tall
façade and semicircular rear wall of the fountain were indented with
niches for sculptural decoration. Fragments of the statues that stood in
these niches have been found near by and some of them are now
exhibited in the Agora Museum. A study of these and other remains
of the Nymphaion indicate that it was built in the middle of the second
century AD.

Just behind the Nymphaion and the South-east Temple there are the
remains of a building that has been identified as the Argyrokopeion,
the mint of ancient Athens. The Argyrokopeion was built c. 400 BC,
and it continued to serve as a mint until late in the first century BC.
According to tradition, the Athenians first began to strike their own

silver coins in the first decade of the sixth century BC, during the archonship of Solon. The silver used in Athenian coins came from the state-owned mines at Lavrion, on the east coast of Attica, which were worked by slave labour. The silver ore was then shipped to the mint in the Athenian Agora, where it was refined and fabricated into coins, stamped on the obverse side with a representation of Athena and on the reverse with her sacred symbols, the owl and the olive tree. The Athenian drachmae were the most highly valued coins in the ancient world, prized because of the extreme purity of the silver from which they were made.

Just to the west of the mint there are the remains of a rectangular structure called the South-east Fountain-house. This building, which has been dated to the last quarter of the sixth century BC, consisted of a long, rectangular structure in which shallow basins at either end flanked the fountain proper; this consisted of a series of water-spouts, probably in the form of lion heads, with a small colonnade of three columns creating a front porch to shade the pool.

The South-east Fountain-house abuts the east end of a structure called South Stoa I, which dates from the early fifth century BC. This stoa, which stood on a terrace that compensated for the steep slope of the hillside, extended for some 75 m to the west of the fountain-house. It consisted of a two-aisled Doric arcade with a series of fifteen square rooms behind, each of them with an off-centre door. This asymmetric location of the doors was characteristic of communal dining-rooms in ancient Athens, the reason being the way in which the dining couches were laid out along the walls. In one of the rooms there was found an inscription dating from the Athenian year 221/20 BC; it recorded the transfer of an official set of standard weights and volumetric measures from one board of the Metronomoi, the Commissioners of Weights and Measures, to another group that succeeded them when their term of office was completed. Thus it is evident that South Stoa I served as the headquarters for these and other high-ranking civil servants, perhaps as an adjunct to the *archaeia* in the south-west corner of the Agora. It has been suggested that this stoa or part of it was the place referred to by ancient sources as the Thesmotheteion, the headquarters of the archons, which was one of the most important civic institutions in the city.

We now return to the courtyard of the church of the Holy Apostles, from which we walk down to explore the extensive ruins that lie to its north and west. The ruins and foundations we see here are the remains of a group of buildings that together make up what is called the South Square, a complex that took shape in the mid second century BC. The first of these buildings to be constructed was the so-called Middle Stoa, an immensely long building that extended from the Panathenaic Way to the road running along the western side of the Agora, passing just behind the south end of the Odeion of Agrippa. The next building to be erected was a structure known as the East Stoa, which extended from the east end of the Middle Stoa back to what is now the terrace wall of the church of the Holy Apostles. After that South Stoa I was demolished and South Stoa II was erected, extending for nearly 100 m westwards from the Panathenaic Way. At its western end it abutted a large rectangular building, which we will identify subsequently and which formed the principal structure in the south-western corner of the South Square.

The Middle Stoa, which was completed *c.* 150 BC, was at that time the largest building in the Agora, with a ground plan measuring 147 × 17.5 m. It stood on a three-stepped platform atop a broad terrace, which served as the principal pedestrian walkway across the southern side of the Agora. The stoa was enclosed on all sides by a colonnade of unfluted Doric columns, 160 in all, with seventy-three on each side and nine on the ends. The columns along the ends and the first seven along the front and back were connected by a thin parapet that rose to about three quarters of the height of the colonnade, thus enclosing the two ends of the building but allowing light and air to enter from the spacious apertures above. There was an internal colonnade of twenty-three columns, probably Ionic; these were connected with thin screen walls so as to divide the arcade into two equal aisles. The main purpose of the Middle Stoa seems to have been to provide a shaded promenade along the southern side of the Agora, though later it would serve as an ambulatory for those going to and from the Odeion of Agrippa. Little remains of this once splendid stoa today except for the stumps of part of its colonnade. The bottom sections of the columns near the south-eastern corner of the colonnade were discovered *in situ*, while the others were found here and there among the ruins and re-erected; they are all of Piraeus poros, and many of them show evidence of the fire that destroyed the Stoa during the Herulian sack in AD 267.

The East Stoa, which was completed in the third quarter of the second century BC, was designed to close the eastern side of the square and to serve as its formal entrance. The eastern front of the building was preceded by a broad terrace that extended out to the Panathenaic Way. The façade of the building of that side was a blank wall pierced by five doorways. These gave entry to a longitudinal vestibule that formed the eastern half of the building. The western half of the structure had five compartments, the central one of which had a stairway that led down to the South Square. The rooms to either side of this seem to have been exedrae with a façade of two columns and with a marble bench running around the other three sides, but the end rooms were so ruinous that it has not been possible to determine their plan or function.

South Stoa II was the last building in the South Square to be completed, probably in the third quarter of the second century BC. It stood on a two-stepped platform and consisted of a colonnade of thirty Doric columns along its north front, while to the rear there was a blank wall with a small niche for a fountain. Like the Middle Stoa across the square, the main purpose of this building was to provide a shady promenade for pedestrians, and anyone strolling across the archaeological site of the Agora in mid summer will appreciate the need for such covered walkways.

Let us now walk over to the south-western corner of the South Square, where one can see the foundations of a large rectangular structure that once stood there. Little remains beyond the foundations themselves, along with the northern part of the stepped platform on which it stood, but from these one can make out the ground plan of the building. The original structure on this site, erected early in the fifth century BC, was simply a rectangular wall, somewhat higher than a man's head, enclosing an area of 31 × 26.5 m, which was open to the elements. At about the middle of the second century BC a square colonnade was erected within the courtyard, which was then covered by a roof, with a raised turret in the centre to provide light and air. The main entrance was from the north, where it opened on to the South Square.

This structure has been identified with some certainty as the Heliaia, the largest and most important of the lawcourts in ancient Athens. Originally, the Heliaia was a popular assembly of the people called together to deliberate on judicial matters. Later, perhaps after the reforms of Cleisthenes, the Heliaia was formalized into a regular jury with carefully defined functions. The normal size of the jury was originally 500, with fifty jurors selected from each of the ten tribes of Attica, but in very important cases two or even three panels of that size might sit together in deliberation. This may very well have been the case in the trial of Socrates, which was almost certainly held in the Heliaia after his indictment in the Royal Stoa. Plato was present at the trial, and several years later he wrote of this in the *Apology*. In this dialogue Plato gives his version of the three speeches that Socrates made during his trial. The last of these was the one that Socrates addressed to the jurors after he had been condemned to death, a noble valediction that ended with these elegiac lines:

Wherefore, good judges, be of good cheer about death, and know of a certainty that no evil can happen to a good man, either in life or after death. He and his are not neglected by the gods, nor has my approaching end happened by mere chance ... The hour of departure has arrived, and we go our ways – I to die and you to live. Which is better God only knows.

When Socrates finished his last speech he was taken away to the state prison, where he was confined for a month before the death sentence was finally carried out. The location of the prison was for long a matter of conjecture, but recent excavations have identified it with some foundations about 100 m to the south-west of the Heliaia. We will proceed there in a moment, but let us first look at the remaining structures in the south-west corner of the Agora.

Near the north-west corner of the Heliaia there are the remains of a large water-clock dated to *c.* 350–325 BC. At the centre of this device there is a vertical shaft with a small hole in its bottom through which the water leaked slowly, and as it did so a float on the upper surface activated a pointer that indicated the passing hours on a scale. It has been calculated that the tank of this water-clock would take seventeen hours to empty, more than enough to record the time of the longest summer day in Athens.

Just to the west of the Heliaia there are the remains of a structure called the South-west Fountain-house. This was a fountain contained in an L-shaped portico that was designed to shade those who stopped there to have a drink or to fill an amphora. This must have been one of the most familiar landmarks in the lower city, for it was the largest fountain in the city and stood beside one of the principal entrances to the Agora. The fountain-house has been dated to the last quarter of the fourth century BC.

We now leave the site of the ancient market square, following the path that leads to the south-west. About 20 m past the South-west

Fountain-house we come to the remains of a tiny sanctuary known as the Triangular Shrine. At the east end of the triangular enclosure wall there is an ancient marble boundary-stone with the following fragmentary inscription: '[Boundary] of the Sanctuary', but, unfortunately, the name of the shrine itself is missing. The lettering of the inscription is characteristic of the late fifth century BC, but excavations indicate that the shrine was founded at a much earlier date than the boundary-stone, perhaps as far back as the seventh century BC. It has been suggested that this shrine, like the Leokorion, was part of a very ancient cult of the dead.

About thirty metres south-west of the Triangular Shrine we come to the extensive remains of a structure that has been identified as a public bath-house. Excavations have revealed that this was founded in the late second century BC, and that it continued in existence until the late sixth century AD. It was customary for a Greek city to have such bath-houses near its principal gateways, so that travellers could cleanse themselves before entering the temples and lawcourts and other public institutions of the *polis*.

Taking the path that goes past the ruins of the bath-house to the right, and just beyond them, we find the remains of a large structure that has been identified as the state prison. Most of the walls and floors that one sees here date from the Roman period, but the foundations go back to the mid fifth century BC. The prison was an irregular rectangle in plan, with a watch-tower on the left as one entered, a row of three rooms beyond that, and another row of five rooms to the right. The two rooms immediately to the right as one enters formed a suite, with the entrance in the second room, and with the inner chamber apparently serving as a bathroom. From the account of the last hours of Socrates in Plato's *Phaedo*, this would seem to fit the description of the chambers in which he was confined before the death sentence was carried out. The narrator of the dialogue is Phaedo, who was with Socrates when he died. The conversation begins when the narrator's friend Echecrates asks, 'Were you yourself, Phaedo, in the prison with Socrates on the day when he drank the poison?' To which Phaedo answers, 'Yes, Echecrates, I was.' And Echecrates then says, 'I would like to hear about his death. What did he say in his last hours?' Phaedo responds by telling Echecrates of what Socrates said to him and his friends during the last hours before he drank the cup of hemlock that would kill him. The dialogue then ends with Phaedo's memorable tribute to the spirit of their departed friend and teacher: 'Such was the end, Echecrates, of our friend; concerning whom I may truly say, that of all the men of his time whom I have known, he was the wisest and justest and best.'

And with that we end our long stroll through the Agora, walking back through the ruins of the ancient market square and departing through the northern gateway of the archaeological site.

6

From the Agora through the Kerameikos

Our next stroll will take us from the Agora out through the Kerameikos, the principal cemetery of ancient Athens. We start in the square outside the northern entrance to the Agora, walking westwards along Odos Adrianou to look down again on the excavations beside the railway line.

Just to the west of the Royal Stoa there are the remains of a colonnade extending westwards parallel to the modern street. This was part of a two-aisled stoa that flanked the Panathenaic Way on its southern side along the stretch between the Agora and the Dipylon. This stoa was built early in the second century AD, not long before Pausanias passed this way *en route* from the Dipylon to the northern entrance of the Agora (which, like so many other ancient writers, he also calls the Kerameikos):

There are colonnades running from the gates to the Kerameikos, with bronze statues along the front, of men and women whose stories are glorious. One of the colonnades has sanctuaries of the gods in it, and a gymnasium named after Hermes. It also includes Poulytion's house, where some distinguished Athenians are supposed to have carried out a parody of an initiation at Eleusis; in my time the place was consecrated to Dionysos. This Dionysos is called the Harp-singer, for the same sort of reason as Apollo is called the Dance-leader of the Muses. They have here an image of Athena the Healer, and one of Zeus and of Mnemosyne and the Muses, an Apollo dedicated by its artist Euboulides, and an Akratos, one of Dionysos's train of divinities: nothing but a face let into the masonry of a wall. Behind Dionysos's enclosure is a building that houses clay figures: Amphiktyon king of Athens giving a banquet to Dionysos and the other gods. Pegasos of Eleutherai is there too, who introduced the god into Athens.

Pausanias gives us much to reflect upon here, endowing these

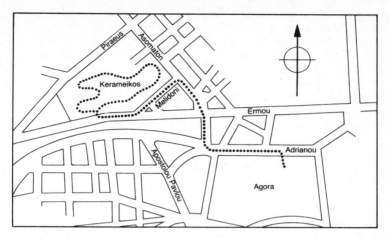

From the Agora through the Kerameikos

meagre ruins with a fascination they might not otherwise possess. The Akratos that he mentions being set into a wall was undoubtedly a terracotta representation of the theatrical masque of a stock character of the Middle Comedy (comedies produced in the period *c.* 404 − *c.* 321 BC), the 'drinker of unmixed wine'. (This character took his name from the krater, the bowl for mixing wine and water, so that Akratos means literally 'the one without a krater'.) Such a comic masque is represented on an ancient krater, now in Glasgow, with the name Akratos painted on it.

The sculptor Euboulides whom Pausanias mentions flourished in the second century BC. Excavations made near the western end of Odos Adrianou in 1837 unearthed a huge statue base and a block bearing the following inscription: 'Euboulides, son of Eucheiros of Cropia, made it.' The base was subsequently covered up with earth and built over, but the inscribed block and fragments of statuary were preserved and are now in the National Archaeological Museum. A colossal marble head found in the same area in 1874 may be the statue of Athena the Healer mentioned by Pausanias.

But the most intriguing of all the things mentioned by Pausanias as standing along this street is the house of Poulytion, where Alcibiades and his companions allegedly profaned the Eleusinian Mysteries one summer night in 415 BC, just before they went on to mutilate the Herms. Thucydides describes this scandal:

Some slaves and servants gave information, not indeed about the Herms, but about the mutilation of other statues which had shortly before been perpetrated by some young men in a drunken frolic; they also said the Mysteries were repeatedly profaned by the celebration of them in private homes: Alcibiades was one of those accused. The persons who disliked Alcibiades because he hindered them from establishing themselves as leaders of the people thought that if they could expel him, they would be supreme; they took this up and exaggerated it, clamorously insisting that both the mutilation of the Herms and the profanation of the Mysteries were part of a conspiracy against the democracy, and that he was implicated in all these affairs. In further proof they spoke of the general and undemocratic lawlessness of his habits and the excesses of his ordinary life, which were unbecoming in the citizen of a free state.

We now walk westwards along Odos Adrianou, which here follows the course of the ancient Dromos, passing on our right a recent excavation site that has unearthed part of a Roman stoa that flanked the Panathenaic Way. This part of the Dromos must have been extremely impressive in late Roman times, when the roadway was 20 m wide and flanked by porticoed stoas on either side. These stoas were destroyed in the Herulian sack, but they were afterwards rebuilt and remained in use until c. AD 590, when they were wrecked again in the Slavic raid that effectively ended the world of ancient Athens.

Odos Adrianou ends two blocks farther along, at the Theseion station on the Athens–Piraeus railway. Here we turn right and cross the square diagonally to turn up Odos Asomaton. At the next corner we cross the busy Odos Ermou, passing on our right the church of Ay. Asomatoi, which we will visit on our stroll through Byzantine Athens. The north-west corner of this intersection was where excavators unearthed the Euboulides Monument in 1837, and in 1874 the colossal marble head thought to be that of Athena the Healer was also found here. This indicates that the corner site is on the course of the ancient Dromos, which would have ended about 150 m farther on at the Dipylon, the main gate of Athens to the north-west.

At the next corner we turn left on Odos Melidoni, and half-way down the street on the left side we come to the Jewish Synagogue of Athens. On the far side of the modern synagogue is its nineteenth-century predecessor, the Old Synagogue. This formerly housed the Jewish Museum, but that has now been transferred to a new home at 36 Leoforos Amalias (see p. 272).

After passing the synagogues, we continue in the same direction along Odos Melidoni and then turn right at the next corner on to Odos Ermou. This avenue borders on its right side the site of the Kerameikos excavations, the entrance to which is about 200 m farther on. After entering, let us stroll over to the brow of the hill to the right of the gateway, where we can look down upon the ancient cemetery and study its topography and history.

The Kerameikos was one of the demes of ancient Athens and extended from the Agora to the Academy, a mile to the north-west of where we now stand. The deme took its name from Keramos, the reputed son of Dionysos and Ariadne, who was the eponymous hero of the potters (in Greek, *kerameis*) who lived in this area. The potters settled here along the banks of the Eridanos because the local river banks were an excellent source of clay, and also because the cemetery itself provided one of their principal markets, with its constant need for burial urns and funerary pottery. When the Themistoclean walls were built in 479/8 BC they cut the deme in two, after which the part within the walls became the Inner Kerameikos and that without was referred to as the Outer Kerameikos, which is where the cemetery and the potters' quarter were located. The site that we look down upon was used as a cemetery as early as the twelfth century BC. In the oldest graves here the deceased was cremated and the ashes were placed in an urn, which was then buried in a shaft cut into the ground. But in the late eighth century BC the mode of burial began to change and cremation took place in the grave itself. In such burials the grave consisted of a narrow pit for the *kline*, or bier, with shallower trenches on either side for the grave-offerings. The grave-offerings were usually contained in vases of various sorts; these were almost always shattered in the course of the cremation, but a great many of them have been reconstructed wholly or in part. They are always richly decorated with figures of sphinxes, sirens, winged lions and large birds – the demons of the dead – along with scenes of mourning and lamentation. These vase-paintings shed much light on the funerary rituals in ancient Athens. The details of the ceremonies involved differed somewhat depending on the age, sex and station of the deceased, so what follows is a description of the funeral of an ordinary Athenian man, one who presumably departed life in the fullness of his years.

The first phase of an Athenian funeral was known as *prothesis*, or lying-in-state. In preparation for this the deceased was washed in perfumed water by his women relatives, after which he was dressed in festive robes of white linen and crowned with a wreath of vine leaves.

In earlier times he would have been laid out on a *kline* (bier) in the outer courtyard of his house or in the street outside, where his relatives and friends would come and pay their last respects to him. But the reforms of Solon in the first decade of the sixth century BC required that this part of the *prothesis* be carried on inside the house, the first in a series of sumptuary laws designed to make funerals less expensive and ostentatious. Thereafter the deceased was laid out in the main salon of his house, lying on his right side facing the door, as if to greet those who entered. The mourners who came to say farewell to him were dressed in black and had their heads shaved, even the women-folk, unless the deceased in his will had expressly directed his wife and female relatives not to do so. This *prothesis* lasted for a full day, during which time his widow was liable to beat her breasts repeatedly and shriek in grief, tearing out handfuls of her hair, gouging her cheeks and pouring ashes over her head, while the other women and hired mourners wailed and keened funeral laments.

The second stage of the funeral, the *ekphora*, began before sunrise on the following day. The deceased was first prepared for his long journey: a flask of oil was placed under his head, an obol was put into his mouth so that he could pay Charon for his passage across the River Styx, and in his hands there was placed a honey-cake to present to the subterranean deities who would greet him in the Underworld. The sturdiest of the male relatives then carried the *kline* out of the house and the funeral procession formed up on the street, led by torch-bearers to light the way and serenaded by flautists playing wild funeral dirges, with the mourners following in the rear. They proceeded thus to the cemetery, where the grave had been dug and the pit filled with a pyre of dry, oil-soaked wood. The *kline* was placed on the pyre and grave-offerings were put into the shallow trenches on either side, after which the clothes of the deceased were laid out over his remains. Then, after one last mass demonstration of grief, the eldest son of the deceased threw a torch into the pyre and the cremation took place. When the fire died down the eldest son threw a handful of earth on the grave, after which the other mourners did the same. Then they all departed from the cemetery and returned to the house of the deceased, where a great feast was held in his honour.

After the funeral was over the grave-diggers heaped a large mound of earth over the grave, after which a layer of limestone plaster was laid down to prevent the earth from being washed away by the elements. During the seventh century BC tombs of mud-brick began appearing for the first time in the Kerameikos, and in the following century stone masonry was sometimes used to create a more monumental sepulchre.

The earliest tombs in the Kerameikos were marked by a simple tapering stele on which was inscribed the name of the deceased, his deme and perhaps an epitaph. Later these stelai were decorated with carved designs and scenes in low relief, usually showing the deceased bidding farewell to his or her loved ones. By the seventh century BC many of the graves in the Kerameikos were surmounted by large terracotta vessels. For the graves of men, the most popular funerary vessel was in the form of the kotyle krater, a type of drinking-cup. For those of women the decoration was usually in the form of a lustral vase such as the two-handled loutrophorus or the single-handled lekythos, the latter being traditionally used for the graves of unmarried maidens. These monumental funerary urns are known to art-historians as Dipylon vases, so called because the earliest examples were found in graves near that gateway.

The funerary sculptures in the Kerameikos remained relatively modest in scale throughout the sixth century BC and through most of the century that followed, perhaps because of restrictions imposed by Solon's sumptuary laws. But in the late fifth century BC funerary sculpture began to become more elaborate and of higher artistic quality. Then in the following century this art form reached the apogee of its greatness, with wealthy clients commissioning some of the best sculptors of the age to carve reliefs on stelai or even to decorate tombs with statues in the round. These monumental sculptures stood on walled terraces along the streets of the cemetery, as do the tombs one sees today along the three paths that cut through the archaeological site, creating a city of the dead just outside the living city.

As time went on these tombs became increasingly expensive, as wealthy Athenians vied with one another in erecting grandiose monuments to the dead. But finally this was stopped by Dimitrios of Phaleron, who ruled Athens in the period 317–307 BC. Dimitrios was concerned about the amount of money that was being wasted on burials, and so, c. 310 BC, he promulgated a law stating that 'no tomb shall be built with more elaboration than can be effected by three men in ten days'. He also forbade the decoration of tombs with reliefs or statues, directing that graves should be covered over by a mound of earth and marked with a plain stele no more than five feet tall, or by a simple vase. This effectively put an end to the development of Attic funerary pottery and its associated sculpture, and throughout the remainder of antiquity the tombs in the Kerameikos were simple and unadorned.

The Kerameikos archaeological site is only part of the ancient cemetery, for tombs flanked both of the roads that led into the country from this side of the city. The first of these was the Dromos, which inside the city was also called the Panathenaic Way; outside the walls this extended from the Dipylon to the Academy. The second was the Iera Odos, or Sacred Way, so called because it was the road taken by the sacred procession to Eleusis. The Iera Odos diverged from the left side of the Dromos at the north-western corner of the Agora, and from there the two roads ran parallel to one another out to the city walls. The Iera Odos passed through the walls at Iera Pyle, the Sacred Gate, while the Dromos went through the Dipylon, the two gateways having their centres only about 150 m apart. After passing through the gates the roads diverged, with the Iera Odos bending more to the west than the Dromos. About 50 m outside the walls a route named the West Road branched off to the west from the Iera Odos to join the Piraeus highroad, completing the pattern of roadways on this side of the city's environs. One can easily identify these roads from the vantage-point on the hilltop near the entrance to the Kerameikos; the nearest of them is the West Road, which diverges from the Iera Odos just below, while the farthest one is the Dromos. The latter two roads disappear at the north-western side of the archaeological site, which is bounded there by Odos Piraeus. The landmark at that end is the large modern church of Ay. Trias, with the Iera Odos bounding its precincts on the left and the Dromos on the right as they disappear from view under Odos Piraeus. Another feature of the landscape that one can discern from the hilltop is the River Eridanos, which emerges from its canal to enter the archaeological site just to the right of the Sacred Gate, flowing beside the Iera Odos until it disappears again just to the left of Ay. Trias under Odos Piraeus.

From the sixth century BC onwards some of the most notable figures in Athenian history were buried along both sides of the Dromos, as well as many nameless warriors who gave their lives fighting for their city; this was known as the Demosion Sema, the state burial-ground. Thucydides describes the ceremony that was held here in the Kerameikos in 431 BC to honour the Athenians who had died in the early days of the Peloponnesian War:

During the same winter, in accordance with traditional custom, the funeral of those who first fell in the war was celebrated by the Athenians at the public

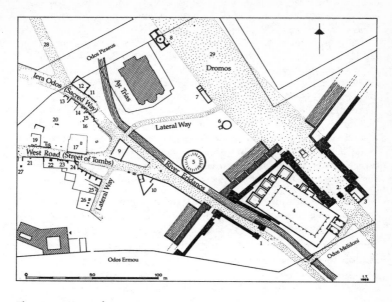

The ancient Kerameikos cemetery

1 Iera Pyle (Sacred Gate)
2 Dipylon Gate
3 Dipylon fountain house
4 Pompeion
5 Round grave monument
6 Round bath
7 Tomb of the Lacedaemonians
8 State burial monument
9 Tritopatreion
10 Unidentified shrine
11 Family grave lot
12 Grave enclosure
13 Family grave lot
14 Lethykos of Aristomache

15 Stele of Antidosis
16 Loutrophorus of Olympichos
17 Memorial altar of Hipparete
18 Aedicula of Hegeso
19 Monument of Bion
20 Aedicula of Eukoline
21 Family grave lot of Lysimachides
22 Grave monument of Dionysios
23 Temenos of Agathon and Sosikrates
24 Memorial of Dexileos
25 Aedicula of Demetria and Pamphile
26 Family grave lot of Philoxenos
27 Shrine of Hecate
28 Wheeled traffic road to the Academy

expense. The ceremony is as follows: three days before the celebration they erect a tent in which the bones of the dead are laid out, and everyone brings to his own dead any offerings that he pleases. At the time of the funeral, the bones are placed in chests of cypress wood, which are conveyed on hearses, one for each tribe. They also carry a single empty litter decked with a pall for those whose bodies had not been found and recovered. The procession is followed by anyone who chooses to do so, whether citizen or foreigner, and the female residents of the deceased are present at the funeral and make lamentation. The public sepulchre is situated in the most beautiful suburb of the city; there they always bring those who fall in war; only after the battle of Marathon, in recognition of their pre-eminent valour, were the dead interred in the field. When the remains of the dead have been left in the earth, a man chosen by the city for his reputed sagacity or judgement or eminent prestige delivers the appropriate eulogy over them, after which the people depart.

This was the setting for the funeral oration which Pericles gave that day, speaking to the assemblage from a stage that had been erected in front of the tomb. He began with these words: 'Most of those who have spoken here before me commend the lawgivers who added this oration to our funeral customs, thinking it right for an oration to be delivered at the funeral of those killed in wars.' Thus began the historic speech in which Pericles rallied his fellow Athenians to make the supreme effort that would be needed to preserve their state, reminding them of how they had reached their present eminence, and telling them of the many ways in which their society and its institutions surpassed those of any other city in the Greek world. As he said in conclusion:

Such is the city these men fought and died for and nobly disdained to lose, and every one of us who survives would naturally wear himself out in her service. This is why I have dwelt upon the greatness of Athens, showing you that we are contending for a higher prize than those who have no like advantage, and establishing by manifest proof the merits of those men whom I am now commemorating.

The part of the ancient cemetery that we look down upon from the hilltop was not visible when Pausanias made his visit to Athens, for by then it had been covered to a depth of 3–10 m with earth washed down upon it by the Eridanos. This part of the cemetery suffered great damage in two of the sieges that Athens endured in the Hellenistic period: the first of these was an unsuccessful attack by Philip V of Macedon in 200 BC, and the second the one that ended with Sulla's sack of the city in 86 BC. The siege operations in Sulla's attack destroyed many of the great funerary monuments in this part of the cemetery, which thereafter fell into disuse and began to silt over. Excavations on the site began in 1863 under the direction of the Greek Archaeological Society; then in 1913 the German Archaeological Institute took over the project and has continued work here ever since. Many of the objects found in the earlier excavations are on exhibit in the National Archaeological Museum, while those discovered by the German Institute are on display in the Oberlaender Museum, which is housed in the building just to the left of the entrance to the Kerameikos site. We will look at these exhibits later, after we have explored the cemetery.

We now take the path that leads downhill to the right, bringing us to the south-eastern corner of the archaeological site. Here we come upon the remains of a double line of ancient walls that cuts across that side of the cemetery, a stretch of some 200 m interrupted only by the Sacred Gate and the Dipylon. The inner wall from the embankment of Odos Ermou to the Dipylon is part of the original defence system built by Themistocles in 479/8 BC and reconstructed by Conon in 394 BC. The lower courses of blocks that you see here are from the original Themistoclean wall, while the upper courses of well-fitted polygonal blocks of bluish limestone are from the reconstruction by Conon, as are the sun-dried bricks in the upper section. These limestone blocks formed only the inner and outer faces of the lower part of the wall, which was nearly 2.5 m thick at this point, with its core consisting of filled-in rubble. When the Themistoclean wall was first excavated, some early tombstones were found built into it. This corroborates the statement by Thucydides, that in the building of the Themistoclean wall 'many tombstones and other blocks from earlier edifices were pressed into service'.

The outer line of walls along this stretch is of a somewhat later date, and it has been suggested that it was part of the construction programme carried out by Lycurgos in the period 338–334 BC. This outer wall, the *proteichisma*, was merely a breastwork at the inner edge of a dry moat, designed to blunt the thrust of an enemy attack and to allow defenders on the inner wall more time to fire down upon them.

At the end of the first stretch of the inner wall we come to the remains of one of its defence towers, which is separated from the curtain-wall by a small sally port. This was one of a pair of towers that flanked the Iera Pyle; the remains of the second one can be seen on the other side of the Eridanos. Looking to the left here, we see the last remaining section of the vaulted tunnel through which the Eridanos flowed, after which it emerged at the inner end of the Iera Pyle to pass through the gateway beside the Iera Odos. If you glance to your left in crossing the brook, you can follow its course as it runs through the cemetery and disappears under the retaining wall of the church of Ay. Trias.

The two lines of ancient walls stretch on for another 50 m from the Sacred Gate to the Dipylon. About 3 m before the far end of the inner wall there is a stela inscribed ODOS KERAMEIKOY, the Road of the Kerameikos, the name by which the Dromos was known locally. At the end of this stretch of the inner wall we see the foundations of one of the pair of defence towers that flanked the outer end of the Dipylon. The Dipylon, as its name implies, was a double gate in both senses of the word, for it had an inner and outer gate, separated by a courtyard, and each of these two gateways had two arched portals separated by a central pier. The piers were not centrally located, but were placed closer to the right-hand curtain-wall, looking at the gate from the cemetery. The outer pier was set back 10 m from the defence tower at that end, and cross-walls ran from the pilaster that formed the other side of the two portals, so that the actual entry-way was rather narrow compared to the width of the Dipylon. The design was intended to create the greatest possible difficulty for an enemy force trying to storm the Dipylon, for they would have to crowd through the two narrow outer portals while under fire from the defenders on the two defence towers that flanked that end of the gate. Then, if they actually made their way into the central courtyard, they would be trapped there by the inner gates and held under fire from all sides. Such was the fate of Philip V of Macedon when he attempted to storm the Dipylon in 200 BC, and he extricated his force only after suffering heavy casualties, leading him to give up his siege of the city. But Sulla, in 86 BC, bested the defenders by heaping huge mounds of earth and stone in front of the walls; his artillery then fired down from these on the fortifications around the Dipylon until they destroyed them, after which his army broke into the city and sacked it.

Outside the outer pier of the Dipylon there is the foundation for the base of a quadriga, and inside the inner one there is the base of another monument, an altar of Zeus Herkaios. To the left of the inner gateway, approaching from the cemetery, there are the remains of a fountain-house, whose L-shaped water basin was fronted by a portico carried on three columns, providing a pleasant, shady spot for those stopping for a drink on their way in and out of the city.

We now pass through the gate and turn right to look at the foundations that fill the irregular area between the Dipylon and the

Sacred Gate. This structure has been identified as the Pompeion, the building that served as the mustering-place for the two great festive processions in Athenian life. (In Greek, the word for processions is *pompai*, and the objects used in these processions are called *pompeia*.) This would have been the ideal place for such a building, since the Panathenaic procession used the Dromos and the procession to Eleusis went along the Iera Odos, the two streets flanking the Pompeion.

The first construction phase of the Pompeion began *c*. 400 BC, but soon after the foundations were laid the design was changed somewhat. The altered design called for a much more substantial structure, 43 m in length and 17 m wide, with a monumental propylon in front and subsidiary chambers at the back and side. The colonnade that supported the portico around the central courtyard had six Ionic columns to front and rear and sixteen along the sides. The propylon was displaced towards the north-east (to the right as one entered the building from the city) in order to line it up with the Dromos, so that one entered and left the central courtyard along a ramp that passed between the first two columns on that side. The propylon was rectangular in plan, measuring 12.5 × 9.8 m, with pedimented porches and a façade formed by four Ionic columns. Wheeled traffic passed through the large central door that connected with the ramp that led down to the courtyard, while pedestrians used the smaller doors on either side or a door near the left-hand corner of the building.

Behind the courtyard there was a row of four square chambers, diminishing in size as the space between the Themistoclean walls and the Pompeion narrowed. There were three more rooms along the side nearest the Dipylon, with the largest room at the far right-hand corner, followed by a paved courtyard with a well, next to which two smaller rooms were squeezed into the narrowing space between the Dipylon and the central courtyard of the Pompeion. The last and smallest room has been identified as a kitchen, and the others as dining-rooms with couches laid out head-to-foot along the walls. The room next to the kitchen was sumptuously decorated, and this may have been the dining-room reserved for the Archon Basileus and his guests, while other high state officials would have dined in the remaining chambers. The greatest feast of the Athenian year was the one that followed the climax of the Panathenaic festival, when the cattle slaughtered in the Hekatomb, the sacrifice offered on the Acropolis to Athena, were served here, with the dignitaries of the city dining in the Pompeion and the rest of the populace feasting in the central courtyard of the Dipylon. At other times of the year the Pompeion served as one of the public stoas of the city, and it must have been a pleasant place to sit or promenade for those entering or leaving the city. The philosopher Diogenes of Sinope once remarked cynically that the Pompeion was one of the two homes that had been provided to him by Athens, the other being the Stoa of Zeus.

Because of its exposed position, the Pompeion was totally destroyed in Sulla's sack of the city in 86 BC, and it was thereafter abandoned as a public building. In the mid second century AD a basilical storehouse was erected on its ruins, standing athwart the central courtyard of the classical building, and with its façade running past the fourth column from the front of the Pompeion's colonnade. By that time the classical Pompeion was known only from the literary tradition, but it is quite possible that the Roman structure continued to perform the same function as the original building, for the processions of the Panathenaea and the Eleusinian Mysteries continued until late antiquity.

Let us now return to the Dipylon and walk back into the cemetery. But before we begin strolling through the site, let us briefly note the various types of grave markers that we will encounter. Some of these have already been mentioned: the plain stele; the stele adorned with a funerary scene in low relief; and the most commonly used funerary urns, namely the kotyle krater, the loutrophorus and the lekythos. In addition to these we will see the following: the pillar stele, often supported by a sphinx or siren; the shorter and broader stele adorned with a funerary scene and surmounted by a palmette antefix; the column topped with a figure or design; the naiskos, in which the lamentation scene is set in a miniature temple; the aedicula, in which the naiskos is reduced to a frame for the relief; the trapeza, a table-like monument whose upper surface is decorated with a relief; and the kioniskos, a small, unadorned column, the grave marker that was most commonly used after the enforcement of the sumptuary laws of Dimitrios of Phaleron.

We will begin our exploration of the ancient cemetery with the section that lies in front of the moat between the Dipylon and the Sacred Gate.

Just in front of the moat, about midway between the two gates, we find a naiskos, and about 10 m behind that the remains of a Hellenistic brick-kiln. The kiln lies at the foot of a burial mound dating from the early classical period. Directly across the way, on the right bank of the Eridanos, there is an even larger burial mound, dated to the fourth century BC. Between the two mounds there are the foundations of structures believed to be workshops, and also a large pithos, which was one of many that were set into the earth in front of the Themistoclean Walls as booby traps to impede besieging armies. Just beyond the smaller of the two mounds there are the remains of a circular bath dating from the classical period. Ten metres beyond the bath we come to the cross-path known as the Lateral Way. We will head this way shortly, but let us first explore the remaining stretch of the Dromos.

Just beyond the Lateral Way, on the left side of the Dromos, we come to a long, rectangular walled terrace surmounted by a funerary monument. This is the Tomb of the Lacedaemonians, the grave of thirteen Spartan soldiers who died in Athens during the civil war that led to the overthrow of the Thirty Tyrants in 403 BC.

On the roadside below the Tomb of the Lacedaemonians there is a boundary-stone marked ODOS KERAMEIKOY, indicating that this is the course of the ancient Dromos. Some 50 m farther along we come to yet another marker stone of the Dromos, this one standing below an elaborate tomb, half of which is still buried beneath the hillside. The façade of this tomb, which dates from the mid fourth century BC, had the figures of guardian hounds at each end and a huge loutrophorus at the centre. The ruins lying along the left side of the road between the two boundary-stones are believed to be the remains of ancient potteries, whose workers and artisans carried on their activities within the graveyard itself, building and decorating tombs.

We now return to the Lateral Way, where we turn right and walk around the retaining wall of Ay. Trias. We then cross the Eridanos brook on an ancient bridge, after which we turn left and walk a short distance down the Sacred Way. This brings us to an enclosure in the form of a truncated triangle, at whose apex the West Road branches off from the Sacred Way. This has been identified as the Tritopatreion, a shrine of mysterious deities called the Tritopatores, who were connected with an ancient Attic cult of ancestor worship. The sacred enclosure of the shrine is demarcated by classical boundary-stones at three points around its periphery.

Just to the south of the Tritopatreion, at the foot of a burial mound, there are three stelai and the foundations of an unidentified shrine of triangular cross-section. One of the stelai stands on a stepped pyramid; this marks the grave of the consul Pythagoras, who in the early fifth century BC was the Athenian representative in Selymbria, near Byzantium. The other two stelai mark the graves of Thersandros and

Simylos, two consuls from the island of Corcyra (the modern Corfu) who died in Athens during the first year of the Peloponnesian War. Thersandros and Simylos came to Athens in 433 BC, at a time when Corcyra and Corinth were at war over their common colony, Epidamus, and their mission was to persuade the Athenians to enter into an alliance with their island. After a public debate, the Athenians agreed to form a defensive alliance with Corcyra, a decision which Thucydides believed to be the immediate cause of the Peloponnesian War, which broke out less than a year later.

After looking at these stelai, we make our way back along the Sacred Way to look at some of the tombs and grave-markers along its final stretch before it disappears into the retaining wall of Odos Piraeus.

On the terrace above the right side of the Sacred Way there are some grave monuments from the classical period, none of them exceptional. After glancing at them we might clamber up on to the terrace on the left side of the road, for there are several interesting classical grave monuments there. The first of these, beginning at the far (west) end, is the sculptured lekythos of the maiden Aristomache. Just to the east of this there is a stele inscribed with the name Andidosis, and behind that the tomb of Olympichos, surmounted by a loutrophorus.

We now return to the Tritopatreion and begin walking up the right-hand side of the West Road. This is also known as the Street of Tombs, because of the large number of burial sites and grave markers in its vicinity, all of them dating from the classical period.

Starting along the right-hand side of the Street of Tombs, we come first to the funeral plots of Phanokles and Philocrates of Kydathenaion, both of them containing a number of funerary slabs, stelai and columns. Beyond these we see a small memorial commemorating Hipparete, a granddaughter of Alcibiades. Then we see the stelai of Menakion and Menes, both of which are decorated with reliefs showing the deceased on horseback, indicating that they were Athenian knights. After this we come to the enclosure of Koribus of Melite, with his stele in the centre, the loutrophorus of his grandson Kleidomus to the right, and to the left a copy of the aedicula of his wife Hegeso. The relief on Hegeso's monument shows her seated on a chair, looking pensively at a piece of jewellery that she has taken from a *pyxis*, or jewel-box, which is being held by her maid, who looks down upon her with an expression of profound sadness. The original of this superb relief, which is dated c. 410 BC, is exhibited in the National Archaeological Museum; it is considered to be one of the very finest examples of Athenian funerary sculpture.

The last grave-plot on this side of the Street of Tombs is that of Eubios of Potamos, in the left side of which we see the stele of his sister Euphrosyne and on the right the monument of his nephew Bion, a Doric column topped with a loutrophorus.

At this point we might climb up the hill to look at the tombs in the angle formed by the Street of Tombs and the Sacred Way. Here we find the aedicula of Aristion, decorated with the figures of a boy, his slave and his puppy. Beyond that is the aedicula of Eukoline, a little girl who is shown in the relief with her pet dog. Also on the hill there is the base of a funerary monument dating from the archaic period.

Let us now make our way back to the west end of the Street of Tombs, from where we will stroll eastwards to look at the monuments along its southern side. The first grave plot on that side belonged to a man named Kephisodoros and his wife Nikostrate. Next to that is the enclosure of Lysimachos of Acharnai, with the marble figure of a huge guard-dog on one side and on the other a funerary relief showing Charon's boat on the River Styx. The next plot is that of Dionysos of Kollytos, which is marked by one of the most striking monuments in the cemetery, a plain naiskos surmounted by the splendid figure of a bull. Adjacent to this is the temenos of the brothers Agathon and Sosikrates of Heracleia in Pontus, in the centre of which stands their tall palmette stele and to its left the aedicula of Agathon's wife, Korallion.

The next monument is the most famous in the Kerameikos, the Memorial of Dexileos. This is a large aedicula decorated with a relief showing a young knight on horseback in the act of spearing a prostrate foe; this is a copy of the original, which is exhibited in the Oberlaender Museum. Below the relief there is this inscription: 'Dexileos, son of Lysanides from Thorikos, was born in the archonship of Teisandros [414 BC] and died in that of Euboulides [394/3 BC], in Corinth, one of the five knights.' An inscription in the Epigraphical Museum of Athens records the names of Dexileos and the other four knights who lost their lives in that action, in which the Athenians and their allies were decisively defeated by the Spartans. Two tall stelai beside the memorial of Dexileos honour the warrior's brother Lysias and his sister Melitta, while to the side a trapeza marks the grave of another brother, Lysanias, who is buried there along with his wife Kallistrate and their son Kalliphanes.

Turning right off the Street of Tombs we go up the Lateral Way, passing a cluster of grave sites to our right. The first of these is that of the actors Makareus and Hieronymos. Other tombs adjacent to theirs are identified as those of Glykera, Dorcas, Hegetor and Demetria; the latter is shown in her aedicula as a seated figure sadly holding the hand of her mother Pamphile, whose own tomb is near by. Beyond these is the tomb of Philoxenos of Messenia, who is buried there along with his wife and other members of his household, including his slaves.

We now make our way up into the complex of graves above the Lateral Way and the Street of Tombs, walking back towards the retaining wall of Odos Piraeus. About half-way in from the Lateral Way we come to the boundaries of an enclosure that extends almost all the way to the retaining wall, with a small projection to the north between the first two grave plots on that side. Here we see a statue base with a triangular cutting, next to which there is a rectangular *eschara*, or hearth. Close by there are also the remains of a podium with two steps on its north side, near which there were discovered inscriptions dedicating the enclosure to Artemis under the name of Soteira (the Saviour) and Kalliste (the Best). Along with the inscriptions there was also unearthed here a votive relief showing a man and woman following a boy who is leading a sacrificial sheep to an altar. All of this has led to the conclusion that the enclosure was a temenos of Hecate, an ancient fertility goddess closely connected with Artemis. This identification was based partly on the triangular cutting on the statue base next to the *eschara*, for the archetypal statue of the goddess represents her as a terrifying figure with three faces: Selene, goddess of the moon; Artemis, goddess of the earth; and Hecate, goddess of the underworld. The identification was supported by the fact that Hecate was also a goddess of crossroads, for the temenos here occupies the angle between the Street of Tombs and another ancient road that branched off from it to the south-west.

Returning to the southern side of the site, we pass the tombs of Poseidonios, Sosibios, Daphnos, Asia, Philon and Isidoros, along with numerous sarcophagi, loutrophoroi and kioniskoi, many of which were assembled here after being unearthed elsewhere on the site. Then finally we reach the Lateral Way and make our way up to the Oberlaender Museum.

In Room I, the first of four exhibition halls in the museum, we see the original relief that adorned the Monument of Dexileos, a superb work in Pentelic marble. Notice also the striking Sphinx Acrotirion and the Boxer Stela, both of the mid sixth century BC, the latter with a relief showing a pugilist with a cauliflower ear and the thongs of his glove still tied to his wrists. Another famous exhibit here is the Stele of Ampharete, which was seen by millions when it was exhibited at

the Greek Pavilion at the New York World Fair and later at the
Metropolitan Museum of Art. The relief shows the lady Ampharete
looking sadly at a little boy whom she is holding in her lap. The
epitaph on the stele was translated thus by Stephen Spender:

> My daughter's dear child I hold on my lap: so
> I used to hold him of old in those days
> When with living eyes we both looked on the sun;
> Now that he's dead, I still hold him: for I
> Am dead too.

Room II contains funerary urns and grave pottery dating from the
twelfth to the seventh centuries BC. Also on exhibit here, dating
from the same epoch, are terracotta votive figurines, as well as painted
plaques called *pinakes*. These plaques were hung as ex-votos on the
walls of tombs, usually decorated with painted scenes of *prothesis* and
ekphora, the two stages of an ancient Athenian funeral.

Room III contains funerary urns and grave pottery dating from the
archaic, classical and Hellenistic periods. The most noteworthy of the
vases exhibited here is a lekythos from a shaft-grave that has been
dated to *c.* 550 BC, and which has been attributed to an artist known
as the Amasis Painter.

Room IV contains a selection of fragments from the amphorae that
were awarded as prizes in the Panathenaic Games. These amphorae,
each of which contained almost forty litres of olive oil when full, were
awarded with their contents to victors in the athletic and equestrian
contests that were held during the games. The organization of the
Panathenaic Games and the awarding of their prizes is described in the
Aristotelian treatise on the Athenian constitution:

The archons also elect by lot ten men known as *athlothetai* . . . who administer
the procession of the Panathenaic festival and the contest in music, the
athletic competition, and the equestrian events. They also supervise the
weaving of the *peplos* and, together with the Council, have the prize vases
manufactured and distribute the olive oil to the victorious competitors. The
oil is procured from the holy trees and the archon collects it from the owners
of the grove . . . The prizes for the victors in music are silver coins and gold
wreaths, the winners in the contest in manly beauty receive shields, and those
who win the athletic and equestrian contests receive olive oil.

The Panathenaic prize amphorae were decorated by some of the
best painters in Athens, who used as their themes the contests and
myths associated with the games. The fragmentary vases exhibited
here are a representative collection of Panathenaic prize amphorae

ranging in date from the second quarter of the sixth century BC to
the fourth century AD, a span of time almost as long as the lifetime
of the games themselves. Thus they constitute a unique and fascinating
record of a very important aspect of life in ancient Athens. Pindar
mentions these vases in one of his Nemean odes, where he sings the
praises of Theaeus of Argos, the city of Hera, who was twice victorious
in the wrestling competition at the Panathenaic Games: 'Yet amid the
sacred rites of the Athenians, twice did voices sweet exalt him in the
prelude of a triumphal ode, and in earth baked by fire came the olive
oil in richly painted vases to the manly people of Hera.'

7

Around the Walls of Ancient Athens

On this stroll we will trace out the circuit once followed by the walls of ancient Athens (see map on p. 13). We have already seen the best-preserved stretch of these walls in the Kerameikos cemetery, along with two of the principal entry-ways to the ancient city, the Dipylon and the Sacred Gate. Besides these remains, very little survives of the defence walls with which Themistocles encircled Athens in 479/8 BC. But a stroll around the circuit of the fortifications gives one some idea of the extent of the ancient city, as well as bringing one to the sites of some interesting monuments that are seldom seen by visitors to Athens.

We will begin this stroll where we ended the last one, at the entrance to the Kerameikos cemetery. But before we set out on our walk, we might pause for a few moments to study the history and topography of the fortifications of ancient Athens.

We learn from both Herodotus and Thucydides that the Athenians had built a wall round their city before the Persian invasion in 480 BC; however, no trace of these fortifications has ever been discovered. (Traces of earlier walls have been found on the Acropolis itself, as we have seen, but not of the outer fortifications.) Nor is there any evidence as to what course this pre-classical wall followed, other than a statement by Thucydides that it surrounded the Acropolis and was 'wheel-shaped'. Perhaps these earlier walls were utterly destroyed by the Persians, as suggested by the account that Thucydides gives of the aftermath of their occupation of the city: '. . . the Athenian people, after the departure of the barbarian from their country, at once proceeded to carry over their children and wives, and such property as they had left, from the places where they had deposited them, and prepared to rebuild their city and their walls. For only isolated portions of the circumference remained standing, and most of the houses were in ruins.'

When the Spartans learned that the Athenians were rebuilding their walls they sent an embassy to Athens in an attempt to dissuade them from doing so. Their motive was to limit the rising power of the Athenians and to make them more dependent on the Lacedaemonian military alliance. Themistocles persuaded the Assembly to dismiss the Spartan ambassadors and send him as an emissary to Lacedaemonia, where he would stall the Spartans while the Athenians went ahead with the construction of their defence walls. The Athenians agreed, and in a remarkably short period of time they erected a new and more extensive line of fortifications. While they were working, Themistocles dragged on his discussions with the Spartans, breaking off the talks and returning to Athens when he learned that the walls were nearing completion. Thucydides describes this project:

In this way the Athenians walled their city in a little while. To this day the structure shows signs of the haste of its execution; the foundations are laid of stones of all kinds, and in some cases not wrought or fitted, but placed just in the order that they were brought by the different hands; and many columns too, from tombs, and sculptured stones were brought in with the rest. For the bounds of the city were extended at every point of the circumference, and so they laid their hands on everything without exception in their haste. Themistocles also persuaded them to finish the walls of the Piraeus, which had been begun before, in the days of his archonship [493/2 BC] . . . Thus, therefore, the Athenians completed their wall, and commenced other buildings immediately after the retreat of the Mede.

During the Periclean Age a double line of fortifications, the so-called Long Walls, was built to connect Athens with the Piraeus. Later in that period another long wall was erected between Athens and Phaleron, so as to enclose the whole area between the city and its two ports. In 404 BC, immediately after the end of the Peloponnesian War, the Spartans forced the Athenians to pull down the Long Walls, but these fortifications were rebuilt by Conon after his victory at Cnidos in 394. Late in the fourth century BC the circumference of the defence walls was shortened by building a cross-wall, the Diateichisma, which extended between the Hill of the Nymphs and the Mouseion Hill, the heights from which the original Themistoclean walls had extended in a salient towards the south-east to meet the double line of the Piraeus Long Walls. Early in the third century BC Dimitrios Poliorketes built a fortress where the Diateichisma joined the

Themistoclean walls atop the Mouseion Hill, a bastion that proved to be the last defence work constructed around Athens in the Hellenistic period.

The defence walls of Athens and its two ports were severely damaged in 86 BC, when Sulla besieged and sacked the city. The Long Walls and the fortifications of the Piraeus were totally destroyed at that time and were never rebuilt. The Themistoclean walls suffered considerable damage too, particularly in the stretch between the Dipylon and the Peiraic Gate, and they lay in ruins for the next three and a half centuries. The walls were eventually rebuilt in the mid third century AD by the Emperor Valerian (253–60), in order to protect Athens from the barbarians who were pouring into Greece from the north. At that time Valerian extended the line of fortifications in a long arc to the east, so as to include the new quarter built by Hadrian in the first half of the second century AD. But the new walls failed to stop the Heruli, who sacked the city in 267. The Late Roman fortification wall was constructed soon afterwards, enclosing only the area just to the north of the Acropolis. The city eventually recovered and expanded well beyond the confines of the Late Roman wall, particularly during the early centuries of Byzantine rule. The Emperor Justinian (527–65) repaired the Themistoclean and Roman walls during the early years of his reign. But these fortifications gave way before the Slavs, who sacked the city in about 590, after which Athens declined to the point where it comprised little more than the Acropolis and its northern slope. At some time in the eleventh century a new wall, the Rizocastron, was built to enclose this area, including as part of its structure the Odeion of Herodes Atticus, the Stoa of Eumenes and stretches of the Late Roman fortification wall. Athens grew outwards once again during the latter Turkish period, and when Hadji Ali Haseki built his defence wall in 1778 it enclosed an area about half as large as that which had been within the ancient Themistoclean walls. When the Greek Kingdom was established with its capital in Athens in 1833, stretches of all these walls still remained standing, monuments spanning a period of more than twenty-three centuries. The growth of the modern city has obliterated almost all traces of the walls that in times past protected the Athenians from their enemies; nevertheless, fragments of these fortifications emerge from time to time in archaeological excavations or construction projects, and we will see these in the course of our stroll.

The total length of the original Themistoclean walls is thought to have been about eight and a half kilometres, although this was

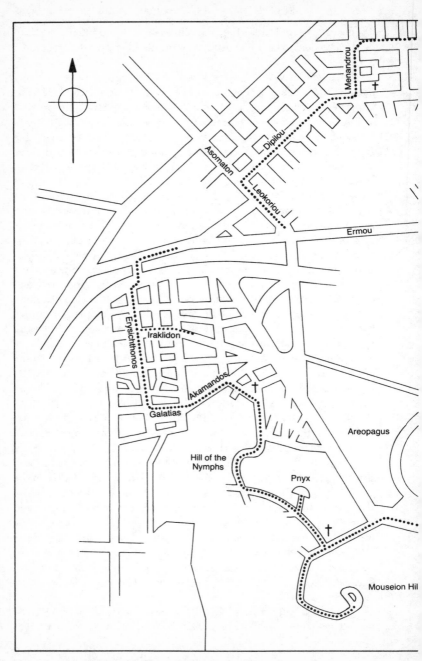

Around the walls of ancient Athens

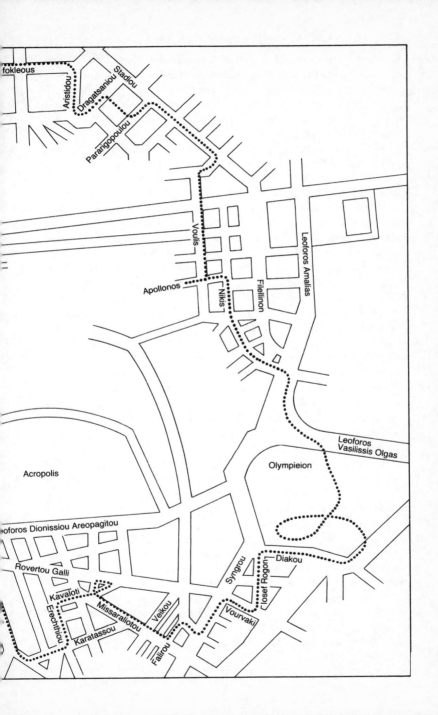

shortened somewhat with the construction of the Diateichisma. There
are known to have been about fifteen main gates, of which the most
famous were the Dipylon and the Sacred Gate. On our stroll along the
circuit of the Themistoclean walls we will come upon the foundations
of a few of these gates, and in other places we can locate their sites
through archaeological or literary evidence.

The first part of our stroll will take us from the vicinity of the Dipylon
and the Sacred Gate as far as the Peiraic Gate, following as closely as
possible the course taken by the Themistoclean walls. After leaving the
Kerameikos we turn right on Odos Ermou, following that avenue as far as
the footbridge across the railway line. We cross the footbridge, and on
the other side we see the little chapel of Ay. Athanasius perched on an
outcrop of rock above the railway line. Then we turn right on Odos
Thessalonikis and after a few steps take the first left on to Odos
Erysichthonos, walking down the left side of the street. We pass Odos
Poulopoulou and Odos Iraklidon, and then half-way down the next
block, at No. 29 Erysichthonos, we come to a grating at street level
through which we can see a section of the ancient Themistoclean wall that
was unearthed in the basement of a house. The courses of stone that we
see here are believed to have been part of the defence wall just to the
north of the Peiraic Gate, which would have been at the right-hand end of
this section as we view it from the street.

The ancient road that led into the city from the Peiraic Gate would
thus have passed midway between Odos Iraklidon and Odos Nileos,
the next street to the south. This supposition has been confirmed by
the discovery of a short stretch of an ancient roadway just to the east
of where we now stand. Further confirmation came with the unearthing
of a sanctuary of Artemis some 200 m to the east on the same line, for
this is known to have stood on the road that passed through the
Peiraic Gate. The sanctuary has been covered over and is no longer
visible; nevertheless the site is still worth a visit because of its
interesting historical associations.

So let us walk back along Odos Erysichthonos and turn right on to
Odos Iraklidon, going down the right-hand side of the street and
across Odos Akteou. We then stop half-way down the street at the
site of the sanctuary, which lies under the block of apartment houses
between Odos Iraklidon and Odos Nileos. The sanctuary of Artemis
that was discovered here was dedicated to the goddess under her
attribute of Aristoboule, or Good Counsel. According to Plutarch, this
little shrine was found by Themistocles, apparently just before his
ostracism in 471 BC:

Themistocles himself gave offence to the majority by founding the shrine of Artemis. He called the goddess Aristoboule, on the ground that he had given the best advice to the city and to Greece, and he built the shrine near his house in Melite. A portrait of Themistocles stood in the temple of Aristoboule even in my day, and it was clear that he was a man heroic not only in spirit but also in appearance. He built this temple near his own house, where now the public officers carry out the bodies of such that are executed, and throw the halters and clothes of those who are strangled or otherwise put to death.

The place to which Plutarch refers was the infamous Barathron, a deep ravine outside the Peiraic Gate where the bodies of condemned criminals were thrown after their execution. According to the testimony of several ancient writers, the public executioner lived just outside the Peiraic Gate, and it was he who disposed of their bodies. Plato, in the *Republic*, tells of how Leontius, one of the characters in his dialogue, was walking to Athens from the Piraeus one day when he saw some corpses lying on the ground outside the executioner's house, thus giving us a glimpse of the darker side of Athenian life in classical times.

Let us now retrace our steps and return to 29 Odos Erysichthonos, the site of the ancient Peiraic Gate, where we will pause for a moment to get our bearings and to study the topography of the next stretch of the Themistoclean walls. The Peiraic Gate was the westernmost point in the Themistoclean walls, and from there the fortifications curved off to the south-west and ascended the Hill of the Nymphs. We will follow the course of this section of the walls by continuing along Odos Erysichthonos to its southern end, where we ascend a flight of steps. At the top of the steps we turn left on to Odos Galatias, which at the next corner changes its name to Akamandos. Here we might pause for a moment, for this intersection has been identified as the site of the Demian Gate, the next entry-way to ancient Athens south of the Peiraic Gate. The Demian Gate was situated just to the north of the point where the northern Long Wall from the Piraeus joined the Themistoclean wall, at the north-west spur of the Hill of the Nymphs. Some years ago a short stretch of an ancient road was discovered under the intersection, its paving stones still bearing the ruts of wagon wheels. This road passed through the Demian Gate along the route of the modern Odos Akamados, after which it led south-west along the outside of the northern Long Wall, following much the same course as the present Athens–Piraeus railway line.

We now continue along the left side of Odos Akamandos to the next corner, where it meets Odos Amfiktionos. There we turn right to cross the street and ascend the steps on the other side. At the top of the steps we find ourselves in the Plateia Ay. Marina, named after the two churches on the far side of the square. The smaller church of Ay. Marina was built early in the nineteenth century, when this part of Athens was still out in the country, while the larger one was erected in recent years when the area around the Hill of the Nymphs became a densely populated residential quarter. The ground on which the two churches stand must have been a sacred spot since ancient times; on a rock face below the chapel there is an inscription of the sixth century BC reading HOROS ZEUS, recording that this was the temenos of a sanctuary of Zeus. Another inscription, dating from the fourth century, indicates that the cult epithet of Zeus here may have been Exopsios, which means 'looking out'. R. E. Wycherley, in *The Stones of Athens*, has suggested that this derives from the fact that 'from the hillside Zeus could look out and view the agora and the city as a whole'.

We now take the road that winds uphill to the right of the two churches. This takes us up towards the summit of the Hill of the Nymphs, ending in a little square beside the garden of the Astronomical Observatory, the Asteroskopion. (On the hillock to the left of the square is the new observatory, built in 1905.) The Asteroskopion was founded in 1842 by Baron Simon Sinas, a philanthropist who endowed several cultural institutions that were influential in the renaissance of learning in modern Greece. The structure was designed and built in the years 1843–6 by the Danish architect Theophil von Hansen. Hansen, who was also a gifted painter and sculptor, was one of the intellectual leaders of the group of brilliant architects and city-planners who were commissioned by King Otho and his government to design and build the new capital. Hansen's studies of the monuments of the ancient city were a major influence in the development of neo-classical architecture in modern Greece, a style that was to adorn nineteenth-century Athens with some of its most distinguished buildings.

The Asteroskopion was the first institution of its kind to be built in Athens since antiquity, when the earliest Greek astronomers laid the foundations of that science. The astronomer Meton worked in Athens in the second quarter of the fifth century BC, and he may have had an observatory on the Pnyx Hill, as suggested by a rock-cutting there that may be his famous Heliotropion, or sundial. Meton is famous in the history of science for having formulated a calendar that reconciled the disparate periods of the sun and the moon, for a lunar year of twelve months comes to twelve days less than a solar year of 365 days. Meton solved the problem by combining artificial years of twelve lunar months in an alternating pattern with years of thirteen months, the so-called Metonic cycle, in such a way that his calendar came into phase with the actual celestial calendar every seventy-two years. According to tradition, Meton was also an accomplished astrologer. In 415 BC, on the eve of the ill-fated Sicilian expedition, Meton's analysis of the celestial configurations led him to predict disaster for the Athenians, whereupon he feigned madness and set fire to his house, which was near the Stoa Poikile, so as to avoid being sent with the force that set sail for Syracuse.

The Hill of the Nymphs is a modern name. This stems from an inscription found near the summit reading HOROS NYMPHAI, now in the garden of the Asteroskopion; this is one of several rock-carvings indicating that the hill was sacred to the Nymphs. As R. E. Wycherley writes:

These particular Nymphs were probably the daughters of Hyakinthos, sacrificed according to legend for the good of the city. Hyakinthos himself, as we learn from an inscription, had a shrine at Athens, and this may have been in association with his daughters; indeed the hill may be what was known in antiquity as the Hill of Hyakinthos ... If the identification is correct, these Nymphs were known as *genethliaia*, i.e. concerned with childbirth; and it is worth noting that St Marina, to whom is dedicated the church which stands just below and a little to the east, is also concerned with birth and children, and may well be a true successor to the Nymphs.

We now ascend the flight of steps at the end of the road, bringing us to a path that leads around the fenced-in summit of the Pnyx Hill to the west. (The summit is officially open to the public only during performances of the 'Sound and Light' show, when it serves as an auditorium for the spectators.) Here we pass the site of the Melitides Gate, the next gateway through the Themistoclean walls. The gate took its name from the deme of Melites, which extended from the Pnyx Hill as far as the Kerameikos. At this point a road, still to be seen today, passed over the saddle between the Hill of the Nymphs and the Pnyx Hill; here one entered the enceinte formed by the Diateichisma, the two Long Walls to the Piraeus, and the westernmost arc of the original Themistoclean walls. This area was densely settled in ancient times, as indicated by the number of primitive rock-cut dwellings that have been discovered there. But after the building of the Diateichisma it ceased to be a residential area, since it was then outside the city walls.

The Diateichisma is the longest and best-preserved stretch of the ancient city walls, and so we might take this opportunity to study its structure and topography in some detail. It extended from the north-west spur of the Hill of the Nymphs to the summit of the Mouseion Hill, following the natural contours of the hills and valleys in between for a total distance of about one kilometre. The original cross-wall was started in the last quarter of the fourth century BC, and was probably completed in the first decade of the following century. About a century later the stretch of wall on the Pnyx was reconstructed along a slightly different line, being shifted a short distance outwards so as to follow more closely the western brow of the hill. The new walls on the Pnyx were 2 m thick and were almost solid masonry, constructed of ashlar blocks. This stretch of wall was anchored at its northern end by a defence tower that stood just to the south of the Melitides Gate. This tower was rectangular in cross-section, projecting outwards 6.6 m from the wall and measuring 9.3 m in width. This was the first in a series of seven towers of similar dimensions that were arrayed along the western brow of the Pnyx, separated by intervals of approximately 40 m and connected by a curtain-wall strengthened by buttresses 1.35 m square and about 4.6 m apart. The Pnyx defence wall terminated at the western end of the summit, where it joined the northernmost tower of the original Diateichisma.

Let us now walk along the Pnyx defence walls, beginning at the site of the Melitides Gate; from there we will follow its course as it first heads south, then turns south-east at the second tower (whose outer face is circular, rather than rectangular as in all the other towers), and finally veers east to meet the northernmost tower of the original Diateichisma. In following the course of this stretch of wall we pass the foundations of two stoas that formed part of the Pnyx, the Athenian assembly place from which the hill originally took its name. (During the classical period the hill was popularly known as 'ai Petrai', or 'the Rocks'.) We will look at these stoas more carefully a little later on, after we have studied the Pnyx itself.

In ancient Greek *pnyx* means 'crowded together', an appropriate word to describe a place where thousands of Athenians gathered to discuss the affairs of their city. The Ekklesia, or popular assembly, probably began meeting here after the restoration of democracy under Cleisthenes in the last years of the sixth century BC. The leading figures in Athenian history during the classical and Hellenistic periods spoke here, most notably Aristides, Themistocles, Pericles and Demosthenes. The Ekklesia continued to use the Pnyx as its principal place of assembly until the last vestiges of democracy vanished under Roman rule, after which the impotent Ekklesia met in the Theatre of Dionysos.

The Pnyx Hill was undoubtedly chosen because of the advantages offered by the site: a hillside forming a natural theatre from which the Athenians could look out over their city during meetings of the Ekklesia. In the earliest period of construction, dating to c. 500 BC, the surface of the hill sloping gently to the north was smoothed by quarrying out the hard limestone from which it was formed, while at the north side a straight retaining wall was built to contain the earth that was brought in to form a level space for the *bema*, or speaker's platform. This completely reversed the orientation of the theatre, so that the audience faced south, towards the hillside, while the orators on the *bema* now looked out over the city as they spoke. In order to accomplish this, a high semicircular retaining wall was built to the north, after which earth was filled in to create a *cavea* sloping down gently to the south, in the opposite direction to the natural slope of the hill. The *bema* was then placed on a level area at the southern end of the theatre, on what had formerly been the uppermost level of the *cavea*. The theatre was enlarged in a second reconstruction during the period 330–326 BC, retaining the same orientation as the previous structure, with the circular retaining wall extended another 10 m farther out in all directions. At that time the two stoas that we passed earlier were laid out along the south side of the upper terrace; these were intended to shelter the citizens from the sun or rain during intermissions in the Assembly, but apparently they were never finished.

The plan of the Pnyx as we see it today is essentially the same as it was at the end of the last rebuilding period, although time and the elements have ruined and eroded much of its structure. The southern or upper side consists of a large terrace, about 60 m in length and 40 m in breadth at its widest part, bounded on the south by a wall 3–4 m high cut out of the rock. To the north of this terrace we come again to the foundations of the two unfinished stoas, a long one on the west and one of half that length on the east, the two structures making an angle of about 135° with one another. This orientation was made necessary by the contours of the hillside, which has a natural bend just above the central axis of the theatre, where the lines of the two stoas intersected. The western stoa was 148 m long and 17.9 m wide, and was designed to have a façade of fifty-four Doric columns between antae, while the eastern stoa measured 65.8 × 16.5 m and was to have had twenty-two columns *in antis* on its façade, but neither structure progressed beyond its foundations. It is thought that the construction of the two stoas began in the last quarter of the fourth century BC, and that work was halted when the decision was made to build the original Diateichisma across their site, incorporating part of their foundations within the base of the fortifications.

At the centre of the terrace, standing exactly on the axis of the theatre, there is a large foundation measuring 5.85×5.10 m. This is believed to have been the base of a huge sundial, the Heliotropion, which is thought to have been erected on the Pnyx in 433/2 BC by the astronomer Meton. To the left of this, as you face the theatre, there is a large rectangular cutting in the rock. This has been identified as the site of the altar of Zeus Agoraios, which we saw earlier in the Agora, and which was removed from the Pnyx in the Augustan era.

Let us now walk over to the northern edge of the terrace to look out over the theatre, the ancient place of assembly of the Athenians. The front end of the theatre lies 4–5 m above the level of the upper terrace, separated from it by a scarp some 120 m in length. The scarp does not form a straight line, its two sides making an angle of 158° with one another. The semicircular *cavea*, now much eroded, has a diameter of 70 m and is held in place by a massive retaining wall made of large blocks of limestone. Originally this wall is thought to have risen some 11 m above bedrock to contain the earth that was poured in to create the artificial downward slope from north to south. Access to the theatre was from the north, where a staircase 12 m wide led up from the road below along the central axis of the cavea. On assembly days Scythian archers were sent out into the Agora and adjacent streets to urge reluctant citizens towards the Pnyx, stretching between them a rope daubed with red paint which rubbed off on those who lagged behind; those who were found to be so marked were deprived of their stipend of one drachma (after *c.* 330 BC) when they were checked at the entrance. Such measures were apparently necessary to convene the required quorum of five thousand citizens, without which no legal decisions of the Assembly could be made.

The *bema* stands in the angle formed by the two sides of the scarp at the front of the theatre; it is a large platform reached by three steps with a combined height about 1 m above the floor of the theatre. At the back of the platform there is a cube of living rock 3 m high projecting from the scarp, with a flight of five steps ascending to its top on either side. The orators at the Assembly gave their speeches from the broad platform below, while the rock probably served as an altar where a public sacrifice was made at the beginning of every session of the Assembly. Several ancient sources refer to this sacrifice, in which suckling pigs were slaughtered and their blood sprinkled over the seats of the theatre by the priest of Zeus Agoraios. Only after this lustration had been performed and the ritual prayers read by the herald could the Assembly begin its discussions.

To the left of the *bema*, as we face it from below, there is a large niche cut into the scarp, with scores of smaller niches all around it. Marble tablets found in these niches (twelve of which are in the British Museum) have led to the identification of this sacred place as a shrine of Zeus Hypsistos (the Highest). These tablets and other ex-votos found in the niches have been dated to the Roman period, but there is evidence that there was a small temple of Zeus Hypsistos here in very early times, before the original construction of the assembly-place on the Pnyx Hill. This temple was probably destroyed when the first theatre was carved out of the hillside. At that time the large niche was undoubtedly carved in the scarp to hold a cult-statue of Zeus Hypsistos, so as to perpetuate the worship of the god in his ancient temenos.

The lustration previously mentioned was undoubtedly associated with an annual religious festival held on the Pnyx Hill; this was the Thesmophoria, a mysterious and primitive fertility rite whose origins must date back to very ancient times. The Thesmophoria, dedicated to Demeter and her daughter Persephone, was an exclusively feminine cult. When the Thesmophoria was held, in early summer at planting time, the women who celebrated the festival took possession of the Pnyx for four days. An ancient commentator gives this description of the festival in all its primeval mystery and magic:

The Thesmophoria is a Greek feast with a mysterious ritual. The legendary reason for its celebration is that when Kore is carried off by Pluto [the god of the underworld] as she is gathering flowers, there is a certain swineherd named Eubouleus feeding his swine on the spot, and they are all swallowed up in the chasm. So then in honour of Eubouleus, they cast pigs into the chasm of Demeter and Kore. The decayed parts of the pigs that are thrown into the chasm are brought back by the women who have undergone purification for three days. These women go down into the adyton, and, bringing up the flesh, place it on the altar. It is believed that if some of this flesh is taken and sown with the grain, there will be a good crop. They say that down below in the chasm there are snakes who devour the greater part of what is thrown in. Therefore a noise is made when the women are drawing up the flesh and when they are putting the images in place of it, so as to drive back the snakes, whom they consider to be the guardians of the adyton.

The ritual of this cult became less primitive in classical times, when it was amalgamated into the worship of the Olympian deities. This is evident in Aristophanes' comedy, *The Women at the Thesmophoria*, as H. W. Parke points out in his work on the *Festivals of the Athenians*:

In the *Women at the Thesmophoria* Aristophanes succeeds in working in bits of local colour and topical allusion, but carefully manages to avoid anything like serious religion, except for a pair of beautiful lyrics written in the form of hymns. The one invokes Artemis, Hera, Hermes, Pan and the Nymphs and Dionysos; the other Athena and the Two Goddesses Thesmophoroi (Demeter and Persephone). This easy-going polytheism avoided any concentrating on divine mysteries, though by ending with the Two Goddesses Aristophanes rightly pointed to the inner aspects of the festival.

After exploring the ancient hilltop site, we continue along the pathway that brought us up across the saddle from the Hill of the Nymphs. This path takes us around the western slope of the Pnyx and down into the saddle between that peak and the Hill of the Muses. The district outside the walls here in classical times was known as 'Coele', or 'the Hollows', because of the deep ravine along which the road extended. Like many of the roads that led out from ancient Athens, the one that ran through the Coele was flanked with burial sites. One of those who may have been buried here was Thucydides the historian, who died *c*. 400 BC, for Pausanias writes that 'his memorial is not far from the Melitian [i.e. Melitides] gates'.

As the path descends we turn left between the Pnyx Hill and the Mouseion, the Hill of the Muses, walking along a very picturesque old road with stone flagstones. A short way along we see on our left the little church of Ay. Dimitrios Loumbardiaris, which stands in a copse of pines, olive trees and cypresses just beside the road. The road is flanked by a number of ancient architectural fragments; these are the remains of the Dipylon above the Gates, the principal entry-way through the Diateichisma. The southern side of the gate was excavated in 1937, and was then covered over again after its structure was carefully studied, leaving only these few fragments above ground. (The northern side of the gate lies beneath the church, and has not been excavated.) The excavation showed that the gateway was flanked by two large towers in the Diateichisma; between these bastions a curtain-wall was pierced by a portal 3.9 m wide, with heavier spur walls leading inwards to create a courtyard inside the entrance. The scene is evocative, for here you have the feeling that you have come upon one of the gateways of the ancient city, with the old cobbled road approaching Athens over the wooded saddle between the hills and passing between the fragmentary remains of the portal on either side.

The roadside chapel enhances the effect, making this one of the most charming spots in Athens. The church of Ay. Dimitrios was built in 1460, according to one authority, although pious local tradition maintains that it was founded in the ninth century. In any event, it was rebuilt in 1955, a very successful restoration that has preserved the entrancing character of the old chapel, which is still a popular place of pilgrimage, despite its somewhat remote location.

The second name of the church, Loumbardiaris, means the Bombardier, whose origin is explained by a document posted in the narthex:

On 26 October 1656, on the feast day of St Dimitrios, the congregation was assembled here. Yusuf Ağa, the commander of the Turkish garrison on the Acropolis, and a mortal enemy of the Christians, conceived of a diabolical plan to exterminate them. He had all the cannons of the Propylaia ready, including the great cannon known as Loumbardiaris, and he awaited the crucial moment when the Te Deum was in progress to open fire. But at that moment a bolt of lightning struck the Propylaia, blowing up the battery and Yusuf Ağa, killing his family and all of his men. The church takes its name from the cannon.

This incident is also mentioned by George Wheler, who visited Athens two decades later. But by then the church must have suffered some unrecorded catastrophe, for when Wheler passed this way he found it in ruins. The church was finally repaired and re-consecrated after the Greek War of Independence, and it appears in many old prints depicting the area south of the Acropolis.

On the far side of the chapel there is a delightful outdoor café, a perfect place to pause when strolling around the walls of ancient Athens. The café tables are set out in a series of embowered terraces around the chapel, and one can sit there in the dappled shade with a view of the Acropolis through an undulating screen of greenery.

Across the road from Ay. Dimitrios a pathway leads up to the Mouseion, the Hill of the Muses. This path follows the original course of the Diateichisma, and on the way uphill one can see the foundations of this stretch of the fortifications. The stones used in this section of the wall were identical in size to those we have seen in the Pnyx wall, but they were of coarse conglomerate rather than ashlar. The wall here was not solid masonry, as on the Pnyx, for the blocks were laid out in a series of rectangular compartments with a core of earth and rubble. Archaeologists thus refer to this stretch of the Diateichisma as the Compartment Wall.

There were eight defence towers in the stretch of the Diateichisma between the Dipylon above the Gates and the peak of the Mouseion Hill, where the Themistoclean walls joined the southern Long Wall from the Piraeus. Seven of these towers were rectangular in cross-section, the largest measuring 10 × 11 m, with one round tower midway along the line, and they were spaced at intervals of 75–80 m, about twice as far apart as those on the Pnyx Hill. Beginning at the Dipylon above the Gates, this wall headed south-west to ascend the northern spur of the Mouseion Hill. The first stretch of this wall, which was about 100 m long, ended in a large rectangular tower, the most massive on the Mouseion Hill. From there the wall bent off to the south-east, joining the southern Long Wall 250 m farther along, near the summit of the hill. At the junction of the Diateichisma and the Long Wall there was a fortress; this was created by building a cross-wall with two defence towers across the angle formed by the other two lines of fortifications, thus enclosing the summit of the Mouseion Hill. This fortress was built by Dimitrios Poliorketes in 294 BC, when he regained control of Athens. During the Hellenistic period the fortress changed hands several times and was apparently kept in good repair, but in Roman times it was no longer used and gradually fell into ruins. Nevertheless, the site of the fortress continued to be a strong point, for any force that held the summit of the Mouseion Hill could dominate the town below and threaten the Acropolis. It was here that Morosini placed his artillery during the Venetian siege of Athens in 1687, when his bombardiers blew up the Parthenon.

The Mouseion probably took its name originally from the Muses, who may have had a shrine on the hill. But a later Graeco-Roman tradition derived the name of the hill from Mousaios, the companion of Orpheus, as Pausanias tells us in his description of the Mouseion: 'The Mouseion is a small hill opposite the Acropolis, inside the ancient ring-wall, where they say Mousaios used to sing and died of old age and was buried; later a memorial was erected there for a Syrian. At this time Dimitrios built and held his fort on it.'

The memorial that Pausanias refers to is the Monument of Philopappos, one of the most prominent landmarks in Athens. (In fact, the monument is so familiar that this is usually called the Philopappos Hill rather than the Mouseion Hill.) This unusual structure was built in AD 114–16, during the reign of Trajan, and was designed as a funerary monument for C. Julius Antiochus Philopappos. Philopappos was the last titular ruler of Commagene, a small kingdom in south-eastern Asia Minor. This realm was founded in 80 BC by Mithridates I Kallinokos, a descendant of Seleucus I, the founder of the vast Seleucid Empire that encompassed most of the Middle East. The kingdom of Commagene survived until AD 72, when it was annexed to the Roman Empire by Vespasian. Antiochus, the last king to actually rule in Commagene, was allowed to retire to Rome. After his death his eldest son Epiphanes assumed the title of King of Commagene, which by then was purely honorific. After the death of Epiphanes his eldest son Philopappos in turn became the King of Commagene, apparently the last to hold that title. After inheriting the title, King Philopappos settled in Athens, becoming a citizen of the Attic deme of Besa. Evidently he became a very prominent and popular benefactor of the city, judging from the splendid monument erected in his honour. (Plutarch, in one of his essays, mentions a King Philopappos as having executed with great munificence the office of agonothetes, the official in charge of festivals, as well as that of choregos of all the tribes of Attica.)

The monument, which faces the Acropolis, was originally 13 m high, including its 3 m base. The slightly concave façade, of which the lower two thirds remain, was in two storeys separated by a cornice, the lower one 3.51 m high and the upper one 6.43 m. The lower storey is decorated with three scenes in low relief showing a Roman consul in a quadriga preceded by his lictors, or attendants; this undoubtedly represents Philopappos, who served as consul in AD 109. In the upper storey there are three niches, each containing a statue of a seated figure, of which there remain only fragments of those on the left and in the centre. Inscriptions on the monument (first recorded by Cyriacus of Ancona in 1437) have identified the central figure as that of Philopappos himself; the one on the left is Antiochus IV, the last ruling King of Commagene; and the missing figure on the right was Seleucus I Nicator, founder of the Seleucid Empire. Behind this façade there was a funerary chamber that contained the sarcophagus of Philopappos, but only battered fragments of this remain.

The view from the summit of the Mouseion Hill is superb, with all of Athens spread out below. Looking to the south, one can make out the ancient course of the Long Walls, which followed almost exactly the route taken by the modern Odos Piraeus from Athens down to the sea. Turning to the north-east, one commands an incomparable panorama of the Acropolis and its south slope.

From the Mouseion fort the Themistoclean walls headed nearly due east down the spur of the hill. The hillside is quite precipitous here, and so we must proceed by a roundabout route and pick up the course of the walls again at the eastern foot of the hill. We will do so by retracing our steps along the path by which we ascended the hill, after which we will circle round it in the clockwise sense until we return to the circuit of the ancient walls.

Just below the summit of the hill, near the top of the path, there is a large rectangular chamber carved out of the hillside. This is undoubtedly an ancient tomb, but there is no archaeological evidence as to its identity or date. Local tradition holds that this is the tomb of Mousaios, the companion of Orpheus.

We now walk back along the path to the road between the two hills, where we turn right and continue downhill. A short way along we take a path on the right that leads through the park at the foot of the Mouseion Hill. A short distance in from the road we see on our right a large chamber cut into the rock of the hillside, with its opening closed by a metal grille. In times past (and still today, by certain guides) this was pointed out to the credulous as the 'Prison of Socrates', where, according to a completely baseless legend, the philosopher was confined before he drank the fatal hemlock. The chamber is probably a Bronze Age dwelling, but here again there is no definite archaeological evidence to date or identify it.

We now retrace our steps and return to the road, where we turn right and walk out towards the highway that runs past the south slope of the Acropolis. Just short of the highway we turn right on to Odos Rovertou Galli, after which we take the first right on to Odos Garivaldi, the street that runs past the east end of the Mouseion Hill. We walk down the left side of this street until we come to a flight of steps; there we descend to Odos Drakou, where we turn left on to Odos Karatassou. We follow this for two blocks and then turn left on to Odos Erechthiou, where we walk down the right side of the street until we come to No. 20. Here we find a grating at street level though which we can see a section of the Themistoclean wall, which ran in a more or less straight line eastwards from the eastern spur of the Mouseion Hill to this point.

The section of wall that we see here has been identified as part of the South Gate; this was where the main road from Athens to Phaleron left the city, passing between the Long Wall to Phaleron and the southern Long Wall to the Piraeus. Burial sites have been discovered along both sides of this road, dating back as far as *c.* 100 BC, indicating that this route has been used since the earliest days of the city.

We now continue in the same direction along Odos Erechthiou and turn right at the next corner on to Odos Kavaloti. After crossing Odos Parthenon we come to Odos Missaraliotou, which leads off to the right at a 45° angle. If you look down Odos Missaraliotou you will see the stump of an ancient column standing on the right side of the street about half-way down the block. This battered column, which has somehow remained standing despite the assaults of time, is thought to have been part of the colonnade of a Roman bath.

We continue along Odos Kavaloti and at the next corner we turn left on to Odos Karyatidon. We cross to the right of the street, and at the second house from the corner we find a grille that allows us to look into an excavation site that has been preserved under the new apartment blocks that have been erected here. Here we see the foundations and mosaic pavements of a large Roman bath, which has been dated to the second century AD.

Let us now walk up Karyatidon in the same direction as before and then turn right on Rovertou Galli, following it to its intersection with Kavaloti. In the acute angle formed by these two streets there is a little park with an ancient column in its centre; this is believed to be part of the Roman bath whose foundations we saw earlier on Odos Karyatidon.

We now turn right and return along Kavaloti, after which we turn left on to Missaraliotou, passing the ancient column we saw earlier. We then continue along Missarliotou as far as Odos Falirou, where we turn left and follow this street a short way to its intersection with Makriyanni and Donta.

This intersection is thought to be the site of the Halade (Seaward) Gate, where another ancient road connected Athens with Phaleron. Tombs ranging in date from the Mycenaean period to the late Roman era have been unearthed along both sides of this road, which followed the course of the modern Odos Falirou. This was the road taken by the Mystics, the initiates in the Greater Eleusinian Mysteries, during the lustration rites that took place on the second day of the festival. On that day all the initiates marched in procession through the Halade Gate on their way to Phaleron, where they washed themselves and the piglets which on the following day they would sacrifice to Demeter and Kore at the Eleusinion.

We now turn right on to Odos Donta and then at the next corner we come to Leoforos Syngrou. Here we cross over the avenue, heading left up it, and take the second turning on the right, bringing us to Odos Vourvaki, after which we take the first left on to Odos Iosef Rogon. We follow this street for two blocks, crossing Odos Lembesi, and then at the next corner we come to the intersection of Odos Diakou and Leoforos Syngrou. In this last zigzag walk we have been following almost exactly the course of the Themistoclean walls at the south-eastern corner of the ancient city. And in so doing we have just passed on our left, midway between Odos Lembesi and Odos Diakou, the site of the Itonian Gate.

According to one ancient source, the funerary stele of the Amazon Queen Antiope stood just outside the Itonian Gate. This stele was still standing in the mid second century AD, for Pausanias reports that he saw it when coming to Athens from Phaleron. The stelai of Antiope and the other Amazon warriors who supposedly died here perhaps marked prehistoric tombs, which the ancient Athenians associated with one of the mythical campaigns of Theseus. As one version of the myth has it, Theseus joined Heracles in his expedition against the Amazons, and as his share of the spoils he received Antiope, an Amazon princess, who became his first wife and bore his son Hippolytus. In revenge, the Amazons invaded Attica and put Athens under siege, but they were defeated and driven off by Theseus. The Amazons who were killed were buried where they fell, and in later times tradition had it that a stele beside the Itonian Gate marked the grave of Antiope.

Archaeological excavations just inside the site of the Itonian Gate have tentatively identified an important ancient monument that has long eluded discovery. This is the shrine of Codrus, one of the legendary kings of Athens, which is believed to have occupied the area now lying between Leoforos Syngrou and Odos Makriyanni, just opposite the far end of Odos Lembesi. According to the legend, Codrus sacrificed himself to save Athens when Attica was besieged by the Peloponnesians. The Peloponnesians had made a pilgrimage to Delphi before invading Attica, and there the Pythian oracle had told them that the winning side would be the one whose king died in battle. When Codrus learned of this he disguised himself as a peasant and made his way outside the city walls, where he provoked a fight with the enemy soldiers who were besieging the city and was killed. The tide of battle then turned in favour of the Athenians and the Peloponnesians withdrew from Attica, fulfilling the prophecy of the Delphic oracle. Long afterwards the Athenians dedicated this shrine to the hero whom they believed to have been their last king, venerating him there along with Neleus, a son of Poseidon, and the nymph Basile.

We now cross Odos Diaku, underneath which the River Ilissos flows in a canal. After crossing the avenue we turn right and walk along it as far as the little chapel of Ay. Photini, where a path leads off to the left towards the archaeological area south of the Olympieion. Just to the right of the church, as one faces it from the avenue, there is a scarp on which is carved a relief of the god Pan. (The relief is extremely faint and hard to make out; it can be seen to best advantage when the sun is high in the sky and the figure is accentuated by a slight shadow.) It is believed that this relief was part of a sanctuary of Pan, for several ancient sources place one of his shrines in the vicinity of the Ilissos. One of these sources is Plato, who ends his *Phaedrus* near this shrine, to which Socrates and his young friend for whom the dialogue is named have come after walking along the banks of the Ilissos. Socrates concludes this dialogue with a prayer 'to the local deities': 'Beloved Pan, and all ye other gods who haunt this place, give me beauty in the inward soul; and may the outward and inward man be at one. May I reckon the wise to be wealthy, and may I have such a quantity of gold as a temperate man and he only can bear and carry.'

We continue along the path as it crosses the former bed of the Ilissos. (Water still flows here at times of torrential rains.) Most archaeologists now agree that this crossing-place, which was probably a ford across the Ilissos, was near the site of the Kallirhoë spring, one of the most famous landmarks in ancient Athens. This spring had been the principal source of water for Athens since the earliest days of the city, and it was here that Athenian maidens drew the water that they used in their premarital lustration rites. The spring was sacred to the nymph Kallirhoë, whose name means 'lovely stream'. She is believed to have been represented in the southern angle of the Parthenon's west pediment, balancing the figure of the river-god Ilissos in the northern angle. During the time of the Peisistratids, a monumental Fountain-house was built around the spring; some authorities believe that this was the celebrated Enneakrounos, the 'Nine-Spouted Fountain', but others identify that landmark with the South-east Fountain-house in the Agora.

The ford across the Ilissos forms the background for a particularly lyrical passage in Plato's *Phaedrus*, evoking the vanished beauty of what was then the countryside around Athens. When they reach the Ilissos ford Socrates congratulates Phaedrus for having led them to such a beautiful place:

By Hera, a fair resting-place, full of summer sounds and scents. Here is this lofty and spreading plane tree and the agnus-castus high and clustering, in the fullest bloom and the greatest fragrance; and the stream which flows beneath the plane tree is deliciously cold to the feet. Judging from the ornaments and images, this must be a spot sacred to Achelous and the Nymphs. How delightful is the breeze – so very sweet – and there is a sound in the air shrill and summer like which makes answer to the chorus of the cicadas. But the greatest charm of all is the grass, like a pillow gently sloping to the head. My dear Phaedrus, you have been an admirable guide!

Let us now look at the fragmentary remains of the antiquities that have been unearthed in the area between the Ilissos and the Olympieion. Most of these sites consist of mere foundations, or even just the bedding trenches for foundations, and the identification of the monuments is not absolutely certain in all cases. Nevertheless, the area is worth exploring, for it has interesting associations in architecture, history and mythology.

After crossing the Ilissos, we walk west until we are about midway along the retaining wall of the Olympieion and about 100 m to its south. There we find ourselves within what was once the enclosure of a sanctuary. The temple enclosure, revealed only by the existence of the deep bedding-trenches for its foundations, was quite extensive, measuring about 40 × 60 m, with its entrance at a propylon on the east side. The temple itself, which stood near the western end of the temenos, was relatively small compared to the size of the enclosure, measuring approximately 5 × 8 m. All that remains of the temple is the outer north-west corner of its temenos, the rest lying under the modern highway. The temple has been dated to the reign of Hadrian (AD 117–38), and has been identified tentatively as the Panhellenion. This sanctuary was designed to serve as the centre for the celebration of the Panhellenia, an annual festival instituted by Hadrian at the time of his first visit to Athens, in 124/5. The Panhellenion seems to have been completed in 131/2, when the Temple of Olympian Zeus was dedicated by Hadrian. The deified Hadrian was worshipped at the Panhellenion under the epithet Zeus Panhellenios, while his wife Sabina was venerated as the goddess Hera. The temple and the peristyle that bordered its temenos were destroyed when the Valerian defence wall was built in the mid third century AD.

The section of the Valerian wall that passed through this area can easily be traced on the site. Beginning just north of the Itonian Gate, the wall extended almost due east to include the southern precinct wall of the Panhellenion within its structure, as well as the south-eastern corner of the temenos as far as the propylon; then it cut north-east for 60 m, after which it turned due north and extended to the retaining wall of the Olympieion. We shall find traces of the Valerian wall on both sides of the Olympieion later on, but now let us continue with our exploration of the archaeological area to the south.

We now walk north from the site of the Panhellenion towards the centre of the retaining wall of the Olympieion. About 30 m short of the retaining wall we come to the remains of a large temple, of which only the poros foundations have been preserved. The structure has been dated to the mid fifth century BC, and has been conjecturally restored as a Doric peripteral temple, distyle *in antis*, with six columns to front and rear and thirteen along the sides. Literary and archaeological evidence has led to the identification of the temple as a sanctuary of Apollo Delphinios and Artemis Delphinia. Pottery shards found on the site date back as far as the Mycenaean period, indicating that the classical temple had a much earlier predecessor, as is suggested by the mythology of Attica. According to tradition, the original sanctuary of Apollo Delphinios in Athens was founded by King Aegeus, and it was still under construction when his son Theseus first appeared in the city. Theseus had long hair at the time, and when he appeared at the Temple of Apollo some of the labourers ridiculed him by saying that he looked like a woman. Theseus was enraged by this, and to show the men his strength he unyoked a pair of oxen and hurled them over the roof of the temple.

The cult of Apollo Delphinios may have been introduced to Athens in Mycenaean times, perhaps having been brought there under Cretan influence. There are several different legends as to why Apollo was worshipped under the epithet Delphinios, but in all of them the story revolves around the god taking on the form of a dolphin (in Greek, *delphini*), and similar legends are related about his sister Artemis. Apollo Delphinios was the patron god of sailors and colonists, and as such there were sanctuaries dedicated to him in many of the Greek ports and islands, particularly in those that had been settled by the Ionians, as at Miletus in Asia Minor. So his original temple here in Athens may very well have been connected with the migration of the first Ionian colonists from Attica to the Aegean coast of Asia Minor. To the west of the temple of Apollo Delphinios there are the remains of a complex of archaic buildings, all of them built up against the side of the hillock below the south-west corner of the Olympieion precinct wall. This complex has been identified as the Law Court of the Delphinium, and it has been dated to *c.* 500 BC. Pottery dating back to the Mycenaean era has also been found on this site, and so this complex too must have had a much earlier predecessor. Once again the archaeological findings are in agreement with mythology, for tradition holds that the lawcourts here were also founded by King Aegeus. These courts had jurisdiction over cases of justifiable homicide, and, according to legend, Theseus himself was tried here for some of the murders he committed during his campaigns. The lawcourts and the Temple of Apollo were probably all part of the same complex of buildings, known as the Delphinium.

According to Plutarch, the Delphinium was within the palace of King Aegeus, and it was there that he welcomed Theseus at a festive banquet when the young hero first arrived in Athens. Medea, the wife of Aegeus, was aware that Theseus was the king's long-lost son, and was thus fearful that he would supplant his father as ruler. So she persuaded Aegeus to give Theseus a cup of poisoned wine to drink at the banquet. But before he drank the wine Theseus drew his sword to cut the meat, that had been placed before him, whereupon Aegeus realized that the young man was none other than his son, for the weapon was the one that he had years before placed under the Rock of Troezen. Then, as Plutarch tells the tale:

Aegeus, at once recognizing the token, threw down the cup of poison, and, questioning his son, embraced him, and having gathered together all his citizens, owned him publicly before them, who, for their part, received him gladly for the fame of his greatness and bravery; and it is said, that when the cup fell, the poison was spilt there where is now the enclosed spot within the Delphinium, for in that place stood the House of Aegeus . . .

A short distance to the south-east of the temple of Apollo Delphinios we come to the precinct wall of another enclosure, within which we see the foundations of a structure raised upon a rectangular podium. This has been identified as a sanctuary of Kronos and Rhea and has been dated to the mid second century AD; it has been restored conjecturaly as a peripteral Doric temple *in antis*, with a peristyle of six columns to front and rear and thirteen along the sides. Some remnants of an earlier sanctuary of the fifth century BC have been found on the site, as well as pottery dating back to the Mycenaean era. So here again we are probably standing on ground that has been sacred since the early years of Athens.

Just outside the north-east corner of this temenos we see the foundations of what was once a gateway in the Valerian wall, along with those of the defence towers on either side of it. When the

Valerian wall was erected, the Themistoclean wall in this area had long since vanished, but there is evidence that the two lines of fortifications followed the same course in the region near the Ilissos. In that case the gateway here would have stood on the site of the original entrance through the Themistoclean walls at this point, the Diomeian Gate. This gate took its name from the fact that the road which passed through it led to the deme of Diomeia, which was situated just outside the city walls on the banks of the Ilissos. The Kynosarges, one of the most famous gymnasia in Athens, was located in the deme of Diomeia, and its site is probably just across the highway from the modern chapel of Ay. Photini. According to ancient literary sources, Socrates was a frequent visitor at the Kynosarges, where he went to engage the young men of the gymnasium in conversation. And several of these sources tell us that when he went to the Kynosarges he always left by the Diomeian Gate.

We now leave the archaeological area south of the Olympieion, making our way along the path that leads around the retaining wall at the east end of the temple precinct. The entrance to the Olympieion grounds is just beyond the north-east corner of the precinct wall, and we will go in there just briefly to look at the site of another gateway in the walls of ancient Athens. (We will look at the Olympieion in detail on our next stroll through the city.) If we follow the northern precinct wall of the Olympieion for about 60 m, we find the site of another gate in the Valerian wall; it lies just to the west of the propylon to the temple grounds and intersects the temenos wall. This too had been originally an entry-way in the Themistoclean walls, and has been identified as the Hippades, or Cavalry, Gate. This gate undoubtedly took its name from the cavalry drills and equestrian displays that took place on the grounds of the Lyceum, the famous gymnasium that stood outside the gate in the countryside to its north-east.

Let us now retrace our steps to the entry-way of the Olympieion grounds, from where we walk out to Leoforos Vasilissis Olgas. There we cross the street and turn left to walk along the outside of the park to Leoforos Amalias. Then we cross the avenue, turn right, and walk as far as Odos Nikis. We turn left and walk as far as Apollonos; there we turn left and go to the corner of Pendelis on the right, where we pause momentarily to get our bearings.

During the course of our stroll from the Olympieion to this point we have followed almost exactly the course of the Themistoclean walls along the south-eastern arc of their circuit. And here at the corner of Apollonos and Pendelis we have come to the site of the

Diochares Gate, identified as such by an inscription and by the chance discovery in the vicinity of sections of the ancient Themistoclean wall and its encircling moat. (These remains have since been covered over and are not visible.) The Diochares Gate was the main entry-way in the western side of the city walls, and was used by those going to and from the Lyceum and the countryside east of Athens.

From the Diochares Gate the Themistoclean wall swung out in an arc to enclose the north-eastern corner of the city. We can follow the course of this part of the walls by going back one block along Apollonos to Odos Voulis, where we turn left and follow the street to Odos Stadiou. Then we turn left and walk down the avenue until we come to Plateia Klafthmonos, where we turn left on to Odos Paparigopoulou. About half-way down this street we turn right and walk across the park to Odos Dragatsaniou. In so doing we pass an array of massive ancient building blocks that were unearthed during the excavation of the underground car-park beneath the square. These were evidently part of the Themistoclean wall, and at present the stones are arrayed in approximately the line in which they were originally found, at some depth below the present ground level.

A long and well-preserved section of the Themistoclean wall was discovered in 1954 when excavating for the foundations of modern commercial buildings on Odos Dragatsaniou. These walls were preserved and left exposed when the buildings were completed, and they can be seen now in the interconnected basement between them. The most convenient approach is to enter the building at No. 4 Dragatsaniou and go down the basement steps immediately to the left of the inner doorway. At the foot of the steps we see on our right an impressive section of the walls, which are standing to a height of several courses of the same massive stone blocks that are on view in the square above. We then turn left and walk along the basement corridor there, which has an arcade of shops on the right and on the left is bounded from floor to ceiling by a section of the Themistoclean wall. This section of the wall continues around the corner and extends for some distance along another corridor that leads off at an angle to the first one. At this point where the two corridors intersect there are the well-preserved remains of an ancient entry-way, which has been identified as the North-east Gate.

After leaving the building at 4 Dragatsaniou, we turn right on the street outside and then afterwards turn sharp right at the corner on to Aristidou. We turn left at the next corner on to Sofokleous, after which we walk one block to its intersection with Aiolou and there pause for a moment. This is the site of the Acharnian Gate, discovered in the mid eighteenth century but subsequently lost and buried under the modern streets. The gate was in the northernmost stretch of the walls; it took its name from the fact that through it passed the road to Acharnai, the deme north of Athens on the slope of Mt Parnes.

From the Acharnian Gate the Themistoclean walls continued due west for about half a kilometre, after which they turned south-west in a series of zigzags to complete the circuit at the Dipylon. We start along this last stretch of wall by continuing in the same direction along Sofokleous until we come to Menandrou, where we turn left. Then, just before the second turning on the right, we see on the right side of the street one of the most picturesque and unusual monuments in Athens; this is Ay. Ioannis stin Colonna, the church of St John of the Column.

This tiny chapel takes its name from the column that protrudes through its tiled roof, an unfluted marble monolith with a huge Corinthian capital. This column has been a talisman since medieval times, when a widespread 'pillar cult' attributed magical powers to such impressive survivors from an ancient world of which virtually all knowledge had been lost. At some time in the medieval era the column here became part of a healing shrine dedicated to St John the Baptist, and it acquired the reputation of being able to cure fevers and other diseases, a powerful attraction at a time when medical care in Athens must have been virtually non-existent. The earliest reference to the monument is in 1678 by Spon and Wheler, who write of a 'column of St John that stood on the northern side of Athens'. The first detailed description of the column is by Edward Dodwell, writing in 1819:

At the northern extremity of the town is a single plain Corinthian column of Euboean marble, and of considerable dimensions. It stands in its original position, and as there are no other remains near it, and as it is of coloured marble, it probably never formed part of any building, but supported a statue, like the Corinthian column in the Roman Forum, which was surmounted by a statue of Phocas. The Greeks have dedicated this column to St John, and a poor Albanian woman living near it piously lights a lamp with oil, which is placed in a hole of the column every night.

Some of the beliefs and cult practices associated with the Column of St John are described by James Rennell Rodd in his *Customs and Lore of Modern Greece*, published in 1892.

This column is looked upon as exerting a magical and miraculous power over fevers and other diseases. In August and September when fevers are rife, patients throng to it, and fastening a silken thread to the column with a piece of wax, have the firm conviction that the fever will be drawn out along the thread and into the column.

The church of St John of the Column is no longer as popular a healing shrine as it was in times past, though the cult is still alive, as evidenced by the talismanic strings tied around the column and the ex-votos hanging from the walls of the chapel. Each year on 29 August, the feast day of the Decapitation of St John the Baptist, the little chapel and its courtyard are filled with worshippers, most of them old women, who obviously continue to believe in the magic powers of this column.

After leaving the church we continue for a few steps along Menandrou and then turn right on to Evripidou. We walk along the latter street for a block and then take a half-left on to Dipilou, passing on our right Plateia Eleftherias. One block beyond the square we come to the intersection of Dipilou with Leokorion on the left, where we pause for a moment. This intersection is thought to be the site of the Eriai Gate, the last of the gateways of ancient Athens that we will encounter on our stroll.

Excavations in the vicinity show that Odos Leokoriou is laid out over a very ancient road. This road began at the Altar of the Twelve Gods in the Agora, passing through the Eriai Gate on its way to Kolonos Hippios, the Knoll of Horses, a rocky eminence about a mile outside the walls of Athens in the valley of the Kephissos river. Sophocles was born and raised in the vicinity of Kolonos Hippios, and it was there that he set the final scene of his last play, *Oedipus at Kolonos*, which he wrote when he was ninety years old. So the Eriai Gate would have been the portal through which Sophocles passed on his way between Athens and his birthplace throughout his long life. Sophocles has his chorus sing the praises of this once beautiful countryside in a lyrical passage of *Oedipus at Kolonos*, here translated by William Butler Yeats:

> Who comes into this country, and has come
> Where golden crocus and narcissus bloom,
> Where the Great Mother, mourning for her daughter
> And beauty-drunken by the water
> Glittering among grey-leaved olive trees,
> Has plucked a flower and sung her loss;
> Who finds abounding Cephisus
> Has found the loveliest spectacle there is.

We now walk one more block along Dipilou to where it ends at Odos Asomaton, which borders the ancient Kerameikos cemetery on the east. There we look down on the Dipylon and the Sacred Gate, along with the section of the Themistoclean wall that joins them, having completed our stroll around the walls of ancient Athens. We may turn left here and follow Odos Asomaton to its intersection with Odos Ermou, where we turn left to stroll back to the centre of the modern city.

8

Roman Athens

This stroll will take us through Roman Athens, to visit the monuments erected in the city when it was ruled by Rome. A few of these edifices are comparable in grandeur and historic interest to all but the supreme masterpieces of the classical and Hellenistic periods. They also represent the last flowering in Athens of Greek architecture, as the city enjoyed one more period of glory before the collapse of Graeco-Roman civilization and the beginning of the Dark Ages.

The Roman period in Athenian history began disastrously for the Greeks with Sulla's sack of the city in 86 BC. But Athens soon regained the favour of Rome, and in the imperial Roman era old monuments in Athens were restored and new ones were erected, with the emperors themselves initiating the most ambitious of the building programmes. Augustus endowed a new market-place in Athens, the so-called Roman Agora, a project that had been started some years before by Julius Caesar. Augustus also transferred the Temple of Ares from its original site in Acharnai and rebuilt it in the Greek Agora, where his chief minister Agrippa built a vast new odeion in the centre of the ancient market square. And so by the beginning of the Christian era the Roman presence in Athens was already evident in the architecture of the city.

Roman Athens reached its prime during the reign of Hadrian (AD 117–38). The Athenians had honoured Hadrian even before he became emperor, for he was a favourite of Trajan and a likely successor to the throne. In 112 the Athenians made Hadrian a citizen of Athens and elected him archon, even though he had never set foot in the city. (Athens was technically a free city under Rome and the Athenians had the right to elect their archons and other officials, but the titles were purely honorific and involved no real political power.) When Hadrian

succeeded to the throne in 117, the Athenians made him the eponymous founder of a new Attic tribe created in his honour, and when he
came to the city for the first time in 122 he was venerated as a god
under the name of Zeus Olympios. Hadrian responded to these
honours by becoming the greatest civic benefactor in the history of
Athens, literally rebuilding the city in the process.

At the time of Hadrian's first visit to Athens the older residential
quarters of the city had deteriorated markedly, particularly in com-
parison with the magnificent monuments that they surrounded, as
Heracleides of Crete remarked at that time:

The road to Athens is a pleasant one, running between cultivated fields
the whole way. The city itself is dry and ill-supplied with water. The
streets are nothing but miserable old lanes, the houses mean, with a few
better ones among them. On his first arrival a stranger could hardly believe
that this is the Athens of which he has heard so much. Yet he will soon
come to believe that it is Athens indeed. A music hall, the most beautiful
in the world, a large and stately theatre, a costly, remarkable and far-seen
Temple of Athena rising above the theatre, strike the beholder with admira-
tion. A Temple of Olympian Zeus, unfinished but planned on an astonishing scale; three gymnasiums, the Academy, Lyceum, and Kynosarges,
shaded with trees that spring from greensward; verdant gardens of philosophers; amusements and recreations; many holidays and spectacles – all
these the visitor will find in Athens.

Hadrian's reconstruction programme began at the time of his second
visit to Athens, in 125. Since the older parts of Athens had become
crowded and run-down, the emperor decided to build a new city, to be
called Hadrianopolis, outside the Themistoclean walls to the east. The
showpiece of this new city was the magnificent Temple of Olympian
Zeus, which was completed in AD 131/2 and dedicated by Hadrian.
In addition to this Hadrian endowed both the new and old parts of the
city with numerous civic and religious buildings, including an aqueduct,
as well as restoring older structures that had fallen into disrepair. Thus
by the end of his reign Athens had regained much of its former
grandeur, which it would retain until late antiquity. Pausanias pays
tribute to Hadrian's good works in his description of the Monument of
the Eponymous Heroes, which he saw just a few years after the
emperor's death, and then, in his description of the Olympieion, he
mentions other Hadrianic foundations in Athens:

These Athenian name-heroes were ancient, but in later times they have
named tribes after Attalos the Mysian, Ptolemy the Egyptian, and now in my

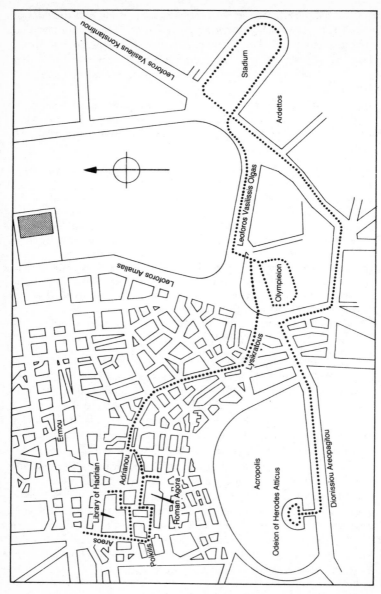

Roman Athens

own day the emperor Hadrian, who has gone furthest to honour religion, and
among all sovereigns done most for the happiness of each of his subjects . . .
All the sanctuaries of the gods he himself has built, and the ones he himself
has improved with furnishings and decorations, and all his gifts to Greek
cities and, when they asked him, to barbarian cities as well, have been
inscribed in Athens in the common sanctuary of all the gods . . . Hadrian built
other things in Athens, a shrine for Panhellenic Zeus and Hera and a temple of
all the gods: but his most famous things are the hundred columns of Phrygian
marble, with walls built just like the columns, and pavilions with gilded
roofwork and alabaster, decorated with statues and paintings. Books are kept
in them. Then you have Hadrian's gymnasium, which also has a hundred
columns, from the quarry in Libya.

Remains of all but one of these works can still be seen in Athens —
the single exception being Hadrian's gymnasium — and we will visit
them on our present tour.

Let us begin our stroll in Monastiraki Square, from where we walk
south along Odos Areos, the street that leads uphill towards the
north-west spur of the Acropolis. As we start down the street and pass
the old mosque, we see on our left the massive wall of an imposing
ancient structure behind a picket fence. This is what remains of the
western enclosure wall of the Library of Hadrian, the largest civic
structure erected in Athens by Hadrian.

The library complex was rectangular in plan, measuring approximately 75 × 112 m, with its long axis running east–west.
This vast space was surrounded by massive walls, which in places are
still standing to their full height; those on the north, east and south
sides being built of large poros blocks, while the west side, which was
the principal façade, was made of marble. The main entrance to the
enclosure was through a doorway in the centre of the western wall.
This was preceded by a simple propylon approached on three sides by
a flight of six steps, with four Corinthian columns in front and antae at
the ends of spur walls on the sides supporting a pedimented roof. On
either side of the propylon there were seven unfluted columns slightly
detached from the wall behind them; these supported an architrave, a
frieze and a cornice that extended out over each column, probably to
serve as statue bases, and with short spur walls terminating in antae at
each end of the façade. All that has survived of this west wall is its
northern half, along with the seven columns on that side and the
column at the left-hand corner of the propylon, as well as the spur wall
and anta behind it.

The library buildings were situated at the east or rear end of the

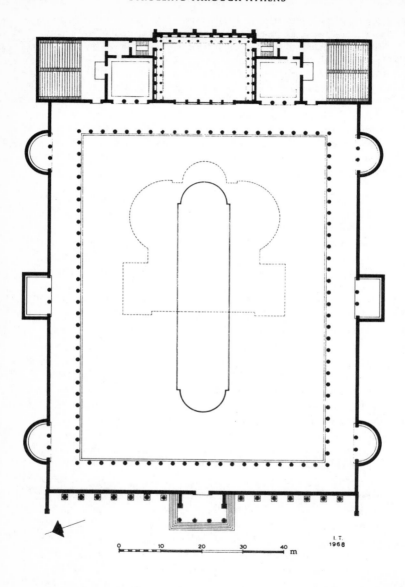

I. T.
1968

The Library of Hadrian, *c.* AD 132, restored plan

enclosure, and were joined to the front façade by the north and south walls. Both of these side walls had three large exedrae, the central ones rectangular in form and the others semicircular, with a diameter of nearly 10 m. The south wall has vanished, but a large part of the north wall and two of its exedrae are still standing; these can be seen on Odos Pandrossou, the street that leads off to the east from beside the mosque at the corner. A large part of the east wall of the complex has also survived, and this can be seen on Odos Aiolou, the street that runs parallel to Areos on the west. The back of the main library room there can be recognized from the fact that it projects slightly from the rest of the wall and is supported by buttresses; it differs from the other parts of the enclosure wall in that bricks and concrete were used for parts of its inner construction.

The interior of the library complex can best be seen either from Odos Aiolou or Odos Adrianou (named for Hadrian), the street that runs by the south side of the archaeological site. From either of these two vantage points we can see where the library proper was situated at the eastern end of the enclosure, though nothing now remains of it except its foundations. The library building itself was in the centre, and may have been on two storeys, as were the slightly lower wings on either side of it that housed the reading-rooms and archives. This building looked out on to a vast courtyard bordered on all four sides by a peristyle standing on a stylobate with a single step. This peristyle was 7.5 m deep and measured about 82×60 m, with a colonnade of thirty columns on either side and twenty-two at the ends, a hundred in all, supporting an architrave and a sloping roof. (These were 'the hundred columns of Phrygian marble' described by Pausanias.) The six exedrae within this peristyle were divided from it by two columns each along the line of the enclosure wall. Not a single one of the columns from the peristyle or the exedrae have survived; they were undoubtedly carried off to be used in the construction of later buildings elsewhere in Athens. Much of the destruction and loss surely occurred during the Herulian sack and in the subsequent erection of the Late Roman fortification wall, which incorporated the southern enclosure wall of the library within its structure.

In the centre of the garden there was originally a long and narrow pool which later fell into disuse, perhaps at the time of the Herulian raid; early in the fifth century AD a large quatrefoil building with a mosaic pavement was erected over the eastern half of the site. This building may have been an institution of higher learning, similar to other schools that were founded in late antiquity in the Agora and the Academy. It is believed that the library complex was also reconstructed at the same time, and that perhaps the quatrefoil building may have been associated with it as a lecture-hall. At the end of the fifth century or early in the sixth a Christian basilica was erected within the quatrefoil building, and this structure continued in use until the late eleventh or early twelfth century. At that time the basilica was destroyed and a much smaller Byzantine church was constructed on the site, occupying the eastern part of the nave and the north aisle of the older sanctuary. This church, dedicated to the Megali Panayia, the Great Virgin Mary, continued in use until 1885, when it was destroyed in the great fire that burned down the market area that then occupied the site of Hadrian's Library. Excavations on the site began later that same year, and in a series of annual campaigns the Byzantine and Turkish structures on the site were cleared away and the plan of the library complex was determined, leaving the Roman ruins as we see them today. In Byzantine times the library was known as the Palace of Hadrian, for its imposing ruins must have indeed looked palatial to the Athenians, whose traditions still recalled the great emperor who had built this and other splendid edifices that survived in medieval Athens.

We now return to Odos Areos and follow it to its intersection with Odos Poikilis. There we turn left, walking along past the archaeological site below us to our right. These are the remains of the colonnaded street that we saw previously on our stroll through the Agora. As we recall, this was built during the Roman reconstruction of the city in the first and second centuries AD, and was designed as a pedestrian mall to connect the old Greek Agora with the new Roman Agora that had been created to the east. The eastern end of this mall ended in a stairway that led up to the main entrance to the Roman Agora. After reaching the end of Odos Poikilis we veer right so as to walk over to that point ourselves, at the centre of the fence that borders the archaeological site. There we stand before the Gate of Athena Archegetis (the Leader), the monumental entry-way to the Roman Agora.

The name Roman Agora is in a sense a misnomer, and is used to describe this archaeological site only because the ruined structures that one sees there today date from Roman times. The market area here actually dates back to the earliest days of the city; according to tradition, the Agora founded by Theseus and re-instituted by Solon would have been just about at this location. It would be

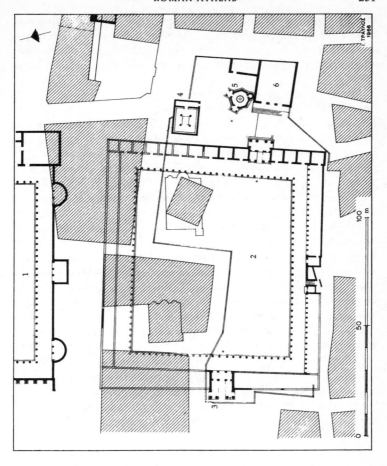

The Roman Agora and its
surroundings

1 Library of Hadrian
2 Roman Agora
3 Gate of Athena Archegetis
4 Public toilet
5 Horologion of Andronikos
   Kyrrhestes
6 Agoranomion

more appropriate to call this the Commercial Agora, for this was always the central market area of the city, whereas the Agora we visited earlier was the civic centre of Athens, the site of the main administrative offices, lawcourts, temples and other public institutions.

An inscription on the lintel of the Gate of Athena Archegetis records that it was erected by the people through donations made by Julius Caesar and (later) by Augustus, and that it was dedicated in the archonship of Nikias, who held that office in 10 BC. The plan of the Roman market was quite simple: a vast outdoor courtyard within which a peristyle provided shade for the arcades of shops along its sides. The courtyard was very nearly rectangular in shape, with a width of 98 m, and measuring 115 m along its north side and 110 m along the south.

Up until recent years it was assumed that the propylaia, the Gate of Athena Archegetis, was situated on the axis of the peristyle, but recent excavations have shown that its axis is displaced to 5.5 m south of the centre. Consequently, earlier measurements of the market's width are short by 11 m. The entry-way itself consisted of a wall with three openings, a wide central portal for carts and animals and two smaller side entrances for pedestrians. In front of this there was a pedimented porch, with four Doric columns in front, two spur walls ending in antae behind the corner columns and two interior columns behind antae half-way back along the spur walls. Drawings made in the seventeenth century show that the acroterion crowning the pediment of the propylaia was a statue of a male figure. An inscription on the base of this acroterion, now lost along with the statue itself, identified the figure as Lucius Caesar, a grandson of Augustus, who held the title of Caesar from 12 BC until his death in AD 2.

Excavations have revealed that the peristyle measured 73 × 84 m and stood on a two-stepped stylobate, with thirty-one unfluted Ionic columns on each side and twenty-four on the ends. The colonnade was approximately 6.8 m deep on all four sides, supporting an architrave, a cornice with lion-headed spouts and a sloping roof. On the south side there was also an interior Doric colonnade separated from the southern peristyle by a single step. Interrupting the inner colonnade at its centre there was a small fountain-house, and also a stairway connecting the market-place with the higher street behind it to the south. Excavations in the south-east corner of the Agora have unearthed six of the shops that once formed the eastern arcade. Between the fourth and fifth shops from the south-east corner the remains of a second monumental entry-way were found. This propylon, which was displaced 20 m to the south of the central axis of the peristyle, was similar in design to the Gate of Athena Archegetis, except that it was somewhat smaller and had a shallower outer porch.

Several inscriptions found in the Roman Agora show that various repairs were done during Roman times, and it was probably then that the entire courtyard of the peristyle was paved in marble. The Agora was probably destroyed during the Herulian raid, and there is no evidence that it was ever rebuilt. But when the Late Roman wall was built the old Greek Agora was outside the fortification, and so from that time on the Roman Agora became the civic centre of Athens as well as its principal market-place. What was left of the Roman Agora's structure fell into ruins during the medieval period, and when the first European travellers came to Athens all that remained above ground was the Gate of Athena Archegetis and a few other ruined structures. The gateway appears frequently in prints of early nineteenth-century Athens, giving a romantic touch to the picturesque scene around it. By that time the site of the Roman Agora had been built over with streets and houses, but it was still the central market of the city, with the ancient propylaia known as the Market Gate. The first large-scale excavation of the site was made in 1890 by the Greek Archaeological Society, uncovering the south-east corner of the peristyle and the eastern propylon. After that no further work was done until 1931, when the first of a series of campaigns was begun to clear as much of the site as possible, a project that continues, with interruptions, until the present day. About half of the Roman Agora has now been cleared, enabling archaeologists to reconstruct the main outlines of its plan as described above. The entire western side and the whole north-western quadrant of the ancient market-place are still underground, covered by the nineteenth-century houses and streets that border the archaeological site to the north. It is interesting to note that this neighbourhood, which overlies the south side of Hadrian's Library as well, is still a market quarter, a testimony to the continuity of life in this old city.

Let us now examine the antiquities at the far end of the archaeological site, beyond the eastern end of the Roman Agora. The best approach is to follow the street that zigzags around the site to the north (it takes on three different names in succession *en route*), passing over the unexcavated northern side of the Roman Agora.

As we approach the north-eastern corner of the site, we see just inside the fence the outline of a rectangular structure paved in marble. This has been identified as a public toilet, built at the same time as the Roman Agora in order to accommodate the crowds who came to shop and do business in the market-place. The building was rectangular in plan, measuring approximately 16 × 18 m, with an oblong lobby on the east side and the almost square toilet area taking up the rest of the building. One entered at the southern end of the lobby, at the centre of which a door led into the main chamber. This was covered by a roof supported by the outer walls and four columns standing at the corners of a smaller rectangular area above the centre of the room; above this a space measuring 3.7 × 2.9 m was left open to the sky so as to provide light and ventilation. Around the periphery of the room there extended a marble bench made up of a series of marble slabs with holes, looking very much like modern toilet seats. A continuous stream of water flowed in a trough around the room and poured through gutters into a deep canal below, which was inclined so that the wastes flushed into the main cloaca of the city. This is by far the most elaborate and well-designed toilet ever found in ancient Athens; nothing like it existed before the Roman period, when toilet and bathing facilities were more primitive.

After passing the Roman toilet, we turn right into the street that leads uphill past the eastern end of the archaeological site. About half-way up the block on the left there is a very pleasant café with its tables arrayed on both sides of the street and with an excellent view out over the archaeological site to the west. The café is called Ai Aerides, which means the Windy Ones; it takes its name from the Tower of the Winds, the conical-topped marble structure just below at the eastern end of the archaeological site. Ai Aerides is an excellent place to sit and have lunch while examining the tower and reviewing its interesting history.

The monument is known to archaeologists as the Horologion, or Clock Tower, of Andronikos Kyrrhestes (of Kyrrhus, a town in Syria). This exceptionally well-preserved structure is believed to date from the second half of the first century BC, and was probably erected when the Romans first began to plan and develop the adjacent market-place. The distinctive building has attracted the attention of travellers and scholars from ancient times to the present day, although, for some unknown reason, Pausanias does not even mention it. The earliest reference to the tower is by Varro in his *De re rustica*, published in

37 BC, and it is described in some detail by Vitruvius in his *Ten Books on Architecture*, which is thought to have been written in the time of Augustus.

The building is octagonal, each side measuring 3.2 m, and is 12.3 m high, with a maximum diameter of 7.9 m. It stands on a three-stepped platform and is built on squared blocks of Pentelic marble of various widths. There are entrances in the north-east and north-west sides, outside which there were rectangular porticoes with two Corinthian columns, while at the south side there projects the nearly circular wall of a water reservoir.

The most interesting aspect of the exterior is the frieze that runs around the top of the building, with each of the eight sides decorated in low relief with a winged figure personifying the wind blowing from that quarter. Athenians have always called them *Ai Aerides*, the Windy Ones. These reliefs formed the faces of an elaborate weathervane, which is described by Vitruvius when he writes of the architects who have investigated the influence of winds on city-planning:

Chief among them was Andronikos of Kyrrhus, who in proof built the marble octagonal tower in Athens. On the several sides of the octagon he executed reliefs representing the several winds, each facing the point from which it blows; and on top of the tower he set a conical-shaped piece of marble and on this a bronze Triton with a rod outstretched in its right hand. It is so contrived to go round with the wind, always stopping to face the breeze and holding its rod as a pointer directly over the representation of the wind that was blowing.

Each of the reliefs bears an inscription giving the mythological name of the wind from that quarter, and the allegorical figures that personify them are represented in such a way as to characterize the weather they bring with them and its effect upon the world. Boreas, the icy north wind, is a rugged and bearded old man, clad in a heavy robe with long sleeves and wearing buskins, and he is blowing through a conch shell to symbolize the howling sound he makes when he roars across the land. Skiron, the north-east wind, is also bearded, heavily dressed and buskined; he carries an inverted brazier, symbolizing the warmer weather he brings to Greece in winter. Zephyros, the balmy west wind, is an almost nude youth, whose only clothing is a loose mantle filled with flowers which he is about to waft down upon the earth. Lips, the south-west wind, is also lightly clad, and he holds in his hands an *aplustre*, the lyre-like stern ornament that adorned ancient Greek ships, signifying the role that he played in filling the sails of those vessels as they journeyed across the Aegean. Notos, the south wind, is a youth dressed in a *chlamys*, a loose cap, holding in his hands an inverted amphora representing the rain that he pours down on the parched Greek countryside when he blows. Euros, the south-east wind, is a bearded old fellow with a fierce expression on his face, for it is he who is responsible for the terrible storms that lash the Aegean when he blows in winter and early spring. Apeliotes, the east wind, is a lightly clad youth who is holding a mantle filled with the fruit and grain that come forth when he brings warmth and rain to the land in spring. And then we finish the circuit with Kaikias, the north-east wind, a bearded and heavily dressed old man, who holds in his hands an inverted bowl full of hailstones, symbolic of the foul weather for which he is responsible.

There was also a sundial on each of the eight faces. This consisted of a gnomon, or shadow-stick, which projected horizontally from the wall and cast its shadow on to a series of inscribed lines below to give the hour of day. In addition, the tower also functioned as a *klepsydra*, or water-clock, an ingenious time-keeping device that was powered by water flowing from the reservoir in the south side of the building, so that passers-by could learn the time by night as well as by day. But the ingenuity of Andronikos Kyrrhestes did not stop even there, for there is reason to believe that the tower also served as a planetarium, in which a mechanical device represented the motion of the sun, the moon and the five visible planets.

The subsequent history of the tower and the legends that sur-round it are as fascinating as its structure and decoration. During the Middle Ages there developed a tradition that this was the prison of Socrates, a rival to the legend that had him imprisoned in the cave at the foot of the Mouseion Hill. The first European traveller to mention the monument was Cyriacus of Ancona, who in 1436 identified it as a Temple of Aeolus, God of the Winds: 'We revisited the octagonal Temple of Aeolus, which has at the top of the walls eight winged figures of the winds, sculpted with their attributes with wonderful art, and each image has above it its name in large letters of Attic style, as we saw from near by.'

Evliya Chelebi, the seventeenth-century Turkish traveller, was told that the tower, which he calls the Tent of Plato, was the tomb of King Philip of Macedon; he also believed that it was a talisman, whose magical powers he thus describes in his *Narrative of Travels*:

Near the Old Mosque stands a building that embodies the knowledge of all the wise men, which is called the Tent of Plato: a model tent, built of single stone blocks, octagonal, with sides facing the eight winds. But beneath its tent-shaped dome there is a tomb. The infidel Greeks all hold it in high esteem, claiming that Philip the Hellene is buried inside it, and they visit it on their accursed days [*paniyiria*]. The head and foot of the tomb are both inscribed with its date in the Greek tongue. The dome of this marble tent is topped by a tall rod. They say that in the time of the ancient sages this supported a mirror of the world, similar to the mirror of Alexander the Great, which was designed to give a reflection of an enemy army advancing on the city from any side, but this mirror is now lost. They say also that in those times the wise men who gathered in this town used to perform strange tricks of magic here . . . And they say that never did plague attack this town nor did snakes remain alive here, nor centipedes either, nor scorpions, storks, crows, fleas, lice, bedbugs, mosquitoes or flies . . .

About a century after Evliya's visit the Tower of the Winds was taken over by a community of Mevlevi dervishes, who used it as their *tekke*, or monastery. The Mevlevi took their name from their founder, the thirteenth-century mystic Mevlana Celaddin Rumi, whose tomb at Konya in Turkey is attached to the original *tekke* of the order. These were the famous Whirling Dervishes, who sought to achieve communion with the divine through their ethereal whirling dance, the *sema*, which was accompanied by the thumping of drums and the haunting wail of the *ney*, or Turkish flute. The Mevlevi dervishes in the Tower of the Winds performed their whirling dance each week on Friday after the noon prayer, a remarkable spectacle described by many foreign travellers to Athens in the latter years of the Turkish occupation. One of the most interesting of these is by Edward Dodwell, who made several drawings of the tower and its interior in 1805, representing the dervishes performing their dances and other rituals:

In the interior of the tower the walls are covered with quotations from the Koran, painted on wood in different colours. The Koran is placed in a cavity of the wall and next to it is a replica of Muhammad's flag and sword. The dance performed in the Tower of the Winds is the strangest religious ceremony of the Muslims. Dervishes and other Turks, irrespective of age and class, participate in this sacred dance. They first sit on the ground in a circle and loudly praise God and Muhammad, accompanied by two small drums. Suddenly they all rise together and begin singing and dancing in a circle at great speed. Shortly after they withdraw, making way for two leading dancers who, held together with a handkerchief or a belt, whirl around in a frantic speed. The leader of the Dervishes dressed in green – the sacred colour of the Muslims – encourages the dancers with his voice, while he beats a large drum. The Dervishes continue to twirl around and cry aloud until they fall exhausted into the arms of the spectators and appear to be unconscious for a while as if seized by divine ecstasy.

Just to the left of the Tower of the Winds, as we look towards it from the café, we see two large arches and the ruined half of a third one. At one time these arches were thought to have been part of an aqueduct that led to the reservoir in the Tower of the Winds, but now they have been identified as being the remains of a structure known as the Agoranomion. This was the building where the magistrates of the market sat in session, handling all the judicial affairs of the Roman Agora and enforcing the regulations involved in its day-to-day operations. These arches formed the southern loggia of the Agoranomion, from which a flight of stairs led down to the eastern propylon of the market.

We now leave the café, walking downhill for a short distance before turning right at the corner of Odos Diogenous. This short street soon veers left and makes its way past an old taverna, the Platanos, which has tables set outside in a little out-of-the way square, a favourite Athenian eating-place for more than half a century.

Thousands of people pass this way each day without realizing that beneath them there are the ruins of one of the most monumental structures ever erected in ancient Athens. We can look down upon the visible remains of this building by peering over the cinder-block wall on the left side of the square. From there we can see part of the massive north wall of the structure, which extended along the rear end of the modern buildings standing on the south side of Odos Adrianou. One authority, John Travlos, has suggested that this was a three-aisled basilica with a large cella and a porch at the east end. The dimensions of the structure were enormous, 85 m in length and 40 m wide, surpassing even the Parthenon in size. Travlos has identified it as the Pantheon, 'the common sanctuary of all the gods' which Pausanias mentions among the edifices built by Hadrian. We can also have a look at these walls from below, after turning left from Diogenous on to Mnesikleos and then left again into Adrianou. The north-west corner of the structure can be seen in a vacant lot below the square above, extending eastwards from there as far as No. 86 Adrianou. The north wall of the Pantheon was incorporated into the Late Roman fortification wall, and if you look towards the right-hand side of the vacant lot on Adrianou you can see the junction between the two walls.

We now begin walking eastwards along Odos Adrianou, following it as it curves in a great arc around the Acropolis. This street, which is named for the Emperor Hadrian, follows the course of the main thoroughfare of Roman Athens. The name of the street changes to Odos Lysikratous one block before emerging on to Leoforos Amalias. Along this last block the Arch of Hadrian suddenly comes into view across the avenue, giving the street scene a grand and Roman look.

This triumphal arch was erected by the Athenians in AD 131/2 to honour Hadrian, who in that year dedicated the Olympieion. The archway stood on the boundary between the ancient city of Athens and the new quarter created by Hadrian. Inscriptions on the frieze of the arch commemorate this historic division. On the side facing the Acropolis the inscription reads: 'This is Athens, the former city of Theseus', while on the other side it says: 'This is the city of Hadrian and not of Theseus.'

The Arch of Hadrian was designed as a free-standing gateway, measuring 13.5 m in width, 18 m in height, and with a depth of approximately 3 m. The single arch of the gateway rests on Corinthian pilasters; these were originally flanked on both faces of the gate by Corinthian columns standing on rectangular bases and connected to the wall by consoles, which still remain in place. The attic, or upper level of the gate, consisted of three openings framed by Corinthian pilasters supporting an entablature, with the middle opening flanked inside and out by Corinthian columns set slightly forward so as to support a pediment. The two side openings were originally closed by marble screens, but these were removed on orders from Queen Amalia, wife of King Otho, so as to open up the view through the archway.

The Arch of Hadrian originally opened on to a road that led around the north side of the Olympieion to the propylon of the temple, which for some unknown reason was situated near the north-eastern corner of the precinct. As we have seen, the entrance to the archaeological site is also at that corner, so we proceed there along Leoforos Vasilissis Olgas. After entering the site we come to the remains of the white marble propylon. This is a surprisingly small entry-way for such a vast enclosure, measuring 10.5 m in width and 5.4 m in depth, with four Ionic columns in front of antae. Then we pass through the propylon and finally enter the temenos of the Olympieion, where we might pause to look upon the remains of this renowned temple and to review its history and architecture.

According to Thucydides, the shrine of Olympian Zeus here was one of the very oldest sanctuaries in the city. Pausanias tells us that the original shrine on this site was founded in the time of Deucalion, who with his wife Pyrrha procreated the human race again after all the rest of humanity was drowned in a deluge sent down upon them by Zeus. As Pausanias tells the tale, the waters of the flood finally drained away through a chasm on this site, flowing through it to the Ilissos and then on into the Saronic Gulf. The remains of a small and very ancient sanctuary have been excavated on the site, and beneath it there was in fact a subterranean passage leading to the Ilissos. According to Pausanias, the salvation of mankind from the deluge was commemorated annually at this shrine, in a primitive ceremony in which cakes of flour mixed with honey were thrown down into the chasm, probably to propitiate the earth-born monsters who dwelt there.

It has always been thought that the first monumental temple on this site was begun by the Peisistratids, but excavations in the late nineteenth century revealed the foundations of a structure that predates their period. Other than that, the date of this pre-Peisistratid temple is not known, nor is it clear whether the structure was ever completed.

In any event, the temple begun by the Peisistratids was far larger in size than its predecessor, though six and a half centuries would pass before it would finally be completed under the sponsorship of Hadrian. Aristotle suggested that Peisistratus conceived of this grandiose scheme as a way of keeping the Athenians so busy that they would have no time to plot against him. We learn from Vitruvius that Peisistratus employed four architects: Antistates, Callaeschros, Antimachides, and Porinos; he tells us that they laid the foundations of the building, and that the project was abandoned when the Peisistratids were overthrown and democracy returned to Athens.

There has been considerable discussion about the plan of the Peisistratid temple and the extent to which it was carried through to completion. Apparently it was a gigantic dipteral sanctuary comparable in size to the colossal archaic Ionic temples in Asia Minor, the Heraeum in Samos and the Artemisium in Ephesus, but here the order would have been Doric. Foundations of polygonal limestone and two steps of the stylobate in Kara stone were actually laid down, and from this the ground plan of the structure can be established. The building would have been 107.7 m long and 42.9 m wide along the stylobate, only very slightly smaller than the temple that we see today. There were to have been eight columns at the front and rear and twenty-one along the sides, with each of them standing to a height of 16 m and having an average diameter of 2.42 m. Some of the lower column drums have survived on the site, while others were used in the construction of the Themistoclean walls and in the foundations of later structures that were erected on the site.

The next building stage on the Olympieion began in 174 BC, under the sponsorship of the Seleucid King Antiochus IV (175–163 BC), who employed the services of a Roman architect named Cossutius. The dimensions of the temple were much the same as those of its predecessor, measuring 107.75 × 41.10 m along the stylobate, but the Corinthian order was used rather than the Doric. The temple was laterally dipteral, with two rows of twenty columns along both sides, while to the front and rear it was tripteral, with three rows of eight columns each, making a total of 104 in all. Vitruvius informs us that the temple was of the type called hypaethral, that is, with a cella open to the elements. From his description and those of other sources it is apparent that the Olympieion was still unfinished when Antiochus died in 163 BC, and it remained uncompleted for nearly three centuries more. According to Pliny, Sulla removed several columns from the Olympieion when he sacked Athens in 86 BC; he took them back with him to Rome, where they were used in the construction of the Capitoline temple.

The third and last building stage on the Olympieion was the one that was initiated by Hadrian. This project began in AD 125, on the occasion of Hadrian's second visit to Athens. Authorities disagree on how much construction remained to be done on the temple, but it seems to have been complete up to the level of the architrave. One part of the structure that can definitely be assigned to Hadrian's reign is the impressive retaining wall that still surrounds much of the Olympieion precinct. This is a massive structure of rusticated poros, 206 m along each side and 129 m along the ends, with buttresses at intervals of about 5.3 m and stronger supports at the corners. The project was completed in AD 131/2, when Hadrian came to Athens to dedicate the temple and the colossal chryselephantine cult-statue of Zeus Olympios, with which he himself was identified as the deified emperor. The dedicatory speech was delivered by Polemos of Smyrna, a distinguished Sophist and a close friend of Hadrian, whom he hailed as 'the Olympian'.

Pausanias visited Athens just a decade or so after the dedication of the Olympieion, and he writes of the numerous statues of Hadrian that were standing in the temple precincts along with the one set up by the Athenians:

Before you go into the Temple of Olympian Zeus, there are two portraits of

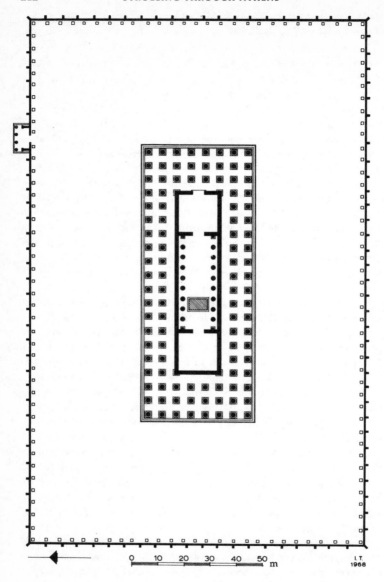

The Temple of Olympian Zeus and the precinct wall, AD 124–32, restored plan

Hadrian in Thasos stone and two in Egyptian stone. In front of the columns are the bronze figures which the Greeks call the Colonies. Hadrian the Roman emperor dedicated this shrine and its statue, which is worth noticing, as it exceeds all other statues in magnitude except the Rhodian and the Roman colossi. Its construction is of ivory and gold, and it has considerable merit if you think of the size of it. The whole enclosure is half a mile round, all full of statues. Every city dedicated a portrait of the emperor Hadrian, but Athens outdid them by erecting the notable colossus behind the temple.

Little is known about the history of the Olympieion subsequent to its completion and dedication. The precinct wall was partly destroyed to supply material for the new line of fortifications built by the Emperor Valerian in the mid third century AD. The temple suffered considerable damage in the Herulian sack of AD 267. And there is little likelihood that it would have been repaired subsequently, given the magnitude of the task and the declining fortunes of Athens during the late Roman period. The Olympieion would have been closed in 435, when Theodosius II issued his edict against the worship of the old pagan gods. Early in the Byzantine era a Christian basilica was erected in the vicinity of the propylon, and later in that period a small chapel dedicated to St John was constructed in the south-east corner of the colonnade. At some time in the Middle Ages a hermit saint, emulating St Simeon the Stylite of Antioch, built himself a little cell on top of the surviving fragments of the architrave in the south-east corner of the temple, living there for the rest of his life. By the end of the Byzantine era the Olympieion was almost totally in ruins, and when Cyriacus of Ancona visited Athens in 1436 he found that only twenty-one of the original 104 columns were still in place. Today only fifteen columns remain standing, all but two of them in the south-east corner of the colonnade, while the drums of another lie neatly arrayed on the ground, having been toppled by a hurricane in 1852. The other columns doubtless disappeared into lime kilns, as did so much of the marble of the ancient world. Such an incident is documented on one of the surviving columns, where an inscription in Greek states that 'on 27 April 1759 he pulled down the column'. This refers to the Turkish voivode Tzisdarakis, who on that date used explosives to demolish one of the standing columns of the Olympieion, using its marble to make plaster for the mosque that he was building in Monastiraki. This incident and other depredations of the voivode are recorded by the Athenian chronicler John Benizelos, quoted by Liza Micheli in *Monastiraki*: 'In 1759 Tzisdarakis the Athenian came as voivode. He erected the Mosque of the Lower Bazaar, he destroyed one of Hadrian's columns with gunpowder and took many marbles from the Old Cathedral.'

In 1778 the western precinct wall of the Olympieion was included in the Serpentzes, the new line of fortifications erected by Hadji Ali Haseki. At that time the Arch of Hadrian was fitted with a massive wooden door and became the principal entry-way to Athens from the east. It was then known to the Greeks as Kameraporta, the Gate of the Arches. During the Turkish period the Olympieion was known to the Greeks as the Palace of Hadrian, a name it shared with Hadrian's Library. The Turks called it the Palace of Belkis, from a Turkish legend that in ancient times the Olympieion was the imperial residence of Solomon's wife.

Before leaving the Olympieion, let us look at some of the ruins that lie scattered around the north side of the site in the vicinity of the propylon. The most interesting remains there are those of a Roman bath, much of whose foundation walls and mosaic pavement have survived. This is the largest and best-preserved Roman bath in Athens, and the only one that can still be seen above ground. It has been dated to the period of Hadrian's great rebuilding programme, AD 125–32. That, together with its proximity to the Olympieion, leads one to speculate that it was built for the use of Hadrian and his entourage, who would then have made use of the bath when the temple was dedicated in 131/2.

The site of the Olympieion was in times past a popular gathering-place for Athenians, particularly on 'Clean Monday', the first day of Lent. This is one of the most joyous days in the Athenian calendar, when everyone goes out into the countryside for a picnic lunch and to fly kites. The first group to begin celebrating Clean Monday at the Olympieion were apparently the milkmen of Athens, beginning in late Ottoman times, and eventually they were joined by the rest of the Greek populace of the city in a day-long festival of drink, dance, music and song. One particularly spirited celebration here was the first Clean Monday after the Turkish garrison finally withdrew from the Acropolis in 1832, a scene depicted by the European artist Perlberg in a magnificent painting now exhibited in the Ethniki Pinakotheke, the National Gallery of Art. Another painting in the museum, an unidentified work dating from the late Ottoman period, shows a large group of black Arabs, slaves of the Turks, gathered for prayer under the columns of the Olympieion. Dimitrios Kambouroglu, the Greek folklorist, has documented these gatherings of the Arab slaves at the Olympieion; he describes their prayers as a continual wailing, and writes that 'when their leader gave the signal, they lifted their arms towards heaven and having their heads and eyes turned heavenwards, prayed with wild cries, appealing to the deaf perception. Sometimes they would even strike their chests.'

We now leave the Olympieion, turning right on Leoforos Vasilissis Olgas once outside the site, and then at the next intersection we turn left on to Leoforos Vasileos Konstantinou. Just before the next intersection we cross the avenue, bringing us to the Panathenaic Stadium.

The Stadium was originally laid out by Lycurgos in the year 330/29 BC. The date comes from an inscription found on the site; this expresses thanks to a certain Eudemos, who donated a yoke of a thousand oxen to be used in the construction project. The first part of the project consisted primarily of levelling off the site, a gulley between two hillocks on the left bank of the Ilissos, after which the slopes of the hillsides were graded to provide a seating area for the spectators. Other than that, there were no seats for the spectators, except for a few marble thrones for notables. The stadium was originally used for performances of the athletic contests connected with the Panathenaic Games. Later, from AD 132 onwards, the Stadium was also used for the contests involved in the Adriana Olympia, a quinquennial festival organized by the Emperor Hadrian when he founded the Panhellenion. The festival also involved gladiatorial contests and the baiting of wild animals, barbarous spectacles that were never seen in Greece before the Roman conquest.

At the opening of the Panatheniac Games in AD 140, the wealthy Athenian Herodes Atticus, who was presiding over the festival, made a speech saying that he would build a new stadium for the people of Athens and have it ready for the next celebration of the Greater Panathenaea. Herodes kept his promise, and the new stadium was dedicated by him at the opening of the Panathenaic Games in 144. Pausanias saw the new stadium just a decade or so after it was completed, and he was impressed: 'A thing not so attractive to hear about, but wonderful to see, is the white marble stadium. The best way of conveying the size of it is to describe the hill above the Ilissos starting from a natural amphitheatre, coming right down to the bank of the river in straight double lines. Herod of Athens built it, and he consumed most of the Pentelic quarry in the process.'

The Stadium of Herodes Atticus continued in use until it was destroyed in the Herulian sack of AD 267, after which the Panathenaic Games and the Adriana Olympia were abandoned. This became official in 393, when a decree of Theodosius I terminated the Olympic Games and all other competitions connected with the old pagan festivals such as the Panathenaea. The Stadium was then abandoned and became a total ruin, hardly recognized by foreign travellers to Athens. One of the first travellers to describe the Stadium was the French artist J. D. Le Roy, who painted a view of the ruins in 1755. Le Roy did his painting from the right bank of the Ilissos, where an ancient bridge still spanned the stream in three round Roman arches. This bridge, which may also have been built by Herodes Atticus, was almost completely demolished in 1778. (Stuart and Revett did a drawing of this bridge in 1751, but it was not published until 1791, with a comment that there was then little left of the span to be seen.) Le Roy describes the scene that he depicted:

The Stadium of Athens, that Pausanias so greatly praised, has lost its beauty today. Its seats are no longer visible, but its shape and its huge size can be clearly traced. In order to complete the picture, I painted the bridge on my left and the part of the Ilissos river in front of me ... While I was drawing the Stadium from quite a distance, I saw Turkish women washing their clothes in the river; I painted them, making every effort not to be seen. They noticed me, however, and angrily told me to go away. I did so, as I did not like to offend the established customs of Athens.

In 1894 an international organization was formed for the purpose of reviving the Olympic Games, and it was agreed that they would be held in Athens. The Greek philanthropist George Averoff contributed a huge sum of money to build a new Panathenaic Stadium for the revived Olympic Games, and a decision was made to construct this on the site of the ancient Stadium beside the Ilissos. The ancient Stadium had been excavated in 1869–79 by Emmanuel Ziller, who was able to determine the original plan of the structure founded by Herodes Atticus. This plan was used in the rebuilding of the Stadium, using the same Pentelic marble from which the original structure had been made. The Stadium was not yet complete when the first modern Olympic Games opened on 5 April 1896, an Easter Sunday, but work had progressed far enough to allow the overflow crowd to be accommodated there. Construction was finally completed in 1906, when a special Olympiad was held in Athens to celebrate the dedication of the new Stadium. Since then the Stadium has been used for national and international sporting events; there were hopes that it would be the focus of the centennial celebration of the modern Olympic Games in 1996, but sadly, Athens was not chosen as the site for the summer games.

Let us now look at the Stadium, which can best be done by climbing up to the top tier of seats. The plan is the normal one for an ancient Greek stadium, an elongated horseshoe shape with one end open, in this case the north, and with the other closed in a semicircular curve, the *sphendone*. The arena is about 204 m long and 83 m wide, the same as in the original structure, which had a straight dromos, or race-track, about 185 m in length. Around the periphery of the arena there is a low marble parapet surmounted by a grille. Inside the parapet there is a broad promenade from which the spectators ascend to their seats, which are reached by 209 flights of steps. There are fifty rows of seats divided half-way up by a *diazoma*, and at the top there is another promenade running around the upper periphery of the stadium. There are seats for 50,000 spectators, the same number that were accommodated in the Roman stadium. In the Stadium of Herodes Atticus, a Doric stoa surmounted the *sphendone*, and between the open northern end and the Ilissos there was a portico with a propylaia. The spectators entered there, after passing over the river on the bridge that Herodes may have built at the same time as the Stadium. The performers entered through a tunnel that led under the *sphendone* to the arena, a design feature that has been retained in the modern structure.

Let us now walk around the upper promenade of the Stadium, pausing at the middle of its eastern side. Here we find ourselves almost level with the peak of the hillock that stands just to the east of the Stadium. Just outside the outer wall of the Stadium there we see a large Roman sarcophagus, on the near side of which there is an inscription in ancient Greek, reading, in translation, 'The Hero of Marathon'. This is believed to be the tomb of Herodes Atticus, who died in his native Marathon *c.* AD 177. Herodes was the greatest figure of his time in Athens. He inherited great wealth from his father and amassed another fortune while administering the Roman province of Asia under Hadrian, and he gave generously of his riches in various benefactions and public works, his principal endowments in Athens being this stadium and the odeion that bears his name on the south slope of the Acropolis. He was a close friend of the emperors Hadrian, Antoninus Pius and Marcus Aurelius, and was the latter's teacher. He was a renowed orator, scholar and writer, though virtually nothing of his work has survived. The principal source for his life is Philostratus in his *Lives of the Sophists*, written in the first half of the third century AD. According to Philostratus, the people of Athens brought the remains of Herodes back to Athens after his death, for they thought it appropriate to bury their benefactor in the stadium that he had built for them. As Philostratus describes the funeral, the ephebes of Athens led the procession for Marathon to Athens and then formed the guard of honour at his burial. The oration at the graveside was delivered by

Hadrian of Tyre, who had been a student and then a colleague and close friend of Herodes Atticus. After the burial a funerary monument was erected over his grave, with this inscription: 'Here lies Herodes of Marathon, son of Atticus, honoured by the whole world and builder of this place.' The funerary monument was later destroyed, probably in the Herulian raid, and all that has survived is this empty sarcophagus, unearthed during Ziller's excavations and placed beside the new Stadium after its completion.

Next to the north-west corner of the Stadium there is a path that leads uphill to the peak of Ardettos, the hillock that flanks the Stadium to the west. In ancient times this hill was where the oath of office was administered to the Heliasts, those who would serve in the Heliaia law court. According to Theophrastus, the hill takes its name from Ardettos, the legendary Attic hero whom tradition credits with being the first to administer the oath. Near the peak of Ardettos we find the remains of a marble platform; this has been identified as part of the stylobate of a Temple of Tyche, the Goddess of Fortune, which was erected by Herodes Atticus while his Stadium was under construction. The view from Ardettos is quite striking, for from here one can see all of the south-east of central Athens, with the Olympieion set against the background of the Acropolis.

The last monument of Roman Athens that we will visit is the Odeion of Herodes Atticus, which we looked down upon at the end of our first stroll through the city. The Odeion is open only during performances of the Athens Festival, which are held on summer evenings. One should enter as early as possible on performance evenings, so that one can see this splendid Roman odeion in the last light of day before the theatre floodlamps are turned on. That was the time of day at which the artist James Skene depicted the Odeion in a painting he did in October 1838, noting his impressions of the scene in his diary: 'This is on the whole a ruined but picturesque monument, one of the world's most beautiful, where the shades and the size of the stone structure dominate. Its colour is sandy with warm tones. The Theatre is still fairly preserved to show the first arrangements of its massiveness.'

Both Pausanias and Philostratus write that Herodes Atticus built this odeion in memory of his wife Regilla, who died in 160 or 161. Pausanias mentions the Odeion only in a footnote, saying that 'In my account of Athens I left out the treatment of the music hall as I finished my Athenian records before Herod began his construction.' This has led John Travlos to date the construction of the Odeion to the period 161–74.

The Odeion was typically Roman in its design. The circular orchestra of the Greek theatre was here reduced to little more than a semicircle, which was 29 m in diameter and paved in marble with a mosaic pattern. The steeply sloped semicircular *cavea* had a diameter of 76 m and was enclosed by a massive retaining wall. There were twenty rows of seats in the lower half of the auditorium, while in the upper tier there were fourteen rows in the wedges. Stairways extended upwards and a semicircular *diazoma* separated the two tiers, with another semicircular aisle extending around the upper rim of the auditorium and connecting it with the second floor of the stage-building. The seats in the auditorium were of white Pentelic marble and accommodated about five thousand spectators.

The three-storeyed stage-building was 92 m wide and 28 m high, measured on its outer façade. The *logeion*, or stage proper, was 35 m wide and 8 m deep; it was raised 1.1 m above the level of the auditorium, to which it was connected by stairways on either side. The rear wall of the stage had eight aisles for statues, four of them arches and four quadrangular. A colonnade standing some 2 m forward of the stage wall supported a second storey, which in the interior may have opened out as a balcony. This storey and the one above had between them arched windows in three rows; these and the south façade through which they opened have survived and constitute one of the most distinctive landmarks on the south slope of the Acropolis. Three doorways led from the stage on to a long, narrow vestibule, paved in a mosaic of variegated marble. On either side of the vestibule arched doorways led through vaulted chambers that gave access to the *paradoi* and thence to the lower tier of seats. Spectators going to the upper tier could enter from the second floor of the Stoa of Eumenes, where a stairway over the main entrance to the east led up to the top *diazoma* of the theatre.

Several ancient writers make reference to the fact that the theatre had a roof of cedar wood. But surely this roof would have covered only the stage, for without internal supports it would have been quite impossible to have roofed the whole vast expanse of the auditorium.

The Odeion of Herodes Atticus was undoubtedly destroyed in the Herulian sack of AD 267, and there is no evidence that it was ever rebuilt in ancient times. During the Turkish period the stage-building formed part of the Serpentzes, the fortification wall built in 1778 by Hadji Ali Haseki. The Serpentzes was dismantled after the Greek War of Independence, and the Odeion was excavated and cleared of later accretions in the decade 1848–58. The theatre was completely restored in the years 1950–61. During the course of the latter restoration the auditorium was fitted out with seats of white Pentelic marble and the orchestra re-paved in a mosaic of white and bluish-grey marble, throughout using the same materials and design as in the original theatre. The setting is superb, particularly for productions of some of the Greek dramas that were performed here in ancient times.

9

Byzantine Athens

This stroll will take us through Byzantine Athens, whose principal monuments were erected during the Dark Ages that followed the collapse of Graeco-Roman civilization. All these monuments are churches or monasteries, for it was the Christian faith that sustained Greek civilization through the long centuries when Athens was virtually lost to history as barbarians overran Greece, cutting off their city from the capital in Constantinople.

The Byzantine period in Athenian history officially began in AD 330, when Constantine the Great shifted the capital of his empire from Rome to Byzantium, thereafter to be called Constantinople. At the beginning of the Byzantine era the Christian community that had been founded two centuries earlier by St Dionysius the Areopagite had barely established a foothold in Athens, where the ancient shrines and schools of philosophy continued to function. But the pagan shrines were closed in 435 by Theodosius II, and in 529 Justinian shut down the Platonic Academy and all the other philosophical schools in Athens and elsewhere in the Byzantine Empire, thus cutting off the cultural roots of Graeco-Roman civilization in Athens.

During the first two centuries of the Byzantine era the Christian church in Athens developed slowly and steadily. By 325 the Bishopric of Athens was sufficiently well established to be represented at the Council of Nicaea, which had been convened by Constantine to create a common doctrine of religious orthodoxy among the Christians in his empire. But Christians were still a distinct minority in Athens and elsewhere in Greece at that time, for of the two hundred bishops at the council only three represented bishoprics in Greece.

Prior to 435 the Christian community in Athens probably congregated in homes or in primitive cave-sanctuaries. The earliest Christian sanctuaries of which traces remain date from after the Theodosian edict of 435. Tradition holds that the earliest known Christian sanctuary in Athens, the church of St Leonides, was founded by the Empress Eudocia, the Athenian-born wife of Theodosius II (408–50). The empress, who was originally known as Athenais, took the Roman name Eudocia when she married Theodosius in 423. Her father was the famous Sophist Leontius, from whom she received a classical Greek education based on the Neoplatonist philosophy current at the time. She converted to Christianity at the time of her marriage to Theodosius, but for the rest of her life she remained true to the cultural traditions of her native city. At the same time she was also a fervent Christian, and during her husband's reign she did much to advance the development of Christianity in Athens. She was also very influential in promoting classical Greek culture in Constantinople. Her success in doing so is shown by the fact that the University of Constantinople, which Theodosius founded largely because of her influence, had more professorships in Greek than in Latin. This was to have a profound effect on the character of the empire, which would combine Greek culture with Christianity to create the civilization that modern historians describe as Byzantine.

The Parthenon and other pagan temples were eventually converted into Christian sanctuaries after their closure by Theodosius, but apparently not before the end of the sixth century. By then the Slavic invasions had totally obliterated what little there was left of ancient Graeco-Roman civilization, and during the next four centuries Athens was for the most part cut off from Constantinople and other centres of culture. This dark period in Athenian history ended in 1019, when the Byzantine Emperor Basil II journeyed to Athens after his final victory over the Bulgars, celebrating his victory with a Te Deum in the church of the Blessed Virgin in the Parthenon. The two centuries that followed represent the apogee of life in Byzantine Athens, a period during which there was a modest renaissance of culture in the city. The great majority of the surviving Byzantine churches in the city date from this period, which ended with the Latin conquest of Athens in 1205.

The last generation of Byzantine rule in Athens produced one of the most remarkable churchmen in medieval Athenian history, Michael Akominatos, who was Greek Orthodox Archbishop of Athens from 1182 until 1205. He was born c. 1140 in north-western Asia Minor, and in his youth he and his younger brother were sent off to study in Constantinople. His brother, who came to be called Nicetas Choniates, became one of the great historians of the Byzantine era, while Michael won renown as a poet, scholar and cleric. But he considered his appointment as Archbishop of Athens to be a personal disaster, for in that provincial town he found himself cut off from his friends and from the rich cultural life he had enjoyed in Constantinople. In one of his letters he describes Athens as 'a God-forsaken hole in a far corner of the empire'. And in another he complains to a friend that 'I have become a barbarian myself since I have been a resident in Athens. The inhabitants are an uncivilized horde who have rejected the search for wisdom. Three years it has taken me to learn their dialect . . .'

Michael's letters and other writings constitute the only surviving description of Byzantine Athens, the first account of life in the city since late antiquity. The brief Athenian renaissance after the Dark Ages was over by the time that Michael ended his tenure as archbishop, for the Byzantine Empire was about to be overrun by the Latins, who conquered Constantinople in 1204. Athens fell to the Latins the following year, and Michael was forced to flee to the Aegean isle of Kea, where he spent the few remaining years of his life in exile, writing to the one or two friends who still survived in Constantinople. In one of his last letters, Michael paints a pathetic picture of what life was like in Athens in the last days of Byzantine rule:

You cannot look upon Athens without tears. Not that the city has lost her ancient glory, it is too long since that was taken from her. Now she has lost the very form, appearance and character of a city. Everywhere you see walls stripped and demolished, houses razed to the ground, their sites ploughed under. Time and its dread ally, envy, have dealt with Athens more barbarously than ever the Persians did. Try your utmost, you will not find a trace of the Heliaia, the Peripatos or the Lyceum, and sheep graze on the meagre relics of the Stoa Poikile . . . Now in Athens there are neither philosophers nor workmen, only women and children, and ill-clad and either naked or in rags. The dying pity those who remain alive.

Although Byzantine rule in Athens ended in 1205, the rich cultural heritage of Byzantium and the deep religious roots of the Greek Orthodox Church sustained the city throughout the more than six centuries of Latin and Turkish occupation. During those centuries the Athenians continued to build churches and monasteries in their city and the surrounding countryside, and these institutions kept alive the spark of Hellenic culture that would be rekindled with the beginning of the Greek War of Independence in 1821. We will visit a number of these later churches in our stroll through Byzantine Athens, for they are elements in the same cultural tradition that created the sanctuaries of the medieval city.

We will begin this stroll in Syntagma Square, from where we will walk along Leoforos Amalias and then turn left on Leoforos Vasilissis Olgas. We then turn right on Leoforos Arditou, and after passing the National Sports Grounds we see below us on the right an archaeological site, the first stop on our stroll.

The overgrown ruins that we see here have been identified as the foundations of a large Christian basilica with an adjoining subterranean tomb, all of which were unearthed in 1917. The foundations are believed to be those of a church founded in the first half of the fifth century AD, while the tomb is dated two centuries earlier. The identification of these ruins is based largely on the testimony of Michael Akominatos, who in one of his letters makes mention of a church and martyrium in this area dedicated to the Corinth Martyrs. Here he is referring to St Leonides, Bishop of Athens, who was martyred in Corinth during the reign of Decius (249–51), along with seven women of his congregation. According to tradition, the church of St Leonides was founded by the Empress Eudocia, wife of Theodosius II. If this is so, and the archaeological evidence supports the tradition, then we have here the oldest surviving remains of a Christian church in Athens. This was a basilica 56 m long and 22 m wide, with an apse in the centre of the east wall and a narthex to the west. Fragments of the mosaic pavement were discovered during the 1917 excavations and are now on exhibit in the Byzantine Museum. The martyrium was attached to the left aisle of the basilica, from which a stone staircase descended into the tomb, a square subterranean chamber covered with a dome and four pendentives. Three graves were discovered within the tomb, and presumably one of these is the last resting-place of St Leonides.

We now cross Leoforos Arditou to look at the fragmentary remains of an ancient structure on the other side of the avenue. The ruins are at the corner of Arditou and Odos D. Koutoula, a short lane running uphill from the avenue just before the traffic lights. There is not much to be seen here, just some cuttings in the bedrock and a few poros blocks protruding from under the foundations of modern building. These have been identified as the remains of the sanctuary of Artemis Agrotera, a small and very beautiful Ionic temple that once stood here on the banks of the Ilissos. This shrine of Artemis took its name from the fact that it was in the district of Agra, which comprised the area on the banks of the Ilissos near the ford by the Kallirhoë spring.

The Temple of Artemis Agrotera is thought to have been built in 448 BC by Kallikrates, the architect of the Temple of Athena Nike on

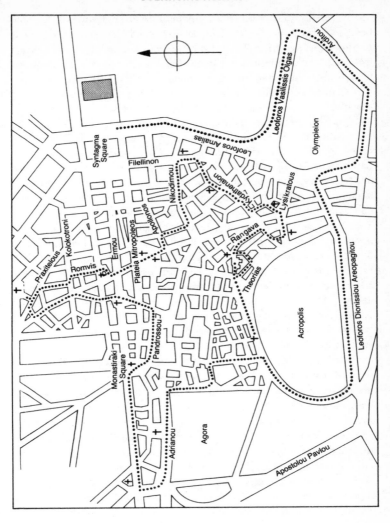

Byzantine Athens

the Acropolis. The sanctuary of Artemis Agrotera appears to have been the prototype for the Temple of Athena Nike, which was built to the same design, differing only in minor details. It was a small (6.1 × 12.8 m) amphiprostyle temple of Pentelic marble standing on a three-stepped crepidoma. The temple was converted into a Christian chapel in the mid fifth century, probably at about the same time that the church of St Leonides was being constructed on the opposite bank of the Ilissos. The church was known as the Panayia stin Petra, the Blessed Virgin on the Rock, taking its name from the rocky spur on which it stood. In 1684, three years before the Venetian occupation of Athens, the church was taken over by the Latins and converted into a Roman Catholic chapel. After the Venetians departed in 1688, the Greeks never reconsecrated the church, and consequently it fell into ruins. The structure was still standing when Stuart and Revett were studying the antiquities of Athens in 1751–3, and the drawing of the church in their book has enabled historians of architecture to determine its plan. Then in 1788 it was dismantled on the orders of Hadji Ali Haseki, who used its stones in building the Serpentzes. In earlier times this temple was sometimes identified as the Metroon in Agrai, a sanctuary of the Mother of the Gods where the Lesser Eleusinian Mysteries were celebrated, but that vanished structure is now believed to have stood on the opposite bank of the Ilissos.

All of the other churches that we will see on this stroll are in or near Monastiraki and Plaka. So we now make our way back along the busy avenues that bound the Olympieion to the south and west, bringing us to the intersection of three avenues, Syngrou, Amalias and Dionissiou Areopagitou. We turn left on to the latter and walk past the south slope of the Acropolis, turning in along the road that leads to the open area below the Areopagus. There we follow the course of the ancient Peripatos around the Acropolis as far as the first stairway going down into Plaka. This leads us down into the maze of streets bordering the eastern side of the Agora archaeological site. We make our way along these streets until we come to Odos Adrianou, which brings us along the northern side of the archaeological site to the main entrance of the Agora. We might pause there for a moment to look back towards the south-eastern entrance of the archaeological site. There we see the church of the Holy Apostles, one of the finest of all the surviving Byzantine churches in the city, which we visited on our tour of the Agora.

Directly opposite the main entrance to the Agora we come to the church of St Philip. The original date of foundation of this church is uncertain. One authority has suggested that the first church on this site was erected in the eleventh century, but there is no evidence to support this, and historians of architecture date the founding of St Philip to some time in the Turkish period. In any event, the church was in ruins at the end of the Greek War of Independence, and it was completely rebuilt from the foundations upwards in 1866. The nineteenth-century church was built to the same plan as its predecessor, a basilica with a central nave separated from a pair of side aisles by two rows of four columns each. The structure and decoration are completely modern and have no architectural or artistic interest.

The Athenians believe that this church was founded by St Philip the Apostle, but this legend is almost certainly apocryphal. According to the legend, before this church was built St Philip used to give his sermons here, and when he did so he was always heckled by the secretary to the Jewish High Priest of Jerusalem. One day the saint finally lost his temper, and by a miracle caused the earth to open up and swallow his tormentor, who was never heard from again. After St Philip left Athens the Athenians built this church in memory of him, or so the legend goes.

After leaving the church, we return to Odos Adrianou, where we turn right and continue along the street as far as the square around the Thesion railway station. There we turn right and cross the square diagonally to turn up Odos Asomaton. In doing so we see off to the left the Hephaisteion, which through much of the Byzantine, Latin and Turkish periods served as the church of St George. The Jesuit priest Babin, writing in 1672, makes an interesting observation about this and the other Christian churches in Athens at the time, which were remarkably numerous; as he writes, referring to the Hephaisteion:

The Christians turned it into a church and dedicated it to Aghios George. They assured me, however, that though the Turks refused to use this temple, for it was far from the centre of their city and their homes, they also prevented Christians from performing their worship in such a magnificent church. Its iron doors never open, except on Aghios George's day 'by means of a silver key' which Greeks may offer to the Turks in return for their permission. A lot of people confirm that about three hundred churches are preserved in Athens and its vicinity at about a distance of a league. I would not believe it, if I myself were not astonished at the great number of small churches, some of which are made of marble . . .

At the next corner we cross Odos Ermou and walk over to the handsome Byzantine structure we saw on our earlier stroll this way. This is the church of Ay. Asomatoi, dedicated to the Incorporeal Saints, or Angels.

The church of the Asomatoi has been dated to the second half of the eleventh century. The structure was clumsily rebuilt in 1880, but an excellent restoration that began in 1959 cleared away the modern accretions and returned the church to its original condition. The plan is a Greek cross inscribed in a square, with a hexagonal dome supported internally by four columns; there is a shallow narthex to the west, and to the east the nave ends in an apse with smaller apses on either side. The decorative stonework on the exterior is similar to that which we have seen before in the church of the Holy Apostles, as is the design of the windows in the dome and in the arms of the Greek cross. These are all typical design features in Athenian churches of the eleventh century. The fragmentary frescos on the wall were uncovered during the restoration of the church; these have been tentatively dated to the seventeenth century. To the left of the entrance to the nave there is an oil-painting depicting the removal of Christ from the Cross; the parishioners say that this is a work of El Greco, but art historians say that it is not.

After leaving the church we turn left on Ermou and walk on to Monastiraki Square. There we cross the square to visit the church of the Panayia Pandanassa, known to Athenians as Monastiraki, or the Little Monastery. Local tradition traces the church back to the tenth century, but there is no evidence to support this. According to Liza Micheli, in her excellent book *Monastiraki*, the earliest reference to the church is in a document bearing the seal of the Patriarch Dionysios and dated 1678; this records that the founder of the convent attached to the church was one Nicholaos Bonefadzis, who established it under the aegis of the monastery at Kaisariani, on Hymettos. A marginal note in the document adds the following statement: ' ... As concerning the affairs of the Monastery of Our Lady at Kaisariani and its subsidiary house, of that called the Great Monastery of the All-Holy Mother of God and Mistress of the Universe, the Pandanassa ... May this holy Monastery of Kaisariani, together with its dependency, the Pandanassa, in accordance with its ancient privileges exist until the end of time.'

The nuns at the Pandanassa convent cared for the poor of Athens, who earned their keep by weaving; Micheli quotes the Athenian chronicler Panighis Skouzes:

In the other cells lived poor people, homeless and destitute. They went there to live permanently, and the people of the parish employed them, the men and women both, in house and farm work, and that way they were able to make a living. The lady-parishioners took the women on as day-servants to do errands and to do other jobs like spinning and weaving cotton. Every woman of the parish who needed temporary service at home and out of doors would hire these poor women to spin thread, work at silk-making, weave clothes and do every kind of labour, such as in the season of the olive harvest, picking olives, carrying ladders, and other light work outside, picking grapes, etc. And so they made a living, the poor who had no property and the homeless old, so that none of them had to go out and beg.

The church as we see it today is the product of a heavy and tasteless rebuilding in 1911, when the present bell-tower was erected. In plan the church is a basilica, with the barrel-vaulted nave separated from the two cross-vaulted side aisles by two rows of four columns each. Unfortunately, the modern rebuilding destroyed whatever architectural interest the church might once have possessed. The monastery of the Pandanassa was also demolished at that time, though its name is perpetuated in that of the market quarter around the church.

After leaving the church we walk to the south-eastern corner of the square and then turn left on to Odos Pandrossou, passing on our right the Tzisdarakis mosque. We continue along Pandrossou as far as Odos Kapnikareas, where we turn left and walk for two blocks to Odos Ermou. At the intersection there we come to the Kapnikarea, one of the most interesting churches that has survived from Byzantine Athens.

The origin of the name Kapnikarea is uncertain, and no satisfactory derivation has been given for it; in any event, it is dedicated to the Panayia Theotokos, the Virgin Mother of God. It has been dated to the eleventh century, for its architecture and decorative brickwork are typical of Athenian churches of that period. As originally constructed, the plan of the church was cruciform, with the octagonal dome supported internally by four columns surmounted with Roman capitals; there is a three-bayed apse to the west, and to the east a central apse terminating the nave and smaller apses on either side. Later, a chapel dedicated to St Barbara was added on the north, extending along the full length of the building on that side, with its central bay covered by a dome that rises to the height of the base of the main dome beside it. Later still an exonarthex was added on the west side, extending along the width of the church and the side chapel; this consists of four large bays separated by columns framing wide arched openings, the central pair of which are double, and covered by a series of gabled roofs. At the south end of the exonarthex, where the modern entrance is located, there is a small porch supported by a pair of arches and a high circular arch of Moorish aspect, above which there is a modern mosaic. From there we pass into the exonarthex, in the western wall of which there have been set some inscriptions and fragments of ancient sculpture. Then we pass through the narthex into the nave, the interior decoration of which is entirely modern but none the less effective. The frescos are by Alekos Kontoglu (1898–1965), a modern Greek painter who was the leading spirit in a return to Byzantine motifs and styles.

After leaving the church, we cross the street and head north on Odos Kalamiotou. At the intersection with Kolokotroni we bear slightly to the left on Odos Ay. Markou, continuing on that street for two blocks until we come to Odos Chrysospiliotissa. We turn right here, then right again at the next corner on to Praxitelous, after which we take the first left on to Skouleniou. This brings us to an impressive old church standing in the middle of a crossroads at the south-west corner of Plateia Klafthmonos; this is Ay. Theodoroi, another of the renowned Byzantine sanctuaries of Athens.

The church of Ay. Theodoroi has been dated to the mid eleventh century, and its plan and decoration are typical of the Athenian churches of that period. It is a cruciform structure, with a three-bayed narthex to the west and to the east a large central apse flanked by smaller apsidal recesses on either side. But here the high octagonal dome is supported internally by longitudinal walls rather than four pillars, as in the other churches of that time that we have seen; these transverse walls enclose the central arm of the cross and open up through high circular arches into the side arms. The entrance is through an arched doorway in the centre of the narthex, with the modern bell-tower above. Above the entrance there is an inscription giving a date; when this is computed according to the Byzantine chronological system it translates to AD 1049, but the alternative Alexandrian system used in some cases gives AD 1065, and architectural historians now lean towards the latter date. Another and longer inscription above the entrance records a repair or restoration by a Nicholas Kalomalos, who is identified as a Spatharocanditos, a high-ranking officer in the Byzantine imperial court in Constantinople.

After leaving the church, we retrace our steps along Skouleniou and turn left on Praxitelous. Then we turn right on Leocharous, left on Kolokotroni and right on Romvis. We continue past the next intersection on to Ktena, which curves sharply left round the back of a church, ending at Odos Evangelistrias. Finally we turn right and enter the church, the Panayia Romvis.

Virtually nothing is known about the history of this fine old church, although local tradition has it that it dates to the sixteenth or seventeenth century. This tradition has it that the second name of the church comes from that of its founder, and indeed a family of that name is known to have lived in this neighbourhood during that period. The nave is barrel-vaulted and the roof is supported internally by four columns and two piers, with a five-bayed narthex to the west and an apse to the east. To the north there is a side chapel with two aisles and five bays; this appears to be of later date than the main body of the church.

After leaving the Panayia Romvis we turn left on to Evangelistrias, and at the end of the block we come to the Plateia Mitropoleos. This large square is dominated by the Metropolis, a huge modern church which serves as the cathedral of Athens. We will visit the Metropolis on a later stroll, but now let us walk around to its southern side to look at the ancient church called the Little Metropolis, the most interesting Byzantine structure in Athens.

The church is called the Little Metropolis because in the eighteenth century it stood within the enclosure of the Archbishopric of Athens, and during that time it served as the metropolitan church, that is, the cathedral. The true name of the church is the Panayia Gorgoepikoös, the Virgin Who Grants Requests Quickly. This attribute stems from a miracle-working icon of the Virgin that is the church's most prized possession. The Archbishopric and the Panayia Gorgoepikoös were abandoned during the Greek War of Independence, and the church remained unused for two decades. Then in 1841 it was converted into a library, a function that it continued to serve until 1868, when it was reconsecrated as a Christian sanctuary. At that time it was dedicated to Christ the Saviour, but after a few years that name fell out of use and it came to be called the church of Ay. Eleutherios. However, architectural historians continue to refer to it by its original name, the Panayia Gorgoepikoös. The church was restored in 1856 (and again more recently), when the modern bell-tower and all later accretions were removed, so that the structure we see today is in essentially its original state.

Most authorities date the church to the twelfth or thirteenth century, although some authorities and local tradition attribute its founding to the Empress Irene, who was born in Athens and ruled the Byzantine Empire in her own right during the years 797–802. But this tradition can probably be discounted, for Irene is credited with founding several of the Byzantine churches of Athens, and in no case is there any evidence to substantiate the claim. In any event, there is definite evidence that there was an earlier church on this site, a structure that has been dated to *c.* 600, for many of its stones have been built into the present structure. In fact, the walls of the Panayia Gorgoepikoös are constructed entirely of ancient marble blocks, many of which are decorated with interesting inscriptions and reliefs. These reliefs are the most fascinating aspect of the church, for they make it a veritable museum of decorative stonework, dating from the classical period up through the medieval Byzantine and Latin eras.

The church is quite small, just 7.6 m long and 12.2 m wide, and its plan is very simple. It is cruciform, and its high octagonal dome was originally supported internally by four columns, replaced in the nineteenth-century restoration by piers. It has the usual narthex at the west end, and at the east a large central apse flanked by two smaller ones, with two side apsidal areas separated from the central area by a pair of piers, thus creating side chapels. The main entrance to the church is at the centre of the narthex, where the marble door-frame is believed to be part of the earlier church on this site; besides this there are somewhat smaller doors of similar design at the side arms of the cross. The church was originally decorated throughout with frescos, but only one of these has survived; this is the figure of the Virgin in the apse, which has been dated to the thirteenth or fourteenth century.

Let us now look at the outside of the church, to examine some of the very interesting reliefs with which it is decorated. One of the most intriguing of these is on the west side above the arch of the entrance, where we see a pair of slabs framed by Roman *anta* capitals. These are decorated with reliefs depicting the Attic calendar of festivals, in which each month is personified by figures carrying out the activities of that time of year and celebrating its holidays, with the signs of the zodiac also shown. The scene representing the month Hecatombaion is extremely important, for this was the time of year in which the Panathenaic festival was held. (This was the first month of the Attic year, beginning with the new moon before the summer solstice.) The relief shows the Panathenaic ship, on whose mast the sacred *peplos* was draped; this is the only extant depiction of this renowned vessel, but, unfortunately, it has been largely obliterated by two Maltese crosses added in the Latin period.

There is another unusual relief on the north wall of the church, on the left side under the cornice. There we see the naked figure of a bearded man with wild hair standing between two crosses. It is evident that the figure is part of an ancient relief, the rest of which has been erased and replaced by the two crosses.

There are also a number of ancient marbles collected around the church. Behind the apse there are inscriptions and a relief with dancing figures; on the north side there are ancient ex-votos; and outside the south wall there is a block of grey marble known as the Stone of Cana; its name deriving from a late inscription stating that it was used at the marriage feast of Cana.

After seeing the Little Metropolis, we cross over to the south-eastern corner of the square and turn right on to Odos Ay. Filotheis. Now we set off on a zigzag route, taking the first left on to Apollonos, then the first right on to Thoukididou, and then the first left on to Navarchou Nikodimou, which we follow until we come to Odos Filellinon. There we cross the street and walk a few steps to the right to Ay. Nikodemos, another of the Byzantine churches of Athens.

Inscriptions on the walls of the church, the earliest of which date to 1031, indicate that it was built in the first half of the eleventh century. The original name of the church was the Soteira (Saviour) Lycodimou, and it served as the chapel of a large convent. The convent was destroyed in 1778 by Hadji Ali Haseki, who used its stones in the construction of the Serpentzes. The church was severely damaged in 1827, when it was struck by shells fired by Turkish cannon on the Acropolis. After the War of Independence it was abandoned and left in ruins, but then in 1847 Tsar Nicholas I expressed an interest in acquiring the church to serve the Russian community in Athens. The Greek government sold the church to the tsar on the condition that it be rebuilt according to the original plan. The reconstruction was carried out in the years 1850–55, but the architect did not rebuild it entirely to the original design, and consequently it has a somewhat different appearance from the other Byzantine churches of that period in Athens. The church is cruciform in plan, with a dome carried on a circular drum supported internally by eight piers, two spur walls and the walls framing the extremely high apse. The bell-tower, which is separate from the church, is an entirely modern construction, dating from the restoration of 1850–55.

There is an ancient marble throne beside the outer door of the church. This originally stood in the Theatre of Dionysos, and it was probably brought here to serve as the abbot's throne when the church and convent were first built. There is also an inscribed marble block near the door. This has been dated to the first century BC and has been identified as part of the Lyceum, the famous gymnasium which is known to have been located near by. This stone was discovered in 1961 when excavations were carried out beneath the church. These excavations revealed the remains of a Roman bath of the second century AD, which is thought to have been part of the Lyceum. There was also evidence that a church was constructed on this site early in the Christian era. It has been suggested that the original second name of the church, Lycodimou, may have been passed on to it by its predecessor, which was so called because it was built within the enclosure of the ancient Lyceum.

Ay. Nikodemos is still used by the Russian community of Athens. This dwindling congregation turns out *en masse* for the service on the eve of Orthodox Easter, when the old church is a wonderful sight to see, thronged with parishioners singing the resonant Russian Orthodox liturgy and the beautiful Easter hymns, and then passing in procession three times around the courtyard at midnight, when the shout goes up all over Athens that Christ has risen.

After leaving Ay. Nikodemos we cross the street and turn left, turning right at the next corner on to Odos Kydathenaion, entering Plaka. We walk along Kydathenaion for two blocks until we see on our right the church of Soteira tou Kottaki, which has in front of it a very pretty garden. This church was built in the eleventh or twelfth century, although local tradition holds that the original Christian sanctuary on this site was founded in the sixth century. In any event, the present church was completely rebuilt and considerably enlarged in 1908, so that for the most part it does not look like a typical Byzantine structure. The original church, which now forms the eastern end of the structure, was the usual cross-in-a-square, with the dome resting on an octagonal drum supported internally by four columns. The modern structure that has been added to this consists of a very long nave from which four barrel-vaulted chambers open off to form the side aisles, with a narthex at the western end.

When leaving the church notice the marble column lying in the courtyard; it is almost certainly from an ancient structure that stood on this site before the church was erected, but there is no evidence to support this. Notice also the little fountain in the garden; in late Turkish times and on into the early days of the Greek Kingdom this was the principal source of water for the quarter around the church, which is one of the older parts of Plaka.

We now continue on along Kydathenaion in the same direction. At the second intersection we come to the Plateia Etaireias, where there is a pleasant park with several cafés around it. At the near end of the park there is a monument honouring Dimitrios Kambouroglu, a distinguished scholar who devoted his life to a study of nineteenth-century Athens and its Ottoman past. Returning to the corner of Kydathenaion, notice the stump of an ancient column embedded in the pavement. There is a similar stump embedded at the next corner, where Kydathenaion intersects Odos Farmaki. Both columns are undoutedly from an ancient structure that once stood on the site of the park, but there is no evidence as to its date or identity.

We now turn left off Kydathenaion on to Farmaki, after which we turn right at the next corner on to Chairophontos. This brings us to the church of Ay. Aikaterini (St Catherine), which stands at the end of another pretty garden. This structure has been dated by archaeologists to the late eleventh or early twelfth century, although there is evidence that it is built on the site of an earlier church, which was itself erected on the ruins of an ancient building. The present church was originally dedicated to St Theodore and served as the chapel for an adjacent monastery of that name. The church and monastery of St Theodore are mentioned in a document dated 1219; this is in a letter to Berard, the Latin successor to Michael Akominatos as Archbishop of Athens, confirming his right to a score of churches and monasteries in Athens and its environs, including St Theodore. The monastery was destroyed at some time early in the Turkish period, after which the church was abandoned for a time and fell partly into ruins. Then in 1769 the church was acquired by the Monastery of St Catherine on Mount Sinai, at which time it was restored and dedicated to Ay. Aikaterini. The church was rebuilt and enlarged in 1927, so that only the dome and the central apse remain from the original structure. The church is cruciform in plan, with the dome resting on a very high octagonal drum which is supported internally by four columns, with the usual narthex to the west and to the east a large central apse flanked by smaller apses on either side. Ay. Aikaterini is one of the most popular churches in Athens, and its spacious courtyard and pretty garden make it a favourite for weddings and baptisms.

Let us now walk along Chairophontos, pausing at the far end of the garden to look down at a smaller archaeological site in the trench beside the street. The identity and date of the ancient structure of which they were a part is not known, but it is thought that they were reused in the construction of the earlier church on this site, which has been dated tentatively to the sixth century.

We now turn right from Chairophontos on to Odos Lysicratous; in a few steps this takes us to the square of the same name, where we see once again the Monument of Lysicrates. We walk through the park and start up the stepped street at its upper corner, Odos Epimenidou, one of the most picturesque byways in Athens. A short way up the street we come on our left to the little chapel of Ay. Dimitrios tou Paraklissi. The façade of the church is totally modern and from outside the structure appears to be of no interest, but when we make our way inside we find ourselves in what is quite evidently a very old sanctuary. Ay. Dimitrios is given only passing mention in works on the old churches of Athens, and it is usually dated to the Turkish period. But there is a local tradition that the church was founded by a Byzantine princess, a sister of the Emperor Nicephorus Phocas, who ruled in the years 963–9.

We continue up Epimenidou for a few steps and then turn right at the next corner, which brings us on to a picturesque lane unidentified by a street sign. At the end of the lane we bear right on Odos Thespidos and then take the second left on to Odos Rangava. At the top of the street we turn left and then right, walking along the lower side of a little park near the base of the Acropolis. At the far corner of the park we turn right and then left on to Odos Pritaniou, which brings us to the large church of Ay. Nicholaos tou Rangavas, one of the landmarks in this part of Plaka.

The core of the present church, which was rebuilt and expanded earlier in the present century, has been dated to the eleventh and twelfth century. The original church had the usual Athenian cruciform plan, but in the modern reconstruction the nave was extended to the west, doubling its length, and a side chapel dedicated to Ay. Paraskevis was constructed along the full length of the north side of the church. Local tradition holds that the original church on this site was founded by Prince Theophylact, son of the Byzantine Emperor Michael I Rhangave, who ruled in the years 811–13. Theophylact was the heir apparent, and in 812 he was wedded to Adelinda, a bastard daughter of Charlemagne, a dynastic marriage that was arranged to strengthen ties between Byzantium and the new empire that was developing in western Europe. But in 813 Michael I was deposed when Leo V, the Armenian, usurped the throne of Byzantium. The royal family was sent off into exile and in addition Theophylact was castrated, so as to disqualify him as a possible future contender for the throne. He then became a monk and apparently retired to a monastery in Athens, at which time, according to the local tradition, he founded this church. The church has recently been restored, and it now looks much more like a Byzantine structure than it did in times past, with its beautiful brickwork exposed to view.

We now continue along Pritaniou, which soon devolves into Odos Theorias, the lane that runs along the northern slope of the Acropolis above Plaka. After a short walk we come to a small Byzantine chapel standing on the left against the bedrock of the Acropolis. This is the church of the Metamorphosis tou Soteros, the Transfiguration of the Saviour. This little chapel has been dated to the late fourteenth century, when Athens was ruled by the Latin dynasty of the Acciajuoli. The plan is a slight variant on the usual one, in that the south aisle of the church opens into a side chapel, at the back of which there is a grotto hollowed out of the Acropolis. This chapel is dedicated to Ay. Paraskevis, and tradition has it that this is where the saint spent her latter years as a recluse and where she was buried. Another tradition holds that this is also the tomb of Odysseus Androutsos, who commanded the Greek troops on the Acropolis when it was besieged by the Turks in 1827. One night shortly before the garrison surrendered, Androutsos was murdered by some of his own men, who flung his corpse from the northern wall. The next morning his body was found on the rocks near the church by some local Greeks, and they secretly buried Androutsos in the chapel of Ay. Paraskevis so that the Turks would not learn that he was dead.

We now retrace our steps back along Theorias and Pritaniou until we come to Odos Erechtheos, a steep street of steps which we descend as far as the first crossing. At the near corner on the right we find another of the Byzantine churches of Athens, Ay. Ioannis Theologus, St John the Theologian. Virtually nothing is known of the history of this little chapel, but from its architectural plan and the style of its typically Byzantine brickwork it would appear to date from the eleventh or twelfth century. The design is a very slight variation of the usual one for Byzantine churches of that period in Athens, in that the dome is supported internally by two piers and two columns, rather than the usual four columns. The two columns, which stand to the west of the piers, are capped by unusual columns, which may have been taken from an ancient structure and reworked.

The setting of Ay. Ioannis is very evocative, for it stands on a charming little square that is probably as old as the city itself, with the north cliff of the Acropolis towering above the picturesque old houses that cluster around the chapel. Two venerable tavernas share the square with the church, and in good weather their tables are set out on the square itself and on the first few broad steps of Odos Erechtheos. Our own favourite is the Palaia Athena, 'Old Athens', which is located on the corner directly opposite the church. This taverna has been run by the same family for more than a century, and it is frequented by people who live or work in this part of Plaka. Ay. Ioannis is still used by old residents of Plaka, particularly on the saint's feast-day, and after services in the church many of them go on to dine in Paleia Athena, bringing with them their lighted candles and the lingering smell of burning incense. And so in this way the modern city still retains its connections with Byzantine Athens, which lives on in ancient churches like Ay. Ioannis Theologus.

10

Plaka

Several of our strolls have taken us through some of the narrow, winding streets of Plaka, the picturesque 'Old Athens' that lies below the north cliff of the Acropolis. The present stroll will take us on a more extensive tour of this part of town, particularly to see the monuments that have survived from the early days of the Greek Kingdom, as well as a few from Turkish Athens.

Starting out from Syntagma Square, we follow Leoforos Amalias as far as Odos Nikis. There we come to the Anglican church of St Paul, the first stop on our tour, though it lies somewhat outside the bounds of Plaka.

St Paul's has been the principal church of the Protestant community in Athens since the early years of the Greek Kingdom. The original plans for the church, a neo-Gothic structure, were completed in 1838 by the English architect C. R. Cockerell. But before construction began, Christian Hansen was put in charge of the project and altered the design somewhat. The cornerstone was laid on 16 April 1838, Easter Sunday in the Western calendar, and it was dedicated on Palm Sunday in 1843 by Dr Tomlinson, Bishop of Gibraltar. The first minister was the Revd John Hill, pastor of the American Episcopal church in Athens.

The stained-glass composition in the east window of St Paul's commemorates the victims of the so-called 'Dilessi murders'. These were three Englishmen and a Frenchman who were killed in April 1870 after being kidnapped by brigands on their way back from Marathon to Athens. The north and south windows were dedicated to the memory of Sir Richard Church, a former British officer who in 1827 was appointed to command the Greek forces then fighting for their independence from the Turks. After the war was over Church became a Greek citizen and was appointed to high positions in the new government. He lived on in Athens until his death in 1873, and his funeral service in St Paul's was attended by George I, King of the Hellenes, and a crowd that included a number of Greek veterans who had fought under Church's command in the War of Independence. A brass tablet on the wall of the nave records a tribute to Church by Gladstone.

On the wall of the north transept there is a tablet honouring another Philhellene, perhaps the most valiant of them all. This is Frank Watney Hastings, a former British officer who commanded a squadron of the Greek navy in several important victories over the Turks. He destroyed a Turkish fleet in the Bay of Salona in 1827, was wounded near Mesolongi in the spring of 1828, and died of his wounds on the island of Zante on 1 June of that year. He was buried on Zante, but his heart was first removed and placed in a small casket, which was later immured in St Paul's, just behind the brass tablet honouring his memory.

To the left of the entrance there is a funerary inscription that once marked a tomb in the Hephaisteion. This is a memorial to three British sailors, George Stokes, Thomas Roberts and Captain William Fearn, who died in 1685 while their ship was anchored in Porte Leone, the name by which the Piraeus was known during the Latin and Turkish periods.

There are two more memorials in the transept. On the right there is a tablet honouring Henry Wodehouse, a Philhellene of a later period, who died fighting with the Greek forces against the Turks in Epirus in 1897. On the left there is a plaque commemorating four members of the Leeves family, English residents of Euboea, two of whom were murdered by a group of their Greek neighbours on 28 August 1854 in a dispute over title to their land. Those villagers who had been directly involved in the murders were executed the following year by the guillotine, one of the many Western innovations that the Greeks put to use when they became a modern European nation.

After leaving St Paul's we cross Filellinon to walk up Odos Nikis. We take the first left on to Kydathenaion and a block later on we pass on our right the church of Soteira tou Kottaki, which we visited on our last stroll. A short way past the church and on our left we come to No. 17 Kydathenaion, which houses the Museum of Greek Popular Art. The museum has an extremely interesting collection of the local folk arts and crafts that have now all but vanished in modern Greece, and it has a particularly rich collection of the native costumes that were worn on the Greek islands and mountainous areas on the

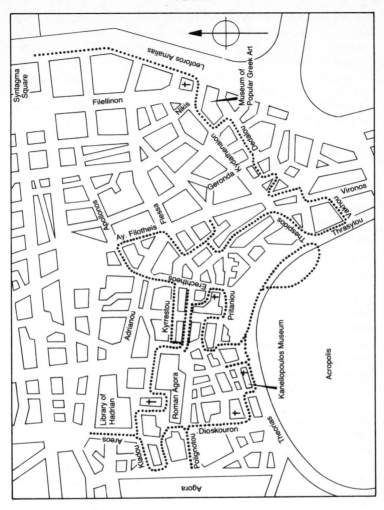

Plaka

mainland up until quite recent times, and even in a few rare cases still today. The museum also has one room whose walls are entirely covered with paintings by the primitive Greek artist Theophilus Hadzimichail (1870–1934) of Mytilene.

We continue along Kydathenaion as far as the next corner, where we turn left on to Monis Asteriou. We follow this street for one block and turn right at the next corner on to Odos Dedalou and then right again on to Odos Angelou Geronda, which brings us out on to a corner of Plateia Etaireias. At our left, at No. 1 on the street that runs along that side of the square, a particularly handsome neo-classical house of the early Greek Kingdom has recently been restored, giving one an idea of how elegant the Athens of King Otho's time must have been.

We turn left and walk to the next corner, where we turn left again on to Odos Farmaki, passing an old-fashioned *kafenion*, or coffee-house. At the next corner, where we see the church of Ay. Aikaterini just ahead, we turn right on to Odos Aphroditis, where there is a fine Othonian house at No. 11 and two others, unnumbered, farther along the quiet street.

At the end of the street we turn left on to Adrianou and then right for a few steps on Lysikratous. There we turn left on Vironos and then right on Vakhou, a picturesque lane lined with simple whitewashed stone houses and walled gardens. The street takes its name from the Taverna Vakhou, or Bacchus, which occupies the buildings that flank the lane at its far end. Vakhou is one of the oldest and most famous tavernas in Athens, though in recent years tourists have far outnumbered locals among its clientele, and so Greeks on an evening out tend to go to a much simpler place at the other end of the street, the Taverna Theophilus.

At the end of Odos Vakhou we turn right on Thrasylou, the lane that borders the archaeological zone at the foot of the Acropolis. After passing Odos Epimenidou on our right we immediately bear right on to Thespidos, and at the second intersection we turn left on to Tripodon. Then we turn right at the first intersection on to a short and narrow lane that in a few steps brings us on to Odos Scholeiou, where we turn right again and walk a few steps more to where the street bends and becomes Odos Hill. This little street, which leads down to Adrianou, is named for John Henry Hill, an American missionary who lived in Athens from 1830 until his death in 1883. Hill and his wife Frances devoted their lives to setting up schools for the education of poor Athenian children. One of their institutions, the Hill School, which is located at the intersection of Thoukididou and Nikodimou, is still functioning today.

At the corner of Hill and Scholeiou there is an old tower-like house, now empty and in poor repair, which once belonged to George Finlay (1799–1875), the distinguished historian and Philhellene. Finlay, who fought with the Greek partisans under Androutsos and who was with Byron at Mesolongi, moved into this house with his wife soon after the War of Independence. During the half-century that Finlay lived here, he devoted himself to writing a multi-volumed history of Greece from Roman times up through the Byzantine, Latin and Turkish eras and concluding at the War of Independence. He then followed this with an enormous tome on the War of Independence itself, one that is still the definitive work on the subject.

At the end of Scholeiou we turn right on to Flessa, continuing as far as Adrianou. At the corner on the left we see the Demotic School, a small neo-classical building erected in 1875.

We now cross Adrianou and bear left on Odos Ay. Filotheis, a street lined with shops selling icons and other religious merchandise. These shops are concentrated here because the Archbishopric of Athens is midway down the street on the right-hand side. Alongside the main building of the Archbishopric we see the church of Ay. Andreas, a modern building constructed from white Pentelic marble. The other structures of the Archbishopric date from the end of the nineteenth century. They replaced the residence erected when the Archbishop of Athens moved here in the last decade of the seventeenth century, after the abandonment of the church of St Dionysius the Areopagite under the Areopagus Hill. During those two centuries the Archbishopric was inside a walled enclosure as long as the present Odos Ay. Filotheis and as wide as the two blocks on either side of it, with the church of the Panayia Gorgoepikoös standing just inside its northern wall.

During Ottoman times the Archbishop of Athens ruled like a despot over his clergy and had considerable power over the other Greeks in Athens. John Cam Hobhouse writes of the situation at the Archbishopric in 1810, when he and Byron were visiting Athens:

The Archbishop of Athens exercises an absolute authority over the whole of the clergy of his see, and has a prison near his house for the confinement of offenders, whom he may punish with the bastinade, or in any degree short of death. His place is purchased by the Patriarch, and is consequently the object of many intrigues, which not infrequently terminate in the expulsion of the incumbent, and the election of another archbishop. Popular clamour has also sometimes displaced such of those priests as have exceeded the usual bounds of extortion.

The present church of Ay. Andreas is built on the site of an earlier church of the same name. This church was founded in the mid sixteenth century by a nun now venerated as Ay. Filothei, after whom this street and the Athenian district of Filotheia are named. Filothei was born in 1522 to one of the most distinguished families in Athens during the Ottoman period. Her father was Angelos Benizelos, a member of one of the so-called 'archontic' families, those who could trace their lineage back to the aristocracy of Byzantine times, with the added distinction that the Benizeloi could also claim descent from the Latin nobility. Her mother was of an even more distinguished lineage, for she was a Palaeologina, a descendant of the Palaeologus dynasty, who ruled the Byzantine Empire during the last two centuries of its existence. Filothei became a nun when she was still in her teens. Later she founded her own convent on the site of the present Archbishopric, dedicating it and its chapel to Ay. Andreas. She was the greatest philanthropist of her day, supporting all the charities of Athens, and in the precincts of her convent she also built a guest house, a hospital and a workhouse that provided employment for two hundred young nuns in weaving and knitting garments that were provided free to the poor of the city. She apparently received little help or appreciation from the well-to-do Athenians of her time, whom she refers to contemptuously as 'a people without religion, decision or shame, wicked and reckless, with mouths open for insults and reproaches, grumbling, barbarous-tongued, loving strife and trouble and gossip, petty, loquacious, arrogant, lawless, crafty, inquisitive and eager to profit from the mistakes of others'. Ay. Filothei is venerated in the Greek Orthodox Church as a martyr-saint, for she was beheaded by the Turks in 1589, probably because she was too outspoken for them.

We continue along Odos Ay. Filotheis until it meets Apollonos; there we turn left and walk along until we turn into Odos Venizelou, which after a few steps brings us back to Adrianou once again. Almost directly across the street here, at No. 96A Adrianou, we see at the back of a walled courtyard one of the very oldest houses in Athens. According to Dimitrios Kambouroglu, this house belonged to the Benizelos family, after whom the street opposite is named, and it dates to the late Ottoman period. It is a private home, and so one must be satisfied with catching a glimpse of it through the courtyard gate on

Adrianou. The ground floor has an arcade facing the courtyard, with a colonnade of five arches supported by columns between the doorposts on either side. An outside staircase of two flights leads to the second storey of the house, where there is a wide balcony, with five windows looking out over the courtyard. This is a fine example of an *archontiki* house, the only one of its type that has survived in Athens, although there are a fair number of them elsewhere in Greece.

We now walk back to the corner of Adrianou and Benizelou and turn left on Erechtheos, which leads up to the north slope of the Acropolis. At the first intersection we see on our left an unidentified archaeological site, with fragments of ancient architectural members scattered about the excavation area. The ruins that we see here have been dated to the classical period, but the name and function of the monument from which they came is not certain. It has been suggested that this is the Diogeneion, the gymnasium where the ephebes of Athens took their training, but there is no definite evidence for this.

Before we go on, let us turn and look at the back wall of the taverna that stands between the archaeological site and Odos Adrianou. In a moment you can see that part of the back wall of the taverna is built of ancient architectural fragments of all types, obviously erected in haste. Thus there is no difficulty in identifying this as a section of the Late Roman fortification wall. The fragment of the Roman wall that is built into the taverna here was precisely at the south-east corner of the circuit, and if you sight along it you can plot the course that the eastern line of fortifications followed up through Plaka to the Acropolis.

Continuing up Erechtheos, we turn right at the next corner on to Kyrrestou, where we are presented with a dramatic view of the Tower of the Winds framed at the end of the street. At the next corner we cross Odos Mnesikleos, and a short way along we see on our left an old wooden building, now abandoned and beginning to fall into ruins. This venerable structure is known locally as 'to hamami', the Turkish bath. This is the hammam of Abid Efendi, which dates from the late Ottoman period, and it is the only Turkish bath that has survived in Athens. This public bath remained in use up until about 1965, and as late as 1979 there was still affixed to the front door a large star and crescent, the emblem of both the old Ottoman Empire and the modern Turkish Republic. But this emblem has since been removed, and it is only a question of time until the hammam itself disappears. The hammam has apparently no architectural interest, but it does evoke memories of Athens under the Turks, when these public baths were an important part of the town's life. As Evliya Chelebi writes in his *Narrative of Travels*, describing Athens as it was in 1638, 'In this town no one has ever seen women, either Muslim or Christian, circulating in the market-place or other streets by day. But after sunset thousands of women come out with lanterns and go about to other houses and the baths to amuse themselves till morning.'

At the end of Kyrrestou we come to Odos Markou Avreliou, the street that runs past the Tower of the Winds and the eastern side of the Roman Agora. Here we will make a short detour uphill to the far corner of the next street on the left, Odos Lysiou. There we find a little whitewashed chapel dedicated to Ay. Spyridon, the patron saint of Corfu. This simple but charming building dates to the sixteenth century, and seems to have been spared the reconstruction that has spoiled so many of the old churches of Athens. It is very nicely decorated inside, and in front of it there is a pretty garden shaded with an ancient grape-vine. One finds such chapels all over rural Greece, particularly on the islands, and at first one has the impression that Ay. Spyridon is out of place in a metropolis like Athens. But then one realizes that when this church was built Athens was in fact little more than a village, clustering under the north slope of the Acropolis just as Plaka does today.

We now walk back down Markou Avreliou, where we might be tempted to stop at Ai Aerides, the outdoor café-restaurant opposite the Tower of the Winds. There could be no better place to sit down and rest for a while before starting the next part of our stroll, which will take us through the Athens of Turkish times.

The area between the Tower of the Winds and Monastiraki Square was the Turkish quarter of Athens during the Ottoman period. The Turkish quarter clustered around the main market of Athens, which was just to the east of the Tower of the Winds. This was Staropazaro, the Wheat Bazaar, whose shops and stalls were set up on the site of the Roman Agora, all of which was covered over with earth except for the Gate of Athena Archegetis, which was known as Pazaroporta, the Bazaar Gate. The Ottoman town hall of Athens, the Voivodalik, was just to the north of Staropazaro, built into the south-western corner of Hadrian's Library. There were half a dozen mosques in this quarter, of which two still remain standing; one of these is the mosque of Tzisdarakis, which we will see later in this stroll, and the other is Fethiye Djami, which we see at the north-west corner of the Roman Agora. There were at least two Turkish baths in the quarter, the Hammam of Abid Efendi, which we passed on Odos Kyrrestou, and the

Hammam of Oula Bey, which stood in the south-west corner of the Roman Agora. In addition there was the dervish *tekke* in the Tower of the Winds, and the Medrese, or Theological School, whose main gateway can still be seen at the lower end of the street that passes Ai Aerides. But this was not an exclusively Turkish area, for the Greek population of the quarter probably exceeded that of the Muslims, Turks and Albanians included, as there are more than a dozen churches in the neighbourhood dating from the Ottoman period. The Archons Demogerontes, or town councillors, also had their meeting-place here, where they administered the local civic affairs of Christian Athens. The meeting-place of the Demogerontia, as their council was called, was in the Kouseyio, or council house, which was also in the market area. And just as there were Greeks living in the Turkish quarter, so were there Turks living among the Greeks in other neighbourhoods of Athens. As Panaghis Skouzes, quoted by Micheli, wrote, 'Although half of the Turkish houses were in one district, the other half were interspersed among the houses of the Christians. Turks and Christians lived peacefully together.' Micheli, in the same spirit, also quotes an early-nineteenth-century Athenian couplet, a nostalgic memory of the vanished world of Turkish Athens: 'The Kouseyio mourns its archons gone, the market-place its agas; likewise the baths of Rodakio, where ladies go no longer.'

Hobhouse's letters from Athens in 1810 describe Plaka and the market quarter through which we are about to stroll, evoking the atmosphere of the Turkish town at a time when the long Ottoman occupation was drawing to a close:

The number of houses in Athens is supposed to be between twelve and thirteen hundred; of which about four hundred are inhabited by the Turks, the remainder by Greeks and Albanians, the latter of whom occupy above three hundred houses. There are also about seven or eight Frank families, under the protection of the French Consul. None of these houses are well-built, nor as commodious as those of the better sort of Greek at Ioannina or Livadia; and the streets are all of them narrow and irregular. In many of the lanes there is a raised causeway on both sides, so broad as to contract the middle of the street into a kind of dirty gutter. The bazaar is at a little distance from the foot of the hill, and is far from well-furnished; but has several coffee-houses, which at all times are crowded by the more lazy of the Turks, amusing themselves with draughts and chess. It is formed by one street, rather wider than usual, intersecting another at right angles; and a little above where the two meet is an ornamental fountain, the principal one in town, supplied by a stream, which is brought in artificial channels or stone gutters from a reservoir under Hymettos.

From Hobhouse's description of the bazaar, it would appear that one of the two streets that bordered the market is the one that now passes Ai Aerides, while the other is the one that borders the north side of the Roman Agora, which would put the ornamental fountain close to the Tower of the Winds. But this monument still awaits discovery.

Let us now leave Ai Aerides and walk down the street to look more closely at the Medrese, which is known to the Greeks as Mendrese. This theological school was founded in 1721 by a pious Turk named Mehmet Fahri, who was an official in the reign of Sultan Ahmet III, the Tulip King. Like most Ottoman *medreses*, it consisted of a series of cells built around the sides of a colonnaded courtyard, with a large domed chamber surmounting the entrance, which was decorated with elaborate floral and geometric reliefs and calligraphic inscriptions. The large domed chamber was the *dershane*, or lecture hall, and an enclosure within it served as the residence of the *hodja*, or teacher. The *dershane* also served as a *mescit*, or small mosque, where the *hodja* and his students said their prayers and attended the noon service on Friday, the Muslim holy day. The smaller cells around the periphery of the courtyard served as living-quarters for the students, with wall shelves for their books, clothes and bedding. Each room had a single window for light and ventilation, and also a fireplace for heat in the winter, with the smoke let out through tall turret-like chimneys. At the two rear corners of the courtyard there were a pair of larger chambers, one of which was the kitchen and the other the latrine. In good weather the *hodja* and his students took their ease in the courtyard, shaded by a plane tree that was at least as old as the school itself, and which in time came to be the symbol of the Medrese. The school seems to have been closed in the latter years of the Ottoman period, for when the War of Independence broke out the Turks were using it as a prison, and Greeks were hanged from the branches of the old plane tree. The Medrese was badly damaged during the two sieges of the Acropolis. Immediately after the war it was repaired by the new Greek government and converted into a prison once again, used for the confinement of political prisoners as well as convicted criminals. The Medrese became infamous for the inhuman conditions under which the prisoners were confined there, particularly since it was in the heart of Athens and the wretches suffering under the plane tree in the courtyard could be seen by passers-by. And those who were condemned to death were hanged from the branches of the old plane tree just as they had been in Turkish times. The prison was finally closed in 1911, and within the next decade the Medrese was demolished except for its ornate

Ottoman entrance, with its calligraphic inscription recording the date of its foundation and the name of its founder, Mehmet Fahri the Honourable. The plane tree of hateful memory was blasted by lightning in 1919, after which its remains were cut down and removed, as the poet Achilleas Paraskhos had foretold in a bitter poem just a few years before, as quoted by Micheli:

O plane tree of the Medrese, O sign and symbol cursed,
O victory of slavery, grown high inside the prison,
gather your leaves so drenched in tears, gather them all together,
that I may see a bit of sky, again a bit of starlight.
Bastille and dungeon of our land, the time is coming, Plane tree,
when all our people's stifled rage at last will send the woodman
to cut you down, when high and free the axe will shine so brightly.
Old age will never come to you, fire instead will burn you.

Just to the right of the Medrese there is a handsome neo-classical mansion built early in the reign of King Otho. This house was erected by Georgios Lassanis, who served as Minister of Finance throughout almost the entire period of Otho's reign, from 1833 until 1860. Across the street from the Lassanis mansion, at the lower end of Odos Markou Avreliou, another handsome house of the same period has recently been restored.

We now walk along the north side of the Roman Agora to look at Fethiye Djami, the oldest and by far the most important Turkish monument surviving in Athens. Unfortunately, the mosque is fenced off and is not open to the public, so we will have to examine it from outside the fence.

This handsome building was erected by the Turks within two years of their capture of Athens in 1456; and it was personally dedicated by Sultan Mehmet II, the Conqueror, who named it Fethiye Djami, the Mosque of the Conquest. Some scholars have suggested that the building was in fact a converted church, but if so only the foundations of the earlier structure remain, for Fethiye Djami is a typical Ottoman mosque of the mid fifteenth century, of which there are several extant examples in Turkey. The ground plan of the mosque is a 15 m square, with a porch 15 m deep. The shallow dome rests on a low hexagonal drum that is flanked on all four sides by smaller semi-domes; these are supported internally by four columns, with four minor domes over the four corners of the square. Thus we have here a variant of the cross-in-a-square used in the medieval churches of Athens, with semi-domes in the arms of the cross rather than barrel-vaults. The mosque is preceded by a porch of five domed bays, with an arcaded façade formed by four round arches springing between spur walls to the side and in front four columns with Ottoman lozenge capitals. The minaret stood just outside the right-hand corner of the porch, where its base may still be seen. Inside we would find that the appearance of the mosque is quite different from that of the Byzantine churches that we have visited in Athens, despite the fact that their ground plans are so much the same. Here the interior is not divided up into a nave and side aisles, for the domes over the arms of the cross have the effect of opening up the interior so that it all appears to be part of one continuous space. And in the mosque there is no altar or iconostasis; there is only the mihrab, a niche in the wall opposite the entrance; this indicates the direction of Mecca, towards which the faithful face when they perform their prayers.

Fethiye Djami was better known in Turkish times as the Mosque of the Wheat Market, because of its proximity to Pazaroporta, the gateway to Staropazaro. After the War of Independence it was used in turn for a variety of purposes, as Micheli writes, quoting the folklorist Dimitrios Kambouroglu:

... the Mosque of the Wheat Market, still standing today [1881], is sometimes used as a military prison for the Garrison Command, and sometimes as a barracks. In the year 1824, by decision of the Municipality, it was given over to the Philomuse Society for a school of mutual instruction ... Already it has been turned into a storehouse for a quantity of wheat sacks, after the addition of mechanical ovens for the large military bakery ...

The mosque was eventually cleared of later accretions and restored to its original form, after which it became a storehouse for architectural members found in and around the Roman Agora.

After looking at the mosque, we turn left at the corner on to Odos Panos and then right on to Epameinonda, passing the Gate of Athena Archegetis. We might pause here for a moment to look once again at this ancient gateway, the Pazaroporta of Turkish times. Here one entered the Staropazaro, where the stalls and barrows of the Wheat Market were set up among the half-buried ruins of the Roman Agora, of which only this gateway and the Tower of the Winds remained standing. The grain dealers of Athens began doing business here each year at harvest time, buying wheat and corn from the farmers of Attica. Olive oil and salt were among the other commodities sold here, as indeed they were in Roman times; a fragmentary inscription can still be seen on the pilaster behind the column at the right side of the gateway recording a decree by Hadrian regulating the prices of oil and salt in the Athenian market. This pilaster was known in Turkish times as the 'Flat Pillar of the Market Gate', as we read in Micheli's chapter on the Staropazaro:

The sale of olive oil and salt continued here also, as in Roman times. An inscription referring to this trade ('From Hadrian Emperor . . .') can be seen today *in situ* on a pilaster of the entrance, which was habitually called the Flat Pillar of the Market Gate. Drawings of 1809 show Hadrian's inscription built into one wall of a house abutting on the ancient structure. When the house was pulled down in excavations of the site, pilaster and inscription were left standing free in their original position. Close to the gate were a number of houses with small gardens, a communal fountain for the use of people and their pack animals, and a Byzantine chapel now demolished: Our Lady (Soteira) of the Market Gate — one of the tiny churches built next to classical monuments to purify the area of pagan influence. Long since demolished were two other nearby churches, the Archangel of the Market Gate and Prophet Elias. Roman weights for wheat, discovered on the spot, were still in use as late as 1672. The Turkish *meltepi* weights, with one or both sides concave, were the same as those used in ancient times. Next to Hadrian's inscription on the pilaster there also hung a tablet with the *narti* (from the Turkish *nahr*), or officially registered price-list of the wheat.

One of the three churches mentioned by Micheli still has its parish in the neighbourhood of the Staropazaro, though its original building has been replaced by a modern structure. This is the church of the Taxiarchoi, the Archangels, which stands just to the north of the Roman Agora, midway along the street that leads from there to the Library of Hadrian. The original church, the Archangel of the Market Gate, is known to have been founded in the eleventh or twelfth century. But this was completely rebuilt after the War of Independence and restored again in more recent times, so that the present structure of the Taxiarchoi has no resemblance to a Byzantine church and is of little architectural interest.

Prints of late Ottoman and Othonian Athens show that just to the north of the Taxiarchoi there stood a smaller Byzantine church of similar design. This was the church of Profitis Ilias of Staropazaro, which was demolished in 1850, one of the many Byzantine and post-Byzantine churches that were levelled when the new capital was being built. The site of Profitis Ilias is the square just to the north of the Taxiarchoi. In the centre of this square you will notice a small circular fenced-in area, where there is the stump of an ancient column surmounted by a flat slab of marble. This little relic of the past has gone unnoticed by most writers on Athens, for it is indeed insignificant. But it has been identified as being part of the altar of Profitis Ilias, and it was placed here to mark the site of this vanished church. During the demolition of the church its principal icon was removed and is now on show in the Byzantine Museum. This is a representation of the Virgin known as Our Lady of Catalonia, indicating that Prophitis Ilias was the chapel of the Sicilian–Catalan dynasty who ruled Athens from 1311 till 1388. Thus the icon and this fragment of an altar are the only reminders in Athens of the fierce warriors who terrorized Greece for nearly a century before the onslaught of the Turks. As the Florentine chronicler Giovanni Villani (quoted by William Miller) wrote in 1311, just after the Grand Army of Catalonia had annihilated the Latin knights of the Duchy of Athens in the Kopaic marshes, 'Thus the uncontrollable rage of the Catalans destroyed all the pleasures of the French conquerors, who had lived in Athens in greater prosperity and luxury than in any country in the world.' The ferocity of the Catalans made such an impression on the Greeks that it remained in their folk-memory up until fairly recent times. William Miller, in his *Essays on the Latin Orient*, writes that villagers in late-nineteenth-century Greece still spoke of the 'Curse of the Catalans', a malediction in which an angry Greek shouts at his enemy, 'May the Catalans get you!'

We now continue through the square and turn left at the corner on to Odos Dexipou, after which we turn right at the next corner on to Odos Areos. We then walk down Areos until we reach the Library of Hadrian. At the right side of the façade, between the last two surviving columns, we see the remnants of a fresco on the wall of the library. This is all that remains of the former church of Ay. Asomatoi sta Skalia, the Incorporeal Saints on the Steps, so named because in Turkish times the present Odos Areos was a stepped street. It was a tiny chapel, probably dating from the eleventh or twelfth century, built up against the south-western corner of Hadrian's Library. According to tradition, this was the private chapel of the Chalcocondyles, one of the most distinguished of the aristocratic families in late medieval Athens, whose mansion would have been near by. The last generation of this family to live in Athens before the Turkish Conquest produced two renowned scholars. Laonikos Chalcocondyles wrote a history of Byzantium in its latter centuries, linking its fall to the rise of the Ottoman Turks. He continued to live on in Athens after the city was captured by the Turks. His brother (some say his first cousin), Dimitrios Chalcocondyles, left Athens for Italy shortly before the Turkish Conquest, one of a group of Greek scholars who brought classical scholarship to Italy at the beginning of the European Renaissance. Among the enduring contributions of Dimitrios Chalcocondyles are his edition of Isocrates, his translation of Homer from Greek into Latin, which is the *editio princeps* on which all later translations have been based, and his collaboration with Marsilio Ficino on the first modern edition of Plato. The Chalcocondyles family continued to live on in Athens throughout the Turkish period, and their name survives in the modern city. Their ancestral chapel was left in ruins at the end of the War of Independence, and it was demolished in 1842. Now all that is left of it is this fresco, which is fast disappearing in the corrosive atmosphere of modern Athens.

The gate to the right of the façade of Hadrian's Library once led to the Voivodalik, the town hall of Athens during the Turkish period. This was the largest Ottoman building in the Turkish quarter of Athens, and in old prints one sees it rising above the south-western corner of Hadrian's Library, with the Doric columns of the gate of Athena Archegetis framing the street leading to Staropazaro. Hobhouse describes the Voivodalik in one of his letters from Athens in 1810: 'The house of the Waiwode is of the poorer sort, though the entrance to it would become a palace, as it is between the columns of antiquity distinguished by the name of the Doric Portico.' Then Hobhouse explains how the Voivodalik was administered at that time, on the eve of the last decade of the Ottoman period in Athenian history:

The Waiwode interferes but little in the administration of the Christians, and generally contents himself with the receipt of the tribute, which is collected by the Codja-bashees or Archons – the immediate rulers, and, it would seem, the oppressors of the Greeks. The Archons have been, until lately, eight in number; they are at present only five. I did not learn that the whole of these rulers ever assembled at any stated time, or have any regular system for the transaction of business. The regular tax transmitted from Attica to the Porte is between seven hundred and seven hundred and fifty purses; but the Codja-bashees, under various pretences, exact as many as fifteen hundred purses; and as they never give any account to the people of the manner in which their money had been disposed, do not fail to enrich themselves by the surplus amount. Threats, and sometimes punishments, are employed to wring from the peasants their hard-earned pittances; and such is the oppressive weight of the tyranny, that the murmurs of the commonalty have frequently broken out into open complaints; and even a complete revolution, involving the destruction of the Archons, and an establishment of a better order of things, has been meditated by the more daring and ambitious among the oppressed.

The Voivode of Athens in 1810, when Hobhouse and Byron were first there, was an amiable Turk named Süleyman Aga. Byron described him as 'a bon vivant, and as sociable a being as ever sat cross-legged at a tray or table'. They dined together one evening when Byron was staying at the Capuchin monastery. 'The day before yesterday the Woywode ... with the Mufti of Thebes ... supped here and made themselves beastly with raw rum, and the Padre of the convent being as drunk as we, my Attic feast went off with great éclat.'

We now continue down Odos Areos to the end of the street, passing the west side of Hadrian's Library. Just beyond the library, at the corner of Areos and Pandrossou we come to the mosque known as Tzisdarakis Djami, the principal landmark in this quarter, where one passes from Plaka into Monastiraki. This is also known as the Mosque of the Lower Fountain, because of the *cheshme*, or Turkish street fountain, that once stood below it in the market square. The mosque was built in 1759 by the newly appointed voivode, Mustafa Ağa, better known as Tzisdarakis. (Mustafa Ağa took his name from the fact that he had formerly been Dizdar Ağa, commander of the Turkish garrison on the Acropolis.) As we have seen, Tzisdarakis demolished several ancient structures to obtain building material for his mosque, and he blew up one of the columns of the Olympieion to convert it into plaster for the interior of the prayer-room. The mosque is currently being restored, so we must be content to examine it from the street below. It stands on a high platform, with a flight of steps leading up to its front porch which has three domed bays with an arcade carried by four columns in front. Above the entrance there is a calligraphic inscription in old Turkish, recording the name of the founder and the date of dedication of the mosque. On either side of the door there are niches that served as mihrabs, orienting the prayers of those performing their devotions on the porch when the mosque was full to overflowing. The plan of the mosque is very simple, with a shallow dome carried on a low octagonal drum that rests on the walls. The square interior is lighted by two courses of four windows each in both of its side walls, and there are smaller windows in the eight sides of the drum below the dome. The only mosque furniture that remains is the mihrab, a very inferior work. The mosque formerly housed the ceramic collection of the Museum of Greek Popular Art, and these works will probably be exhibited here again when the restoration of the building is complete.

After leaving the mosque we retrace our steps along Odos Areos, pausing just before we reach the first turning on the right. The house at No. 14 has an arched entrance, through which we venture for a moment in order to look at the courtyard inside, where one can still see the façade of a Turkish street fountain built into the precinct wall. This house was built by the Logothetes family, who were prominent in Athens in the late Turkish period.

After leaving the courtyard, we turn right at the next corner on to Odos Kladou. The house at No. 30 originally belonged to the Dragoumis family, who called this the Villa Oleander. The house was built by Marcos Dragoumis, who was born in Istanbul and moved to Athens as a young man. Dragoumis was an early initiate in the Philiki Hetairia, or Society of Friends, the secret society that began the Greek independence movement. He began his political career as a secretary to Count John Capodistrias, the first President of Greece, and in 1862 he became Minister of Finance.

We now continue along Kladou; near the end of the street we see an old building on the left that now houses an antique shop. This shop is the most interesting of its kind in Athens, and while looking at its fascinating assortment of antiques one takes the opportunity of examining the building itself. The house appears to date from the late Turkish period, for the interior courtyard and the arcaded balcony above it are typical of Ottoman houses of the late eighteenth and early nineteenth century.

At the end of Kladou we turn left on to Odos Vrissakiou, the street that runs behind the Stoa of Attalos. Then we turn left on to Odos Poikilis, the street that parallels the excavated area between the ancient Greek Agora and the Roman Agora. We turn right at the end of the street, where we pass the Gate of Athena Archegetis, and then we turn right again on to Odos Polignotou. This is a quiet cul-de-sac graced by a number of mansions dating back to the days of the early Greek Kingdom. The first house on the right is now the residence of the Director of Byzantine Antiquities. The last house on the left, which looks out over the site of the ancient Agora, is now the home of the Director of Classical Antiquities.

We now make our way back along Polignotou and then turn right on to Dioskouron. Towards the end of this street, which climbs steeply up towards the Acropolis, we pass the tiny church of Ay. Anna, reminiscent of some of the little chapels one sees out on the Aegean isles of Greece. Just past the chapel we turn left on to Aretousas, after which we turn right at the next corner on to Panos. This is a very steep stepped street that leads up to the top of Plaka, taking its name from the Cave of Pan, which we can now see directly above in the north cliff of the Acropolis.

At the top of Odos Panos we come to a handsome neo-classical mansion on the left side of the street. This is the Kanellopoulos Museum, which has a very interesting collection of antiquities covering the whole span of Athenian history, ranging from the third millennium

BC to the nineteenth century AD. On the first floor of the museum there is an enclosure containing a large rectangular stone block that was found here when the mansion was built in the mid nineteenth century. This stone appears to have been part of the classical defence walls of the Acropolis, and it probably tumbled down here during one of the several sieges in the city's post-classical history.

After leaving the museum we walk up the few remaining steps of Odos Panos and then turn left on to Odos Theorias, the lane that extends around the uppermost tier of Plaka under the northern cliff of the Acropolis, following the course of the ancient Peripatos. On the slope of the Acropolis just above the Kanellopoulos Museum we see the ruins of the church of the Holy Seraphim, a little chapel dating back to the Turkish period. The façade of the chapel once formed part of a Turkish fortification known to the Greeks as Ipapanti, which ringed the northern slope of the Acropolis just below the cliff.

Continuing eastwards along Theorias, we pass the church of the Metamorphosis, which we visited on our last stroll. Just beyond the church we turn left for a short detour down Odos Klepsydras, which in a few steps brings us to the largest and most distinguished of the old mansions in Plaka, the Old University (in Greek, Panepistimiou).

This building was already in existence when the War of Independence ended, though there is some disagreement as to when it was first erected. There was once a suggestion that it was a Venetian building, dating from Morosini's occupation of Athens, but authorities now agree that it dates from the late Ottoman period. In any event, the building was acquired in 1833 by Stamatios Kleanthes, one of the architects who planned the new capital of the Greek Kingdom. Kleanthes lived here from 1833 until 1837, after which the building was used to house the newly formed University of Athens, the first institution of higher learning to be established in modern Greece. The Old University was later used for a variety of purposes, serving for some years in the 1960s as a restaurant, the Taverna Panepistimiou, whose romantic atmosphere owed much to the fact that the building was falling into ruins. The building has since been splendidly restored, and it is now open to the public as a museum, with exhibits of memorabilia dating from the years when it was the University of Athens.

After visiting the Old University we return to Odos Theorias, where we continue until we come to a pathway on the right leading uphill to a village-like cluster of old stone cottages perched high on the north-west slope of the Acropolis. This is Anafiotika, so called because those who first settled on this spot in the mid nineteenth century were from Anafi, a small island near Santorini. The Anafiotes built here a village similar to the one they had left behind on their island, a constellation of whitewashed cottages and walled gardens laid out along a labyrinth of marble-paved lanes.

There are two small chapels on the paths leading up to Anafiotika, both of them founded in Turkish times and restored by the Anafiotes when they settled here. The first of these that we see is Ay. Simeon, which we pass on our way up to Anafiotika from Odos Theorias. We pass the second chapel coming down by the path on the other side of the village; this is Ay. Yorgios tou Vrachou, St George on the Rocks, so named because it is perched on an outcrop of rock below the Acropolis cliff.

The second of the two paths leads us down to Odos Stratonos, the continuation of Odos Theorias around the north-eastern spur of the Acropolis. From here we walk back along the peripheral road towards the point where we started up to Anafiotika, stopping at the top of Odos Soterias Alimberti. We turn right here and walk down to Odos Thrassivoulou, the next cross street in the upper tier of Plaka, passing the Old University on our left. This brings us to Chrysocastriotissa, the church of Our Golden Lady of the Castle.

Athenian tradition traces Chrysocastriotissa back to Byzantine times, though the present structure dates from a complete rebuilding in the nineteenth century. According to tradition, the original church on this site was built to house a miraculous icon of the Virgin, the Chrysoca-striotissa, which fell down from the Acropolis in early Christian times. Those who found it attempted to bring the icon back up to the Acropolis, but when they did so it turned up again in the same place below. This happened twice more, and so finally the people of Plaka decided that they would build this church to house the icon. In times past the Chrysocastriotissa was famed for her healing powers, and even today her icon is widely venerated by those seeking relief from illness.

We now walk eastwards on Thrassivoulou and then turn right on Mnesikleos, a steep, stepped street that takes us back up towards the Acropolis. At the top of the street we turn left on Pritaniou, and a short distance along we pass the precinct wall of the Monastery of the Holy Sepulchre, a dependency of the Patriarchate of Jerusalem. The entrance to the enclosure is around the corner on Odos Erechtheos, where we find the monastic chapel of Ay. Anargyroi and the residence of the Exarch of Jerusalem, the emissary of that patriarchate to the Archbishopric of Athens.

According to tradition, the original church of Ay. Anargyroi was founded by the Empress Irene, who ruled the Byzantine Empire in her own right from 797 until 802. Irene is revered as a saint in the Greek Orthodox Church for her efforts in restoring icons to the churches of the empire, from which they had been banned by the Iconoclasts. Tradition has it that Irene was a member of the Sarandapichos family, who lived in this part of Athens during the middle Byzantine period; though an orphan she went on to marry Leo VI and become Empress of Byzantium, at which time she is supposed to have built Ay. Anargyroi and several other churches in Athens. The original church of Ay. Anargyroi was abandoned at the time of the Venetian occupation of Athens, and was not used again until 1760, when it was acquired by the Monastery of the Holy Sepulchre. The church has been heavily restored in modern times, and today it has little of interest except a finely carved iconostasis. But the garden behind the church is one of the loveliest and most serene spots in Athens, a quiet haven shaded by columnar cypresses and brightened by a flower garden that borders the monastery garden, with fragments of ancient columns and capitals lying around from some unidentified ancient structure. There is even an old gas lamp, the last survivor of those that once illuminated the streets of Plaka.

After leaving the courtyard, we turn left on Erechtheos and left again at the next corner on to Erotokritou. This takes us to Lysiou, where we turn left and continue past Mnesikleos to Odos Markou Avreliou, turning right there to come once again to the Tower of the Winds.

One might conclude this tour of Plaka by stopping once again in Ai Aerides, where we began our stroll through Turkish Athens. It is particularly pleasant sitting here in late afternoon, before the crowds begin to throng the streets of Plaka, and in the serene atmosphere of the old quarter you can better imagine what life was like here in times past. The street that passes Ai Aerides is one of the oldest in the city, and in Ottoman times it was the main route between the market quarter and the Turkish village on the Acropolis. The Acropolis was off limits to the Greeks, and only an occasional foreigner could gain admission by paying baksheesh to the guards. And the Turks in the Acropolis tended to keep to themselves, for the men were regular soldiers in the Ottoman army, and probably neither they nor their wives had family connections among the local Turks. The wives of the garrison troops, probably most of them Anatolian peasants, must have looked down with wonderment on the quarter below, with Greeks,

Turks, Albanians and occasional foreigners thronging the lively market area, with each vendor hawking his wares in his own language, a scene so different from the sleepy and backward Turkish villages from which they had come. Hobhouse remarked upon them in one of his letters from Athens in 1810: 'I have seen several Turkish ladies, on a fine day, leaning over the battlements, to enjoy the amusing murmur that arose from the city below.'

The fighting in Athens during the War of Independence ended in 1829, with the Turks continuing to occupy the city for another three years, using it as a pawn while the national boundaries of the new Greek state were being negotiated between the European powers and the Sublime Porte. Liza Micheli quotes the young German archaeologist Ludwig Ross, who came to Athens for the first time in 1832, during the last days of the Turkish occupation; he was appalled to see the condition in which Athens had been left at the end of the War of Independence:

A few Turkish guards, dirty and in rags, sat cross-legged and belching, paying not the least attention to the comings and goings of the inhabitants except when farmers came in with their produce to the market – and then they took the occasion to help themselves to some of it. In this ruinacious setting, how fearsome the scene of devastation! An almost solid, desolate mass of wrecked buildings, a few little low houses of gaping holes, patched up with whatever lay to hand, the splendid remains of Antiquity, several battered churches and mosques, and a few better-preserved houses or new structures that were beginning to rise, and a dozen lone palms and cypress trees. Our laden beasts had difficulty descending through the alleyways between the walls of ancient and later buildings.

One of the last descriptions of Turkish Athens is that of Christopher Wordsworth, who was in the city when the Ottoman garrison was finally withdrawn in 1832, not long after Ramadan, the Muslim month of daily fasting and nightly feasts:

The Muezzin still mounts the scaffolding in the Bazaar to call the Mussulman to prayer at the stated hours . . . The Athenian peasant, as he drives his laden mule from Hymettus through the eastern gate of the town, still flings his small bundle of thyme and brushwood from the load which he carries on his mule's back, as a tribute to the Mussulman toll-gatherer, who sits at the entrance to the town; and a few days ago the cannon on the Acropolis fired the signal at the conclusion of the Turkish Ramazan – the last which will ever be celebrated in Athens.

Such are the memories that are evoked while sitting in Ai Aerides late of an afternoon, as the people of Plaka make their way past the Tower of the Winds on their way to and from their homes under the north cliff of the Acropolis.

11

Central Athens I

Our next two itineraries will take us through central Athens, where we will be principally looking at a number of historic buildings of the last century. On these two strolls we will also visit a number of museums whose collections reflect the culture of Athens from the medieval period up to modern times.

We will begin the first of these two itineraries where we started our first stroll through Athens, in Syntagma Square. But before we start out we might sit for a while in the square, preferably in one of the quieter outdoor cafés in the central garden, where we can review the architectural history of Athens in the early days of the Greek Kingdom.

Plans for the design of the new capital were discussed even before the end of the War of Independence. The architects originally appointed to draw up this design were Stamatios Kleanthes and Eduard Schaubert, whose report to the provisional government in December 1832 called for the complete razing of the old Turkish town and the construction on its site of a modern European capital, with broad boulevards and spacious squares. But this aroused a great deal of controversy, for it would have meant the uprooting of most of the populace, who had returned to Athens at the end of the war and either rebuilt their old houses or erected new ones. A compromise was reached by Otho's father, King Ludwig of Bavaria, who sent his own architect, Leo von Klenze, to modify the plans. The revised plan spared the old town by shifting the course of the boulevards northwards, with what is now Syntagma Square as their focal point, above which the royal palace would be built on high ground about midway between the Acropolis and Lycabettos. The architect Friedrich von Gaertner was chosen to design the royal residence, whose cornerstone was laid in 1836 by King Ludwig. The palace was completed in 1842, by which time the course of the principal boulevards had been laid out, radiating from the main square below the palace. Fortunately for modern Athenians, Queen Amalia had insisted that the plan include a large public park and gardens, which were laid out and planted under her direction in the area between the palace and the Olympieion. By the time that Otho and Amalia moved into the palace the new capital had taken form, and the ruined old Turkish town on the north slope of the Acropolis had been recreated as a modern European city. The transplanted northern Europeans in the royal court seemed delighted with their new capital, as we gather from a letter written by Fräulein von Nordenflycht, one of Amalia's maids of honour, quoted by Liza Micheli:

On Sundays a very good band plays in a large square. Six cafés have been opened there; at six in the evening it was crowded with little tables and surrounded by people in carriages, while the King and Queen usually stopped in their drive or ride to listen to the music. Hydriote ladies in their picturesque costumes, the latest Paris fashions and foreign naval uniforms completed the picture . . . All foreigners are surprised at the great progress made in so short a time.

But the Greeks themselves were quickly disillusioned by the new kingdom, under which many of them had no better life than under the old regime. This led to a popular uprising in Athens on 3 September 1843, when the Greek troops in the garrison marched on the palace and were joined there by virtually the entire population of the city, all of them demanding that the king grant them constitutional rights. Popular pressure eventually forced Otho to accede to their demands, and one day in March 1844 he stood on a balcony of the palace and read the text of the new constitution to the masses assembled below him. Thenceforth the square was called Syntagma, or Constitution Square.

The palace on Syntagma Square continued to be the principal royal residence until 1890, when the New Palace was built on the eastern side of the National Gardens. The Old Palace, as it then came to be called, served as a state residence up until 1909, when it was badly damaged in a fire. In 1922 and 1923 it was used to house thousands of the refugees who ended up in Athens in the population exchange that followed the Greek–Turkish War in Asia Minor. The building was restored in the early 1930s, and in 1935 it reopened as the parliament building, a purpose that it serves again today, after interruptions by wars and dictatorships.

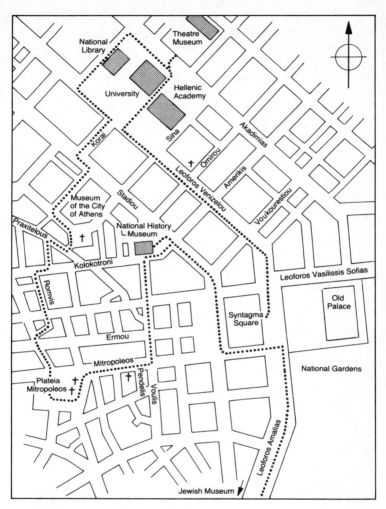

Central Athens I

Let us now walk over to look more closely at the Old Palace, whose east front is distinguished by a Doric portico of Pentelic marble. The ceremonial main entrance to the palace is approached by a small square, on the retaining wall of which we see a memorial to the Unknown Soldier. The relief on the façade, depicting a dying Greek hoplite, was modelled on an original that once decorated the Temple of Aphaia on Aegina; the inscriptions are quotations from the funeral oration by Pericles. The bronze shields affixed to the façade commemorate Greek military victories since 1821.

In the garden in the centre of Syntagma Square, there is a small but very important historical marker that is seldom noticed by visitors to Athens. This is an ancient boundary marker that stands on a modern base near the north-western corner, surrounded by the tables of an outdoor café. This stele, which was discovered just where it now stands, bears the inscription HOROS MOUSON KIPOU, meaning 'the Boundary-Stone of the Museum Gardens'. This and other stelai found in the vicinity, as well as several references in ancient literature, identify the site as part of the famous Garden of Theophrastus, which is known to have included a shrine of the Muses. The land on which this garden was laid out had been given by Dimitrios of Phaleron to the Lyceum Gymnasium, of which Theophrastus became director after the death of Aristotle in 322 BC. The Lyceum was founded in the late sixth century BC, the largest of the three gymnasia that were established at that time in the countryside outside Athens, the other two being the Kynosarges and the Academy. The Lyceum took its name from the fact that it was a shrine of Apollo Lykios, the Wolf-God, one of several animal forms under which Apollo was worshipped.

We now leave Syntagma by the north-eastern corner of the square, where we start walking down the right side of Leoforos Eleftherios Venizelou, better known as Panepistimiou. At the beginning of the avenue we pass on our left the Hotel Grande Bretagne; this was originally begun in 1842–3 by the architect Theophil von Hansen as the mansion of Antonius Demetriou, but it was completely rebuilt and enlarged in 1958. After the first crossing, at Odos Voukourestiou, we see on our left one of the oldest and most famous *zacharoplasteia* in Athens; this is Zonar's, which has been doing business here for more than half a century.

Half-way up the block we pause before the handsome neo-classical building identified by an inscription as ILIOY MELATHRON, the Palace of Ilion. This is the mansion that Ernst Ziller built in the years 1877-80 for Heinrich Schliemann, the discoverer of Troy and

Mycenae. Schliemann lived here during the latter years of his life with his Greek wife Sophie and their children Agamemnon and Andromache. Since 1935 the Palace of Ilion has housed the Areopagus, the Supreme Court of Greece, which is named after the ancient council that assembled on the Areopagus Hill in the early years of Athens.

A little way beyond the Palace of Ilion an arcade on the right leads to Apotsos, the oldest and most famous *ouzeria* in Athens. (An *ouzeria* is a drinking place that serves ouzo and *mezedes*, small snacks and appetizers.) Apotsos was founded in 1900, and was housed in several other locations in the vicinity before it moved to its present location in the 1970s. This is a favourite meeting-place at lunchtime for those who work in central Athens, and when it is closed in August, for the staff holidays, it is greatly missed. Apotsos has become an informal museum of poster art, for its walls are covered with old-fashioned advertisements, mostly for alcoholic beverages, which have accumulated there over the years, along with playbills and notices of exhibitions long past.

We continue along the avenue, crossing Amerikis and then Omirou, where we come to the Roman Catholic Cathedral of Athens, St Denis (the Latin form of Dionysius) the Areopagite. The original plans for this Italianate basilica were drawn up in 1844 by Leo von Klenze, who modelled them on a Roman Catholic church in Munich. Lack of funds delayed the laying of the cornerstone until 1853, but the building was still incomplete when construction halted two years later when the money ran out. An international fund-raising campaign led to a resumption of construction in 1858 under the Greek architect Kaftandzoglu, who radically altered the design to produce the present building, which was completed in 1887. The interior decoration was done by Italian artists in the first decade of the present century, and is thus totally different in style and spirit from the decor of Greek Orthodox churches in Athens of the same period.

Just beyond the cathedral of St Denis we pass the Ophthalmic Hospital. This was originally designed as a single-storeyed building by Christian Hansen, under whose supervision the foundations were laid in 1847. But here too the money ran out soon after the project started, and Hansen left Athens when construction was halted. Sufficient funds were eventually raised and Kaftandzoglu took charge of the project, completing the original building in 1854; then a second storey was added in 1869. The building is still used as an Ophthalmic Hospital.

After crossing Odos Sina, we come to the most grandiose complex of buildings erected in nineteenth-century Athens; these are, in the order that we pass them: the Hellenic Academy, the University of Athens and the National Library. All three edifices are designed in the neo-classical style.

The Hellenic Academy was founded by Baron Sinas, a Viennese philanthropist who in the mid nineteenth century endowed several cultural institutions and buildings in Athens, of which we have already seen the Astronomical Observatory. The Academy was designed by Theophil von Hansen; construction began in 1859 and the building was completed in 1887. The sculptured pediment represents the birth of Athena, the two exceedingly tall columns in front of the building are surmounted by statues of Athena and Apollo, on either side of the main entrance there are seated figures of Plato and Aristotle, and in the entrance hall there is a statue of Baron Sinas: all are works of the Greek sculptor Drosos. The Hall of Conferences in the Academy is decorated with frescos by Griekenperi: on the front wall there is depicted a Gigantomachy, and on the side walls there are scenes from the myth of Prometheus. This is the meeting-room of the Hellenic Academy, a society of scholars modelled on the French Academy.

The University was designed by Christian Hansen, and it was constructed in the years 1839–42. The frieze in the Ionic portico, which was designed by Karl Rahl and executed by Eduard Lebiedzky, shows King Otho among personifications of the Arts and Sciences. Directly in front of the building there is a statue of Gladstone; to the left of the steps stands a figure of Capodistrias, who founded the University of Athens shortly after the declaration of Greek independence in 1821; and to the right of the steps there is a statue of Alexander Korais, one of the leading figures in the cultural renaissance of modern Greece. In front of the façade there are statues of the poet Rigas Pherios, who was executed by the Turks in 1797, and the Patriarch Gregory V, who at the outbreak of the War of Independence was attacked by a Turkish mob and hanged from the front gate of the Patriarchate in Istanbul. The main university building here on Leoforos Panepistimiou contains administrative offices, classrooms and the great Hall of Ceremonies, where faculty meetings are held. On the street behind, at No. 25 Acadimias, there is a science building named for its founder, Baron Sinas; this houses a Museum of Natural History, which is open to the public.

The National Library, which was designed by Theophil von Hansen, was built in the years 1888–91. Its founder was Paul Vallianos of Kephalonia, whose statue stands in front of the library. This building houses the collection of both the National Library, founded by King

Otho, and the University. It is estimated that the library's collection includes more than half a million books, including some 2,500 from the sixteenth century and 130 dating from before 1500, among which are two illuminated gospels from the eleventh or twelfth century.

Behind the University, at No. 50 Acadimias, a large building houses the Cultural Centre (Pneumnatiki Kentron) of Athens. In the ground floor of this building, behind a modern statue of Pericles, we find the entrance to the Theatre Museum. This museum houses a fascinating collection of theatrical costumes, playbills and other memorabilia of the Athenian theatrical world. The most interesting exhibits are the dressing-rooms of seven of the most celebrated stars of the Greek stage and cinema in modern times. Each of these rooms is decorated as it might have been on the opening night of a play, complete with costumes, make-up kit and script, along with photographs of the performers at the height of their careers.

After visiting the Theatre Museum, we walk back through the University grounds to cross Panepistimiou. We then continue straight ahead on Odos Korai and cross Stadiou, where we turn left to walk along Stadiou to the next corner, turning right there on to Odos Paparigopoulou, which forms one side of Plateia Klafthmonos. Half-way down the block, at Nos. 5 and 7, we come to two handsome old mansions connected together by a covered walkway. This is now the Museum of the City of Athens, with its entrance at No. 7.

The house at No. 7 originally belonged to Stamatios Dekozis-Vouros, a merchant from Chios who settled in Athens in 1834. This is believed to have been the first modern house erected in Athens after the War of Independence. The house at No. 5 originally belonged to the Aphtonides family and was built soon after the erection of the Vouros mansion. In 1836 King Otho bought the two houses and joined them together, and they served as the royal residence until the palace on Syntagma Square was completed. This was the residence to which Otho brought his new bride Amalia after their wedding in Bavaria. The royal couple landed in the Piraeus on 14 February 1837, after which they and their entourage were driven to Athens. The entire population of Athens was waiting to meet them at the Kerameikos, and the girls of the Hill School serenaded them with a hymn of welcome written by the poet Rhangavas, after which Otho and Amalia were escorted to their residence on what is now Odos Paparigopoulou.

The mansions here were restored and reopened in 1980 as the Museum of the City of Athens. The museum has a wonderful collection of exhibits associated with Athens in the early days of the Greek Kingdom, including old prints, paintings, photographs, maps and memorabilia. The central exhibit is a model of Athens as it was in 1842, a work of the eminent architect and archaeologist John Travlos. One could spend hours studying this extraordinary recreation of Old Athens, a city that had been resurrected from the ruins of its past to begin a new life in the modern world.

If we continue down Paparigopoulou and turn left at the corner, we see a large church standing in the middle of the square a short distance ahead. This is Ay. Yorgios Karytsis, one of the largest churches in Athens. The present edifice, which was designed by Ernst Ziller and completed in 1852, replaced a much smaller church that was founded in the last decade of the eleventh century. The founder of the original church was a Byzantine general named Karytsi, who was governor of Crete during the reign of Alexius I Comnenus, 1081–1118. In 1092 Karytsi led a revolt against the emperor, but he was decisively defeated and was forced to flee from Crete. He was eventually reconciled with the emperor, who allowed him and his family to settle in Athens, where Karytsi built this church and its associated monastery.

After leaving the church we take the short street that leads off from the south-west corner of the square. This brings us out on to Odos Praxitelous, where we turn right; a short way along, we cross the street and take a sharp left. This brings us on to a short street that leads us out on to Odos Kolokotroni, which we cross and turn left on to Odos Romvis. We continue past the next intersection on to Odos Ktena, which cuts sharply around the rear of the church of the Panayia Romvis, bringing us out on to Odos Evangelistrias. There we turn left, and after a short walk we come to the Plateia Mitropoleos. Here we come once again to the Metropolis, the Cathedral of Athens, which we will now spend some time visiting.

The cathedral was designed by the architects Theophil von Hansen, Franz Boulanger and Dimitrios Zezos. The corner-stone was laid on Christmas Day in 1842 by King Otho and Queen Amalia. The construction and decoration of the building were finally completed in 1862, and on Sunday 21 May it was formally dedicated by Otho and Amalia as the Church of the Annunciation of the Theotokos, the Mother of God. It is better known as the Metropolis, so called because it is the seat of the Metropolitan Bishop of Athens.

The cathedral is the largest church in Athens, with a nave 40 m in length and 20 m wide, and 24 m high measuring from the floor to the crown of the dome. The church is cruciform in plan, with its dome rising from a very high quadrangular drum which is supported internally by four huge pillars. Four great arches spring from these pillars, and between them four pendentives make the transition to the circular cornice from which the drum rises to the dome. To the west of the nave there is a narthex flanked by two tall quadrangular bell-towers. This narthex consists of six domed chambers, in two rows of three each, supported by four double columns between pilasters, with polychrome decorations on the capitals, the voussoirs of the arches, the pendentives and the dome. The walls of the cathedral are built almost entirely of marble taken from the seventy-two churches in Athens and its environs that were demolished during the construction of the cathedral, with the sale of their lands providing much of the revenue for the project. The marble iconostasis and baptistry and the wooden bishop's throne were carved by the sculptor Constantine Foneli and decorated by the artist Zeitz, who was responsible for the iconography of the church. Zeitz also painted the fresco in the dome, which represents Christ Pantocrator, the All-Powerful, as well as that in the conch of the apse, which depicts the Panayia Platytera, the Virgin Broader than the Heavens. To the right of the apse there is a side-chapel dedicated to Ay. Filothei; this contains several relics of the saint which are carried in procession each year on 19 February, the anniversary of her martyrdom by the Turks in 1589. (In this procession the reliquary of Ay. Filothei is always carried by a member of the Benizelos family, of which she was a member.) To the left of the entrance inside the nave there is a shrine dedicated to the New Martyrs, those saints who died for their faith at the hands of the Turks. There in a barrel-vaulted niche we see the marble sarcophagus of the Patriarch Gregory V, whose remains were brought here from Odessa in 1871. The martyred patriarch was canonized as St Gregory V on 8 April 1821, the centenary of his execution by the Turks.

The cathedral has been the scene of some of the great ceremonial occasions of the modern Greek state, including the coronation of its kings and the swearing-in of its prime ministers. The dedication ceremony itself was a historic occasion, for it was one of the very last affairs of state presided over by King Otho; just five months later a popular revolt in Athens led to his overthrow, after which he and Amalia left Greece and spent the remainder of their lives in exile. In the autumn of 1862 a provisional government organized a national convention that framed a new constitution and elected a king to replace Otho. The man they chose was Prince Christian William

Ferdinand Adolphus George of Holstein-Sonderburg-Glücksburg, whose father subsequently became king of Denmark. His accession was confirmed by the Protecting Powers of the Treaty of London, and in 1863 he was crowned in the Cathedral of Athens as George I, King of the Hellenes. All six of King George's successors were crowned here as well, the last being Constantine II, who reigned from 1964 until 1973. King Constantine spent the last six years of that period in exile, and his reign officially ended in 1973 when a national plebiscite abolished the monarchy.

We now walk east on Odos Mitropoleos, the street that passes the left side of the cathedral. Just behind the cathedral we pass on our right a marble monument commemorating Bishop Chrysostomos of Smyrna, who was killed by the Turks on 27 August 1922, in the closing days of the Greek–Turkish War that began in 1919.

Two blocks farther along, at the corner of Mitropoleos and Pendelis, we come upon a most unusual sight, a tiny old chapel standing under the crowded arcade of a modern commercial building. This is the church of Ay. Dynamis, the Divine Power, which dates from the late Turkish period. It is named for an attribute of the Virgin Mary, symbolizing the power that she uses to protect women in childbirth. Her cult has been attracting pregnant Athenian women here for at least two centuries, and it has been the power of their belief that has preserved this little chapel amidst the soulless modern structures that tower above it. Within the church there are vestiges of a faded fresco depicting Ay. Filothei, and so it is possible that this chapel was a dependency of her convent, which stood near by. Just prior to the War of Independence the chapel was seized by the Turks and converted into a munitions works, where a Greek named Mastropavlis made cartridges for the Ottoman garrison on the Acropolis. But Mastropavlis gave the Turks only those cartridges that he made during the day, for he also worked secretly at night, and the bullets he made then were smuggled out of the chapel each morning by an old washerwoman named Kyr Manolina Biniari. Kyr Manolina hid the bullets under her washing and took them out each day to the Kallirhoë fountain on the Ilissos, where she passed them on to the revolutionaries then assembling in the Attic village of Menidhi. These were the men who rose in revolt on 26 April 1821, and when they made their first attack on the Acropolis shortly afterwards they were firing bullets that had been made by Mastropavlis in Ay. Dynamis.

After seeing the chapel, we continue along Mitropoleos and turn left at the next corner on to Voulis. We continue along Voulis to its end, at which point we turn right on to Kolokotroni and then left at the next corner on to Stadiou. This brings us to the distinctive old building known as Palaia Voulis, the Old Parliament, which now houses the National Historical Museum.

The Old Parliament stands on the site of one of the first mansions built in Athens after the War of Independence. This grand mansion was built in 1834 by a wealthy merchant named Kontostavlos. Soon after the mansion was built it was purchased from Kontostavlos by the Greek government as a residence for King Otho, who lived there until he and Amalia moved into the two houses on Odos Paparigopoulou. In March 1844 the mansion became the house of the first Greek Parliament, which met here until the building burned down in October 1854. Four years later funds were appropriated for a new House of Parliament, the present building, which was designed by Franz Boulanger and completed in 1874. Parliament met here on Odos Stadiou until 1935, when the assembly moved into its new quarters in the Old Palace on Syntagma Square. After that the building on Stadiou was used to house the Ministry of Justice, which moved elsewhere when the Old Parliament was converted into a museum in 1961.

In front of the museum there is a bronze equestrian statue of Kolokotronis, a copy of the original work in Nauplia by the Greek sculptor Sokhos. In the garden to the left of the entrance there is a marble statue of Charilaos Tricoupis, who was three times prime minister during the last two decades of the nineteenth century.

The exhibits in the National Historical Museum range in date from the Byzantine period up to the nineteenth century, with particular emphasis on the Greek War of Independence, including portraits and memorabilia of the leaders in the struggle against the Turks. The most interesting of the paintings are a series of vivid battle scenes painted by Paniotis Zographos, who was a sergeant in the forces led by Ioannis Makriyannis. These paintings served as illustrations for the *Memoirs* of Makriyannis, the most remarkable account to come out of the war. If you look closely you can see that the various units in the paintings are numbered, so that readers of the *Memoirs* could follow the action in each of the battles. Other interesting exhibits include Byron's sword and helmet; figureheads from ships of the Greek navy during the War of Independence; and an extraordinary painting on wood of the battle of Lepanto (1571), which was apparently done from memory by an eyewitness from Kephalonia.

After leaving the museum we turn right on Stadiou to return to Syntagma Square; then we make our way round the square to emerge on Leoforos Amalias, passing the National Gardens on our left, and continue along Amalias until we come to No. 36, which houses the Jewish Museum. This museum was formerly in the Old Synagogue in Monastiraki, and moved to its present location in 1977. The founder and director of the museum, Nikos Stavrolakis, has organized here an extremely important and interesting collection of historical documents, records, works of art, handicrafts, religious articles and memorabilia associated with the Jewish community in Athens, an aspect of the city's life that has hitherto been almost completely neglected.

Our first stroll through central Athens concludes with our visit to the Jewish Museum. From there we might cross Amalias to sit for a while in the National Gardens, where our next stroll will begin.

12

Central Athens II

<hr/>

Our second stroll through central Athens begins where the last one ended, in the National Gardens.

These were originally known as the Royal Gardens; they were sponsored by Queen Amalia and were planned by a team of landscape designers, architects, sculptors and gardeners under the direction of the Prussian Frederick Schmidt. This is one of the most pleasant and interesting parks in Europe, with an enormous variety of trees, plants and flowers, along with a small but charming aviary, the remains of Roman baths and fragments of the architrave of Hadrian's aqueduct; above all there is shade, blessed shade, so that in the high noon of summer one can escape here from the relentless Attic sun.

The remains of the Roman baths are at the north-east corner of the park, to the left of Leoforos Amalias just beyond the Old Palace. The ruins are difficult to find and very fragmentary, since Queen Amalia destroyed most of what remained of the baths' mosaic pavement in laying out the Royal Gardens.

The remains of the architrave of Hadrian's aqueduct are also difficult to find, but more rewarding; they are in the north-east corner of the park some distance behind the Old Palace, recognizable by the finely carved inscription in Latin, a fragment of the original that Cyriacus of Ancona copied when he visited Athens in 1437. This recorded the names of the emperors who contributed to the establishing of the Roman water-supply system of Athens, which was begun by Hadrian in AD 125 and completed fourteen years later by Antoninus Pius. The architrave was then still in place on the propylon of a Roman reservoir high on the south-east slope of Lycabettos; it remained there until 1778, when it was taken down to be used in the construction of Ali Haseki's defence wall, the Serpentzes, serving as the lintel of the

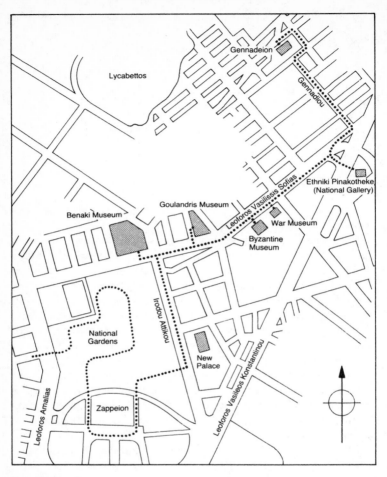

Central Athens II

Boubounistra Gate. The site of this gate is at the beginning of Leoforos Amalias on the left, just to the south of the Old Palace. The gate was named for the Boubounistra Fountain, a Turkish *cheshme* that stood just inside the Serpentzes at the terminus of the road leading into Athens from the north. The gateway was demolished to make way for the construction of the palace on Syntagma Square, but the surviving block of the architrave was preserved as part of the sculptural decoration of the Royal Gardens. The Turkish gateway and fountain were still standing in 1809, and Hobhouse noticed them when he and Byron one day walked the circuit of the Turkish walls 'in a brisk pace in forty-seven minutes'. As Hobhouse writes of the gateway and its ancient architectural members:

Two large blocks formed the jambs, a third even larger, the lintel, its form declaring that it once stood as an architrave and frieze alongside an arch, its inscription that it was from the aqueduct begun by Hadrian and finished by his successor Antoninus Pius. Just within the walls is a Turkish fountain, nicely placed to greet the traveller in Athens from Marathon or Kifissia.

Off to the southern side of the park we find the Zappeion, founded by Kossos and Voutos Zappos as an exhibition hall. The corner-stone of the building was laid in 1874 from plans prepared by the architect Franz Boulanger, but then Theophil von Hansen took over and completed the building in 1878, using his own design.

We wander through the park and make our way out to the street that forms its eastern boundary, Odos Irodou Attikou. There we find the New Palace, designed by Ernst Ziller and completed in 1890. Since the monarchy was abolished in 1973, the New Palace now serves as the official residence of the President of Greece.

On Irodou Attikou we turn left and make our way along the eastern side of the park. Towards the end of the street on the left we pass the Evzones' barracks. During the days of the monarchy the Evzones, dressed in their colourful Epirote costumes, served as the palace guard for the royal family, while today their main duty is to act as a guard of honour on ceremonial state functions. Also quartered here are the Cretans of the Royal Guard, whose duties have similarly changed.

Directly across Leoforos Vasilissis Sofias on the left we come to the handsome neo-classical mansion that houses the Benaki Museum.

The mansion itself was built in about 1900 by the architect Anastasios Metaxas for Emmanuel Benaki, a Greek who made a fortune in Egypt before settling in Athens. The museum is named for his son, Antonios Benaki, who in 1931 gave this house to the Greek nation for the purpose of exhibiting his incomparable collection of works of art and Greek handicrafts. Antonios Benaki spent the remaining twenty-three years of his life organizing the museum, whose collection has been considerably augmented by generous gifts from his relatives and other prominent Athenian families.

Most of the antiquities and works of art in the Benaki Museum fall into three categories, which are as interwoven with one another as the cultures that produced them. The first of these are works of Greek art from the Bronze Age up to the present day, with special emphasis on ancient Greek jewellery, Byzantine and post-Byzantine art, and modern Greek folk arts and crafts, particularly folk costumes. The second category consists of memorabilia of the War of Independence and the early Greek Kingdom, including works of art by foreign painters. The third group consists of Christian and Islamic works of art, principally from the eastern Mediterranean area, but there is also a large collection of Chinese porcelains, as well as textiles and embroideries from the Far East. The museum has a research library of some 80,000 volumes, as well as an immense archive of photographs dealing with modern Greek history and culture. The shop on the first floor sells an excellent guide to the various collections in this incomparable museum, so what follows is just a leisurely first stroll through the building to identify the collections in its various rooms.

The tour starts in Room I, which is immediately to the left of the entrance hall as one enters the museum. Here we see a collection of Greek art from the early Bronze Age to the fifth century BC, including a Mycenaean krater of Attic workmanship dating from the thirteenth century BC, and also an amphora of the Geometric period from the Kerameikos potteries. Room II has exhibits ranging in time from the fourth century BC to the fifth century AD, with the most outstanding works deriving from Alexandria in the Hellenistic and Roman periods, including two of the finest examples of the mummy portraits known as Fayyum paintings. Room III has exhibits of the early Christian period in the Greek world, including examples of Coptic textiles. Room IV contains the Benaki's small collection of Byzantine art, including a number of sacred objects brought to Greece in 1923 by refugees from Asia Minor, whose treasures are also exhibited in other galleries of the museum. The collection includes a number of icons dating from the Palaeologian era (1261–1453), when Byzantium flowered in a last renaissance before Constantinople fell to the Turks. Room V has part of the Banaki's extraordinary collection of Islamic art, including examples of the renowned Iznik ceramics, along with Bursa velvets, Turkish armour, Mameluke glass and Arab metal-work, the most notable exhibit being a bronze astrolabe from Aleppo dating from the fourteenth century. Room VI is devoted to ec-clesiastical objects of the Ottoman period, many of which were made for churches in the Pontus, eastern Thrace and Asia Minor, brought to Greece by the refugees in 1923. Rooms VII and VIII exhibit the Benaki's renowned collection of post-Byzantine icons, most of which are by painters of the Cretan school, which flourished until the Great Island was captured from the Venetians by the Turks in 1669. Room VIII also contains examples of nineteenth-century icons, the final stage in the post-Byzantine artistic tradition. Room IX is dedicated to the memory of Eleftherios Venizelos, the great Cretan who was the first statesman of international stature in modern Greece, serving as prime minister three times in the years 1910–35. Room X, which is at the base of the stairs leading up to the first floor, is devoted to paintings on Greek subjects by foreign artists in the eighteenth and nineteenth centuries; these works, which are also exhibited on the walls of the stairway itself, include a number of romantic views of Athens and its monuments.

The stairway brings one first to Room XI, which exhibits works of art from western Europe, principally Italian renaissance furniture and Italian and Spanish velvets dating from the fifteenth, sixteenth and seventeenth centuries. Room XII, which is endowed by the Damianos Kyriazis bequest, is devoted to paintings depicting Greece in the Ottoman period and in the early years of the Greek Kingdom, including a watercolour of Corfu by Edward Lear and a number of views of Athens and its monuments. Room XIII is devoted to Coptic textiles and Room XIV to Islamic art, continuing the exhibition of the collec-tions to which we were introduced on the ground floor. The theme of Room XV is the Greek War of Independence, which includes portraits and memorabilia of the revolutionary heroes, vivid battle scenes, including one by Zographos, and personal articles belonging to Byron, including the writing-desk that he used at Mesolongi. Room XVI is devoted to the reign of King Otho, and Room XVII to the reigns of George I and Constantine I. Room XVIII continues the collection of Islamic art, principally in silks from Bursa, while Room XIX extends the exhibit into works from Asia Minor, Iran and India. Room XX contains part of the George Eumorphopoulos collection of Chinese art, the remainder of which is divided between the British Museum and the Victoria and Albert Museum; on the walls there are carpets from Asia Minor, the Caucasus and central Asia. Room XXI is devoted to an exhibition of household embroideries from the Greek islands, Crete, Cyprus, Epirus and Asia Minor, along with similar works from other places as far away as the Portuguese colony of Goa in India.

The basement of the Benaki Museum is almost entirely given over to an exhibition of folk costumes from all over Greece. Also exhibited here are other examples of Greek folk art, including jewellery, earrings, bracelets, necklaces, belt clasps, embroideries, carved wooden distaffs, musical instruments and ceramics. In the far corner of the basement we come to the Helene Stathatos Room, which is the reconstructed salon of a late eighteenth-century house in Kozani, in northern Greece. This is an exceedingly handsome room, with superbly carved wooden panelling and furniture, and hung with a number of excellent paintings. This and the other exhibits in the museum are a testimony to the richness and depth of the culture that sustained the Greek people through the long centuries of occupation by the Latins and the Turks.

After leaving the Benaki we continue up the avenue for another two blocks, crossing Odos Douka and walking a short distance down the street to the modern glass-fronted building that houses the Goulandris Museum of Cycladic and ancient Greek art.

This very attractive new museum houses the Nicholas P. Goulandris collection, which covers a time span ranging from the beginning of the Bronze Age down to the end of antiquity, with particular emphasis on the earliest art of the Cyclades. The first floor has 230 examples of Cycladic art dating from the third millennium BC, the most distinctive being the abstract marble figurines known as *idoles*, which were buried with the dead as votive offerings. Many of these are representations of the Great Earth-Mother, the fertility goddess who was worshipped in the Aegean world from the Neolithic period to the end of the Bronze Age; her *idoles* are strange and haunting, evoking the primitive power of her cult, and there is nothing else like them in the world. On the second floor there are three hundred works of art dating from *c.* 2000 BC to the fourth century AD; these include works in clay, gold, bronze, glass and marble, the most notable being unique vases of the classical and archaic periods. Many of the objects on these two floors have never been exhibited to the public before the opening of the Goulandris Museum, and so a first visit there is very exciting for anyone interested in the art of ancient Greece.

We now return to Sofias and continue in the same direction to the next corner, where we cross the avenue and continue half-way up the next block. This brings us to the Byzantine Museum, which is housed

in an exceedingly handsome mansion at the rear of a courtyard off the
avenue.

The mansion that houses the Byzantine Museum was originally
known as the Villa Ilissia, standing as it does on a bluff above the
Ilissos river. The building was designed and built in 1848 by Stamatios
Kleanthes, who modelled it on a renaissance Florentine palace. It was
built for Sophie de Marbois, Duchesse de Plaisance (1785–1854), who
was probably the most eccentric woman to set foot in Athens during
the early years of the Greek Kingdom. Sophie was born in Philadelphia,
the daughter of a French consul to the new republic of the United
States. She later married one of Napoleon's generals and served as
lady-in-waiting to the Empress Josephine. In 1829 she left her husband
and went off to Greece, taking with her their only child, a daughter.
She set up house in Athens, but left after two years, moving to the
Lebanon and settling in Beirut. Her daughter died there two years
later, and this apparently led Sophie to leave Beirut and return to
Athens, taking the child's remains with her in an ornate casket. She
bought a mansion in what is now Omonia Square, but not long
afterwards the house was completely destroyed in a fire, which
cremated her daughter's remains. Sophie recovered her daughter's
ashes from the fire and preserved them in a smaller casket, which she
carried about with her wherever she went, talking to it as if the child
was still alive. After the fire she moved into a large villa she had built
in Pendeli, and which is still standing, and she lived there until the
Villa Ilissia was completed. Sophie entertained a circle of French
intellectuals there, including David d'Angers, Théophile Gautier, and
Edmond About, who would later write about her and her life in
Athens. According to About, Sophie loathed the poor and admired the
wealthy, turning her huge sheep-dogs loose on the beggars who came
to her door, but lending large sums of money to aristocratic families
who were short of funds. She despised all the Germans and Scan-
dinavians in the royal court in Athens, particularly Otho and Amalia,
and never had anything to do with them. As About describes Sophie,
her dress was as odd as her manner, a 'sort of classical costume: a large
veil over her head, and her dress fastened on her shoulder with a kind
of fibula'. She dictated the terms of her will to About, telling him how
she wanted to be laid out after her death. She said that she wanted to
be buried in a large and airy mausoleum near her villa in Pendeli, with
the caskets of her daughter and her two beloved sheep-dogs beside
her, and that each day an open bottle of burgundy and a bouquet of
flowers should be placed beside her coffin by a good-looking young

Greek shepherd. Sophie's tomb can still be seen today near her villa in Pendeli, but there are no wine and roses beside her sarcophagus, which is inscribed with this laconic epitaph in French: 'Sophie Marbois, Duchess of Plaisance, born in Philadelphia on 3 April 1785, died in Athens 14 May 1854.'

The Villa Ilissia began a new life in 1930 as the Byzantine Museum, whose foundation and restoration were the work of the architect George Sotiriou. Another architect, Aristoteles Zacos, was principally responsible for the conversion of the building into the museum, which Sotiriou created 'to provide a picture of the evolution of the art developed in the Greek world from the close of antiquity to the time of the deliverance of the Greek nation from the Turkish yoke'. Zacos reconstructed the ground floor of the villa so that it could be used to recreate the three archetypal plans that were used in Greece from the early Christian period onward; these are described by the director of the Byzantine Museum, Manolis Chatzidakis, in his excellent illustrated book on the art works exhibited there, as 'the Early Christian basilica, the Byzantine church with dome and the post-Byzantine single-space religious building'.

The vestibule of the museum, Room I, contains architectural fragments from churches dating from the fourth to the sixth century, the most notable being from the early basilica of Ay. Dimitrios in Thessalonika and from an early Christian basilica that stood on the Acropolis. Room II, which takes up the whole right-hand side of the museum, has been laid out to reproduce the floor-plan of a three-aisled basilica of the fifth or sixth century, using architectural members from Ay. Dimitrios and other churches of that period. Room III is given over to an exhibition of sculptures from the later Byzantine era, the ninth to the fifteenth centuries, including some works from the centuries when the Latins dominated Greece. Room IV is laid out in the form of a Byzantine cruciform church of the eleventh century. Room V reproduces the architecture and decoration of a post-Byzantine church, with a painted iconostasis dating from the late Turkish period.

On the upper floor, Room II is devoted mostly to an exhibition of Byzantine portative icons; these are arrayed chronologically and range in date from the twelfth to the mid sixteenth century, though most are from the Palaeologian renaissance of the thirteenth and fourteenth centuries. There are also three large frescos from the late Byzantine period, as well as a number of documents and liturgical objects of that era. Room III is given over to an exhibition of frescos that were removed from churches in Athens and elsewhere in Greece before their demolition, or, in some cases, taken from ruined churches to protect them from the elements. One fresco of particular interest is exhibited to the left of the doorway leading into Room IV. This is a portrait of Our Lady of Catalonia, taken from the church of Profitis Ilias in Staropazaro, whose site we saw on our stroll through Plaka; it is the only known work of art associated with the Catalan period in Athenian history.

Room IV contains examples of silver-clad icons and minor works of art in metal, wood and ivory, mostly liturgical, as well as pottery excavated from Ay. Dimitrios in Thessalonika. Room V exhibits vestments and other liturgical objects arrayed in chronological order, including Coptic embroidery dating from the fifth century to the seventh. The most noteworthy exhibit here is the celebrated Epitaphios of Thessalonika, a beautiful embroidery that is thought to have been made in Constantinople in the fourteenth century.

The buildings that form the two sides of the courtyard are used to exhibit the museum's collections of Byzantine and post-Byzantine icons, arrayed in chronological and geographical order. These include Byzantine icons of the twelfth to fifteenth centuries; icons of northern Greece dating from the sixteenth and seventeenth centuries; Cretan icons of the sixteenth and seventeenth centuries; Venetian icons from seventeenth-century Crete; and post-Byzantine icons from the early Ottoman period. A new gallery of the museum is devoted to Greek folk art, including a number of secular paintings and other works of art from the Turkish period and also from the early years of the Greek Kingdom.

After leaving the Byzantine Museum we continue walking up the avenue as far as the next corner, where we come to the large and unattractive building that houses the War Museum.

In the courtyard of the museum there are a number of tanks and fighter planes of the Second World War, including a Spitfire. On the porch there is a replica of the first Greek fighter aircraft, appropriately named the Daedalus, which on 5 October 1912 was flown by Lieutenant Dimitrios Kumberos over the Turkish lines in Thessaly.

On the ground floor of the museum there are cases containing armour, weapons and armaments from the Byzantine, Latin and Turkish periods in Greece, as well as firearms and dress armour from the War of Independence and the early Greek Kingdom. In the basement there is a display of Greek military uniforms from ancient times up to the present. On the mezzanine there are Greek armaments from the Second World War. The various galleries on the upper floor contain exhibits devoted to Greek military history through the ages, illustrated with prints, paintings, battle plans, dioramas, weapons, uniforms, battle flags and weapons. These are arranged in chronological order; the first gallery deals with warfare from Mycenaean times down to the classical period, while the others are dedicated to the campaigns of Alexander the Great; the Byzantine period; the Latin and Turkish occupations; the War of Independence; the period 1828–1911; the Balkan Wars; the First World War; the Greek–Turkish War of 1919–22; the 1940 campaign against the Italians in Albania; and the German invasion of Greece in 1941.

After leaving the War Museum we continue walking up the avenue, turning right at the major intersection beside the Hilton Hotel. There we make our way across Leoforos Vasileos Konstantinou to the Ethniki Pinakotheke, the National Gallery of Art, which also houses the Alexandros Soutzos Museum. The permanent collections here are principally Greek painting and sculpture of the nineteenth and twentieth centuries. The best known of these are works by the painters N. Hadzikyriakos-Ghikas, C. Parthenis, Alekos Kontoglu and Theophilus Hadzimichail, and the sculptors P. Prosalentis and Y. Halepas. The museum also has a number of works by major European artists, including a sculpture by Rodin and paintings by Breugel, Caraveggio, Delacroix, El Greco, Picasso and Utrillo. Besides these, there are also a number of paintings, by both Greek and foreign artists, depicting Athens in the late Ottoman period and in the early years of the Greek Kingdom, showing the monuments of the ancient city as they looked when Greece was rediscovered by the western world.

We now make our way back to Leoforos Vasilissis Sofias and cross to the opposite side, where we turn right and continue walking up the avenue. We then turn left at the next corner on to Odos Gennadiou, walking uphill past the Evangelismos Hospital and the grounds of the American School of Classical Studies and the British School of Archaeology. At the upper end of the street we see a handsome edifice of white marble at the base of Mount Lycabettos; this is the Gennadeion, known in English as the Gennadius Library, the last stop on this second stroll through central Athens.

The Gennadeion houses one of the world's richest collections of books on Greek subjects, the core of which is the 24,000 volumes that once belonged to John Gennadius (1844–1932), the founder of the library. Gennadius, the son of a schoolmaster, served for sixty years in the diplomatic service of Greece, and for two decades he headed the Greek legation in London. Throughout his career he used a large part of his modest income in buying antiquarian books on Greek subjects. As he wrote in his memoirs, referring to his early years in London, 'But then, as always ever since, I denied to myself many other luxuries, and even necessities, in order to buy books. And although I neither gambled nor betted, I ran into debt through a love which was growing into a passion.'

Gennadius ended his distinguished diplomatic career as the Greek representative to the Naval Disarmament Conference, which met in Washington, DC, in 1921–2. It was then that Gennadius made his decision to donate his books to the American School of Classical Studies. On 29 March 1922 the American School formally agreed to accept his donation, supported by a generous grant from the Carnegie Foundation. The Greek government provided a site adjacent to the American School, and construction of the building began on 1 September 1923. The project was completed in 1926, and on 23 April of that year John Gennadius dedicated his library to the memory of his father, George, who had instilled in him the love of learning that had made him a bibliophile. During the remaining six years of his life Gennadius continued to add to the library's collection, and when he died in 1932 his estate amounted to minus £1,500 sterling, which he still owed to various booksellers for works that he had purchased for the Gennadeion, a debt soon settled by the foundation that was established in his memory. During the years since then the number of books in the Gennadeion has been doubled, and it has become a world centre for the study of Greek culture during the Byzantine and Turkish periods.

Some of the most important books in the Gennadeion's collection are exhibited in the main reading-room of the library. These include a copy of the first edition of the Greek Bible, printed in Milan in 1481; a first edition of the New Testament in modern Greek, printed in Basle in 1516; and the *Lascaris Grammar*, printed in Milan in 1476, the first Greek book known to have been published in western Europe during the Renaissance. In addition to these and other rare antiquarian books the display cases contain a number of Byron memorabilia. There are also several interesting paintings on the walls of the reading-room, including the last portrait ever made of Byron; this was painted by Robert Seymour from a sketch made by Major Parry, and it shows the poet playing with his huge dog, Lion, with some of his Suliote guards in the background.

Beyond the stacks to the left of the entrance there are more display cases with rare books and other exhibits. The most interesting exhibit here is a work entitled 'Marche Triomphale du Sultan, la Musique', which consists of thirty-eight drawings of scenes from an imperial procession in Istanbul, dating from the second half of the sixteenth century. The walls around the stacks are hung with some of the 190 watercolours of Greek landscapes done in the mid nineteenth century by Edward Lear, all of which Gennadius bought in London in 1924 for a total price of £24. There are also several battle scenes of the War of Independence painted by Paniotis Zographos, done as illustrations for the *Memoirs* of Makriyannis.

Beyond the stacks a door leads into the left wing of the library, where there is an extraordinary room that one can visit by asking permission from the librarian. This is the Helene Stathatos room, another chamber from the same house in Kozani whose salon we saw at the Benaki.

After seeing the Stathatos Room we leave the Gennadeion, concluding this second stroll through central Athens. When departing we might reflect on the inscription over the entrance; this records the concluding sentence of the speech that John Gennadius made when he dedicated the Gennadeion: 'They are called Greeks who share in our culture.'

13

The National Archaeological Museum

This penultimate chapter will be devoted entirely to the National Archaeological Museum, which is some 600 metres north of Omonia Square along Leoforos 28 Oktombriou, formerly known as Patission. The museum is surrounded by a tree-shaded park with outdoor cafés, a pleasant place to stop and take a break during this tour.

The main museum building was designed by the architect Ludwig Lange and its foundations were laid under his direction in 1866. But when Lange died two years later Theophil von Hansen was placed in charge of the project, which was completed in 1889 by the Greek architect Kalkos. A new wing, started in 1925 and completed in 1939, was built to house the vast amount of material that had accumulated in the meantime. Formerly, virtually all of the finds from archaeological explorations in Greece were stored and exhibited here, but in recent years local museums have been built all over the country so that antiquities can be kept at or near their original sites. But even so, the number of the antiquities on display in the National Archaeological Museum, and their variety, is so great that there will only be time to look at a few of the major exhibits on a first stroll through its various rooms. At the reception desk one can buy an excellent illustrated guide to the museum's collections by Professor Manolis Andronicos, so that the present chapter will for the most part point out only the more famous exhibits, particularly those that have associations with ancient Athens.

From the entrance lobby we pass into Room 4, the Mycenaean Hall. This long gallery contains some of the most important finds made at Mycenae and other sites of the Mycenaean age in Greece, beginning with the pioneering excavations made by Heinrich Schliemann in 1874–6. Most of the objects here range in date from 1600 to 1200

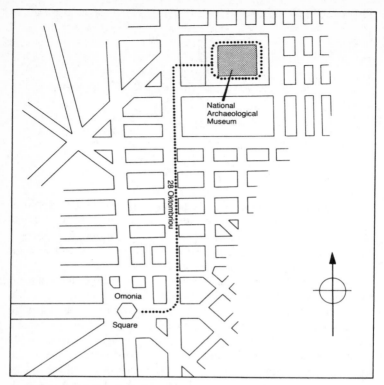

28 Oktombriou

National
Archaeological
Museum

Omonia

Square

To the National Archaeological Museum

BC. The most prominently displayed of the exhibits are those that Schliemann excavated from the shaft-graves at Mycenae. There he unearthed nineteen skeletons, which he identified with Agamemnon and his companions, who were murdered on their return to Mycenae by Clytemnestra and her lover, Aegisthus. The most famous exhibit here is the gold funerary masque which Schliemann believed to be that of Agamemnon himself. Other notable exhibits are the gold tiara of a Mycenaean princess; a silver rhyton, or drinking cup, in the shape of a bull's head with golden horns; a golden rhyton in the shape of a lion's head; two gold cups found at Vapheio; and a golden goblet known as the 'Cup of Nestor' because of its supposed resemblance to the 'fine two-handled beaker' of which Homer writes in the *Odyssey*, describing the welcoming feast that King Nestor gave for Telemachus. There is also a case of clay tablets from the archives of the Mycenaean palace at Ano Englianos, near Pylos, all of them inscribed with the script known as Linear B, now recognized as the earliest form of the Greek language. Another notable exhibit is the plaster head of a woman with painted features; this dates from the thirteenth century BC, and is one of the very few sculptures in the round that have survived from the Mycenaean world.

We now enter Room 5, the Prehistoric Room, which is to the left of the Mycenaean Hall. The antiquities here come mostly from excavations north of Attica as far as Macedonia, ranging in time from the Neolithic era down to the Mycenaean age. The exhibits consist mostly of pottery and votive objects found in tombs, including numerous statuettes of the Great Earth-Mother, the fertility goddess who was worshipped throughout the Aegean world in the prehistoric era.

The Cycladic Room, Room 6, is on the other side of the Mycenaean Hall. The antiquities here are all from the Cyclades, the beautiful archipelago in the central Aegean, and they date mostly from the third millennium BC. As we have seen in the Goulandris Museum, the most distinctive works of Cycladic art are its famous marble *idoles*, most of which are stylized representations of the Great Earth-Mother. But the statues take other forms as well, the most notable being the one known as the Harp-player, found on the isle of Keros. The player is shown seated on a marble throne, his harp resting on his knee and his blank, prow-nosed face looking upwards, much the same attitude that is assumed by folk musicians in the islands even today. This is undoubtedly the greatest and most imaginative work of art that has survived from the Cycladic period.

We now return to the lobby and go to Room 7, which is to the left of the main doorway as one enters the museum. This and the seven rooms beyond it are devoted principally to works of the Archaic era, along with some from the Geometric period (750–700 BC).

The principal exhibit in Room 7 is a huge clay funerary amphora from the Kerameikos cemetery in Athens. This superb vase, dated *c*. 750 BC, is decorated in the geometric style that gave its name to the second half of the eighth century BC; here it consists of bands of geometrical designs, principally meanders, along with two bands on the neck depicting grazing fawns. On the front, between the handles, is depicted a *prothesis* – laying-out and wake – while at the back there is a scene depicting eight mourners.

The outstanding exhibit in Room 8 is the Sounion Kouros, the colossal statue of a naked youth with long hair braided down over his shoulders. This kouros, which in Greek means 'youth', was set up towards the end of the seventh century BC in the precincts of the Temple of Poseidon at Cape Sounion, a memorial to a young man who had died before his time in battle. The kouroi are idealized statues of youths represented as if they were Apollo, their hair braided down over their shoulders, their lips curved and their eyes rounded in the haunting smile that characterizes the faces of the Archaic age. The Pythian Hymn to Apollo was written at just about the time when the Sounion Kouros was created, and one can see the form of the god in the statue: 'He is like a youth, lusty and powerful in his bloom, his hair spread over his shoulders.'

In Room 9, we see another kouros, the Melos Kouros, a work of the mid sixth century BC, named for the Cycladic isle on which it was found. Also outstanding is the beautiful Myrrhinous Kore, discovered in 1972 near Markopoulo, a village in Attica; an inscription identifies this as a statue of the maiden Phrasikleia done by Aristeion of Paros, a sculptor who is known to have worked in the last quarter of the sixth century BC.

A door at the far right-hand corner of Room 9 leads into Room 10. The principal exhibit here is the Myrrhinous Kouros, found near Markopoulo in 1972 along with the kore we have just seen in Room 9. In the smaller chamber beyond, Room 10A, we see the slender Volomandra Kouros, here again named for the Attic village in which it was found. This is considered to be one of the archetypes for a large group of such dedicatory statues done in the mid sixth century BC.

We now make our way back to Room 8, and then straight ahead into Room 11. The principal exhibit here is the muscular Kea Kouros, found on the northernmost island of the Cyclades, where it was carved c. 530 BC. Another outstanding sculpture in this room is a tall funerary stele, decorated in low relief with the figure of a lightly bearded warrior in armour, dated to c. 510 BC.

The most outstanding exhibit in Room 12, at the far left-hand corner of the museum, is the Stela of the Hoplitodromos, a funerary relief with the naked figure of a running hoplite. This superb work, another masterpiece of archaic art, is dated to c. 510 BC.

In Room 13 we see the Anavyssos Kouros, a funerary monument discovered in Attica in 1938, dated c. 520 BC. The base of the statue bears this inscription: 'Pause and lament at the tomb of the dead Kroisos, whom furious Ares slew when he was fighting in the forefront.' Two other interesting exhibits are kouros bases with reliefs showing ephebes in several lively scenes; these were carved c. 500 BC, and just two decades afterwards they were built into the Themistoclean walls of Athens in the vicinity of the Dipylon.

Room 14 is devoted almost entirely to an exhibition of funerary sculpture dating from the first half of the fifth century BC. The exhibits here were all found outside Athens, for during this period the sumptuary laws of Cleisthenes prohibited Athenians from building elaborate funerary monuments in the Kerameikos cemetery.

Room 15 is dominated by the colossal bronze statue known as the Poseidon of Artemision. This magnificent work of art, one of the few large-scale moulded bronze statues that have survived from the ancient Greek world, was found in 1928 at the bottom of the sea off Cape Artemision in northern Euboea. It is an original work dated to *c.* 450 BC, and may have been done by Kalamis, one of the famous sculptors of that period. Another remarkable sculpture in this room is the Eleusis Relief, a large votive panel found in the Temple of Demeter in Eleusis. This shows Demeter and her daughter Persephone with Triptolemos, the young King of Eleusis, who was sent off to teach the arts of agriculture to all mankind. This is a very moving work of art, its beauty enhanced by the deep religious feeling that it conveys; it is dated to *c.* 440 BC, contemporary with the Parthenon sculptures, which obviously influenced the unknown artist who created this masterpiece.

A door to the right leads into Room 16, the first of three rooms devoted to an exhibition of funerary monuments and votive sculptures of the fifth century BC. Many of these date from the latter part of the fifth century, when the sumptuary laws of Cleisthenes had been allowed to lapse, and include some of the most beautiful Attic funerary sculptures in existence.

In the centre of Room 16 there is a large white lekythos, which adorned the tomb of a maiden identified by an inscription as Myrrhine. A relief on the vase shows Myrrhine's living relatives looking on as she is led into the Underworld by Hermes Psychopompos, the Conductor of Souls. This lovely vase, which was found in an excavation at Syntagma Square, is dated to 420–410 BC. Another notable exhibit in this room is a funerary stele showing an ephebe with his slave boy, his cat and his pet birds, who mourn his departure to the Underworld. This stele was found in Salamis and is dated 430–420 BC; the extremely high quality of the relief has led to the suggestion that it was the work of one of the artists who did the Parthenon frieze.

We now enter Room 17, which is devoted to an exhibition of Attic votive sculpture of the fifth century BC. In the centre of the room we see the most spirited work of this type in the museum, a double votive relief from Phaleron dated to the end of the fifth century BC. The central figure in the front scene is Hermes, who here appears in his role of Nymphagogos, the Leader of the Bride, so this relief must have been dedicated in a shrine of Hermes and nymphs to commemorate a wedding.

A door at the right side of the room leads into Room 20, where there is an exhibition of sculpture from the Classical period. One of these is a relief showing an ephebe with horses; this is dated to the period 430–420 BC, and appears to be strongly influenced by similar figures on the Parthenon frieze. Another interesting relief shows a man praying at an outdoor altar in the presence of two nymphs, while Pan looks down from his cave above. This relief, which dates to c. 410 BC, was restored from fragments found on the north slope of the Acropolis, and undoubtedly came from a shrine in the Cave of Pan that we have seen on two of our strolls. This room also has a number of Roman copies of original works by Pheidias and his school. One of these is the Varvakeion Athena, so called because it was found near the Varvakeion Lycée in Athens. This is a small marble copy of the chryselephantine statue of Athena Parthenos by Pheidias, one twelfth of the size of the original cult-statue that once stood in the Parthenon; it is an inferior work of the second century AD, but it is of great interest to those trying to reconstruct the Pheidian masterpiece. Another such work exhibited here is the Lenormant Athena, an unfinished Roman copy in miniature of the statue of Athena Parthenos by Pheidias. Still another work of some interest here is an Amazon caryatid from Kynouria, in Arcadia. It is thought that the Amazon is a Roman copy of an original made by Pheidias for the famous Artemis-ium in Ephesus, one of the Seven Wonders of the World.

Room 19, on the left, is also devoted to sculptures of the Classical period, and Roman copies of Greek originals of that era. One of the most interesting originals is a relief showing ephebes doing the Pyrrhic war-dance. The most interesting of the copies is perhaps a small statuette of Aphrodite, a copy of an original work dated c. 420 BC. This was a popular representation of the goddess, for quite a number of copies of it have survived, the finest being those in the Louvre and the Naples Museum.

From Room 20, a flight of steps leads down into the atrium, an open courtyard between the central hall and the left wing of the museum. Under the colonnade that borders the courtyard there are stored a number of antiquities; these include marble statuary recovered from the sea bed off the island of Antikythera, as well as some Roman sarcophagi and several tombstones of the fourth century BC.

We now make our way back into Room 17, where we turn left into Room 18, which contains more funerary monuments of the fifth century BC. One of the principal exhibits here is the funerary monument of Hegeso, whose grave we saw earlier on our stroll through the Kerameikos cemetery. The monument is a naiskos, in which the relief is framed by the representation of a temple. This masterpiece of Attic funerary sculpture is dated to c. 400 BC, and it has been suggested that it is a work of Kallimachos.

In Room 21, just beyond the Mycenaean Hall, the principal exhibit is the group known as the Horse and Jockey of Artemision, one of the most striking works of art in the museum. This is a life-size bronze statue of a horse being ridden at full gallop by a small and very young jockey, who is mounted bareback. This splendid group was found on the sea bed off Cape Artemision at the same time as the bronze statue of Poseidon we saw earlier, and was later reassembled from many fragments; it is dated to the second century BC, and is one of the most original works of Hellenistic sculpture in existence. Another famous work exhibited in this room is the Diadoumenos, a representation of Apollo as a handsome youth. This is a good marble copy, made c. 100 BC, of the original bronze statue done in the fifth century BC by Polykleitos, one of the great sculptors of the Periclean Age. Another notable work is the Hermes of Andros, a large marble statue of the god represented as guardian of the dead; this is another good copy, made in the first century BC, of an original dating from the fourth century BC, a work attributed to the great Praxiteles. Of the many reliefs exhibited in this room the most interesting is perhaps one representing an Amazonomachy, a work discovered in Athens and dated to the fourth century BC. This is similar to the Amazonomachy that decorated the famous Mausoleum in Halicarnassus, another of the Seven Wonders of the World, and it has been suggested that it may be the work of one of the sculptors who decorated that tomb, perhaps Bryaxis.

We now turn left to pass through the colonnade and enter Room 34, a long hall that connects the older part of the museum with the new addition to its rear. This hall is called the Room of the Altar, and it is arranged in the form of an ancient outdoor sanctuary. The central exhibit here is an altar dedicated by the Athenian Boule in 197/6 BC to Aphrodite Hegemone, Leader of the People, and to her attendant Graces. This altar was found at the foot of Kolonos Agoraios during the excavations for the Athens–Piraeus railway. The altar stood in a small sanctuary of Demos (the People) and the Graces, in which the goddess Roma was also worshipped in Roman times. Among the many exhibits here there are several from monuments in Athens; these include two votive reliefs and a small cult-statue from a sanctuary of Heracles at Agra on the Ilissos; fragments from a frieze found in the cave-sanctuary of Aphrodite and Eros on the north slope of the Acropolis; a marble slab from the choregic monument of Thrasyllos on the south slope of the Acropolis; and a marble statue group found in the Theatre of Dionysos on the south slope of the Acropolis. The latter group depicts an old Papasilenos carrying on his shoulders the young Dionysos, who holds in his hands a tragic mask, a work dating to the late Hellenistic period.

At the far end of Room 34 we pass through the colonnade and enter Room 35, where we turn left to go on into Room 36. The latter room houses the Karapanos Collection, an exhibition of antiquities discovered by the archaeologist Constantine Karapanos during the years 1875–7. A large number of these antiquities are from the Panhellenic sanctuary of Zeus in Dodona, whose oracle was second only to that of Pythian Apollo at Delphi in its influence throughout the Greek world.

Next we come to Room 37, which is devoted to a display of bronze objects from the Geometric, Archaic and early Classical periods. The most notable of these is a superb statuette of Athena Promachos, distinguished by the incredibly tall crested helmet she is wearing as she strides forward, about to hurl a thunderbolt at the advancing foe. This was found on the Acropolis of Athens and is dated to the mid fifth century BC.

Room 37 opens into Rooms 38 and 40, the only galleries that are currently open at the north-west corner of the museum on the ground floor. The most famous of the works exhibited here is the Ephebos of Marathon, a superb bronze statue of a naked youth found in an ancient shipwreck in the Bay of Marathon. This masterpiece is believed to be a work of Praxiteles, and is dated to the third quarter of the fourth century BC.

We return through the Room of the Altar to Room 21, and then turn right to enter Room 22, which is devoted mostly to an exhibition of sculptures from Epidaurus. Many of these objects formed part of the sculptural decoration of the Temple of Asklepios, a Doric edifice completed c. 370 BC.

Room 23 is devoted to funerary monuments of the fourth century

BC. The most noteworthy of these is the Ilissos Stele, so called because it was found on the bed of the Ilissos river. The stele, which is dated to *c.* 430 BC, is decorated with a large relief that was once framed in a naiskos. The deceased is shown as a naked ephebe who is being gazed upon sadly by a bearded older man who is undoubtedly his father, while at the feet of the youth we see his disconsolate slave boy and hound. This masterpiece has been attributed by some scholars to the great Scopas or a sculptor of his school.

Turning right, we enter Room 25, which is given over to funerary and votive reliefs as well as inscribed stelai. Many of the votive reliefs here and elsewhere in the museum's collection were found in the Athenian Asklepieion, on the south slope of the Acropolis, placed there in gratitude by patients who had been cured of their ailments at the shrine. On one interesting relief we see Hygieia blessing a suppliant at the shrine's altar, while her father Asklepios sits on a stool behind her, with one of his sacred serpents raising its head beside him.

In Rooms 26 and 27 there are more votive reliefs. The most unusual of these reliefs, in the first of the two rooms, shows a bearded man holding the lower half of a huge leg that is bigger than he is. A varicose vein in the leg establishes the ailment suffered by the donor, identified by an inscription as Lysimachides, son of Lysimachos. The inscription, which is dated to the end of the fourth century BC, records that the offering is being made to the hero-physician Amynos, whose sanctuary has been identified on the west slope of the Athenian Acropolis.

We now make our way back into Room 24, which is given over to funerary reliefs of the fourth century BC. The finest of these is a funerary stele in the form of a naiskos found in the Kerameikos cemetery; an inscription identifies it as a memorial to Prokleides, a youth who is shown with his grieving parents.

A noteworthy exhibit in Room 28, which is devoted to a collection of late Attic funerary stelai and other sculptures of the fourth century BC, is the monument of Aristonautes. This is a naiskos in which the figure of the deceased is represented almost entirely in the round. He is a mature and muscular man, wearing a thin chiton, a leather breastplate and a conical helmet, and holding his shield in his left hand; his missing right hand would have been wielding his sword. This stirring work was found in the Kerameikos cemetery and is dated to *c.* 320–310 BC. Another outstanding funerary sculpture here is a large relief in which a young black groom is shown trying to control a high-spirited stallion; this lively and imaginative work was found in Athens and is dated to the Hellenistic period.

Elsewhere in this room we see one of the most famous works of art in the museum, the Ephebe of Antikythera. This is a bronze statue of a young man discovered in 1900 on the bottom of the sea off the isle of Antikythera. The muscular youth is shown nude, his right arm raised with the fingers curled down to hold a round object, now lost, which he is offering to someone at whom he is looking in apparent adoration. It has been suggested that the youth is Paris, son of King Priam of Troy, and that he is offering the apple of Eros to Aphrodite in the contest of beauty that was held on Mt Ida in the Troad, judging her the winner over Hera and Athena. If so, this would be the famous statue of Paris done by the sculptor Euphranor c. 340 BC.

Beside the door at the far end of the room we see the lovely marble head of a deity identified as Hygieia, goddess of health, the daughter of Asklepios. This was found in the sanctuary of Athena Alea at Tegea, in the Peloponnesus, and is dated to c. 360 BC. It is thought to be a work of Scopas, and if so it is one of the very few of his sculptures that have survived in the original.

We now go on to Room 29, the first of two galleries in this wing devoted to Hellenistic sculpture. This is also known as the Room of Themis, one of the goddesses of justice, whose marble statue is one of the principal exhibits in this gallery. This statue was found at Rhamnous, near Marathon, where Themis was worshipped along with Nemesis, the goddess of divine retribution. An inscription on the base of the statue identifies the donor as Megacles of Rhamnous and the sculptor as Chairestratos, son of the famous artist Chairedomos, and consequently the work is dated to the third century BC.

The exhibition of Hellenistic sculpture continues in Room 30, the last gallery in the south-east wing of the museum. There are a number of famous bronzes here, including the head of a philosopher, c. 240 BC, found off Antikythera with the ephebe we have just seen; the head of a man, early first century BC, from Delos; and the head of a pugilist, from Olympia. It is thought that the latter may represent Satyros, who won first prize in boxing at one of the Olympic Games, c. 330 BC, and dedicated a statue of himself done by the well-known Athenian sculptor Silanion.

We come finally to one of the most delightful works in the museum, the famous 'Sandal Slapper'. This is a marble group representing Aphrodite, Pan and Eros. Aphrodite is represented nude, her hair worn high on her head, an amused smile on her pretty face as she holds aloft her left sandal, ready to slap the amorous Pan as he tries to embrace her, while the sweetly smiling Eros hovers between them, holding the goat-god by one horn. This charming group was found in Delos and is dated *c.* 100 BC.

Room 31, on the right, is used to house temporary exhibitions illustrating various aspects of life in ancient Greece. Beyond this in the south-east wing are Rooms 32 and 33, which house the Stathatos Collection. This collection is another donation of Helene Stathatos; it consists mainly of antiquities from Thessaly, Chalcidia and Macedonia, ranging in date from the Bronze Age to the Byzantine era. The collection is particularly rich in jewellery and gold ornaments. The most outstanding exhibit here is an ornament decorated in high relief in a jewel-studded gold naiskos; the central figure is Dionysos, flanked by a young satyr and a panther; this was found in Thessaly and is dated to the late Hellenistic period.

We now make our way to the upper floor of the museum, which is approached by the stairway at the far end of the central area of the building. At the top of the stairway we proceed straight ahead to enter Room 48, which is devoted to the extraordinary Minoan frescos from Akrotiri on Thera.

Thera, the Cycladic isle known also as Santorini, was part of the maritime empire of Minoan Crete in the mid second millennium BC, the period recalled in the myth of Theseus and Ariadne. A Cretan settlement dating to *c.* 1600 BC was excavated at Akrotiri during the years 1967–74 by Professor Spyridon Marinatos, who discovered the extraordinary frescos that are now exhibited here at the National Archaeological Museum in Athens. (There are plans to build a new museum in Santorini to house the frescos and other antiquities excavated at Akrotiri.) The frescos are largely depictions of daily life on Thera in Minoan times, vivid and charming scenes painted in bright and fresh colours. The most remarkable fresco is a vast panorama depicting a naval expedition about to set off on a campaign, an expedition that Professor Marinatos suggested was a Minoan invasion of Libya mounted from Thera.

The other galleries on the upper floor are devoted to the museum's vast collection of pottery and to its numismatic collection, the latter housed in the north-east wing. (The north-east wing also houses the epigraphic collection, which has a separate entrance on Odos Tositsa.) Most visitors to Athens content themselves with a brief stroll through the rooms on the upper floor after seeing the Thera frescos, for the enormous number of exhibits is far too much to absorb after seeing the rest of the museum. But it is worth spending some time in these galleries on a later visit, particularly in the almost deserted rooms where the vases are exhibited, because there are masterpieces of Greek art to be seen there, many of them evocative of the life and culture of ancient Greece.

14

Strolling through Athens

This last chapter consists of a number of strolls to various places in Athens, some of them in the centre of town, others in more remote parts of the city seldom seen by foreign visitors.

Our first stroll will take us to Monastiraki Square, the centre of the market quarter. We have passed through this busy square several times on our various strolls through the city, but now we will just wander at random up and down the narrow, crowded streets that lead off from the old mosque of Tzisdarakis, one of the two landmarks of the quarter, the other being the old Monastiraki church itself. One little byway to look for is a flight of steps off Odos Pandrossou just behind the mosque; this is now just a dead end, but it was once the main market street leading up from Monastiraki to Staropazaro. This vanished street, the famous Steps, is vividly described by Nikolaos Makri in his novel, *Vasiliki, the Lady of Athens*, published in 1878, as quoted by Liza Micheli in her book on Monastiraki:

The street of shops was the busiest and most important in the town, and was called either agora, *charshi*, or bazaar. It cut through the lower fortress wall, the Rodakio district, the square with the Judgement Hall, and the Upper and Lower Bazaars as far as the blacksmiths' quarter on the hither side of the Piraeus Gate. The shops themselves stood between the two fountains. This stone-paved street, hardly more than two metres wide, became almost impassable on weekdays, when the way was blocked by the door panels used for stalls and benches, the textiles strung out on projecting poles and the throng of people shopping; and happy was he who could thread his way through them without being knocked to the ground amidst the cries of the shop apprentices shouting to customers, the banging of the cobbler's hammers and the quarrels.

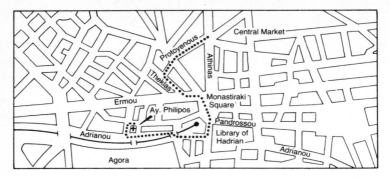

Monastiraki and the Central Market

The main street of the Monastiraki market quarter is now Odos Adrianou. Many of the shops on street level sell workaday items or worthless trash for the tourist trade, but there are a number of good antique shops in the basements, and there is also a rather interesting secondhand bookshop in one of the side alleys. Sunday morning is the best time for a stroll through Monastiraki, for then an outdoor flea-market is set up off Adrianou in the little square around the church of Ay. Philipos. The flea-market never ceases to be fascinating, for every imaginable product of modern society is sold there secondhand, evidence that the poor of Athens never throw anything away, but sell or trade it in Monastiraki.

Walking along Adrianou to Monastiraki Square, one realizes with some sadness that this lively quarter is not as plebeian or colourful as it was in times past, though the variety of goods for sale there is still astonishing. An evocative description of Odos Adrianou as it was at the turn of the century is given by Emmanuel Roidis, in another quote from Liza Micheli's *Monastiraki*:

... In it you find whatever you want, or (more particularly) don't want, to find: Greek and Roman ruins, wreckage from the Turkish period, food frying in the open, coach-builders', potters', palm and plane trees, chicken coops, boys' schools, girls' schools, a primary school, stables, slaughterhouses, pharmacies, doctors, coffin-makers', cypresses and whatever else you need as long as you are alive or after you are dead.

Let us now head towards the Central Market, starting our stroll by walking north from Monastiraki Square to the intersection of Odos Ermou and Odos Athinas. But at that point let us make a short detour to visit a nearby site of some sentimental interest, though there is

nothing tangible to be seen there. We turn left on Ermou and then take
the second right on to Odos Theklas, a short and nondescript street
that is just one block long. Half-way down the street on the left we
come to our destination, a vacant lot on which once stood the house
marked No. 11. (By the time this book is published there will doubtless
be a new building here.)

The original house on this site, built late in the Turkish period, was
where Byron and Hobhouse lived when they first came to Athens in
1809, remaining there for ten weeks. Hobhouse describes the place:
'We occupied two houses separated from each other by a single wall
through which we opened a doorway. One of them belongs to a lady
named Theodora Macris . . . Her lodgings consisted of a sitting-room
and two bedrooms, opening on to a courtyard, where there are five or
six lemon trees.'

From this house Byron and his friend set out each day, as Hobhouse
put it, to contemplate 'the noble monuments of Grecian genius, that
have outlived the ravages of time, and the outrage of barbarous and
antiquarian despoilers'. The house adjoining their lodgings was also
part of the Macris estate and belonged to Theodora's sister-in-law, the
widow Tarsia, who lived there with her three daughters, whom Byron
described in a letter to his friend Henry Drury, dated 3 May 1810: 'I
almost forgot to tell you that I am dying for love of three Greek girls
of Athens, sisters. I lived in the same house. Teresa, Marianna and
Katinka are the names of the three divinities, all of them under fifteen.'

Teresa, the youngest, was Byron's favourite, and when he left
Athens a few months later he wrote her a touching letter of farewell.
When Byron returned to Athens, in July 1810, Tarsia Macris confronted him about his relationship with Teresa, an incident that he
described in a letter to Hobhouse, who was still in England. As he
wrote: 'Intrigue flowers; the old woman was mad enough to imagine
that I was going to marry the girl, but I have better amusement.'
Nevertheless, Teresa Macris seems to have lingered on in Byron's
mind; she was the one to whom he addressed his poem, *Maid of
Athens*, whose first lines are evoked by the site of the house where she
once lived:

> Maid of Athens, ere we part
> Give, O give me back my heart.

Let us now continue on towards the Central Market, taking back
streets all the way. We continue walking down to the end of Theklas,
turning right at the corner, then at the first crossroads we continue in

the same direction on Odos Protoyenous. Two blocks farther along we come to Odos Athinas, which we cross to enter the Central Market.

During the hours when it is open, from early morning until midday, the Central Market is the noisiest, liveliest and most colourful place in all of Athens, with fishmongers, poulterers and butchers in one of the market halls, and greengrocers in another across the street, all of them hawking their products to the passing throng. Many of the men who shop here linger on with the market people in one or another of the raffish little tavernas and stand-up bars that have long been established in among the stalls and barrows of the butchers and fishmongers, or at the very old *oinomagerion*, or wine-house, that has been doing business out on Odos Athinas since the Central Market was first established here. There is no more entertaining place in Athens to have lunch than one of these old bars, watching the endless parade of Athenian life passing through this bedlam of a market.

THE FIRST CEMETERY

The First Cemetery of Athens, the Proto Nekrotafeion, is situated a short distance to the south-west of the Olympieion. To go there, we walk first to the intersection of Kallirois, Arditou and Anapafseos, just across from the little chapel of Ay. Photini, which we passed on our stroll around the walls of ancient Athens. From there we walk up Anapafseos to the end of the street, where we come to the main entrance of the Proto Nekrotafeion.

The First Cemetery is a veritable outdoor museum of modern Greek funerary architecture and sculpture. Some of the sepulchral sculptures are authentic works of art, the most notable being perhaps the famous 'Sleeping Maiden' by Halepas, which adorns the tomb of Sofia Afendaki. This statue, along with most of the other nineteenth-century sculptures and mausoleums, is in the neo-classical style. Many of the great figures of modern Greek history are buried here, as well as a few distinguished foreigners. One of the most conspicuous tombs in the cemetery is that of Heinrich Schliemann, a temple-like structure in the neo-classical style that stands high on the bluff to the left of the mall inside the entrance.

At the far end of the cemetery and to the left there is a separate burial-ground for the Protestant community of Athens. The most notable tomb in this graveyard is that of George Finlay, the Philhellene and

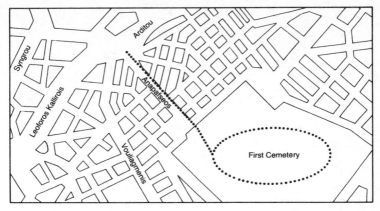

The First Cemetery

historian of Greece, who is buried there with his wife Nectar (an Armenian woman whom he met in Istanbul), and their daughter, who died at the age of ten. The tomb is in the form of a sarcophagus, with a fine bust of Finlay; he is shown as he looked in his later years, with long hair, full moustaches, bristling beard, aquiline nose and large eyes, a proud and defiant look on his face as he stares towards the city where he lived for virtually the whole of his adult life.

KOLONAKI SQUARE AND LYCABETTOS

After the Acropolis, Lycabettos is the most prominent topographic landmark in central Athens, a steep, conical peak covered with pines and crowned with the white chapel of Ay. Yorgios. The peak of Lycabettos is 278 m above sea-level, making it the highest hill within the city, surpassing the Acropolis by 22 m. According to mythology, the rocky mass of Lycabettos was torn from Mt Pendeli by Athena, who planned to use it in fortifying the Acropolis, but as she did so she was startled by a crow's cry and dropped the rock where it lies today. Lycabettos was not included within the walls of Athens, and no ancient source refers to any ancient monument erected upon it until Hadrian built a reservoir on its south-east slope in AD 125. Both Plato and Xenophon describe it as rocky, barren and dry, as indeed are the rest of the Tourkovounia, or Turkish Mountains, of which Lycabettos is the southernmost peak. At some point in the Byzantine period it

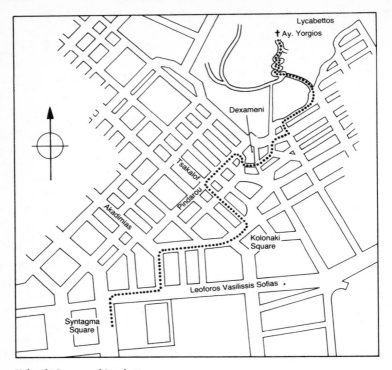

Kolonaki Square and Lycabettos

was planted with olive trees, of which a few survive, while the pines with which it is now covered were planted only in 1882. The hill suffered considerable damage at the turn of the century, when it served as a quarry. Most of the damage has been repaired in recent years, and the hill has been converted into an extremely pleasant park.

If we are approaching Lycabettos from Syntagma, we walk first to Kolonaki Square, which in the evening is the favourite gathering place of fashionable Athens. The square takes its name from the stump of an ancient column, now vanished, that once stood there. Our route takes us through the square to its upper corner, turning left on to Tsakalof, after which we take the second right on to Pindarou. At the top of Pindarou we come to a little park called Dexameni, which in Greek means 'Reservoir'. The park takes its name from the fact that it is laid out on top of the main tank of the water-distribution centre of modern

Athens. The modern Dexameni is to a large extent a rebuilding of the Roman reservoir, which was begun by Hadrian in AD 125 and finished fifteen years later by Antoninus Pius. The monumental façade of the Roman reservoir was located at the upper left-hand side of the present park, where there is now a modern structure with an arcaded niche. The façade consisted of an Ionic propylon with four columns, with an architrave over each pair of columns and an arched entrance at the centre. The columns and their architrave remained standing until 1778, when Ali Haseki pulled them down to use in his defence wall, the Serpentzes. As we have seen, part of the architrave survives in the National Gardens. All that is left *in situ* in the Dexameni can be seen just in front of the modern structure at the top of the park; the remains consist of two column bases of the propylon and part of the stepped platform on which they stood.

We leave the Dexameni by the stairway at the top of the park; there we turn right and take the uppermost street, which winds around the base of Lycabettos. A short way along we come to one of the park entrances, from which there are several paths leading to the summit. Alternatively, one can ride to the top on the funicular railway, whose lower terminus is a little farther along the street that goes round the periphery of the park.

The peak of Lycabettos is crowned by the chapel of Ay. Yorgios, one of the landmarks of Athens. This was built soon after the establishment of the Greek Kingdom, probably on the site of a medieval Byzantine church dedicated to Ay. Profitis Ilias. Later in the nineteenth century the church was enlarged to create two side-chapels, one dedicated to Ay. Yorgios and the other to Ay. Profitis Ilias. The feast-days of both saints are celebrated in the church, and there is also a special service on the eve of Easter Sunday, after which there is a candle-lit procession down from the peak of Lycabettos, a beautiful sight from the lower city.

The view from the peak of Lycabettos is magnificent, for one can see all Athens and the Kephissos plain with its surrounding mountains, as well as the Saronic Gulf and its islands, with Salamis, Aegina, Poros and Hydra visible on a clear day against the background of the Peloponnesus.

PLATO'S ACADEMY AND KOLONOS HIPPIOS

The site of Plato's Academy is about two and a half kilometres north-west of the Dipylon, the ancient gateway of Athens in the Kerameikos

cemetery. We begin our stroll at Ay. Trias, the large modern church
that stands outside the cemetery to the north-west, and from there we
cross Odos Piraeus and start walking out along Odos Platonos. We
will follow this street, persevering across railway tracks and other
obstacles, almost all the way to our destination.

Odos Platonos follows the course of an ancient road for wheeled
traffic that extended from the Dipylon to the Academy. A section of
this ancient road was excavated some years ago near the large modern
church of Ay. Yorgios, which we pass about two kilometres along in
our stroll. The same excavation revealed a number of ancient tombs,
some of which can still be seen in the open area below the church on
its far side. This confirms the supposition that the road from the
Dipylon to the Academy was flanked by the Demosion Sema, the
state burial-ground, where many of the leading figures in the history
of ancient Athens were buried, along with the heroic dead of the city's
many wars. Pausanias took this road on his way from the Academy to
the Dipylon, and he mentions that along the way he saw numerous
war memorials and the tombs of many of the leading statesmen of
ancient Athens, namely Solon, Cleisthenes, Pericles, Cimon, Conon,
Thrasybulus and Lycurgos; as well as those of the philosophers Zeno
and Chrysippos and the tyrannicides Harmodius and Aristogeiton.

We continue along Odos Platonos as far as Odos Alexandrias,
where we turn left on the final approach to the Academy, and at the
third turning on the right we come to the modern church of Ay.
Tryphon. Ay. Tryphon stands at the south-east corner of the
Academy's precincts, a large area of which has been excavated just to
the north of the church. Before exploring this and the other excavated
areas of the temenos, let us pause for a moment to review the history
of the Academy.

The Academy takes its name from Hekademos, an earth-born hero
of Attic mythology; according to tradition he planted here twelve
olive trees that were cuttings from Athena's sacred olive on the
Acropolis, her gift to the people of Attica. Another myth has it that
Hekademos aided the Lacedaemonian heroes Castor and Pollux when
they were searching for their sister Helen, and so whenever the
Spartans invaded Attica they always spared his sacred olive grove.

The temenos of the shrine of Hekademos was vast, judging from
the extent of the excavations, with a periphery of about a thousand
metres. Hipparchus, the younger son of the tyrant Peisistratus, is
credited with building the first enclosure wall around the temenos. He
may also have diverted the Kephissos river to irrigate the temenos,

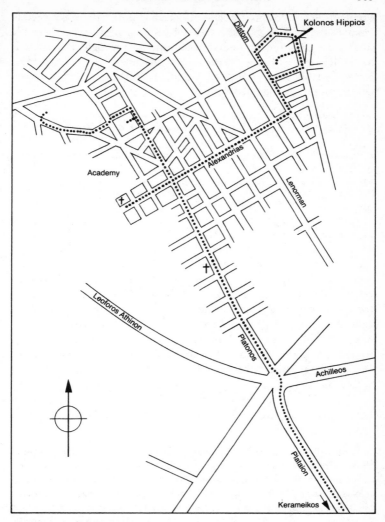

Plato's Academy and Kolonos Hippios

although Plutarch attributes this to Cimon, writing that he changed it 'from a bare, dry and dusty spot into a well-watered grove, with shady walks and running-tracks'. There was already a gymnasium here by the time of Aristophanes, for he describes the foot races that took place within the 'groves of Academe' in a lyrical passage in his *Clouds*, which was produced in 423 BC:

But you below to the Academe go, and under the olives contend
With your chaplet of reed, in a contest of speed, with some excellent rival and friend;
All fragrant with woodbine and peaceful content, and the leaf which the lime-blossoms fling,
When the plane whispers love to the elm in the grove in the beautiful season of spring.

Ancient sources refer to several other deities who were worshipped here, including Athena, who was the patron goddess of the Academy, as well as Zeus, Hermes, Heracles, Eros, the Muses, Hephaistos and Prometheus. Prometheus, the god of fire, was worshipped at an altar which was the starting-point for the nocturnal torch race that took place on the eve of the Panathenaic Procession. As Pausanias describes the race, mentioning some of the other shrines in the vicinity of the altar of Prometheus, 'In the Academy is an altar of Prometheus; they run to the city from it with burning torches. The contest is running while keeping the torch alight; if the first man's torch is out he loses and the second man wins; if his is not burning either, the third man wins; if all the torches are out no one wins.'

Pausanias also describes an altar of Eros, the little god of love, known in Latin as Cupid, telling a bizarre tale about the foundation of this cult in Athens:

In front of the entrance to the Academy is an altar of Love with an inscription that Charmos was the first Athenian to dedicate to Love. They say the altar of 'Love Returned' in the city was dedicated by foreign residents, when an Athenian named Meles spurned an alien lover named Timagoras, and told him to climb to the top of the rock and then jump; Timagoras had no love for his life and wanted to give the boy absolutely everything he asked for, so he really did throw himself off: but Meles was so remorseful when he saw Timagoras killed that he fell to his death from the same rock. From that day to this foreign residents have believed in the demonic spirit of 'Love Returned' which avenged Timagoras.

Peter Levi, in his excellent translation of Pausanias, adds a footnote explaining that Charmos was in love with his son-in-law Hippias, who succeeded his father Peisistratus as tyrant of Athens. Levi also notes that this scandal was quoted by Athenaeus from an inscription on the altar of Love that Charmos founded at the Academy.

> Complicated love, Charmos built you this altar
> among the shadowy boundaries of the playing-fields.

The Academy is celebrated in history as the site of Plato's gymnasium, which he founded c. 386 BC. Other schools and institutions functioned within and around the sacred temenos of Hekademos, but in time the gymnasium founded by Plato became so famous that the name Academy came to be applied to it alone. Plato's Academy was one of the most influential intellectual centres in the Greek world, and many of the great names in the history of Greek philosophy, science and mathematics taught or studied there. The Academy continued in existence for more than nine centuries, and its closure by Justinian in AD 529 is an event that many historians take to mark the end of Graeco-Roman culture and the beginning of the Dark Ages.

Archaeological excavations, here and elsewhere in the vicinity, show that the area of the Academy was first settled in the late Neolithic period, probably at about the same time as the region around the Acropolis. Pottery shards indicate that the area was continuously inhabited throughout the prehistoric era, and foundations excavated in the vicinity of Ay. Tryphon indicate that there was considerable building here during the latter part of the Bronze Age.

The archaeological site next to Ay. Tryphon has been identified as a gymnasium complex, dating to the late Hellenistic or early Roman period. The central part of the complex consisted of a large rectangular court, with a smaller rectangular area in the middle for the *palaestra*, or exercise ground, and an enclosed space at the north end for the baths. Closed halls adjoined the court on the east, south and west sides, serving as dining areas for the students.

Let us now examine the other archaeological sites in the area of the Academy. We begin by retracing our way along Alexandrias to Odos Platonos, where we turn left and continue as far as the fourth turning on the left. This is a little lane that leads immediately to another archaeological site, which has been identified as a square peristyle, though its precise function has not been determined.

After looking at the peristyle we return to Odos Platonos and continue to the next corner, where we turn left on to Odos Evklidou; we follow this for three blocks until it intersects with Odos Dracontos, a road through what is here open countryside. We follow this road for a short way, passing on the right a vast fenced-in area that in places shows evidence of archaeological digs, with fragmentary ancient structures visible here and there in the fields. The entrance to the site is a few hundred metres along on the right. Just inside the entrance and to the right there is a roofed-over area in which some ancient foundations have been identified as belonging to the 'Sacred House', where Hekademos and other chthonic deities were apparently worshipped during the Bronze Age. Elsewhere on the site there is a splendid Roman sarcophagus standing by itself in the middle of a field, quite an extraordinary sight to see in this little-known and almost rural quarter of modern Athens.

The three archaeological sites that we have just seen represent only a small fraction of the total area of the Academy grounds. There is no evidence as to where on this vast site the Academy gymnasium stood, or where Plato himself lived. Plato is known to have built a house within the enclosure of the Academy when he founded his school, and he is thought to have dwelt there until his death in 347 BC. We learn from Diogenes Laertius that 'Plato was buried in the Academy, where he spent most of his life. Possibly his tomb was in the garden beside his school, which was often identified with the Academy itself.'

Many who would later become renowned scholars studied at the Academy during the nine centuries of its existence, including foreigners as well as Greeks. The most distinguished of all the foreign students who studied here was perhaps Cicero, who enrolled in the Academy in 74 BC, when he was twenty-seven years old. Years later, when Cicero was writing one of his philosophical treatises, he reminisced about an afternoon stroll he and some friends took through the grounds of the Academy when they were students there. As he writes:

We arranged to take our afternoon stroll in the Academy, chiefly because the place would be quiet and deserted at that time of the day ... When we reached the walls of the Academy we had the place entirely to ourselves, as we had hoped. Thereupon Piso remarked: 'Whether it is a natural instinct or mere illusion, I can't say; but one's emotions are more strongly aroused by seeing the place that tradition records to have been the favourite resort of men of note in former days, than by hearing about their deeds or reading their writings. My own feelings at the moment are a case in point. I am reminded of Plato, the first philosopher, we are told, who made a habit of holding discussions at this place; and indeed his garden close at hand yonder not only recalls his memory, but seems to bring the actual man before my eyes.'

Pausanias tells us that there was a memorial to Plato near the Academy in his time, and this may very well have been on the site of the philosopher's house. Then, after recounting a strange legend concerning Plato and his mentor Socrates, Pausanias describes some of the other monuments in the vicinity of the Academy:

At this point in the country Timon's tower can be seen; he was the only human being who could find no kind of happiness except in flight from the rest of humanity. They show the place called Kolonos of the Horses, where they say Oedipus entered Attica. This is not what Homer wrote, but they say it. They show you an altar of Poseidon of Horses and Athena of Horses and a hero-shrine of Peirithous and Theseus and Oedipus and Adrastos. Among the damage Antigonus did to the countryside in his invasion was to fire the grove of Poseidon and the shrine.

Pausanias gives us much to think about here. The places that he mentions would all have been between the Academy and Kolonos Hippios, the Hill of Horses, a rocky knoll some 800 m to the north-east of Ay. Tryphon. The first place that he mentions, the Tower of Timon the Misanthrope, was in times past placed conjecturally about midway between the Academy and Kolonos Hippios. But although there may have been a tower there at some point it has long since vanished, and Timon himself is an apocryphal figure, a literary invention of Roman date. Shakespeare would have read about him in Plutarch and Lucian, which gave him the background for his tragedy, *Timon of Athens*, whose closing scenes are set in the misanthrope's tower – or, as Shakespeare has it, cave – outside the walls of Athens.

We might now stroll from the Academy to Kolonos Hippios, beginning at Ay. Tryphon and walking back along Odos Alexandrias. After crossing the busy Odos Lenorman we turn left on Odos Distomou. Three blocks along this street on the right we come to a park centred on a rocky eminence, a place known since antiquity as Kolonos Hippios, the Hill of Horses, one of the least-known of all the historical topographic features in Athens.

Kolonos Hippios is renowned as the birthplace of Sophocles. It was also the setting for his last play, *Oedipus at Kolonos*, which he wrote when he was nearly ninety, and which was not produced until four years after his death in 405 BC. In the last scene of this play Sophocles has Oedipus disappear into the underworld at a shrine of Pluto on Kolonos Hippios, whose site is now occupied by the little chapel of Ay. Elousa. Just before he disappears Oedipus says goodbye to Theseus, in elegaic lines that can be taken as Sophocles' own farewell to the land and people of Attica:

> O sunlight of no light! Once you were mine!
> This is the last my flesh will feel of you;

For now I go to shade my ending day
In the dark underworld. Most cherished friend!
I pray that you and this land and all
Your people may be blessed; remember me,
Be mindful of my death, and be
Fortunate in all time to come.

At the peak of Kolonos Hippios there is a small fenced-in enclosure, within which there are two tombstones in the neo-classical style. These mark the graves of Karl Ottfried Müller (1797–1840) and Charles Lenormant (1802–59), two European archaeologists who worked in Athens during the reign of King Otho. (One of the streets that leads off to the north of the park, Odos Myller, is named after Müller, and the main avenue just to the west, Odos Lenorman, is named after Lenormant.) The rare foreigner who passes this way must wonder why two scholars from northern Europe would come to be buried here, in this remote and characterless quarter of Athens. But when Müller and Lenormant were buried here Kolonos Hippios was far out in the verdant Attic countryside, more than a mile from the city limits, in an area which had been renowned since antiquity for its natural beauty. Sir James Frazer, in his translation of Pausanias published in 1898, quotes J. P. Mahaffy's description of the countryside between the Academy and Kolonos Hippios as it was before it was engulfed in the urban mass of Athens:

I have wandered whole days in these delightful woods, listening to the nightingales, which sing all day in the deep shade and solitude . . . and seeing the white poplar show its silvery leaves in the breeze, and wondering whether the huge old olive stems . . . could be the actual sacred trees . . . Now and then through a vista the Acropolis shows itself in a framework of green foliage.

The nightingales have long since flown from Kolonos Hippios, but their presence there is still evoked by the lyrics that Sophocles wrote for the chorus of *Oedipus at Kolonos*:

Of all the land far-famed for goodly steeds,
Thou com'st, O stranger, to the noblest spot.
Kolonos, glistening bright,
Where ever more, in thickets freshly green
The clear-voiced nightingale
Still haunts and pours her song . . .

KAISARIANI AND MT HYMETTOS

The beauty of the Attic countryside in outer Athens can still be seen at

Kaisariani, a medieval monastery near the peak of Mt Hymettos (see map on p. 2). Kaisariani is some 16 km from the centre of Athens by road, putting it beyond the range of most walkers, so we must resort to public transport, taking bus 39/52 from the terminal beside the University, on Odos Akadimias. The bus takes one to the upper part of the Kaiseriani neighbourhood, a working-class quarter on the lower slopes of Hymettos, from where one can walk up to the monastery in about half an hour. The walk is very pleasant, for Hymettos is covered with a thick growth of trees, plants and aromatic herbs of all varieties, and as one ascends the mountain one commands ever-widening panoramas of the teeming city below. Then finally we come to a broad bend in the road, where a sign points the way to Kaisariani. We ascend by a natural stone staircase that leads up to the monastery, a walled enclosure of medieval aspect built in a verdant glen shaded by pines and cypresses, reminiscent of what the outskirts of Athens must have been like in centuries past.

Just to the left of the entrance there is an extremely picturesque old fountain, with water pouring into a basin from an orifice in the form of a ram's head, part of an ancient sarcophagus. This gave its name to the monastery in Ottoman times, for the Turks called it Cochbashi, the Ram's Head. The origins of the name Kaisariani are obscure, and in times past it was also referred to as Siriani. (An old Athenian folk-song refers to it in the latter form in describing the delights of pilgrimages to the three famous monasteries in the outskirts of Athens: 'A slow walk to Siriani, and honey at Pendeli, and the cool water of angels at Daphni.')

George Wheler, in his *Journey into Greece*, published in 1672, refers to the monastery as Hagios Kyriani; as he writes, describing his visit there six years before with Spon:

After we had staid a month at Athens, our first expedition was to climb Mount Hymettus . . . We passed by three monasteries that lay on that side of the mountain . . . The third is called Hagios Kyriani by the Greeks and Cosbasi by the Turks because of a sheep's head engraved on a marble sepulchre now made use of for a cistern to the fountain arising there whose stream falls into the Ilissos. The present Abbot is called Ezekiel Stephaki and is a learned man; understanding the ancient Greek very well and Latin indifferently, with a little Italian. He understands Philosophy too, so far as to be esteemed a Platonist; and notwithstanding that he is an Abbot, yet he professes not to be a Divine, but a Physician.

As we enter the courtyard of Kaisariani we see on our right the *catholikon*, the church of the monastery, which is dedicated to the Presentation of the Virgin. This courtyard is one of the most beautiful and serene enclosures in the environs of Athens, and so we might pause here while we review the history of this holy place.

There is evidence of human habitation in the area of the monastery going back to Neolithic times, with settlers undoubtedly drawn here by the presence of the spring. There is also considerable evidence for the existence of both pagan and early Christian shrines in and around the site of the monastery; some fragments of these sanctuaries are built into the structure of the *catholikon* and the other monastic buildings or lie scattered around the courtyard. One of these, a marble stele standing in the courtyard, is inscribed with the names of the priests and other officials involved in the Eleusinian Mysteries, indicating that there was a sanctuary of Demeter and Persephone here in ancient times. The earliest Christian church that has been found in the vicinity dates to the fifth or sixth century; the remains of this sanctuary and two other medieval chapels of somewhat later date are located on a hill to the south-west of the monastery, a site that we will visit later on our tour.

The monastery of Kaisariani is believed to have been founded in the eleventh century; this was built on the foundations of an earlier structure of unknown function, traces of which are still visible behind the *catholikon*. The earliest historical reference to Kaisariani is dated 1208, when it appeared on the list of churches and monasteries granted by Pope Innocent III to the Latin Archbishop Berard, who displaced the Greek Orthodox Archbishop Michael Akominatos as head of the church in Athens. But the abbot of Kaisariani appealed directly to the Pope, and succeeded in keeping the monastery independent of the Catholic archbishopric, a status that it maintained throughout the Latin period, with the added privilege of being exempt from taxation by either church or state. When the Turks surrounded Athens in 1456, the abbot of Kaisariani was chosen to come forth and present the keys of the city to Ömer Pasha, as a result of which the monastery maintained both its independence and its tax exemption throughout most of the Ottoman period. During the dark ages of the Turkish occupation Kaisariani was the cultural centre of Attica, renowned for its library and its highly educated monks, who as teachers and scholars kept alive the ancient tradition of Greek learning. One of those educated here was a youth of humble origin who became the Ecumenical Patriarch Gregory V, killed by the Turks in 1821 at the outbreak of the Greek War of Independence.

Kaisariani lost its privileged status in 1792, when the Ecumenical Patriarch Neophytos placed the monastery under the jurisdiction of the Metropolitan of Athens. The loss of its ancient privileges soon brought about the decline of the monastery and its subsequent closure. When Edward Dodwell and his party visited the monastery in 1802 they found it abandoned, though from the quantity of food that they found stored there it must still have been in use by people in the surrounding area, probably herdsmen. As Dodwell wrote in his *Views in Greece*, published in 1821:

With a great deal of difficulty we scaled the lofty walls; we entered when night was closing in and a deep silence prevailed throughout the cells. But the storehouses were open and well furnished with jars of Hymettan honey ranged in neat order; next were large tubs of olives and from the roof hung rows of grapes, pomegranates and figs. The only inhabitants left in the convent were some cats which seemed to welcome us in the absence of the masters. We took complete possession of the place and feasted on the produce of the deserted mansion which seemed to be prepared for our reception.

The monastery remained empty until after the War of Independence, when for a time it was used as a convent. But the convent was closed in 1855, after which Kaisariani was abandoned once again, this time for nearly a century, and consequently it fell into ruin. Even Hymettos itself suffered during that period, particularly during the Second World War, when all the trees on the mountain were cut down for firewood. In 1949, after the end of the Greek Civil War, the Athenian Friends of the Trees Society began a programme of reafforestation, and by 1963 they had succeeded in restoring the indigenous trees, shrubs and flowers in an area of 750 acres around Kaisariani. During that period the society also restored the *catholikon* and other buildings of the monastic complex, so that Kaisariani is now one of the best-preserved Byzantine monuments in Greece.

Let us now examine the *catholikon*, whose plan is a variation of the traditional cross-in-a-square, a design characteristic of all Athenian churches of the eleventh and twelfth centuries. The dome sits on a high octagonal drum supported internally by four ancient columns, with four barrel-vaults roofing the arms of the cross. Pendentives between the intersection points of these four vaults make the transition to the circular cornice that supports the drum and the dome. At the eastern end of the church the circular apse is flanked by two smaller apses, each of them semicircular within and three-sided on the exterior, surmounted by conches. Between the eastern columns and the pilasters that flank the central apse there is a pair of piers that flank the iconostasis; from each of them there springs a pair of arches, low ones to the east, very tall ones to the west, matched by a pair of tall arches between the western columns and the piers engaged in the west wall of the naos. The narthex at the western end of the church, which is a later addition, has a central bay covered by a dome carried on a low octagonal drum, with barrel-vaulted bays to either side. To the right of the narthex there is a side-chapel, whose façade is surmounted by a bell-tower; this was constructed during the Latin period and is dedicated to St Anthony of Padua.

The main entrance to the church is at its western end, but there is an even grander entrance on the north side. This north doorway has an ancient marble threshold and a sculptured lintel reused from a Roman structure. This is surmounted by a projecting arch over the end wall of the north transept, the top of which is pierced by a double-arched window divided at its centre by a column. There is an identical window over the door at the end of the south transept, but there the external arch is missing. In addition to these doors, there is a fourth entrance into the chamber beneath the bell-tower, which is connected with the south end of the narthex.

We now enter the church through the main door at the western end of the narthex, the upper surfaces of which are decorated throughout with frescos. An inscription over the inner entrance to the narthex gives the date of the frescos and identifies their sponsors and painter:

This pronaos has been decorated at the expense of those who sought refuge in the monastery for fear of the plague, through the mighty hand of the all-praised Trinity and the protection of the Blessed Virgin; they being the noble and learned Benizelos, son of John, together with his noble sisters and mother and all the rest of his retinue; in the terms of the most learned monk, the abbot Hierotheos: by the hand of John Hypatos of the Peloponnesus. The year 1682 on the twentieth day of August.

A door at the southern end of the narthex leads into the side chapel dedicated to St Anthony. Here, on what was once the outer surface of the side wall of the narthex, there is a painting of the Virgin, all that remains of a Deësis, in which Christ would have been flanked by the figures of his mother and St John the Baptist. This is the earliest of the surviving frescos in Kaisariani, dating to the fourteenth century; all the other paintings in the church are from the Turkish period.

We now return to the narthex and pass into the nave, where we pause to examine the frescos there. These have been dated to the latter part of the seventeenth century, and are based on original works by

Cretan painters, primarily Emmanuel Tzanes. The arrangement of the paintings follows the traditional iconographic cycle of the Byzantine church, centring on the figure of Christ Pantocrator in the dome. In the upper drum of the dome there are the figures of the Virgin, St John the Baptist and angels; and in the lower zone, between the windows, there are eight prophets; while the pendentives have the figures of the Four Evangelists. The conch of the apse shows the Virgin Platytera, the Virgin Broader than the Heavens; below this is a representation of the holy liturgy, and beneath that the Communion of the Apostles. The four vaults of the cross, the end walls of the two transepts, and the west wall are decorated with scenes from the cycle of the life of Christ and also representations of the Twelve Feasts of the Orthodox Church (three of these, the Annunciation, the Crucifixion and the Assumption, are now missing); with portraits of the prophets in a band along the top of the vaults.

We now return to the courtyard, where we pause to examine the other buildings in this part of the monastic complex. The domed structure that one passes in entering the courtyard is a bath-house, part of the eleventh-century monastery. The structure to the rear of the courtyard housed the refectory and kitchen of the monastery; the first of these is in the long building with a peaked roof, and the second is in the domed annexe with the tall chimney projecting from its roof. The two-storeyed building with the arcade on the right side of the courtyard was the dormitory; this, as well as the refectory and the kitchen, date from the sixteenth or seventeenth century. The *pyrgos*, or tower, at the right end of the dormitory was built by the Benizelos family as their residence in 1682, when they took refuge in Kaisariani to avoid the plague in Athens.

We now leave the monastery through the archway at the south-west corner of the courtyard. This opens on to a path that leads up to the peak of a hill to the south-west of the main part of the monastic complex. During the Byzantine era the cemetery of the monastery was located here, and some of the tombstones of the monks can still be seen near the ruins of the large church. This church was dedicated to the Taxiarchoi, the Archangels, and was erected during the Turkish period on the ruins of a tenth-century church. Near by are the ruins of a vaulted Byzantine chapel dedicated to Ay. Markos, which was converted into a Roman Catholic chapel at the time of the Venetian occupation of Athens in 1687. Just to the left of this we see an early Christian church dating from the fifth or sixth century, the earliest-known Christian sanctuary in the vicinity of Kaisariani.

We might pause here to enjoy the incomparable view, one that takes in the whole of the Kephissos plain from Mts Parnes and Pendeli to the Saronic Gulf, where we can again see the islands of Salamis, Aegina, Poros and Hydra, with the Peloponnesus in the background. Dodwell praised this as the most magnificent panorama he had seen on his travels in Greece, and during the few days he spent at the deserted monastery he rode up here every morning 'over the bare and shining rocks' to enjoy the view: 'I had already seen in Greece many surprising views of coasts and islands, and long chains of mountains rising one above the other, and receding in uncertain lines as far as the eye could reach: but no view could equal that from Hymettos, in rich magnificence or attractive charms.'

We now make our way back to the monastery, where we pass through the courtyard and turn right on to the path that leads up to the Aghiasmos, or 'Consecrated Water', the sacred spring that feeds the ram's-head fountain. William Leake identified this as the ancient Kallia fountain, the principal source of the Ilissos river and the site of an ancient temple of Aphrodite, now vanished. The spring issues from a rock-hewn fountain in a secluded glen above the monastery, a place called Pera, or 'Beyond'. This is one of the most beautiful settings around Athens, still looking much as it did when Dodwell and his party were here; as he writes, after describing their night in the deserted monastery:

The next morning we rose with the sun, anxious to examine our situation . . . The Convent stands in a glen; the surrounding rocks are adorned with scattered pine; and the general verdure of this sequestered locality forms a striking contrast with the parched and yellow hue of the Athenian plain. Above the Monastery is a clear and copious fountain of perennial water, which is the source of the Ilissos. The surrounding grass is of a lively green and speckled with the cyclamen, the starry hyacinth, the *Amaryllis lutea* and the purple crocus. The sun penetrates so little into this sheltered glen, that throughout the summer it preserves its lively green.

The spring has been renowned since antiquity for its therapeutic powers. It is still a popular place of pilgrimage, and Athenian mothers bring their sick children here to bathe in its healing waters; pregnant women also drink from it to ensure good health for their unborn children. The Aghiasmos is the site of a very ancient cult ritual that is celebrated each year on 15 August, the feast-day of the Assumption of the Blessed Virgin, when the Kaisariani monastery has its *paniyiri*. After the celebration of Holy Mass in the *catholikon*, the clergy lead a procession from the monastery up to the Aghiasmos, where they wait to catch a fleeting glimpse of the dove that descends from heaven and hovers over the spring; this epiphany renews the healing powers of the spring's waters, and all of the faithful thereupon drink from the sacred fountain.

The Kallia fountain is believed to have been the setting for Ovid's version of the myth of Cephalus and Procris, which he writes of in his *Ars amatoria*, the *Art of Love*. Cephalus, the son of Hermes, is the lover of Procris, the daughter of Erechtheus, and in the beginning of his tale Ovid has them living blissfully together here on Hymettos. But they become terribly jealous of one another, and Procris believes that Cephalus is having a love-affair with a mountain-nymph named Aura, whose name means 'Breeze'. Procris follows Cephalus one day when he is out hunting on Hymettos, and when he stops at the fountain she hides herself in the bushes there, thinking that he is waiting for Aura. It is a hot day and Cephalus sighs for a breeze; Procris, thinking that he is calling for Aura, rushes from her hiding-place to confront them. The startled Cephalus, thinking that she is a creature of the wild, flings his spear at Procris and mortally wounds her, but she dies happily in his arms when she learns that he has not been unfaithful to her.

The first scholar in modern times to identify the Aghiasmos as the Kallia fountain was William Leake; as he writes in his *Topography of Athens*:

The source of the Ilissus at Syriani seems to be the fountain Callia at Pera, where was a temple of Venus, probably upon the spot now occupied by the Monastery. There is no other place near Mt Hymettus which will so well suit the scene of the death of Procris described by Ovid. It is rare to meet with such accuracy of description in a Roman poet. We not only find the soft turf, which the fountain maintains in verdure in the season when everything around is parched with the excessive heat, but even all or nearly all the trees and shrubs that the poet enumerates.

William Congreve's translation of Ovid perhaps best evokes the scene:

> Near where his purple head Hymettus shows
> And flow'ring hills, a sacred fountain flows,
> With soft and verdant turf the soil is spread,
> And sweetly-smelling shrubs the ground o'ershade.
> There rosemary and bays their odours join,
> And with the fragrant scent combine.
> There tamarisks with thick-leav'd box are found,

And cytisus and garden pines abound
While through the boughs, soft winds of Zephyr pass,
Tremble the leaves and tender tops of grass.
Hither would Cephalus retreat to rest,
When tir'd with hunting, or with heat opprest;
And, thus, to Air, the panting youth would pray;
Come, gentle Aura, come, this heat allay.

After leaving Kaisariani, we continue up the mountain road to look at the remains of the two other monasteries mentioned by Wheler, with ever-widening prospects opening up below us as we approach the peak of Hymettos.

Three kilometres above Kaisariani we see on our left the monastery of Asteriou, founded in the eleventh century. The *catholikon* of this little monastic complex, which has recently been restored, has some well-preserved and interesting post-Byzantine frescos. The monastery is believed to have been built on the site of an ancient pagan sanctuary whose name it perpetuates, that of Asteria, who was the mother of Hecate. According to the local version of the myth, Zeus tried to make love to Asteria on Hymettos, but she escaped from him by jumping from the mountain and changing herself into a quail; the crag from which she leaped was thereafter known by her name and a shrine was built there, later to become the Asteriou monastery.

The third monastery on Hymettos is 2 km or so beyond Asteriou. All that remains of this is the chapel of Ay. Ioannis Kynigou, St John the Hunter, which also dates from the eleventh century. Unfortunately, the church is in a military area, and so it is off-limits to the public. In times past the festival of the saint was celebrated here on the peak of Hymettos, where in ancient times there was a statue of Zeus.

KIFISSIA

Our last stroll will take us through Kifissia, the celebrated garden suburb in the northernmost metropolitan area of Athens (see map on p. 2). The quickest and most convenient way to get there is by the Underground, known in Greek as the 'Elektrikos', whose most centrally located station is in Omonia Square; from there it takes just twenty-one minutes to reach Kifissia, the last stop on the line.

The moment one leaves the station in Kifissia one has the feeling of being in quite another world than that of central Athens. The air is clearer and cooler, the sky is a more brilliant blue, and one sees here the pellucid Attic light that is seldom visible now in Athens itself. Kifissia has been a suburban retreat for wealthy Athenians since Roman times. It is about a thousand feet higher than central Athens, and this, together with its celebrated greenery, gives it a cooler and more salubrious climate than the rest of the city. Thus it has long been a very popular summer resort, and in the high season its many hotels are booked to capacity by older people who come here to escape the stifling heat and pollution of Athens. Kifissia has lost some of its beauty and old-world charm in recent years, spoiled by the construction of modern apartments and the opening of innumerable shops catering to the wealthy Greeks and foreigners who now live in this fashionable suburb or congregate in its expensive restaurants and cafés; nevertheless it is still very attractive and, although frequently maddening, there is no place quite like it in all Greece. Many handsome old mansions and villas of the nineteenth century still remain standing along the quieter back streets of Kifissia, shaded by the tall pines and columnar cypresses that give a Roman look to the skyline, particularly at twilight, with Mt Pendeli always looming in the background to lend its grandeur to the scene.

After leaving the station we walk up through the public gardens of Kifissia, which are among the prettiest in Greece. At the upper end of the park we cross Leoforos Kifissias, the main road from Athens. After crossing the avenue we start up the left side of the street directly opposite the park. A short way up the block we come to Varsos, the oldest *zacharoplasteion* in Athens, which has café tables both on the pavement and in its tree-shaded rear garden. In the inner salon of the café there are large photographs of Kifissia as it was at the turn of the century.

After leaving Varsos we cross the street and walk back towards the main avenue, crossing the first side street and then pausing to examine the ancient remains there. There we notice that the retaining wall of the side street is constructed of huge squared blocks dating from the Roman period. A shed at the corner covers four Roman sarcophagi which were discovered near by in 1961; a second excavation at the same site in the years 1972–6 unearthed some fragmentary sculptures and the remains of what are believed to be Roman baths. Reliefs on the sarcophagi identify them as being from the family vault of Herodes Atticus; and so these and the other remains are undoubtedly part of his country mansion, the Villa Kifissia. This renowned villa is described in the *Attic Nights* of Aulus Gellius, a Roman writer who was a guest of Herodes Atticus here during the year that he studied in Athens, *c.* AD 150; as he writes:

When we were students at Athens, Herodes Atticus, the Consul, of true Greek eloquence, often invited me to his country house near the city, with several other Romans who had come to Greece in search of culture. At that time, when we were at his villa called Kifissia, we were protected against the unpleasant heat in the summer or autumn by the shade of his spacious groves, the long avenues, and the cool position of his home. It had elegant baths with an abundance of sparkling waters; and on the whole it was a charming place, with the melodious sounds of running water and bird-song.

Traffic signs guide one to Kefalari Square, the centre of Kifissia and the site of its most fashionable cafés. At one side of the square we see the modern but rather attractive church of the Panayia; behind it is the very pretty Kefalari Park, a pleasant place to while away a summer afternoon. Here one can hire a *phaetoni*, an old-fashioned horse-drawn carriage, perhaps the best way to tour Kifissia on a first visit. One interesting place to visit in the vicinity of Kefalari Square is the Goulandris Natural History Museum, which is at No. 10 Odos Lividou, housed in a handsome neo-classical mansion of white marble. This is one of the finest institutions of its type in Europe, with exhibits illustrating the flora and fauna of Greece and its Aegean and Ionian isles.

Those who have the time and stamina might consider a hike up Mt Pendeli, whose summit is about 9 km by road from Kefalari Square. Beginning at the square, we take Odos Deliyannis past the park, after which we turn left on Odos Harilou Trikoupis and then right on Odos Pendelis. The latter street goes beyond the uppermost houses of Kifissia and then winds all the way up to the summit of Mt Pendeli.

On the way up to the summit we pass on our left a little chapel in a grove of trees, and about 500 m farther along we cross a bridge over the bed of a winter torrent, the principal source of the Kephissos river. Here one might be tempted to take a pathway on the left just above the bridge, leaving the road and walking the rest of the way to the summit along a series of goat trails. Off to the right you see the scars of the quarries that have been worked since antiquity, and then you remember that the Parthenon was built with marble from Mt Pentelikon, as it was known in classical times. One of the ancient quarries, now worked out, is called Spilia, or 'the Cave'. This takes its name from a large cavern which has obviously been a sacred spot since antiquity, and one can see there the remains of two chapels dating from the Byzantine period. One of the chapels still has faded and fragmentary remnants of its fresco decoration, including a representation of Michael Akominatos, the last Greek Orthodox Archbishop of Athens before the Latin Conquest.

The summit itself is a Greek army radar site and thus off-limits to the public, but we can climb to the top of the rocky crag just beside the peak. When we reach it we are suddenly confronted with a sweeping view of the plain of Marathon and its historic bay, while in the other direction we can see the whole of the Kephissos plain, with the massed buildings of metropolitan Athens stretching all the way down from Kifissia to the Piraeus and the Saronic Gulf, bounded on the north by Mt Parnes, on the west by Mt Aigaleos, on the east by Hymettos and here on the north-east by Pendeli. Off in the distance to the south we can see the peaks of some of the Cyclades. Midway between Aigaleos and Hymettos the treeless spurs of the Tourkovounia range rise from the urban mass in a series of peaks terminating in Lycabettos, and these guide our line of sight southwards to the Acropolis, where on the clearest of afternoons we can see the oblique light of the falling sun gleaming on the columns of the Parthenon.

And so our last stroll ends here, looking down on the vast modern megalopolis that Athens has become, yet knowing that at its heart the ancient city of Athena is still there, resplendent. Here one recalls the lines from Milton's *Paradise Regained*, in which Satan offers Christ dominion over the kingdoms of the world:

> Look once more e're we leave this specular Mount
> Westward, much nearer by Southwest, behold
> Where on the Aegean shore a City stands
> Built nobly, pure the air, and light the soil,
> Athens the eye of Greece, Mother of Arts
> And Eloquence, native to famous wits
> Or hospitable, in her sweet recess,
> City or Suburban, studious walks and shades;
> See there the Olive Grove of Academe,
> Plato's retirement, where the Attic Bird
> Trills her thick-warbl'd notes the summer long,
> There flowrie hill Hymettus with the sound
> Of Bees industrious murmur oft invites
> To studious musing; there Ilissus rouls
> His whispering stream; within the walls then view
> The schools of antient Sages; his who bred
> Great Alexander to subdue the world,
> Lyceum there, and Painted Stoa next;
> There thou shalt hear and learn the secret power
> Of harmony in tones and numbers hit
> By voice or hand, and various-measur'd verse . . .
> These here revolve, or, as thou lik'st, at home,

Till time mature thee to a Kingdom's waight;
These rules will render thee a King compleat
Within thy self, much more with Empire joyn'd. (IV, 236–56, 281–4)

Appendices

I CHRONOLOGY

BC

c. 5000: First Neolithic settlers around Acropolis

c. 3000–*c.* 1125: Bronze Age. Continuous settlement around Acropolis

c. 1400–*c.* 1125: Mycenaean Age. Kings rule from palace on Acropolis

c. 1300: Mycenaean defence wall built on Acropolis

c. 1230: Union of Attica under Athens

c. 1150–*c.* 750: Dark Ages of the ancient Greek world

c. 1050: Ionian migration to Asia Minor

c. 1000–900: End of hereditary kingship in Athens, oligarchy rules

c. 750–*c.* 700: Geometric period

c. 700–480: Archaic period

c. 621: Reforms of Dracon

c. 594: Reforms of Solon

561: Peisistratus seizes power in Athens

555: Peisistratus deposed

546: Peisistratus again seizes power in Athens

546–528: Peisistratus rules as tyrant; institutes festival of Greater Panathenaea; begins construction of Olympieion

528: Peisistratus dies and is succeeded as tyrant by his son Hippias

514: Hipparchus, brother of Hippias, is assassinated by Harmodius and Aristogeiton

510: Hippias deposed

508: Constitutional reforms begun by Cleisthenes

499: Beginning of Ionian revolt against Persia in Asia Minor

494: Persians crush Ionian revolt and burn Miletus

493: Themistocles first elected as archon

490: Persian invasion of Greece, defeated by Athenians at Marathon

480: Persians, led by Xerxes, invade Greece; battles of Thermopylae and Artemision. Athenians abandon their city, which is sacked by Persians. Greeks defeat Persians at battle of Salamis

479: Greeks defeat Persian army at Plataea and Persian fleet off Cape Mycale; Athenians return to their city and begin rebuilding it

479–323: Classical period

479/8: Construction of outer defence walls of Athens

478: Establishment of Delian League under Cimon of Athens

472: Pericles pays for production of Aeschylus' *The Persians*

471: Themistocles ostracized

468: Sophocles wins his first victory in drama competition

466: Birth of Socrates

461: Cimon ostracized; Pericles begins rise to power

461–451: War between Athens and Spartan alliance

458–456: Construction of Long Walls between Athens and the Piraeus

455: First production of play by Euripides

454: Herodotus at Athens

451: Five-year truce between Athens and Sparta

449: Peace with Persia

449–444: Construction of Hephaisteion on Kolonos Agoraios

447: Parthenon begun

442: Odeion of Pericles opened

442–438: Parthenon frieze carved

441: Sophocles elected general; his *Antigone* produced

438: Statue of Athena by Pheidias dedicated in Parthenon

437–432: Construction of Propylaia on Acropolis

435: Work begins on Erechtheion

432: Sculptural decoration of the Parthenon completed

431: Start of Peloponnesian War

430: Plague in Athens

429: Death of Pericles

428: Birth of Plato

427–425: Building of Temple of Athena Nike on Acropolis

423: Aristophanes' *Clouds* produced

421: Peace of Nikias; truce in Peloponnesian War

416: Peloponnesian War resumes

415: Athenian expedition to Sicily sets off

411: Production of Aristophanes' *Lysistrata*

410: Sculptural decoration of Temple of Athena Nike completed

405: Death of Sophocles

404: Peloponnesian War ends with surrender of Athens. Athenians forced to destroy the Long Walls, with Spartan garrison on the Acropolis. Athens ruled by the Thirty Tyrants

403: Return of democracy to Athens

401: Posthumous production of Sophocles' *Oedipus at Kolonos*

399: Death of Socrates

395–393: Athenians rebuild the Long Walls

394: Athenians under Conon defeat Spartans in naval battle off Cnidus. Conon rebuilds defence walls of Athens

387: Establishment of Second Maritime League, headed by Athens

c. 386: Plato establishes his school at the Academy

384: Birth of Aristotle and Demosthenes

367: Aristotle joins Plato's school at the Academy

359: Philip II becomes King of Macedon

356: Birth of Alexander the Great

351: Demosthenes makes his first speech against Philip of Macedon

347: Death of Plato

343–342: Aristotle in Macedonia as tutor to Alexander

338: Philip II of Macedon defeats the Greek allies at Chaeronea. Aristotle establishes the Lyceum at Athens. Alexander at Athens

338–334: Lycurgos in charge of finances of Athens and inaugurates major construction programme

336: Philip II of Macedon assassinated and succeeded by his son Alexander

335: Aristotle establishes his school at the Lyceum

334: Alexander begins his campaign of conquest in Asia

c. 330: Completion of the Panathenaic Stadium on the Ilissos and the new Theatre of Dionysos on the south slope of the Acropolis

323: Death of Alexander

323–86: Hellenistic Period in Athens

323–322: Athens and her allies revolt unsuccessfully against Macedonian rule; Antipater takes Athens

322: Deaths of Aristotle and Demosthenes; Theophrastus becomes head of Lyceum. Democracy in Athens suppressed

321: First production of play by Menander, greatest poet of the New Comedy

317: Athens captured by Cassander, King of Macedon, who installs Dimitrios of Phaleron as governor of Athens

317–307: Dimitrios of Phaleron rules Athens as Macedonian governor

307: Athens captured by Dimitrios Poliorcetes; Epicurus establishes his philosophical school in Athens

294: Dimitrios Poliorcetes builds fortress on Pnyx

287: Death of Theophrastus

279: Greeks defeat barbarian Gauls at Thermopylae

271: Death of Epicurus

267–262: Ptolemy unsuccessfully supports Greek independence from Macedon; Athens taken by Antigonus Gonatas, King of Macedon

200–197: Philip V of Macedon invades Greece and attacks Athens

197: Philip V defeated by Greeks and their Roman allies

197–159: Stoa on south slope of Acropolis built by Eumenes II, King of Pergamum

175–163: Seleucid king, Antiochus IV, advances building of unfinished Olympieion

159–138: Stoa in Agora built by Attalos II, King of Pergamum

146: Romans sack Corinth and annex Macedonia and Greece

88: Athens sides with Mithridates VI, King of Pontus, in his first war against Rome

86: Roman army under Sulla sacks Athens

86 BC–AD 330: Roman period in history of Athens

47–44: Julius Caesar establishes Roman Agora in Athens

31: Octavian defeats Antony and Cleopatra at Actium

31/30: Octavian at Athens with Agrippa

27: Octavian given the name Augustus

c. 15: Agrippa builds Odeion in Agora

10: Dedication of Roman Agora

AD

49: St Paul preaches on the Areopagus; Dionysius the Areopagite consecrated as first Bishop of Athens.

114–116: Philopappos Monument built on Mouseion Hill

124–5: Hadrian begins building programme in Athens

131–2: Hadrian completes the Olympieion in Athens

140: Antoninus Pius completes water-supply system in Athens

139/40–143/4: Herodes Atticus builds new stadium in Athens

c. 160–74: Herodes Atticus builds odeion on south slope of Acropolis

253–60: Valerian builds defence wall around Athens

267: Heruli sack Athens

c. 267–80: Late Roman fortification wall built around Athens

325: Bishopric of Athens represented at Council of Nicaea

330: Constantine the Great shifts his capital from Rome to Byzantium, thereafter to be called Constantinople, beginning the Byzantine period in Greek history

396: Alaric the Visigoth attacks Athens and damages the Agora

c. 400: 'Gymnasium of the Giants' built on Agora on site of Odeion of Agrippa, last major edifice erected at Athens in antiquity

c. 425: Empress Eudocia builds church of St Leonides in Athens

435: Edict of Theodosius II closes all pagan temples

485: Death of Proclus, last great philosopher in Athens

529: Edict of Justinian closes the Platonic Academy

c. 590: Sack of Athens by the Slavs

c. 590–600: Parthenon coverted into church of the Blessed Virgin

1019: Basil II celebrates his victory over Bulgars with Te Deum in church of the Blessed Virgin in Parthenon

1182–1205: Michael Akominatos serves as last Greek Orthodox Archbishop of Athens before Latin Conquest

1204: Latin knights of the Fourth Crusade capture and sack Constantinople, ending Byzantine period in history of Athens

1205: Latins take Athens, beginning Latin period in Athenian history. Othon de la Roche, French noble, rules as Megaskyr, or Great Lord; his successors rule as Dukes of Athens

1205–1311: De la Roche dynasty rules Athens (dukes after 1260)

1261: Greeks recapture Constantinople from Latins

1311: Latin knights under Walter de Brienne, Duke of Athens, wiped out by Catalans at battle of the Kopiac marshes. Catalans take Athens. Manfred, second son of Frederick II of Sicily, accepted by Catalans as Duke of Athens

1311–88: Catalans control Athens

1388: Nerio Acciajuoli, a Florentine, captures Athens, ending Catalan control of the city

1394: Acciajuoli becomes Nerio I, Duke of Athens

1394–1456: Acciajuoli dynasty rule as Dukes of Athens

1453: Ottoman Turks under Sultan Mehmet II capture Constantinople, ending Byzantine Empire. Constantinople renamed Istanbul, which becomes capital of Ottoman Empire

1456: Turks under Ömer Pasha capture Athens; mosque built in Parthenon

1456–1833: Ottoman period in history of Athens

1458: Mehmet II visits Athens and dedicates Fethiye Djami, the Mosque of the Conquest

1466: Venetians take Athens, but then city is recaptured by Turks

1656: Propylaia destroyed in explosion of Turkish powder magazine

1686: Temple of Athena Nike destroyed by Turkish garrison on Acropolis

1687: Venetians under Morosini besiege Athens and blow up Parthenon

1688: Venetians abandon Athens, which is virtually empty for two years after their departure

1690: Turks re-occupy Athens and populace returns to city

1759: Tzisdarakis builds mosque in Monastiraki

1778: Hadji Ali Haseki, Turkish governor of Athens, encircles Athens with new defence wall, the Serpentzes

1801–11: Lord Elgin removes sculptures from Parthenon and other monuments

1821: Beginning of Greek War of Independence; Greek revolutionaries from Attica attack Turkish forces in Athens but fail to take Acropolis

1822: Greeks under Androutsos besiege Athens and capture the Acropolis

1826–7: Turks under Kütahya Pasha besiege Athens and capture the Acropolis

1832: Convention of London (signed 11 May) creates independent Greek Kingdom, with Otho as first King of the Hellenes

1833 (March): Turkish garrison evacuates Acropolis, ending Ottoman period in history of Athens. Athens becomes capital of independent Greek Kingdom

1833–62: Reign of King Otho. Athens is rebuilt as a new European capital, while at the same time work begins on the restoration of the monuments of ancient Athens

1843: Bloodless revolution in Athens forces King Otho to accept Constitution

1862: Otho deposed, George I becomes second King of the Hellenes

1864: Ionian Islands become part of Greece

1881: Thessaly becomes part of Greece

1896: First modern Olympic Games held in Athens

1897: War between Greece and Turkey

1910: Venizelos becomes prime minister for first time

1912: Greece fights in alliance against Turkey in First Balkan War

1913: Greece fights in alliance against Turkey in Second Balkan War. Greece acquires southern Epirus, Macedonia, Samos and Crete. George I assassinated and is succeeded by Constantine I

1917: Constantine I is deposed and replaced by Alexander I; Venizelos brings Greece into the First World War on the side of the Allies

1918: Greek troops join Allies in final drive to victory over Germany and her allies

1919: Alexander deposed and Constantine I regains throne. Greek troops enter Istanbul as part of allied army of occupation. Greek army lands at Smyrna and begins invasion of Asia Minor. Atatürk leads Turkish nationalists to create new nation out of dying Ottoman Empire

1919–22: War between Greece and Turkey in Asia Minor

1922: Greeks defeated by Turkish nationalists under Atatürk. Greek army abandons Asia Minor and Smyrna is destroyed by fire. Ottoman Empire ends with the abolition of the sultanate. Constantine I abdicates and is replaced by George II

1923: New Republic of Turkey formed with Atatürk as first President. Population exchange of minorities between Greece and Turkey; a million Greeks from Asia Minor arrive in Greece, many of them settling in Athens and the Piraeus

1933: Venizelos prime minister for last time

1940: Italians invade Albania and are stopped by the Greeks

1941: Germans invade Greece and defeat Greek and allied forces

1941–44: German occupation of Athens

1944: Liberation of Athens; beginning of civil war in Greece

1949: End of civil war

1947: George II dies and is succeeded by Paul

1964: Paul dies and is succeeded by Constantine II

1967–74: Military dictatorship in Greece; King Constantine in exile

1974: Return of democracy to Greece; new constitution effectively ends monarchy

1981: Greece becomes a member of the European Community

II GLOSSARY

ACROPOLIS. Fortified upper city

ACROTERIA. The sculptural decoration at the lower angles or apex of a pediment

ADYTON. Inner sanctuary of a temple

AEDICULA. Funerary monument in the form of a framed relief

AEGIS. Cloak, shield or cuirass with Gorgon's head and ring of snakes

AMAZONOMACHY. Mythical battle between Greeks and Amazons

AMPHIDISTYLE *IN ANTIS*. A temple with two columns *in antis* at both front and rear

AMPHIPROSTYLE. A temple with portico of columns at front and rear only

AMPHORA. A two-handled vase

ANTA (pl. ANTAE). The slightly projecting pilaster of a cella wall; columns placed between antae are said to be *in antis*.

ANTEFIX. The decorative termination of the covering tiles on a roof

APSE. The semi-circular or polygonal termination of a church sanctuary

ARCHAEIA. Public offices in an ancient Greek city

ARCHITRAVE. A lintel carried from the top of one column to another; the lowest element of an entablature

ASHLAR. Large building blocks of squared stones

BARREL-VAULTED. A continuous vault of semicircular cross-section

BASILICA. An oblong rectangular building usually with aisles at the sides and an apse at one end

BEMA. Speaker's platform

BOULEUTERION. Meeting-place of the Boule, the legislative council of a city

CAPITAL. The crowning feature of a column

CARYATID. Statue of a maiden taking the place of a column or pilaster

CATHOLIKON. The church of a monastery

CAVEA. Auditorium of a Greek city, so called because originally it was dug out of a hillside

CELLA. The enclosed central chamber of a temple; also called the naos

CENTAUROMACHY. Mythical battle between Lapiths and Centaurs

CHESHME. Turkish fountain

CHOREGIC. Monument erected to commemorate a victory in a choral competition

CHRYSELEPHANTINE. Statue with a wooden core overlaid with gold and ivory

CHTHONIC. One who dwells on or under the earth

COFFER. A sunken panel in a wall or ceiling

CONCH. Domed roof of semicircular apse

CORINTHIAN. An architectural order differing from the Ionic principally in having its capitals decorated with volutes and acanthus leaves

CORNICE. The upper member of the entablature

CREPIDOMA. The stepped platform of a temple

CRUCIFORM. Cross-shaped

DEME. A political subdivision of the Athenian city-state, the equivalent of an English parish

DERSHANE. Lecture-room of a Turkish medrese, or theological school

DIAZOMA. Aisle of a Graeco-Roman theatre

DIPTERAL. A temple surrounded by a double row of columns; a double colonnade

DISTYLE. Temple front or porch with two columns

DORIC. The order of architecture originally developed by the Dorian Greeks

DROMOS. Road or running-track

EGG-AND-DART. The decorative pattern (also called tongue-and-dart) applied to the convex moulding of Ionic columns known as the ovolvo profile

ENTABLATURE. The upper part of an order in architecture, comprising architrave, frieze and cornice, supported by a colonnade

THE ORDERS OF GREEK ARCHITECTURE

The Doric order

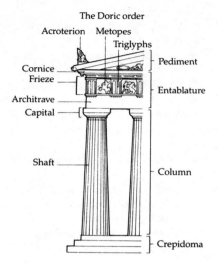

Acroterion   Metopes
            Triglyphs
                        Pediment
Cornice
Frieze
                        Entablature
Architrave
Capital

Shaft
                        Column

                        Crepidoma

The Ionic order

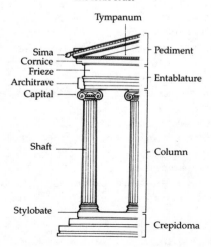

Tympanum

Sima
Cornice
Frieze
Architrave
Capital
            Pediment

            Entablature

Shaft
            Column

Stylobate

            Crepidoma

THE ORDERS OF GREEK ARCHITECTURE

The Ionic order (details)

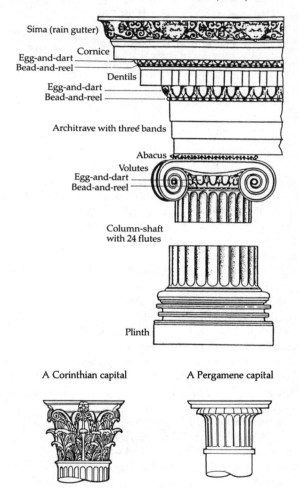

Sima (rain gutter)

Cornice
Egg-and-dart
Bead-and-reel

Dentils

Egg-and-dart
Bead-and-reel

Architrave with three bands

Abacus
Volutes
Egg-and-dart
Bead-and-reel

Column-shaft
with 24 flutes

Plinth

A Corinthian capital   A Pergamene capital

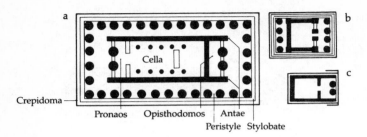

Greek temple layouts

(a) Peripteral (hexastyle)
(b) Amphiprostyle (tetrastyle)
(c) In antis (distyle)

ENTASIS. The slight convex curve given to Doric columns in order to correct an optical illusion; if the shaft were absolutely cylindrical its silhouette would appear concave

EPHEBE. Greek youth undergoing military training

EPISTYLE. The Greek term for the architrave

ESCHARA. A sacred hearth

EXEDRA. A rectangular or semicircular recess

EXONARTHEX. The outer vestibule of a Greek church

EXTRADOS. The exterior curve of an arch

EX-VOTO. Dedicatory offering in a shrine

FRIEZE. The middle division of a classical entablature, often decorated with sculpture in low relief

GYMNASIUM. A school and athletic training centre

HAMMAM. Turkish public bath

HERM. Quadrangular pillar with a phallus in its middle and surmounted by a bust

HEROUM. Shrine dedicated to a deified hero

HEXASTYLE. A temple with six columns in front

HIP ROOF. A roof with sloping ends and sides

HYPAETHERAL. A temple whose cella was open to the elements

ICON. A sacred picture

ICONOSTASIS. The screen on which icons are hung

IDOLES. Cycladic statuettes of the Mother Goddess

INTERCOLUMNIATION. Distance between column centres in a colonnade

IONIC. The architectural order evolved by the Ionians of the Greek cities in Asia Minor

KIONISKOS. Small unadorned column used as funerary monument

KLINE. Funerary bier

KORE (pl. KORAI). Maiden; archaic female figure

KOUROS (pl. KOUROI). Youth; archaic male figure

KRATER. Vessel in which wine is mixed with water

KUFIC. Brickwork frieze imitating angular Arabic calligraphy

LEKYTHOS. Tall single-handled vase used as funerary monument

LEOFOROS. Avenue

LINTEL. The horizontal beam spanning the opening between two columns or piers to make a doorway or window

LOUTROPHORUS. Tall two-handled vase used as funerary monument

MEDRESE. Turkish theological school

METOPE. The recessed panels between the triglyphs in a Doric frieze, often decorated with sculptures in relief

MIHRAB. Niche in a mosque indicating the direction of Mecca

MIMBAR. Pulpit in a mosque

MONOPTERAL. Temple with columns only, lacking a cella, usually circular

NAISKOS. A funerary monument in which a relief is framed in the imitated façade of a miniature Greek temple

NAOS. The inner sanctuary of a temple; also called the cella

NARTHEX. The inner vestibule of a Byzantine church

NAVE. The main body of a church from the entrance to the chancel

NIKE. Winged Victory

NYMPHAION. A fountain or fountain-house; so called because such places were sacred to the nymphs

OCTASTYLE. Temple front with eight columns

ODEION. A theatre designed primarily for musical performances, generally unroofed

ODOS. Street

OPISTHODOMOS. The recessed porch at the rear of a Greek temple, often used as a treasury

OPUS SECTILE. Ornamental paving made from stone or marble slabs cut into various geographical shapes

ORCHESTRA. The 'dancing-place', and hence the place of action for the chorus and at first even the actors in a Greek theatre, generally circular in plan

ORDER. An order in Greek architecture usually comprising a

column with its base (though the Doric column did not have a base), shaft and capital, the whole supporting an entablature

ORTHOSTAT. Upright slabs at the base of a wall

OVOLVO. A quarter-round moulding with egg-and-dart (or egg-and-tongue) carving in the Ionic order

PANIYIRI (pl. *PANIYIRIA*). Religious festival in the Greek Orthodox Church

PARADOS (pl. *PARADOÍ*). Side entrance to a Greek theatre, passing between the stage-building and the auditorium

PARASKENIA. The symmetrical wings of the scene-building which project into the orchestra

PEDIMENT. The triangular termination of a ridge roof

PEPLOS. The robe woven for Athena

PERGAMENE. The style of architecture that developed in Pergamum

PERIPTERAL. A temple whose cella is surrounded by a colonnade

PERIRRHANTERIA. Basins for holy water

PERISTYLE. Covered colonnade surrounding a temple

PILASTER. A mass of masonry, as distinct from a column, from which an arch springs

PITHOS. A huge earthenware vase used for the storage of olive-oil or grain

PLATEIA. Town square

PLINTH. The supporting member of a statue or honorific column

POROS. A soft, coarse limestone

PORTICO. A colonnaded space, with a roof supported on at least one side by a roof

PRONAOS. The porch in front of the naos or cella of a temple

PROPYLON (pl. PROPYLAIA). The monumental entrance to a sacred enclosure (the plural form is used if there is more than one gateway)

PROSCENIUM. A colonnade between the orchestra and stage-building, often terminated at the ends with paraskenia

PROSTOMIAION. Anteroom of a sanctuary

PROSTYLE. Temple with a portico of columns in front

PROTHESIS. The laying-out of a corpse

PRYTANEION. The state dining-room and senate committee building in a Greek city

PYRGOS. A watch-tower

QUADRIGA. A four-horse chariot, often used as a sculptural group on honorific monuments

QUATREFOIL. A structure with four lobes or foils

RHYTON. A chalice

RUSTICATED. Masonry constructed in rustic style, with outer surfaces left unfinished and joints emphasized

SATYR. Follower of Dionysos, usually depicted as half-human and half-animal, with permanently erect penis

SCAENA FRONS. Elaborately decorated façade of a theatre's scene-building

SEKOS. Temple building

SKENE. The stage-building that formed the back scene of a theatre

STELE (pl. STELAI). Upright stone slab bearing inscription or relief, often used as boundary marker or grave monument

STOA. A building with its roof supported by one or more rows of columns parallel to the rear wall

STYLOBATE. The upper step of a Greek temple, serving as the platform for the columns

TEKKE. Dervish monastery

TEMENOS. The sacred enclosure or precincts of a temple

TEMPLE *IN ANTIS.* A temple without a peripteral colonnade but with columns *in antis*

TETRASTYLE. A temple or porch with four columns in front

THYMELE. Altar of Dionysos in theatre

TRANSEPT. The part of a cruciform church which crosses at right angles to the principal axis of the building between the nave and the apse or choir

TRAPEZA. Table or table-like funerary monument

TRIGLYPH. Part of Doric frieze bearing three vertical grooves; triglyphs alternate with metopes

TRIPOD. The base of the trophy won in a choral competition, surmounting a choregic monument

TRIPTERAL. Temple or porch front with three rows of columns

VOUSSOIRS. Wedge-shaped stones that make up an arch

XOANON. Sacred wooden image serving as a cult-image

ZACHAROPLASTEION (pl. *ZACHAROPLASTEIA*). Patisserie

III BIBLIOGRAPHY

About, Edmund, *Greece and the Greeks of the Present Day*, Edinburgh, 1885

Andrews, Kevin, *Athens*, London, 1967; *Athens Alive!*, 1979

Andronicos, Manolis, *National Museum*, Athens, 1987

Antoniou, Jim, *Plaka*, Athens, 1973

Argyropoulo, Kaity, *Mt Hymettus and the Kaisariani Monastery*, Athens, 1962

Ashmole, Bernard, *Architect and Sculptor in Classical Greece*, London and New York, 1972

Barker, Robin, *Blue Guide – Greece*, London and New York, 1981

Beazley, J. D., and Ashmole, B., *Greek Sculpture and Painting*, Cambridge, 1966

Boardman, John, *Athenian Black Figure Vases*, London, 1974
  Athenian Red Figure Vases: Archaic Period, London, 1977
  Greek Sculpture: Archaic Period, London, 1978
  Greek Sculpture: Classical Period, London, 1985

Boardman, John, Griffin, Jasper, and Murray, Oswyn, *The Oxford History of the Classical World*, Oxford, 1986

Bowra, C. M., *Periclean Athens*, Harmondsworth, 1971

Brommer, Franz, *The Sculptures of the Parthenon*, London, 1974

Brouscaris, Maria S., *The Monuments of the Acropolis*, Athens, 1968

Bruno, V. J., ed., *The Parthenon*, New York, 1974

Burn, A. R., *The Pelican History of Greece*, Harmondsworth, 1982

Bury, J. B., *A History of the Greeks to the Death of Alexander the Great*, 3rd ed., revised by R. Meigs, London, 1951

Camp, John M., *The Athenian Agora: Excavations in the Heart of Classical Athens*, London, 1986

Camp, John M., and Dinsmoor, William B., Jr, *Ancient Athenian Building Methods* (Athenian Agora Picture Book, no. 21), Princeton, 1984

Carpenter, Rhys, *The Architects of the Parthenon*, Harmondsworth, 1970

Cary, M., *History of the Greek World from 353 to 146 BC*, London, 1977

Chatzidakis, Manolis, *Byzantine Museum*, Athens, 1986

Chatzidakis, Theano, *The Monastery of Kaisariani*, Athens, 1977

Cheetham, Nicholas, *Mediaeval Greece*, New Haven, 1981

Coldstream, J. N., *Greek Geometric Pottery*, London, 1968

Cook, B. F., *The Elgin Marbles*, London, 1984

Cook, R. M., *Greek Painted Pottery*, London, 1960
  Greek Art, Harmondsworth, 1979

Corbett, P. E., *The Sculptures of the Parthenon*, London, 1959

Coulton, J. J., *Greek Architects at Work*, London, 1977

Dakin, Douglas, *The Unification of Greece, 1770–1923*, London, 1972

Delivorrias, A., *et al.*, *Athens 1839–1900, A Photographic Record*, Athens, 1985
  Guide to the Benaki Museum, Athens, 1988

Desborough, V. R., *The Greek Dark Ages*, New York, 1972

Dinsmoor, William Bell, *The Architecture of Ancient Greece*, London, 1950

Dodwell, Edward, *A Classical and Topographical Tour through Greece . . .*, 2 vols., London, 1819
  Views in Greece, 2 vols., London, 1821

Dontas, George, *The Acropolis and its Museum*, Athens, 1988

D'Ooge, Martin L., *The Acropolis of Athens*, London, 1908

Ehrenberg, V., *From Solon to Socrates*, London, 1968

Evliya, Chelebi, *The Narrative of Travels*, translated by Joseph von Hammer, London, 1834–50

Ferguson, W. S., *Hellenistic Athens*, London, 1911

Finlay, George, *History of Greece*, 7 vols., Oxford, 1877

Frazer, J. G., *Pausanias' Description of Greece*, 6 vols., London, 1898

Frel, Jiri, *Panathenaic Prize Amphoras* (Kerameikos Book, no. 2, German Archaeological Institute), Athens, 1973

French, A., *Growth of the Athenian Economy*, London, 1964

Gardner, Ernest A., *Ancient Athens*, London, 1902

Grant, Michael, *The Rise of the Greeks*, London, 1987

Grimal, Pierre, *The Dictionary of Classical Mythology*, Oxford, 1986

Guthrie, W. K. C., *The Greeks and their Gods*, London, 1950
  History of Greek Philosophy, Cambridge, 1962

Hammond, N. G. L., *History of Greece to 322 BC*, Oxford, 1959

Hammond, N. G. L., and Scullard, H. H., eds., *The Oxford Classical Dictionary*, Oxford, 1970

Harrison, Jane E., *Primitive Athens as Described by Thucydides*, Cambridge, 1906

Harrison Jane E., and Verrall, Margaret, *The Mythology and Monuments of Ancient Athens*, London, 1890

Heller, Charles W., *Athens and its Monuments*, New York, 1913

Herodotus, *The Histories*, translated by Aubrey De Sélincourt, Harmondsworth, 1954

Hignett, C., *History of the Athenian Constitution*, London, 1969

Hill, Ida Thallon, *The Ancient City of Athens, its Topography and Monuments*, Athens, 1953

Hobhouse, John Cam, *A Journey through Albania and Other Provinces of Turkey in Europe and Asia to Constantinople during the Years 1809 and 1810*, London, 1813

Hoepfner, Wolfram, *The Pompeion* (Kerameikos Book, no. 1, German Archaeological Institute), Athens, 1971

Hooker, J. T., *Mycenaean Greece*, London, 1977

Johansen, H. Friss, *The Attic Grave Reliefs*, Copenhagen, 1951

Jones, A. H. M., *Athenian Democracy*, Oxford, 1957
    The Decline of the Ancient World, London, 1966

Karo, George, *An Attic Cemetery*, Philadelphia, 1943

Lawrence, A. M., *Greek Architecture*, Harmondsworth, 1957

Leake, William M., *The Topography of Athens, with Some Remarks on its Antiquities*, 2nd ed., 2 vols., London, 1841

Lesky, Albin, *History of Greek Literature*, London, 1966

Mahaffy, J. P., *Greek Life and Thought from the Age of Alexander to the Roman Conquest*, London, 1896

Marchand, Leslie, *Byron, A Portrait*, London, 1971

Martin, Roland, *Greek Architecture*, London, 1988

Meigs, Russell, *The Athenian Empire*, Oxford, 1972

Meletopoulos, Ioannis, *Athena, 1650–1870*, Athens, 1979

Micheli, Liza, *Monastiraki, Athens' Old Market*, translated by Kevin Andrews, Athens, 1985

Mikalson, J. D., *Athenian Popular Religion*, North Carolina, 1983

Miliadis, Yiannis, *A Concise Guide to the Acropolis Museum*, Athens, 1965

Miller, William, *The Latins in the Levant*, London, 1900
    Essays on the Latin Orient, Cambridge, 1921

Mossé, C., *Athens in Decline, 404–86 BC*, London, 1973

Nielsen, M. P., *Greek Piety*, Oxford, 1928

Parke, H. W., *Festivals of the Athenians*, London, 1977

Pausanias, *Guide to Greece*, translated by Peter Levi, 2 vols., Harmondsworth, 1979

Penrose, F. C., *An Investigation of the Principles of Athenian Architecture*, London, 1988

Peters, F. E., *The Harvest of Hellenism*, New York, 1976

Pickard-Cambridge, A. W., *The Theatre of Dionysus in Athens*, Oxford, 1946

    The Dramatic Festivals of Athens, second edition, revised by J. Gould and D. M. Lewis, Oxford, 1968

Plato, *The Collected Dialogues of Plato*, translated by E. Hamilton and H. Cairns, Princeton, 1973

Reinhardt, Karl, *Sophocles*, Oxford, 1978

Richter, Gisela M. A., *Archaic Attic Tombstones*, Cambridge, Mass., 1944
    The Sculptures and Sculptors of the Greeks, New Haven, 1950
    Handbook of Greek Art, London, 1969
    Portraits of the Greeks, Oxford, 1984

Robertson, D. S., *Greek and Roman Architecture*, Cambridge, 1943

Robertson, Martin, *A Shorter History of Greek Art*, Cambridge, 1981

Robertson, Martin, and Franz, Alison, *The Parthenon Frieze*, London, 1975

Rodd, James Rennell, *The Customs and Lore of Modern Greece*, London, 1892

St Clair, William, *Lord Elgin and His Marbles*, London, 1967

Scheibler, Ingeborg, *The Archaic Cemetery* (Kerameikos Book, no. 3, German Archaeological Institute), Athens, 1973

Smith, A. H., *A Catalogue of the Sculptures of the Parthenon in the British Museum*, London, 1906

Snodgrass, A. M., *The Dark Ages of Greece*, Edinburgh, 1971

Sparkes, R. A., and Talcott, L., *Pots and Pans of Ancient Athens* (Athenian Agora Picture Book, no.1), Princeton, 1958

Stoneman, Richard, *A Literary Companion to Travel in Greece*, Harmondsworth, 1984

    Land of Lost Gods, The Search for Classical Greece, London, 1987

Stuart, John, and Revett, Nicholas, *The Antiquities of Athens*, London, 1762–94 (supplementary volumes by Cockerell and others, London, 1830)

Thompson, Dorothy Burr, *Garden Lore of Ancient Athens* (Athenian Agora Picture Book, no.8), Princeton, 1963

Thompson, H. A., *The Stoa of Attalos II in Athens* (Athenian Agora Picture Book, no.2), Princeton, 1959

    The Athenian Agora, A Short Guide, Princeton, 1980

Thompson, H. A., and Wycherley, R. E., *The Agora of Athens* (The Athenian Agora Series, vol. XIV), Princeton, 1972

Thucydides, *History of the Peloponnesian War*, translated by Rex Warner, Harmondsworth, 1954

Travlos, John, *Pictorial Dictionary of Ancient Athens*, New York and London, 1971

Vacalopoulos, A. E., *Origins of the Greek Nation: The Byzantine Period, 1204–1461*, New Brunswick, New Jersey, 1970

The Greek Nation, 1453–1669, New Brunswick, New Jersey, 1976

Vermeule, Emily, *Greece in the Bronze Age*, Chicago, 1964

Webster, T. B. L., *Art and Literature in Fourth-Century Athens*, London, 1956

Everyday Life in Classical Athens, London, 1964

Athenian Culture and Society, Berkeley, 1973

Woodford, Susan, *The Parthenon*, Cambridge, 1981

Woodhouse, C. M., *Modern Greece, A Short History*, Cambridge, 1977

The Greek War of Independence, London, 1984

Wordsworth, Christopher, *Athens and Attica*, London, 1836

Greece, Pictorial, Descriptive and Historical, London, 1839

Wycherley, R. E., *How the Greeks Build Cities*, London, 1949

The Stones of Athens, Princeton, 1978

Literary and Epigraphical Testimonia (The Athenian Agora Series, vol. III), Princeton, 1957

Sources of Quotations

p. 5: Thucydides, *History of the Peloponnesian War*, trans. Rex Warner, Harmondsworth, Penguin Books, 1954

p. 7 (poem by Solon): Aristotle, *The Athenian Constitution*, trans. H. Rackham, London, Heinemann (LCL), 1935

p. 8: Plutarch, *Life of Solon*, trans. Bernadotte Perrin, London, Heinemann (LCL), 1914

p. 8: Thucydides, op. cit.

p. 9: Herodotus, *The Histories*, trans. Aubrey de Sélincourt, Harmondsworth, Penguin Books, 1954

p. 10: Herodotus, ibid.

p. 17: Dio Cassius of Nicaea, *History of Rome* 9 vols., vol. IX, trans. E. W. Cary, London, Heinemann (LCL), 1927

p. 17: Pausanias, *Guide to Greece*, 2 vols., trans. Peter Levi, Harmondsworth, Penguin Books, 1971

p. 20: Evliya Chelebi, *The Narrative of Travels*, trans. Joseph von Hammer, London, 1834–50

p. 21: Cristoforo Ivanovich, quoted V. J. Bruno, ed., *The Parthenon*, New York, W. W. Norton, 1974

pp. 21–2: Francesco Morosini, quoted V. J. Bruno, op. cit.

p. 22: *Anargyria Apospasmata*, quoted Liza Micheli, *Monastiraki, Athens' Old Market*, trans. Kevin Andrews, Athens, 1985

p. 23: John Benizelos, quoted Liza Micheli, op. cit.

p. 23: Dimitrios Kalephronas, quoted Liza Micheli, op. cit.

p. 24: John Benizelos, quoted Liza Micheli, op. cit.

p. 25: John Stuart and Nicholas Revett, *The Antiquities of Athens*, London, 1762–94

p. 26: Edward Dodwell, *A Classical and Topographical Tour through Greece*, 2 vols., London, 1819

p. 27: Byron, 'The Curse of Minerva', in *The Complete Poetical Works of Lord Byron*, ed. Ernest Coleridge, London, John Murray, 1905

p. 28: Christopher Wordsworth, *Athens and Attica*, London, 1836

p. 29: Pindar's 'Dithyramb to Athens', from *The Odes of Pindar*, trans. John Sandys, London, Heinemann (LCL), 1915

p. 32: Homeric Hymn to Dionysos, from *Hesiod, the Homeric Hymns and Homerica*, trans. Hugh G. Evelyn-White, London, Heinemann (LCL), 1915

p. 32: Byron, *Lord Byron's Correspondence*, ed. John Murray, New York, 1957

p. 36: Pausanias, op. cit.

p. 39: Pausanias, op. cit.

p. 41: Cratinus, 'Thrattae', from *Fragments of Attic Comedy*, trans. J. M. Edmonds, Leiden, 1957–61

p. 53: Pausanias, op. cit.

p. 55: Pausanias, op. cit.

p. 61: Plutarch, *Life of Pericles*

pp. 67–8: Pausanias, op. cit.

p. 73: Homer, *The Iliad*, trans. Richard Lattimore, London, 1951

p. 79: Pausanias, op. cit.

p. 80: Pausanias, op. cit.

p. 85: Michael Akominatos, Ida Carleton Hill, *A Medieval Humanist: Michael Akominatos*, New Haven, 1923

pp. 89–90: Herodotus, op. cit.

p. 91: Pausanias, op. cit.

p. 92: Pausanias, op. cit.

p. 94: Pausanias, op. cit.

p. 99: John M. Camp, *The Athenian Agora: Excavations in the Heart of Classical Athens*, London, Thames & Hudson, 1986

p. 103: Euboulos, from *Fragments of Attic Comedy*, op. cit.

p. 103: Diogenes Laertius, *Lives of Eminent Philosophers*, 2 vols., trans. R. D. Hicks, London, Heinemann (LCL), 1925

p. 104: Demosthenes, 'Oration Against Androtion', vol. III of Demosthenes' *Orations*, trans. J. H. Vince, London, Heinemann (LCL), 1926

p. 107: Cicero, *De Natura Deorum* ('On the Nature of the Gods'), trans. H. Rackham in Cicero's *Works*, London, Heinemann (LCL), 1933

p. 109: Samuel Rickards, Oxford prize poem, quoted Richard Stoneman in *A Literary Companion to Travel in Greece*, Harmondsworth, Penguin Books, 1984

p. 109: Byron, *Lord Byron's Correspondence*, op. cit.

p. 112: Diogenes Laertius, op. cit.

p. 113: Aristotle, op. cit.

p. 118: Pausanias, op. cit.

p. 119–20: Arrian, *The Campaigns of Alexander*, trans. Aubrey de Sélincourt, Harmondsworth, Penguin Books, 1958

p. 123: Strabo, *Geography*, trans. H. L. Jones, 8 vols., London, Heinemann (LCL), 1917

p. 125: Apuleieus, *Metamorphoses*, trans. W. Adington (1566), revised S. Gaselee, London, Heinemann (LCL), 1915

p. 125: Pausanias, op. cit.

p. 126: Thucydides, op. cit.

p. 126: Velerius Harpokration, *Hermai*

p. 126: Herodotus, op. cit.

p. 127: Pausanias, op, cit.

p. 128: John Travlos, *Pictorial Dictionary of Ancient Athens*, New York and London, Thames & Hudson, 1971

p. 131: Xenophon, 'The Cavalry Commander', from *Scripta Minor*, trans. E. C. Marchant, London, Heinemann (LCL), 1922

p. 132: Athenaeus, *The Learned Banquet*, 7 vols., trans. C. B. Gulick, London, Heinemann (LCL), 1927–41

p. 137: Himerios, from *Lives of the Sophists* by Eunapius, trans. W. C. Wright, London, Heinemann (LCL), 1922

p. 146: Pausanias, op. cit.

p. 148: Thucydides, op. cit.

p. 152: Thycydides, op. cit.

p. 154: Thucydides, op. cit.

p. 163: Aristotle, op. cit.

p. 164: Pindar, op. cit.

p. 165–6: Thucydides, op. cit.

p. 166: Thucydides, op. cit.

p. 171: Plutarch, *Life of Themistocles*, trans. Bernadotte Perrin, London, Heinemann (LCL), 1914

p. 172: R. E. Wycherley, *The Stones of Athens*, Princeton, Princeton University Press, 1978

p. 173: R. E. Wycherley, ibid.

p. 177: ancient commentator on the Thesmophoria; known only as 'the scholiast on Aristophanes' Thesmophoriazusae'

p. 178: H. W. Parke, *Festivals of the Athenians*, London, Thames & Hudson, 1977

p. 180: Pausanias, op. cit.

p. 188: Plutarch, *Life of Theseus*

pp. 191–2: James Rennell Rodd, *Customs and Lore of Modern Greece*, London, 1892

p. 195: Heracleides of Crete, 'On the Cities of Greece'; see F. Pfister, *Die Reisebilder des Herakleides*, Wien, 1951

p. 195: Pausanias, op. cit.

p. 199: Pausanias, op. cit.

pp. 206–7: Evliya Chelebi, op. cit.

pp. 211–13, Pausanias, op. cit.

p. 213: John Benizelos, quoted Liza Micheli, op. cit.

pp. 214–15: Dimitrios Kambouroglu, quoted Liza Micheli, op. cit.

p. 215: Pausanias, op. cit.

p. 216: Le Roy, quoted Liza Micheli, op. cit.

p. 223: Michael Akominatos, op. cit.

p. 227: Babin, quoted Liza Micheli, op. cit.

p. 229: Panighis Skouzes, quoted Liza Micheli, op. cit.

pp.243–4: John Cam Hobhouse, *A Journey . . .*, London, 1813

pp. 247–8: John Cam Hobhouse, op. cit.

p. 249: Achileas Paraskhos, quoted Liza Micheli, op. cit

p. 251: quoted by Liza Micheli, op. cit.

p. 253: John Cam Hobhouse, op. cit.

pp. 253–4: Byron, *Lord Byron's Correspondence*, op. cit.

p. 259: Ludwig Ross, quoted Liza Micheli, op. cit.

p. 259: Christopher Wordsworth, op. cit.

p. 262: Fräulein von Nordenflycht, quoted Liza Micheli, op. cit.

p. 275: John Cam Hobhouse, op, cit.

p. 283: John Gennadius, *Memoirs*

p. 297: Nikolaos Makri, quoted Liza Micheli, op. cit.

p. 298: Emmanuel Roidis quoted Liza Micheli, op. cit.

p. 299: John Cam Hobhouse, op. cit.

p. 299: Byron, *The Complete Poetical Works*, op. cit.

p. 306: Pausanias, op. cit.

p. 307: Athenaeus, op. cit.

p. 308: Cicero, *De Finibus*, trans. H. Rackham, London, Heinemann (LCL), 1914

p. 309: Pausanias, op. cit.

p. 310: J. P Mahaffy, quoted Sir James Frazer in his translation of Pausanias, *Description of Greece*, 6 vols., London, Macmillian, 1908–13

p. 113: George Wheler, *Journey into Greece*, London, 1672

p. 313: Edward Dodwell, *Views in Greece*, 2 vols, London, 1821

p. 316: Edward Dodwell, ibid.

p. 317: William M. Leake, *The Topography of Athens* . . ., 2 vols, London, 1841

pp. 317–18: William Congreve's translation of Ovid's *Metamorphoses*

p. 320: Aulus Gellius, *Attic Nights*, trans. John C. Rolfe, 3 vols., London, Heinemann (LCL), 1927

Index